REIMAGINING LEADERSHIP
ON THE COMMONS

REIMAGINING LEADERSHIP ON THE COMMONS

Shifting the Paradigm for a More Ethical, Equitable, and Just World

Edited by

Devin P. Singh,
Dartmouth College, USA

Randal Joy Thompson,
Fielding Graduate University, USA

and

Kathleen A. Curran,
Fielding Graduate University, USA

United Kingdom – North America – Japan
India – Malaysia – China

Emerald Publishing Limited
Howard House, Wagon Lane, Bingley BD16 1WA, UK

First edition 2021

British Library Cataloguing in Publication Data
A catalogue record for this book is available from the British Library

ISBN: 978-1-83909-527-6 (Print)
ISBN: 978-1-83909-524-5 (Online)
ISBN: 978-1-83909-526-9 (Epub)

ISSN: 2058-8801 (Series)

ISOQAR certified
Management System,
awarded to Emerald
for adherence to
Environmental
standard
ISO 14001:2004.

ISOQAR
REGISTERED
Certificate Number 1985
ISO 14001

INVESTOR IN PEOPLE

*To all the Commoners throughout history who have sought
a more ethical, equitable and just world.
May we finally achieve it together.*

CONTENTS

About the Editors   xi

About the Authors   xiii

Foreword by Dr Marco Janssen, Past President of
   the International Association for the Study of
   the Commons   xix

Preface   xxiii

Acknowledgments   xxix

Introduction Part I: Overview of Leading on the Commons   1

Randal Joy Thompson

Introduction Part II: Debt, Obligation, and Care on
   the Commons   31

Devin P. Singh

PART I: THE PARADIGM SHIFT

1. Leading Regenerative Systems: Evolving the Whole
    Instead of a Part   59

    Kathleen E. Allen

2. Leading So All Can Thrive: Commons Leadership for
    Mutualistic Self-Organization   69

    Elizabeth A. Castillo

3. Redefining Leadership Through the Commons:
    An Overview of Two Processes of Meaning-making
    and Collective Action in Barcelona   81

    Antonio Jimenez-Luque

4. Responsible, Relational, and Intentional: A Re-Imagined
    Construct of Corporate-Commons Leadership   97

    Kathleen A. Curran

5. What Favelas Can Teach about Leadership:
    The Importance of Shared-Purpose and Place-Based
    Leadership   119

    Renato Souza, Thomaz Wood and Brad Jackson

6. From Governance to Leadership: Ethical Foundations
    for Value-Infused Leadership of the Commons   137

    *Catharyn Baird, Nancy Sayer, Jeannine Niacaris and
    Allison Dake*

7. Leading Proleptically on the Commons   157
    Randal Joy Thompson

    PART II: LEADERSHIP ON THE COMMONS LIFECYCLE

8. Developing Leadership on the Commons: Animal
    Rescue   177

    Robin Bisha

9. Convening Leadership on the Commons: Initiating
    Stakeholder Networks to Solve Complex Global Issues   191

    Patricia A. Clary

10. Collaborating and Co-Creating Leadership in the Virtual
    and Not-So-Virtual Commons: Road Warriors,
    Communitas, and Culture   205

    Gayla S. Napier and David Blake Willis

11. Using Interorganizational Collaboration to Create Shared
Leadership Through Collective Identity Development   223

Patricia Greer

12. The Role of Leaders in Catalyzing Cooperative Behavior
in the Governance of Nonprofit Sector Shared
Resources: The Case of Early Childhood Education   243

*Wendolly A. Escobar, Angela Titi Amayah and
MD Haque*

PART III: LEADING SPECIFIC TYPES OF COMMONS

13. The Peoples' Voice Cafe: Leading Collectively and
Horizontally for More than 40 Years   257

Susan (Susie) J. Erenrich

14. Open Data, Distributed Leadership and Food Security:
The Role of Women Smallholder Farmers   273

*Éliane Ubalijoro, Victor N. Sunday, Foteini Zampati,
Uchechi Shirley Anaduaka and Suchith Anand*

15. Learning and Leading Together to Transform
the World: Jesuit Higher Education and Ignatian
Leadership Formation at the Margins   295

Dung Q. Tran and Michael R. Carey

16. Traditional Leadership on the Commons: Main
Challenges for Leaders of Community Organizations
to Govern Rural Water in Ránquil, Chile   311

*Camila Alejandra Vargas Estay, Noelia Carrasco Henríquez,
Victor Manuel Vargas Rojas and Luis Gatica Mora*

17. Leadership of the Commons in Bosnia and
Herzegovina: Protecting Natural Resources and
Reclaiming Public Space   329

Edin Ibrahimefendic

18. Hopping the Hoops or Building a Communal Culture as
     the Most Significant Pillar of Leadership of the Commons   345

     Katja Hleb, Miha Škerlavaj and Domen Rozman

19. Job Commons: The Overlooked Dimension of Commons
     Leadership and Global and Local Governance   363

     Jan Hurst

Index   385

ABOUT THE EDITORS

Devin P. Singh (PhD, Yale) is Associate Professor of Religion at Dartmouth College as well as Faculty Associate in Dartmouth's Consortium of Studies on Race, Migration, and Sexuality. He is the author of *Divine Currency: The Theological Power of Money in the West* (2018) and *Economy and Modern Christian Thought* (forthcoming), as well as articles in journals such as *Political Theology*, *Journal of Religious Ethics*, and *Harvard Theological Review*. He is also founder and president of Leadership Kinetics LLC which provides leadership coaching and strategic advising.

Randal Joy Thompson (PhD, Fielding) is a Scholar-Practitioner with 40 years' professional experience in international development, serving in countries around the world. A Fellow with the Institute for Social Innovation, Fielding Graduate University, her research focuses on the commons, on gender, education, evaluation, and organization development. Her publications include *Proleptic Leadership on the Commons: Ushering in a New Global Order* (2020), *Leadership and Power in International Development: Navigating the Intersections of Gender, Culture, Context, and Sustainability* (2018) which won the Human Resource Development R. Wayne Pace HRD Book of the Year Award, and many chapters in ILA books.

Kathleen A. Curran (PhD, Fielding) is a Scholar-Practitioner with 25+ years' professional experience in Asia, and practicing internationally. A Fellow with the Institute for Social Innovation, Fielding Graduate University and principal of Intercultural Systems, she specializes in developing global leadership in mindset and capability for spanning cultural boundaries. Her research focuses on co-creating freedom, equity, and belonging through global responsible leadership and talent development within the global enterprise. Recent publications include "Global Identity and Global Leadership: Knowing, Doing, and Becoming – Differently," *The Study and Practice of Global Leadership* (2021); "Global Identity Tensions for Global Leaders," *Advances in Global Leadership, 12,* (2019).

ABOUT THE AUTHORS

Kathleen E. Allen, PhD, is the Author of *Leading from the Roots: Nature Inspired Leadership Lessons for Today's World.* She writes a weekly blog on leadership and organizations that describes a new paradigm of leadership based in lessons from nature and living systems. She is a Consultant specializing in leadership coaching and organizational change.

Angela Titi Amayah is an Assistant Professor in the Department of Management & Marketing at California State University, Bakersfield. Her research focuses primarily on leaders and their role in readiness for change. Other areas of interest include the experiences of women leaders in various cultures.

Uchechi Shirley Anaduaka is a Lecturer in the Department of Economics, University of Nigeria, Nsukka, and the SDGs Research and Training Associate for Unique Mappers Network Nigeria. She holds a PhD in Economics from Lingnan University, Hong Kong. Her research interests focus on child and youth development, and women's wellbeing.

Suchith Anand is Chief Scientist at Global Open Data for Agriculture and Nutrition. He co-founded GeoForAll with a vision to make geospatial education and digital economy opportunities accessible to all, enabling a better future for everyone. He has mentored over 1,000 emerging leaders in sustainable development programs and initiatives worldwide through GeoForAll.

Catharyn Baird, JD, is the Founder/CEO of EthicsGame, LLC. Her research resulted in the development of the *Ethical Lens Inventory*™, a typology used by more than 550,000 people to determine ethical leadership style. Her TEDx presentation, *Ethics for People on the Move,* explores how to build strong cultures.

Robin Bisha, Professor of Communication Studies at Texas Lutheran University, teaches a course called Leadership for Social Change and participates in community service in animal welfare and rescue in South Central Texas. Her main research interest is the relationship between humans and animals.

Michael R. Carey, PhD, is an Associate Professor and Chairperson of Organizational Leadership in the School of Leadership Studies at Gonzaga University in Spokane, Washington. He has taught leadership studies at the graduate level for over 30 great! years.

Elizabeth A. Castillo is an Assistant Professor at Arizona State University. She studies organization leadership and intangible assets like social, cultural, moral, and political capital. Her mission is to repair the world through research and teaching that promote thriving organizations, engaged employees, connected communities, and a world we can be proud to pass on to our children.

Patricia A. Clary, Doctoral Candidate, is a Scholar-Practitioner who dedicated her life to the common good of people and societies through service in nonprofit, public, and higher education sectors. A C-level executive, she is a skilled convenor through her work with United Way Worldwide, the City of Los Angeles, and Brandman University.

Allison Dake, PhD, is devoted to global development and working with organizations to solve complex issues. She blends her practical experience with her academic work in Values-Driven Leadership and Global Nonprofit Management.

Susan (Susie) J. Erenrich is a Social Movement History Documentarian. She uses the arts for social change to tell stories about transformational leadership, resilience, and societal shifts as a result of mobilization efforts by ordinary citizens. She is also the editor of *The Cost Of Freedom: Voicing A Movement After Kent State 1970; Freedom Is a Constant Struggle: An Anthology of the Mississippi Civil Rights Movement and co-editor of Grassroots Leadership & the Arts for Social Change & A Grassroots Leadership & Arts For Social Change Primer For Educators, Organizers, Activists and Rabble- Rousers.*

Wendolly A. Escobar, PhD, currently serves as the Vice President of Family Engagement at the Partnership for Los Angeles Schools. Her research interests include PK-12 family engagement policies and practices, social justice in education, and teacher preparation to engage families in educational settings.

Patricia Greer began practicing collaboration and leadership on her first-grade playground. She applies scholar practitioner practices honed over decades of teaching graduate students. Her grasp of common-sense solutions to problems strengthens multiple organizations in all three sectors. She earned a PhD in Leadership and Change from Antioch University.

MD Haque is an Associate Professor in the Organizational Leadership Doctoral Program at the University of LaVerne. He carries out research in the areas of Leadership and Organizational Change. His recently published work appears in *Leadership and Organizational Development Journal, Journal of Organizational Psychology, Qualitative Research in Organizations and Management: An International Journal, and Online Journal of Distance Learning Administration.*

Noelia Carrasco Henríquez, PhD, is an Anthropologist and Doctor in Social and Cultural Anthropology. Associate Professor of the History Department at the University of Concepción. Director of the program CIDESAL (Research, Science, Development, and Society in Latin America), Deputy Researcher of the Center of Climate Science and Resilience, and Director of the Project SIMOL.

Katja Hleb is a Board and Ministry level Consultant in the areas of leadership and people development for 20 years. She has served more than 150 top end global or international companies in eight countries. At the moment, she is a PhD Student at SEB UL and her research focii include levels of consciousness in adults and responsible leadership.

Jan Hurst PhD, is an Independent Scholar and former Practitioner. Her academic background is in politics research and the governance of unemployment solutions. She has published an academic book, presented to the Academic Council on the United Nations System AGM (Rome), and the Centre for Ethics and Poverty Research (Salzburg), and attends a University of Cambridge labor market reading group (currently online).

Edin Ibrahimefendic, JD, is a Human Rights Attorney who works for the Ombudspersons Office in Sarajevo, Bosnia and Herzegovina. He focuses on religious persecution and other violations. He has published chapters in ILA books, including "The Cellist of Sarajevo" and "Women's Postwar Activism in Bosnia-Herzegovina: A Human Rights Approach to Peacebuilding and Reconciliation through Liminal Space."

Brad Jackson is Associate Dean Strategic Engagement at The University of Waikato School and Professor of Leadership and Governance. His current research explores the inter-relationship between leadership and governance practices in promoting and sustaining social and economic innovation and the application of place-based approaches to foster cross-sectoral leadership development and education.

Marco Janssen is a Professor in the School of Sustainability and School of Complex Adaptive Systems at Arizona State University. He was President of the International Association for the Study of the Commons in 2019 and 2020. The research interest of Janssen is the study of the conditions of communities to self-govern their shared resources using computational modeling, behavioral experiments, and case study analysis. Recent projects focused on water management in Mexico City, participatory games to save water in rural India, comparative case study of lake organizations, and experiments on collective action in a virtual Mars habitat.

Antonio Jimenez-Luque, PhD, is Assistant Professor at the University of San Diego. His work explores how cultural, social, and historical perspectives influence conceptualizations and practice of leadership understood as a relational process of mobilization, emancipation, and social change. At the intersection of critical theory and intercultural studies, his main research topics are organizational culture and identity, decolonial leadership, and social change leadership.

Luis Gatica Mora is a Graduate in Conservation of Natural Resources from the University of Concepción. Currently is responsible for monitoring and researching for "Foresta Nativa" an ecological restoration project of the University of Concepción and implementing tools to make the restoration process more efficient.

Gayla S. Napier, PhD, obtained her doctorate in Human and Organizational Systems from Fielding Graduate University. With over 20 years of organizational consulting and executive coaching experience, her research focuses on the future of work, communitas, and belonging. She is an Associate Professor at the Jack Welch Management Institute.

Jeannine Niacaris, MA, is the COO of *EthicsGame, LLC*. She brings her passion for creating and sustaining value-based cultures to her work with leadership teams. She has experience as an executive and consultant in human resources, focusing on empowering people to become effective and ethical in the workplace.

Víctor Manuel Vargas Rojas, PhD, is a Researcher at the National Forestry Institute and Forest Engineer with a MSc in Natural Resources Economics and a PhD in Natural Resources and Sustainable Management. With 32 years of experience in Research and Development, he is FSC Lead Auditor. Lines of work include: Clean production, BMPs, Water Basin Management, Forest Certification, Local Monitoring, and Water Governance.

Domen Rozman is a TEDx Speaker and the Leader of the world-famous acrobatic team Dunking Devils. The team has performed more than 2,000 shows in 50 different countries while their amazing videos have been viewed more than 500 million times. The Dunking Devils moto is: "There is one true direction. Up!"

Nancy Sayer, PhD, is currently the CEO of Leadership Evolvement Institute. She provides coaching and consultation to leaders and organizations in the areas of change management, conflict management, leadership skills, team development and appreciative inquiry.

Miha Škerlavaj, PhD, is a Professor of Management at the School of Economics and Business University of Ljubljana and an adjunct professor of leadership and organizational behavior at BI Norwegian Business School. His research has been published in the *Academy of Management Journal*, the *Harvard Business Review*, and the *Journal of Organizational Behavior*.

Renato Souza holds a PhD in Business Administration at FGV EAESP. His research interests include Leadership Theory and Practice, Human Resource Management and Organizational Behavior. He has been working in the private sector as Human Resources Director for several companies in distinct segments such as FMCG, Education and Financial Services.

Victor N. Sunday is a Lecturer-Geospatial Information Science at University of Port Harcourt, Nigeria. National Coordinator at Unique Mappers Network (UMT), Nigeria. GODAN-Nigeria Capacity Development Lead. Member-ISPRS WG IV/4. UNFPA Nigeria Delegate FOSS4G Bucharest. Community leader for OpenStreetMap, GeoForAll & Participatory Citizen Science, Nigeria. Chair of Geoformation Society of Nigeria, Rivers State, Nigeria.

Dung Q. Tran, PhD, is an Assistant Professor in the Master of Arts in Organizational Leadership program at Gonzaga University. He is co-editor of *Servant-Leadership and Forgiveness: How Leaders Help Heal the Heart of the World* (SUNY Press, 2020) and a contributing author to *The Routledge Companion to Mindfulness at Work* (Routledge, 2021).

Éliane Ubalijoro, PhD, is the Deputy Executive Director for Programs at Global Open Data in Agriculture and Nutrition. She is a Professor of Practice for Public–Private Sector Partnerships at McGill University's Institute for the Study of International Development. She is a member of the Supervisory Board of the Capitals Coalition.

Camila Alejandra Vargas Estay, MA, is an English, Spanish, and German translator and master's degree holder in Anthropology. Freelance Researcher in Social Sciences and Academic Research Consultant. Currently works in a project called SIMOL (Monitoring System for Local Community Participation in Integrated Water Basin Management) led by the University of Concepción, Chile.

David Blake Willis, Professor of Anthropology/Education, Fielding Graduate University (2008-Present) and Soai Buddhist University (Japan, 1986–2009), taught and did research at Oxford, Grinnell, and the University of Washington. His interests in anthropology, sustainability, social justice, immigration, leadership, and The Commons come from 38 years living in traditional cultural systems (Japan/India).

Thomaz Wood, Jr, is Full Professor at FGV EAESP. He is also the associate dean for research and directs the DBA program. He has published more than 20 books in the area of management. His research interests include business transformation, organizational change and the social impact of management research.

Foteini Zampati is a Legal Professional with over 18 years of experience. She works for the Association for Technology and Structures in Agriculture (KTBL) as a data rights research specialist, advising the Global Open Data for Agriculture and Nutrition (GODAN) initiative on ethical and legal aspects of open data.

FOREWORD

MARCO JANSSEN, PAST PRESIDENT OF
THE INTERNATIONAL ASSOCIATION FOR
THE STUDY OF THE COMMONS

Biologist Garrett Hardin (1968) argued that overuse of commons was inevitable since users would never self-organize. Hardin envisioned a pasture open to all, in which each herder received an individual benefit from adding sheep to graze on the common land and suffered costs only later (and shared with other herders) from overgrazing. Besides private property rights, an intervention such as taxing the use of common resources is the only possible intervention to avoid overharvesting of the commons.

Hardin's judgment has been widely accepted due to its consistency with predictions from noncooperative game theory, the economics of resource use, and well-noted examples of resource collapses. The consequences of this work were significant, especially due to the privatization and nationalization of natural resources in many places around the world, ignoring existing institutional arrangements.

Communal property was equated with the absence of exclusive and effective rights and thus an inability to govern the commons. However, this was not the observation from scholars doing fieldwork on natural resource governance. In the mid-1980s, a group of interdisciplinary scholars who perform field studies began to discover that the empirical evidence was not consistent with conventional theory. In order to understand the diversity of outcomes from individual case studies, there was a need for synthesis. This happened through meetings of the National Research Council, starting in 1983. A large number of case studies were discovered that showed both successes and failures of self-organization of resource users. The resources included local fisheries, irrigation systems, pastures, and forests. This spurt of activities also led in 1989 to the establishment of the International Association for the Study of the Commons (IASC).

Founding IASC President Elinor Ostrom published her 1990 book *Governing the Commons*, in which an initial analysis of the meta-analysis was provided. She proposed eight so-called design principles that co-occur more frequently with successful governance of shared resources. Those design principles include clearly defined boundaries of the resource and eligible resource users, active monitoring and sanctioning, and inclusion of resource users in defining institutional arrangements to govern the commons. In the years since, subsequential studies have confirmed that those proposed design principles remain key to explain successes and failures (Baggio et al., 2016).

However, with increasing amount of data and comparative analysis of case studies in diverse resource domains, additional social and biophysical factors have been found to be influential. One of those factors for success is leadership (Gutiérrez, Hilborn, & Defeo, 2011). However, the observation that effective leadership correlates with success is of limited practical value. What defines an effective leader, what enables the presence of effective leadership and how we train effective leaders? The role of leadership is an underexplored topic in the study of governing the commons. Therefore, I am pleased to see this volume of leadership scholars focusing on the commons.

Current scholarship on the commons moved past the original focus on natural resources. The study of self-governance of communities to manage their shared resources has been applied to knowledge and data, health care, urban services, education, the use of Earth's orbit, and many more topics. With the increasing spread of application areas, it becomes important to understand the role of leadership in diverse contexts.

At the time of writing this foreword, the pandemic of COVID-19 is in full swing. Handling the COVID-19 crisis requires governing various types of shared resources, from personal protective equipment and sanitizers, to vaccine development and distribution, health care workers, and hospital beds. The variety of ways countries and states are handling this crisis demonstrates the importance of leadership. The ability of leaders to set examples, provide priorities and coordinate between different stakeholders could make an important difference.

To conclude, leadership study is an important aspect in the study of the commons, and this volume provides an important contribution by bringing together a diverse set of studies on this topic.

REFERENCES

Baggio, J. A., Barnett, A., Perez-Ibarra, I., Ratajczyk, E., Brady, U., Rubinos, C., ... Janssen, M. A. (2016). Explaining success and failures in the commons: The configural nature of Ostrom's Institutional Design Principles. *International Journal of the Commons, 10*(2), 417–419. doi:10.18352/ijc.634

Gutiérrez, N., Hilborn, R., & Defeo, O. (2011). Leadership, social capital and incentives promote successful fisheries. *Nature, 470*, 386–389. doi:10.1038/nature09689

Hardin, G. (1968). The tragedy of the commons. *Science, 162*, 1243–1248.

Ostrom, E. (1990). *Governing the commons: The evolution of institutions for collective action.* Cambridge, England, UK: Cambridge University Press.

PREFACE

The year 2020 turned out to be a year of shocks, a global pandemic, the exposure of dysfunctional social, economic, and political systems, protest, riots, extreme climate disasters, and toxic leadership. The pandemic became the defining symbol of a country in crisis. With one fourth of the coronavirus cases and deaths in the world and the virus out of control, journalists queried whether the United States was a failed state (Packer, 2020), whether the revolution was already underway (Spang, 2020), or whether coronavirus killed the revolution (Hamid, 2020). The public murder of African American George Floyd by a Minnesota police officer added to the chaos just as the world was reeling from the pandemic. The grief of losing loved ones to the virus combined with the economic recession and the uncertainty of the future ignited righteous anger and grief flamed by his murder and opened to the world the entrenched and vicious racist underpinning of American society. Fury and the determination to change the broken system spilled into the streets of cities around the world. "Black Lives Matter" became the cry that signified that the people had suffered enough. And just when it seemed like nothing more could go wrong, the presidential election threatened to undermine the foundations of democracy as the groundless cries of fraud and election stealing echoed throughout the country while the President attempted to overturn the election results through scores of baseless lawsuits and a final standoff in Congress. His false claims and inflammatory narrative resulted in the President's insurrectionists shattering their way into the Capitol building in a revolutionary attempt to take over the government, in the "Worst Revolution Ever" (Flanagan, 2020).

Articles appeared during the year that highlighted the dire predictions of doomsayers such as Peter Turchin whose mathematical model predicted that 2020 would be a rough year followed by five or even 10 even rougher years (Wood, 2020). As he told Grame Wood, "the problems are deep and structural – not the type that the tedious process of democracy can fix in time to forestall mayhem" (Wood, 2020, para. 5). Based on the assumption that there are too many elites in the United States and not enough positions for all of them to hold, Turchin's model predicts that competition between elites will ensue and some of them will turn against the others and support the masses whose standard of living has declined because of the growing inequality. As Turchin wrote, the masses will

> accept the overtures of the counter-elites and start oiling the axles of their tumbrels. [People's] lives grow worse, and the few who try to pull themselves onto the elite lifeboat are pushed back into the water by those already aboard. (Wood, 2020, para. 9).

Government hand-outs to quell the unrest and suffering will run out, security will increase as people protest and strike, and finally state insolvency will trigger social disintegration, Turchin concluded.

Well-known leadership gurus responded to the crisis and to the signs of impending doom in dramatically different ways. Margaret Wheatley, for example, who made her name with her 1994 book *Leadership and the New Science*, agreed that it was too late to rectify past mistakes and that collapse was inevitable. She pointed to authors such as William Ophuls (2012) who identified the historical signs of the end of civilizations and paralleled these with what was happening in the U.S. Ophuls (2012) highlighted the biophysical limits reached by ecological exhaustion, exponential growth, expedited entropy, and excessive complexity combined with human error manifested in moral decay and practical failure as signs of collapse. "A civilization declines," Ophuls contended, "when it has exhausted its physical and moral capital" (2012, p. 65). Such was the state of the Western world, he concluded, and a "stupendous" global collapse lays on the near horizon.

> We must salvage as much as possible, Ophuls wrote. Human survival will require a fundamental change in the ethos of civilization – to wit, the deliberate renunciation of greatness in favor of simplicity, frugality, and fraternity. (2012, p. 70)

Wheatley has devoted herself to empowering "warriors of the human spirit" who are called into dying civilizations to stand for what is good in humankind and to help where help is needed during the chaos of collapse. Warriors are to enter when fear pervades the people and wait for opportunities to help rather than to construct their own life course and intentions. Being a warrior requires intensive inner work of being a present, mindful, and calm spirit in a world of chaos capable of offering compassion and care to those suffering the terrors of civilizational collapse.

Other high-profile leadership gurus, such as MIT's Otto Scharmer took the opposite stance during the pandemic. He organized global communities of hope, using the crisis to help create a more sustainable, equitable, and healthy world. Scharmer's GAIA journey united over 10,000 people around the world in an online "impromptu global infrastructure for sensemaking, for leaning into our current moment of disruption and letting this moment move us toward civilizational renewal" (Pendle, 2020, para. 4). Through the practice of presencing, community members opened their minds, hearts, and wills and allowed the future to reveal itself through a process of social emergence and the economics of creation until what arose crystallized, prototyped, embodied, and then performed. Members continue to meet and implement personal, group, and community projects that emerged from the presencing process.

Others have preferred visual imaginations of a positive future that we build after the increasing chaos and possibly collapse. Social critic Naomi Klein's 2020 video *A Message from the Future II: The Years of Repair* boosts the subtitle: *If We Stop Talking About What Winning Looks Like, Isn't It the Same as Giving Up?* (The Intercept, 2020). Her video – a follow up to the award-winning video "A Message from the Future with Alexandria Ocasio-Cortez," which painted a future in which people in the United States pulled together to launch the decade of the "Green New Deal" (The Intercept, 2019) – projects society into the probable future. The animated video paints the second pandemic of COVID in 2023, climate catastrophes, and the final realization that untamed economic growth equals sickness and death. Intensely struggling and fed up with dinosaur politicians, the people start protesting and striking, realizing that the only way forward is to build new systems. The people rebuild society starting with fundamentals such as local food, health, and education systems, while recognizing the importance of maintaining more-than-human systems. They return land to indigenous groups and form local collectives that are prepared for disasters and capable of ensuring that everyone has enough to meet their basic needs (See: https://www.youtube.com/watch?v=2m8YACFJlMg).

The people, that is, build "a commons-centric society," self-organized, self-governed, founded on community and care, and functioning outside the state and the private sector. Indeed, talk of the commons and a possible commons-centric society has become widespread in recent times. The pandemic highlighted the importance of the commons more than ever. Social organizations and groups stepped up to provide commodities and services to their local communities, illustrating the need to organize locally in order to take the provision of our basic needs into our own hands when the state and private sector fail us. In querying whether coronavirus would mean the end of neoliberalism, social critic Jeremy Lent (2020) posited that "this rediscovery of the value of community has the potential to be the most important factor of all in shaping the trajectory of the next era" (para. 33). The pandemic made it clear why people in crises historically have joined in commons in various parts of the world to stave off disaster. The crisis drove home the necessity for communities themselves to develop commons to provide the necessities of life, including food, water, shelter, medical care, among others.

We initiated this volume long before the pandemic shattered our normalcy. Yet, the pandemic and the revelation of crumbling systems made this book more significant than we initially imagined. People of the world may have to look more at local community commons to provide for our own survival as governments increasingly fail to adequately care for their people and the private sector cares only about their high-paid elite. Our intention in editing this book was to highlight the importance of the commons as well as to explore what leading on the commons looks like, since leadership on the commons has not been a focus of study by commons scholars and activists. Indeed, leadership is missing in most of the accounts of the commons by well-known scholars and activists such as Nobel-prize winning, now deceased Elinor Ostrom, David Bollier, Silke Helfrich, Massimo DeAngelis, Michel Bauwens, and others. Many of them have written that leadership will not be required in the future and that governance is all that will be needed. We disagree. We believe that the commons require some form of leadership and that it is important to reimagine leadership on this ancient, yet recently rediscovered form of organizing and acting in community.

Consequently, we published a call for proposals and received a large number of submissions from which we selected 17. We believe we have succeeded in selecting those that provide both theoretical arguments for and practical examples of particular approaches to leading on the commons. Authors hale from the United States, Great Britain, Brazil, Chile, New Zealand, Nigeria, Rwanda, Bosnia and Herzegovina, and Slovenia. We have titled the volume *Reimagining Leadership on the Commons: Shifting the Paradigm for a More Ethical, Equitable, and Just World* because the authors have presented approaches to leadership that challenge the underlying paradigm of the self-maximizing economic man. They have based their leadership on a far more communal, open relational paradigm based on care, compassion, and responsibility toward others and toward the more-than-human.

By the time this book is published in late 2021, the U.S. will have a vaccine against COVID-19, a new administration will be in power, but climate change will still be worsening and the vitriolic partisanship that is tearing the country apart will still be raging. Hopefully, that will not be the time of another global disaster. In any case, we hope that the leadership approaches proposed by the authors will prove useful whatever the future presents, and that leadership on the commons can provide the world a path toward a more ethical, equitable, and just world – the kind of world we all yearn for. That possibility may be in our own hands to create. Studying the commons and leadership on the commons give us some hope, for as Kirwan, Dawney, and Brigstock (2016) wrote:

> *The idea of the commons offers a romance, and through this romance, a way forward, a way to think out of the despondent political narratives of ecological destruction, polarization and dispossession, and a counter-narrative to that of the inevitable and uncontrollable force of neoliberalism. Above all else, it offers a glimmer of possibility that change can occur incrementally, and that small acts matter. (pp. 3–4)*

REFERENCES

Flanagan, C. (2020). The worst revolution ever: Attacking the U.S. capitol is not an act of patriotism. Obviously. *The Atlantic*. Retrieved from https://www.theatlantic.com/ideas/archive/2021/01/worst-revolution-ever/617623/

Hamid, S. (2020). The coronavirus killed the revolution. *The Atlantic*. March 25, pp. 7–26. Retrieved from https://www.theatlantic.com/ideas/archive/2020/03/coronavirus-killed-revolution/608680/

Kirwan, S., Dawney, L., & Brigstock, J. (2016). *Space, power, and the commons: The struggle for alternative futures*. Routledge.

Lent, J. (2020). Coronavirus spells the end of the neoliberal era. What's next? *The Broker: Connecting Worlds of Knowledge.* Retrieved from https://www. thebrokeronline.eu/coronavirus-spells-the-end-of-the-neoliberal-era-whats-next/

Ophuls, W. (2012). *Immoderate greatness: Why civilizations fail.* Create Space Publishing.

Packer, G. (2020). We are living in a failed state. *The Atlantic.* June Issue. Retrieved from https://www.theatlantic.com/magazine/archive/2020/06/ underlying-conditions/610261/

Pendle, D. (2020, May 25). GAIA journey and the healing potential of the social field. *Presencing Institute.* Retrieved from https://medium.com/ presencing-institute-blog/gaia-journey-and-the-healing-potential-of-the-social-field-1e779dc1c588

Spang, R. L. (2020). The revolution is only getting started. *The Atlantic.* April 5. Retrieved from https://www.theatlantic.com/ideas/archive/2020/04/ revolution-only-getting-started/609463/

The Intercept (2019, April 17). *A message from the future with Alexandria Ocasio-Cortez.* [Video] YouTube. https://www.youtube.com/watch?v=d9uTH0iprVQ

The Intercept (2020, October 1). *A message from the future II.: The years of repair.* [Video] YouTube. https://www.youtube.com/watch?v=2m8YACFJlMg

Wood, G. (2020). The next decade could be even worse. A historian believes he has discovered iron laws that predict the rise and fall of societies. He has bad news. *The Atlantic,* December 2020. Retrieved from https://www.theatlantic.com/magazine/ archive/2020/12/can-history-predict-future/616993/

ACKNOWLEDGMENTS

The journey of putting together this volume has been made possible and immeasurably more enriched by the support and commitment of a number of individuals to whom we are deeply indebted. The keen insights into necessary changes in the underlying paradigm that shapes the world and leadership theories and the commitment to the betterment of the world of the chapter authors have made this book both possible and promising. We as editors have benefitted from a life-enhancing learning process catalyzed by the leadership chapters of these contributors. The editors also owe a huge debt of eternal gratitude to Debra DeRuyver, Communications Director of the International Leadership Association (ILA). Debra, a superb editor and savvy production expert, supported us every step of the way, offering sound advice and guidance based on her many years of experience. We also would like to thank Cynthia Cherrey, President and CEO of ILA, Shelly Wilsey, COO, and Bridget Chisholm, Director of Conferences for their faith in us and support for our work. They and the rest of the ILA staff provided the foundation for making this book possible and providing us with the opportunity to make an impact. We are especially grateful for Dr Marco Janssen, Past President of the International Association for the Study of the Commons who agreed to write the Foreword to our book.

We would also like to thank all the reviewers of our book proposal for their insightful comments and recommendations. We greatly appreciate their confidence that our book would make a significant contribution to the leadership field. We would also like to acknowledge all the readers of this volume who we invite to join us on this journey of exploration of leadership on the commons. We look forward to engaging in a dialogue with all of you and in advancing our understanding of the factors influencing leadership in this domain as well as the values, principles, and competences that will help us all work together for a more ethical, equitable, and just world.

INTRODUCTION PART I: OVERVIEW OF LEADING ON THE COMMONS[1]

RANDAL JOY THOMPSON

The last few decades of growing inequality in the world, the loud call of peoples everywhere to have more say in the political machinations of their countries, and the global instability of the financial and economic systems caused by neoliberal capitalism, crowned by recent revelations that many key social and political systems have become dysfunctional, have brought challenges to capitalism and concern for the seeming decline of democracy. Many scholars and activists have posited that the global order is undergoing the process of a radical transformation to a commons-centric society. Social theorist Jeremy Rifkin (2014), for one, argued that technology, especially the 3D printer, the Internet, communications, and energy systems have made such a transformation inevitable, due to production approaching zero-marginal cost. Commons scholars and activists Massimo DeAngelis (2017), Bollier and Helfrich (2019), and Bauwens, Kostakis, and Pazaitis (2019) all posited a transformative process in which commons, as open adaptive systems, form federations and expand to dominate the socio-economic order. Commons, as we shall point out, derive from a distinctive ontology and uphold values and ways of operating that are in sharp contrast to capitalism and are intended to support a more ethical, equitable, and just world.

Commons have existed since antiquity and many ancient practices of communal governance of resources outside the state and the private sector have extended even to the present. New commons are emerging in contemporary society on a regular basis. The communal Spanish *huerta* system of irrigation has lasted for over a thousand years. The village of Torbel in the Swiss Alps established an association to communally manage the village's grazing land and forests in the fifteenth century, an association which continues to function today. The *Bisse de Saviesse* in the canton of Valais, Switzerland, managed since the first half of the twentieth century, is a communal irrigation system in the Swiss mountains that collects melting water directly from glaciers and takes it into villages and the farms in the valley down below. The iconic Boston Common initially served as a common grazing ground for cattle and now serves as a symbol of the community. For many decades, lobster fishermen in Maine have communally managed their businesses to ensure the sustainability of the lobster catch. The Great Lakes Commons, a cross-border community, works to save the water in the Great Lakes. The Agrarian Commons holds lands in various parts of the United States for regenerative agriculture and community building.

The *hackerspace*, *FabLab*, and *Maker* movements are pioneering spaces to develop collaborative innovations in software, customized fabrication, and open hardware design and manufacturing. Examples include the Embassy of the Commons in Poland, the Hack of Good Initiative in Spain, Fabulous St Pauli in Germany, and Move Commons, a tagging system for commons-based Internet projects (Helfrich, 2013).

Software such as the Linux open-source operating system has created a global commons of users who access Linux for free. Peer-to-peer (P2P) and open-source production of houses, automobiles, 3D printers, and many other products have created global commons of individuals anxious to work together, share, and take control of more aspects of their own lives outside of the market. Openly sourced and distributed knowledge such as through Wikipedia and available as through Creative Commons licenses and open-sourced media products through Wikimedia have allowed the free sharing of information, photos, music, and other creations that used to cost to access. Wikispeed has created a milieu for open-access automobile manufacturing. Other commons such as community gardens, time banks, coops, community-run innovation centers, solidarity networks, and so on, are expanding throughout the world. Commons are increasingly using alternative currencies to establish themselves as separate from mainstream financial systems and capitalist logics.

The phenomenon of the commons has undergone tremendous conceptual reframing in recent years. From commons-based laws in ancient Egypt and Rome to common land during feudal times to natural resources, knowledge, culture, Internet, and other commons in contemporary times, the phenomenon of commons has been infused with significant meaning and power to change society. A starting point to think about the meaning of the commons is to consider them as

> *social systems comprised of self-organized communities of commoners*
> *who create and/or use and/or protect and/or share natural, human-*
> *made, or abstract commonwealth governed and sustained by the*
> *practice of commoning which infuses the community with distinctive*
> *values, processes, and actions that differ from those of the state and*
> *private sector.*

Commoners generally also share the belief that the private sector does not have the right to take and "enclose" such commonwealth to make it profit-generating, nor does the state have the right to manage it and determine its access and use, especially within a culture of privatization. Rather, commoners believe that the shared commonwealth belongs to everyone by virtue of it being provided by nature or as a manifestation of general human creativity.

The term *commons* has a wide range of meanings and uses in English (Williams, 1983). Its Latin root word, *communis* is derived from *com*, meaning "together" and *munis*, meaning "under obligation" and from *com*, meaning "and" and *unis*, meaning "one." French political activist Alain Lipietz traced the word *commun* back to the Norman, William the Conquerer. *Commun*, according to Lipietz, derives from *munis*, which means "gift" and "duty," a dualism that describes the two sides of the concept in its contemporary usage (Bollier, 2014). As Dardot and Laval (2019) explained:

> *What we find in the term's etymological meaning is thus the Janus-*
> *face of the debt and the gift, of obligation and recognition. The term*
> *is thus bound up with the fundamental social fact known as sym-*
> *bolic exchange, which – at least since the work of Marcel Mauss –*
> *ethnological and sociological literature has documented in almost*
> *every form of human society. (p. 10)*

Dardot and Laval (2019) also argued that *munis* does not refer only to the formal requirement for reciprocity but that this duty is collective and often political.

The term "commons" has often been inextricably related to the term *community*, referring to a group or to all humankind, a place where the public meets, or to a shared resource. Also derived from the Latin root *communis*, the related term *community* generally refers to a group having direct, even intimate relationships in contrast to terms such as *society* or *state*, where relationships are organized and instrumental (Williams, 1983).

The contemporary interest in the commons was catalyzed by Garret Hardin's now classic article "The Tragedy of the Commons" (Hardin, 1968). Hardin argued that people would naturally overuse and destroy a shared piece of land by overgrazing their livestock in order to maximize their personal benefit. There would inevitably be free riders who would maximize their usage without any sense of responsibility toward others or the land. The only viable option to Hardin would be coercion by the state or private sector to prevent such overuse. 2009 Nobel Prize in Economics Winner Elinor Ostrom disagreed. After studying successfully and communally-governed common pool resources CPRs (CPRs are those resources such as air, water, etc. to which it is difficult if not impossible to deny access), Ostrom found that autonomous communities were capable of independently governing CPRs sustainably (Ostrom, 1990). According to Ostrom, Hardin ignored the possibility that users would communicate with each other and develop rules and practices so that their shared resources would be used equitably. Ostrom and her colleagues spent many years studying approaches to govern CPRs and derived governance principles for successfully managing them. These included: (1) the boundaries of users and resource are clear; (2) there exists a congruence between benefits and costs; (3) users have procedures for making their own rules; (4) there exist the practice of regular monitoring of users and resource conditions; (5) graduated sanctions for members who abuse the rules are established and implemented; (6) conflict resolution mechanisms are agreed to and followed; (7) there must be the minimal recognition of rights by government; and (8) commons are treated as nested enterprises in higher-level systems and that polycentric governance is designed and practiced (Ostrom, 1990).

By the mid-1990s through the 2000s, concomitant with protests against the International Monetary Fund, genetically modified food, the enclosure of water caused by privatization in Bolivia, the Zapatista uprising in Mexico against the privatization of common land, Occupy Wall Street, the Indignados in Spain, the anti-austerity movement in Greece, and many more, the concept of the commons expanded far beyond the governance of CPRs. Scholars, including Ostrom, began writing against the enclosure for profit by the private sector of natural and human resources that should belong to everyone and clamored for the communal management of such resources. They identified resources such as knowledge, information, urban spaces, genes, language, culture, etc. that should be governed by communities outside of the state and private sector. Meanwhile, the environmental movement expanded and helped to change the public's mindset regarding human to more-than human relationships and the responsibility to care for and sustain natural and human resources. As ecologist Andres Edwards wrote (2005), four new concerns entered the international conversations and began to shift the values of environmentally conscious individuals. These included:

(1) An awareness of the profound spiritual links between human beings and the natural world; (2) a deep understanding of the biological interconnection of all parts of nature, including human beings; (3) an abiding concern with the potential damage of human impact on the environment; and (4) a strongly-held commitment to make ethics an integral part of all environmental activism. (pp. 14–15)

Studies emerged that proved that instead of being individual self-maximizers, humans were inherently cooperative and relational. Some scholars recommended that the paradigm underlying economics and capitalism, namely *homo economicus* be replaced by another paradigm similar to *homo cooperantus*. In his 2011 book, *The Penguin and the Leviathan: How Cooperation Triumphs over Self-Interest,* legal scholar Yochai Benkler (2011) argued that the rational man underlying economic theory and based on the view that humans are only self-interested is antedated. He contended that advances in evolutionary biology and experiments in human interaction have illustrated that humans have an innate propensity for cooperation. Furthermore, Benkler concluded that cooperating humans do not require a dictatorial Leviathan looming over them to keep them under control.

As the commons movement expanded the notion of commons from CPRs to communities or social systems that govern a variety of human and natural resources or services, the underlying ontology, values, and principles of commons became unveiled. Rather than an individualist ontology, the commons are founded upon a relational ontology, or as Bollier and Helfrich wrote (2019), an ontology similar to the African *ubuntu*, "I am because we are." This ontology recognizes that the self emerges and develops in relationships and that these relationships impact one's worldview and mindset. As psychologist Kenneth Gergen (2006) wrote in his book *Relational Being: Beyond Self and Community*:

> [W]e exist in a world of co-constitution. We are always already
> emerging from relationship; we cannot step out of relationship; even

in our most private moments we are never alone...The future well-being of the planet depends significantly on the extent to which we can nourish and protect...the generative processes of relating. (p. xv)

Furthermore, especially in recent writings, many authors argue that this relationship includes the more-than-human which also impacts how the self develops and influences the values one embraces vis-à-vis nature and the environment. The more-than-human includes nature, animals, technology, and other things bestowed upon or created by humans.

Commons are self-organized, self-governed, collaborative, and autonomous social systems that can function as loose networks such as internet commons or open systems such as open-access journals or more integrated systems such as cooperatives. Commons are generally considered to be communities based on care, responsibility, sharing, provisioning, and sustainability, in which decisions are made collectively. The process of commoning is that which creates and expands commons and infuses them with their unique set of values.

LEADERSHIP ON THE COMMONS

As previously stated, the commons literature has not systematically explored leadership and many commons scholars and activists reject the concept of leadership as being authoritarian, hegemonic, and derived from a hierarchical unequal worldview (Bollier & Helfrich, 2019; DeAngelis, 2017). Although her emphasis was on governance, Ostrom admitted that "the presence of a leader or entrepreneur who articulates different ways of organizing to improve joint outcomes is frequently an important initial stimulus" (2009, p. 149). Furthermore, a number of studies explored the importance of leadership on various types of local levels commons (Thompson, 2020). These studies highlighted different roles leaders can play on commons, including catalyst, broker, political representative, buffer, bonding element vis-à-vis external forces, functional broker who bridges cultural divides, mobilizer, among others (Thompson, 2020). These studies generally contend that in local level community commons, local leaders play a key role in initiating, leading, protecting, and promoting commons.

Studies of leadership in networks and complex adaptive systems, the models that commons scholars and activists have employed in order to explain the transition to a commons-centric society, have concluded that leadership is both necessary and can take various forms. Although these studies do not focus specifically on commons *per se*, they do illustrate that network and systems models do not negate the need for leadership (Thompson, 2020). A review of some of these approaches will help locate the chapters in this book within certain leadership traditions which have emerged to fit within the knowledge era.[2]

NETWORK LEADERSHIP

Autonomous, self-governed, and self-organized Internet networks are commons and hence such commons can gain insights on leadership from the literature on network leadership. Ogden (2018) proposed a view of network leadership as a shared and multidimensional endeavor required to "hold the whole." Holding the whole, generally titled by Ogden "facilitative leadership," means to perceive the system as a whole and to pay attention to what is required to support the system's resiliency and ensure the system is providing equitable and sustained benefits. "Facilitative leaders" also bring people together for difficult conversations. Ogden (2018) viewed a number of different and complimentary leadership roles in networks that different individuals can play. These included "network guardianship," "network gardeners," "design leaders," "communications and curating leaders," "thought leaders," "coordinating leaders, and "implementation/prototyping" (Thompson, 2020).

Ogden (2018) put governance last and resisted the tendency of network members to want to address governance issues first and foremost. Rather, Ogden proposed a network principle he called "subsidiarity in governance," namely that governance matters "ought to be handled by the smallest, closest to the ground or least centralized competent 'authority'" (para. 15). Hence, contrary to what Ostrom (1990) and Bollier and Helfrich (2019) proposed, Ogden believed that governance should play a secondary role in networks, whereas various leadership roles maintain the dynamism, creativity, resilience, and adaptability of the network.

Schreiber and Carley (2008) highlighted the importance of learning and adaptability in networks. Leadership is essential to support these processes "through activities which foster knowledge flows, enhance interactions, advocate contextual change (structuration) and facilitate aggregation" (p. 298). To stimulate network learning they proposed the concept of "leaders in process" that shape communication flows in the following ways: "enhancing knowledge flows, creating interactions and interdependencies, maintaining relational coupling, increasing the speed of learning, and communicating new knowledge" (p. 298). The leadership role individuals assume depends upon the number and proximity of connections they have within the network and their role in creating the network emergent outcomes. They title some of these leaders "emergent leaders," "boundary spanners," and "network agents." They contended that leadership generates collective action in networks.

COMPLEXITY LEADERSHIP

Complexity leadership, derived from the behavior of complex adaptive systems (CAS), does not only manifest in leadership positions but also manifests

> *as an emergent, interactive dynamic – a complex interplay from which a collective impetus for action and change emerges when heterogeneous agents interact in networks in ways that produce new patterns of behavior or new modes of operating. (Uhl-Bien & Marion, 2008, p. 187)*

Complexity leadership, Uhl-Bien, Marion, and McKelvey (2007) and Uhl-Bien and Marion (2008) argued, comprises three leadership roles, namely administrative or operational leadership, enabling leadership, and adaptive or entrepreneurial leadership. These roles "reflect a dynamic relationship between the bureaucratic, administrative functions of the organization and the emergent, informal dynamics of complex adaptive systems" (p. xxiv) conflicting and connecting in the adaptive space.

Administrative or operational leadership relates to bureaucratic hierarchy, alignment, and control. Enabling leadership enables creative problem solving and learning. Adaptive or entrepreneurial leadership is generative of emergent change. The locus of leadership shifts from individuals to the processes of the system, making the primary role of leaders to ensure that the mechanisms and processes exist in the organization to allow for knowledge generation, emergent change, and adaptability (Thompson, 2020). Whereas the three identified leadership roles may not exist in Internet commons networks or open-access information, they may well exist in more purposefully organized commons such as cooperatives.

LEADING FROM NATURE

Allen (2019) argued that since technology and especially the Internet has connected the world and made organizations more permeable, interdependent, and connected, organizations need to become generative rather than consumptive and driven by collaboration, not competition. Nature, Allen (2019) pointed out, offers lessons that are relevant to the challenges of knowledge organizations. She identified three forms of organizational photosynthesis, namely authentic relationships, shared higher purpose, and reciprocity that help to release positive human energy and create integrative "power with" built on trust and transparency. Cooperation in nature is rewarded by developing mutualistic relationships, she wrote, also a quality discussed by Bollier and Helfrich (2019).

Allen (2019) recommended that organizations modify their cultures to move their conception of leadership from a positional one to an inclusive one in which leadership is distributed throughout the organization, where anyone can emerge with leadership behaviors, and where leadership becomes an emergent process in the organization. Distributed leadership is exercised in nature, Allen wrote, and is critical for living organisms for the following three reasons: First, distributive leadership provides leadership and initiative at all levels of the organization that can be used to serve the larger organization. It provides feedback about changes in the internal and external environments and what adaptations are needed so that the organization can thrive. Second, it provides bench strength, continually developing the next generation of leadership and management, increasing its likelihood to be successful and long lasting. And third, it recognizes and supports more individual capacity and individual initiative (self-organizing) at all levels which increases the organization's adaptive capacity, flexibility, and agility. In this volume, Allen expands her notion of distributive leadership to regenerative leadership, which is based on a whole, adaptive living systems framework. Other authors in the volume propose distributive leadership based on the values commons hold dear.

LEADERSHIP ON PEER-TO-PEER NETWORK COMMONS

Baker (2014) focused on leadership in P2P network commons. P2P, which has also been equated with commoning, is a form of production in which individuals in a commons produce and consume their products and are called "prosumers." She proposed that P2P networks rather than individuals are leaders, and that network leadership derives from the relational dynamic of peers. She based her notion of leadership on the system notions of node communities, equipotency, and relational dynamics. She also based her concept on commons values, asserting that "the P2P network is equivalent to the protective process that researchers say enables resilience – caring relationships with compassion, understanding, respect, and interest – and is grounded in listening, safety, and basic trust" (p. 69).

Baker (2014) contended that P2P as a network of peer nodes that send and receive information is the basis of communication and collaboration and creates a relational dynamic that reflects an egalitarian network and manifests as leadership. The network itself becomes the leader as it computes raw data and turns them into actionable information. She argued that all nodes in a P2P network are equally privileged participants in the network in accordance with the principle of equipotency, which is reflected in mutual respect, confidence, and trust. Networks become leaders, Baker contended, when cooperation and collaboration among equals to achieve a common task in pursuit of common good functions and becomes more effective than the traditional schism between leaders and followers.

Although from an outsiders' view it may look as if the network is the leader, we at this point, are not willing to ascribe agency to networks or commons, but rather are concerned with leader behavior and leadership from the perspective of individuals.

REIMAGINING LEADERSHIP ON THE COMMONS

Although the leadership approaches and theories summarized above are applicable to leadership on the commons, none of them except Baker (2014) specifically claim that they are proposing leadership that is derived from the values of the commons. Moreover, none of them specifically discuss leadership as derived from a relational ontology although Baker (2014) contended that the network becomes a leader as relationships between nodes strengthen, implying that leadership is relational. Many of the leadership approaches discussed serve functional roles for maintaining networks and systems. Hence, they illustrate the multifaceted character of leadership as being viewed as serving a functional purpose, in addition to referring to the way leaders approach leadership, to the knowledge and skills leaders need, to the values they uphold, and to their fundamental worldview which is reflected in how they conceive of leadership.

The authors in our volume have constructed leadership approaches based on a paradigm that has shifted away from an individualistic ontology toward one that is essentially relational, based on an open adaptive and living systems worldview, and founded on the commons' values of self-organization, self-governance, care, obligation, compassion, and sustainability, among others. Chapters in our volume are divided into three parts. Part I. "The Paradigm Shift" includes chapters which purposefully challenge the individualistic, self-maximizing economic man paradigm and propose fresh conceptions of leadership. Authors discuss the importance of viewing systems as a whole and viewing leadership as a relational mutualistic process. In Part II. "Leadership on the Commons Lifecyle," authors describe various leadership approaches that serve to bring into being critical stages of the commons lifecycle. Included are creative leadership approaches exercised to catalyze the emergence of commons; convening leadership required to build stakeholder networks to solve complex global commons challenges; distributive leadership that both develops and emerges from a sense of community and *communitas* critical in order for commons to be sustainable; shared leadership that drives the development of collective identity through collaborative processes both within and between commons; and catalytic leadership that initiates collaborative behavior between commons when resources are scarce and must be shared. In Part III. "Leading Different Types of Commons," authors provide a compendium of appropriate leadership approaches for leading a variety of different types of commons, including an arts-focused communally-run café, an open-access agricultural information system, an educational commons for marginalized groups, locally governed water systems, social movements to preserve natural resources and national culture, an acrobatic basketball commons, and finally a call for commons leaders to recognize the global need for jobs commons.

PART I. THE PARADIGM SHIFT

Kathleen E. Allen compares the mindsets and worldviews that underlie regenerative versus degenerative systems in Chapter 1, "Leading Regenerative Systems:

Evolving the Whole Instead of a Part." She argues that most management and leadership theories have been derived from the notion of degenerative systems and have led to many of the problems facing society today. A degenerative worldview views systems as mechanistic rather than living and focuses only on parts of systems. It conceives of systems as closed and has a short-term, self-interested perspective. This worldview optimizes a part of the system such as profit over the health of the whole and justifies exploitation of people and nature. The emotions of scarcity and fear emanate from such a mindset.

On the other hand, a regenerative systems worldview focuses on open living systems, the evolution of whole systems, and their adaptation to the environment. Benefits and burdens are widely shared in a regenerative system. Such a system has a long-term perspective and is filled with positive emotions of trust and care. Regenerative systems are resilient because they adapt to changing conditions and are able to continually learn.

A regenerative mindset goes beyond sustainability to restoration, Allen argues. From restoration, this mindset moves to regeneration and leadership. And, as she concludes,

> Our core purpose in regenerative leadership is to reset our economy, our education systems, our political system, and create a world that is designed as a regenerative system. To do this, we need to start with critical internal beliefs and worldviews and shift them to support a regenerative outcome.

In Chapter 2, "Leading So All Can Thrive: Commons Leadership for Mutualistic Self-Organization," Elizabeth A. Castillo argues that commons leadership, which is particularly effective in organizational contexts characterized by uncertainty, change, and interdependence, "is a relational, mutually beneficial process of influence rooted in cooperation and reciprocity." Commons leadership differs from conventional leadership approaches based on command and control. Rather, it "promotes autonomy, expands degrees of freedom, catalyzes the capabilities of participants, encourages pluralism, and creates architectures for self-organization rather than imposed order." Castillo outlines guiding principles for core aspects of commons leadership – relationships, power, and resources – derived from complexity science and processes found in nature such as "self-organization, mutualism, and resource flows across tropic levels." After presenting an example of commons leadership in systems engineering, Castillo concludes by describing "social accounting as a strategic accountability tool for enacting commons leadership to make pluralistic values legible, hastening more expansive adoption of the commons approach to leadership."

Like Allen and Castillo, Antonio Jimenez-Luque, contends that a leadership approach for the commons must emerge from a change in the heretofore underlying paradigm of leadership theories. In Chapter 3 "Redefining Leadership Through the Commons: An Overview of Two Processes of Meaning-making and Collective Action in Barcelona," Jimenez-Luque argues that even when scholars explore leadership as change, transformation, mobilization, and the construction of the social order, they have based their theories on a hierarchical top-down individualistic approach. He claims this approach derives from the charismatic paradigm that legitimizes the accumulation of power in a few hands.

Jimenez-Luque applauds recent leadership theories that have laid the groundwork for conceiving of leadership as a relational and collective process of meaning-making and views that commons have the opportunity to challenge the old and to introduce a new underlying ontology of leadership. By exploring two commons in Barcelona, *Som Energia* and *Guifi.net*, Jimenez-Luque employs process philosophy to explore how leadership emerges through a combination of framing for meaning making and collective action to advance a task or goal. Jimenez-Luque focuses on two particular elements in the two commons he explores in order to redefine leadership, including: (1) how the collective frameworks to make sense and meaning of the organization as a commons are designed; and (2) how the collective practices to achieve the commons' goals are developed. Jimenez-Luque concludes that

> leadership emerges in the 'in between' of relations and in the 'in between' of actions of people willing to achieve goals together… [and that] leadership is a relational process of meaning making through collective action and thereby debunks mainstream leadership discourses that legitimize the conceptualization of the solo-leader who exercises leadership from the top.

Kathleen A. Curran challenges the typical adversarial relationship between commons and corporations in Chapter 4, "Responsible, Relational, and Intentional: A Re-Imagined Construct of Corporate-Commons Leadership." As she points out, commons and corporations have traditionally existed at adversarial corners of the fighting ring in four key ways: (1) purpose of entity – profit extraction from resources versus protection of resources; (2) rights of resource ownership - individually controlled versus collectively shepherded; (3) responsibility to shareholders versus collective responsibility to stakeholders, that is, an egocentric attitude of dominance as opposed to an ecocentric concern for the whole interconnected planet; and (4) time orientation – short term with an emphasis on shareholder value versus long term with an emphasis on sustainable care of shared resources. Curran argues that neither the 200-year-old industrial model of business nor the efforts of the less powerful commons can be sustained. She contends that, more importantly, working at odds is less beneficial for all. Her chapter challenges the ongoing conflictual dynamics and explores the possibility of leadership on the commons as a corporate-commons hybrid that shares leadership from an ecocentric commons mindset. The construct of responsible leadership and model of intentionality provide the lens through which to view this re-imagined possibility.

In Chapter 5, "What Favelas Can Teach about Leadership: The Importance of Shared-Purpose and Place-Based Leadership," Renato Souza, Thomaz Wood, Jr, and Brad Jackson explore leadership in the favelas of Brazil. The favelas can be considered as commons because they are self-organized and self-governed and autonomous from the state or private sector. The authors argue that leadership "emerges from a relational ontology and a situated-in-place relational dynamics as a collective construction process and that leadership is embedded in a system of interdependencies." Furthermore, leadership needs to be constantly created in the face of significant odds that favelas inevitably face. By employing the concept of the "leadership moment," which theorizes leadership as an event which occurs when context, purpose, followers, and leaders align, the authors examine how leadership occurs through a process of mutual influence between favela leaders and residents, connected by a shared purpose. The authors emphasize the uniqueness of the favela as a "shared place" as being even more influential than shared purpose. Collective direction, alignment, and commitment in the distinctive place of the favelas emerges. Leadership, the authors contend is "a collective construction process." They argue that

> *the interconnections between place, purpose and leaders/residents combine to create collective leadership as leadership needs to be constantly created in the face of the significant challenge of securing infrastructural necessities for sustaining everyday life.*

The authors conclude that leadership does not lie in the people of the favela but in their relations and recurrent interactions and is a property of the collective.

In their Chapter 6, "From Governance to Leadership: Ethical Foundations for Value-Infused Leadership of the Commons," Catharyn Baird, Allison Dake, Jeannine M. Niacaris, and Nancy Sayer propose a process through which commons can establish their micro-social norms. Such norms comprise one of commons scholar Elinor Ostrom's primary design principles to ensure congruence between rules of appropriation, provision, and local conditions vis-à-vis a particular resource. After exploring the history and theories of ethics, including the narrow vision of ethics derived from the metaphors of science which led to systems to monitor people, track accountability, and balance power, the authors explore a process of "conscious conversations." During these conversations, which involve discursive engagement and hypothetical reasoning, commoners become co-creators of the shared values, organizational solutions, and flourishing systems required for equitable, healthy, and prosperous relationships within a thriving community.

Expanding upon Brian Henning's Ethics of Creativity, an ethical theory using an organic processive worldview as a framework for identifying and harmonizing core values and then resolving conflict, the authors enrich their conscious conversations by elaborating five key practices. These include the practices of (1) empathy and compassion, (2) courageous covenant, (3) curiosity, (4) harmonizing values in tension, and (5) discernment. Through these practices, commoners "create a sense of purpose and meaning, and foster hope and courage for positive action."

The authors argue that benevolent leadership is the most appropriate approach for facilitating conscious conversations. Benevolent leadership, the authors write, is an integrated model of regenerative leadership anchored by four key processes:

> *(1) ethical sensitivity, the process of moral reflection and ethical decision-making; (2) spiritual depth, the search for deep meaning and purpose; (3) positive engagement, an emphasis on care and concern for the stakeholders of an organization, instilling hope and courage; and (4) community responsiveness, where the leader and members of the organization together solve social problems through social innovation.*

Randal Joy Thompson's Chapter 7, "Leading Proleptically on the Commons" builds leading proleptically from a human action framework which contends that individual leadership actions are influenced by and influence four different levels of organization, the individual (micro), the collective (meso), the societal (macro), and the universal (meta). Based on a relational ontology in which leadership is a bridging action between these levels, proleptic leadership leads with glimpses of the future which invade the present and which draw the leader toward its realization. Leading proleptically is leading the transformational process toward a commons-centric world manifesting the values of the commons. Proleptic leaders are called to prepare themselves for leadership; open themselves up to the future; and lead themselves, others, and society with integrity and with hope that they can in fact help bring in a new more ethical, equitable, and just world.

PART II. LEADERSHIP ON THE COMMONS LIFECYCLE

Part II. of the book, "Leadership on the Commons Lifecycle" includes chapters that discuss leadership required for several key occurrences and practices of commons. Robin Bisha's Chapter 8, "Developing Leadership on the Commons: Animal Rescue," provides an auto-ethnographical account of creating a commons to rescue animals, primarily dogs. She traverses the process by which her care for animals developed into leadership in a town that was first negligent of unowned animals into one "poised to adopt shared responsibility and collaboration in managing the relationship of the human community and unowned animals in the city."

Bisha's essay is an example of how one's beliefs in the interdependence of humans and animals and her recognition of the need for an animal rescue commons drew her into vocal leadership through modeling a humane approach toward unowned animals, advocating for community shared responsibility, and persisting in her efforts even while being criticized and not seeing the obvious results of her efforts.

As is no doubt typical with many initiating leaders addressing an issue with a commoner's mindset, she relates that she needed courage to step out on her own and accept both the responsibility and potential sacrifices such a move entailed. What initially felt like hopeless despair to reach a seemingly impossible goal turned into "stubborn optimism" which eventually paid off as collaborators joined her and even the local government came to support what she was leading. Leading on a commons requires love, Bisha concluded. Her love for animals carried her through feeling initially isolated from her community to be rejoined to the community when they embraced her belief that animals were worth caring for. As she concluded, "community members are likely to be inspired to take action by watching a neighbor. My experience in Seguin shows that the contours of a nascent commons are not always visible. Leaders may think they have done little, but other people in the community have been watching their example. Modeling commoning can provide the path out of the wasteland to sustainable collaboration based on shared responsibility."

Patricia A. Clary's Chapter 9, "Convening Leadership on the Commons: Initiating Stakeholder Networks to Solve Complex Global Issues" introduces "convening leadership." This leadership approach is required when complex commons challenges, especially global ones, can only be solved by several organizations who need to collaborate to define and implement an agreed-upon solution. Convenors help to form stakeholder groups who develop mutual respect and trust, share their perspectives, and agree to work together even if they represent different and sometimes conflicting interests. Convenors are especially required to help address the challenges that Ostrom and her colleagues faced in solving global commons issues. These include: (1) scaling up and the increased difficulty of organizing and agreeing on governance principles as the number of stakeholders increases; (2) dealing with the increased magnitude of cultural diversity as commons are scaled up; (3) governing a complicated collaborative process as the commons challenges become global, increasing the complexity between interdependent systems; (4) recognizing that tried-and-true solutions are rarely applicable to commons governance given the rapid rate of technological change and changes in the political, social, and environmental factors means; and (5) facing the reality that the possibility of obtaining unanimity on an agreed upon course of action becomes extremely difficult for global commons.

To address these challenges, convenors will: (1) necessarily have to learn how to facilitate collaboration of larger stakeholder networks; (2) need to develop a keen understanding of cultural differences, develop a global mindset, and be able to facilitate collaboration by highlighting diversity as a positive trait; (3) want to understand how the beliefs, values, and attitudes of all stakeholders factor into a flexible adaptive management model of commons governance; (4) need to facilitate a creative co-learning and co-creating environment in order to assist the stakeholders to think outside of the box and derive a new approach to a major challenge and; (5) need strong negotiation skills to meet challenges associated with collaborative stakeholder networks.

Commons are often close communities in which collaborating and co-creating are essential aspects of their cultures. Yet, in network commons such as on the Internet or in open-source information, or in social movements, participants are more distanced or even virtual and may not have close contact with each other. Virtual work has certainly become standard practice during the COVID-19 pandemic and there are indications that it may become a more accepted arrangement even after the pandemic subsides. In their Chapter 10, "Collaborating and Co-Creating Leadership in the Virtual and Not-So-Virtual Commons: Road Warriors, *Communitas*, and Culture," Gayla S. Napier and David Willis present findings from Napier's study of "Road Warriors" and how they develop *communitas* even in their virtual world.

Road warriors are consultants who travel from one project to another and comprise a virtual, always morphing community with each other. Despite working virtually, they recognize each other and meet from time-to-time in airports, restaurants, or hotels and form a self-organized, self-governed commons based on mutuality and care as well as rituals which help them define themselves as they move through liminal space from one assignment to the next. Road warriors as well as virtual workers during the pandemic and Internet commoners

> *are confronted with their need to create a sense of belonging and inclusion in virtual or near virtual space…where* communitas *can develop, a place for mindful interrelating…*Communitas *is that exquisite and rare occurrence of human connection.*

As they write:

> *When* communitas *exists, it involves that part of the community expressed in unity. Boundaries may be invisible but are known to those in the group. Lines of inclusion are drawn, and there exists an "us" and "them" mentality….* Communitas *is about journeying together through something, where the journey or experience brings people together.*

The authors argue that *communitas* may negate the importance of traditional leadership. Instead, leadership may be more distributed, akin to peer governance, with leaders emerging when their perspectives and qualifications are required. Distributed leadership "is not leadership by a single person" Napier and Willis stress. "It is a group activity that works through and within relationships, rather than individual action...Where a traditional hierarchical organization might have one leader much like a conductor in an orchestra, distributed or shared leadership might resemble a jazz ensemble led by one of the musicians based on the rhythm of the moment," they conclude.

One of the central arguments of the most notable commons scholars and activists, including Bollier and Helfrich (2019), DeAngelis (2017), and Bauwens et al. (2019) is that commons must expand and form federations in order to eventually reach a tipping point at which time society will become predominantly commons-centric. Hence, inter-commons or interorganizational collaboration is a key to this transition. Patricia Greer's Chapter 11, "Using Interorganizational Collaboration to Create Shared Leadership Through Collective Identity Development" describes the interorganizational collaborative process. As she notes, this process is one of shared leadership

> *where members from multiple organizations partake in actions to achieve a joint outcome without any formal hierarchy...Shared leadership requires a shared goal, an internally supported process, and a high level of voice and involvement.*

Given that interorganizational collaboration is so important, Greer conducted a study of collaboration experts who submitted 46 collaborations to the Colorado Collaboration Award competition in 2013 and 2014, to determine what qualities made such collaboration successful. Interorganizational collaboration requires members of the organization to co-construct processes that operate without organizational structural support. Success factors identified by Greer include committed members, resources, time, communication, trust, shared goal, and defined process. The most important factors Greer highlighted that emerged from her study comprise: collective identity, the development of relationships that bring value to communities, and despite challenges and differences, the building of something wonderful together. Greer's study also details a collaborative process that most likely takes place within a commons. No doubt, the process of communicating, developing a shared purpose, creating trust and openness, and eventually collective identity is the process by which commoning creates a commons which is why commoning is a subjective building activity.

Collective identity is an extremely important concept for the commons transition as commons form federations and push for changes to support them. Greer posits a new model of achieving collective identity through collaboration. She found that success in a collaboration may have multiple meanings, ranging from completion of the shared goal to building capacity within a community. Furthermore, as Greer explains, social capital is built during the process and spills out into organizations and the community.

In their Chapter 12, "The Role of Leaders in Catalyzing Cooperative Behavior in the Governance of Nonprofit Sector Shared Resources: The Case of Early Childhood Education," Angela Titi Amayah, MD Haque, and Wendolly A. Escobar also focus on interorganizational collaboration, but are concerned with the sharing of resources in an increasingly resource-scarce world lacking government support for the non-governmental sector. Their example of resource sharing is significant for the commons. Because commons function outside of the state and private sector, they may face times of scarce resources and will need to join together to do more with less. In the case of the interorganizational collaboration to govern scarce resources in the child education and protection sector, the authors argue that a leader is required to be a catalyst of cooperative processes. Based on extensive interviews of a number of nonprofit sector leaders who are responsible for resource-seeking public-private partnerships, they developed a framework of success factors for leaders to catalyze cooperative behavior. They determined that successful catalytic leaders of cooperative behavior need passion, keen relationship building skills, and openness to change by shifting their mindset and outlook and further developing their capacity, knowledge, and skills.

PART III. LEADING SPECIFIC TYPES OF COMMONS

In her Chapter 13, "The Peoples' Voice Cafe: Leading Collectively & Horizontally for More Than 40 Years," Susan (Susie) J. Erenrich employs portraiture, a form of narrative inquiry, to describe her lived experience in preparing for performances and in experiencing how horizontal, collective, and collaborative leadership manifests in the Peoples' Voice Cafe, a New York City Commons that for over 40 years has provided a space for the artistic expressions of humanitarian issues and concerns. Erenrich argues that such shared grassroots ventures comprised of cultural activists and arts organizations are generally excluded from the general conversation. Erenrich provides a personal narrative of planning the last event of the year to be held on May 16, 2020, a concert titled, *The Cost of Freedom* to mark the 50th anniversary of the shootings on the Kent State and Jackson State college campuses. The event was also to launch a new anthology that she edited, *The Cost of Freedom: Voicing A Movement After Kent State 1970.* Yet, the event was not to be: COVID-19 interfered. Although Erenrich eventually held the event virtually, she clearly missed the interpersonal interaction of the cafe.

Describing how leadership is practiced by members of the cafe horizontally, collectively, and collaboratively, she points out that such leadership, although only recently "discovered" in the leadership literature has been practiced among activists for many decades. As she writes, the "We Are All Leaders" paradigm was around long before the cafe existed, and the field of leadership was an accepted area of inquiry. The terminology was different, but the fundamental principles are similar." The Industrial Worker of the World (IWW), otherwise known as the Wobblies, answered Sheriff McRae when he shouted out to them, "Who is your leader?" "We are all leaders!" Since its beginnings, group-centered leadership has also been practiced at the Highlander research and Education Center, founded as the Highlander Folk School. Erenrich notes that the Highlander is a place where "average citizens can pool their knowledge, learn from history ... and seek solutions to their social problems."

In Chapter 14, "Open Data, Distributed Leadership and Food Security: The Role of Women Smallholder Farmers," authors Éliane Ubalijoro, Victor N. Sunday, Foteini Zampati, Uchechi Chirly Anaduaka, and Suchith Anand, explore the work of Global Open Data for Agriculture and Nutrition (GODAN) and partner Unique Mappers Network. They recount how these open-source commons leverage open data mapping to drive GODAN's capacity development efforts, United Nations Sustainable Development Goal (SDG) targets and women-inclusive community engagement in Nigeria. Open-source data is an extremely important commons, which, as the authors illustrate, is key to empowering marginalized groups throughout the world. Once these groups can obtain the richness of information which was previously withheld from them through copyrights and expensive books in foreign languages, people such as the women shareholders highlighted in this chapter can take control of and improve their livelihood and wellbeing. Further, as the authors emphasize "the distributed, inclusive and diverse leadership of Open Data is emerging as an important model for global leadership of the commons, especially networked digital commons."

The authors focus primarily on how open data positively impacts knowledge related to women's land rights, productivity, and agricultural sustainability, as a critical step toward the food sustainability and the end of world hunger. Such open data sources such as GODAN are bringing together experts and leaders from multiple disciplines including geospatial data, agriculture production, postharvest technologies and climate who collaborate to build rich and robust information systems. As the authors write,

> GODON also includes intellectual property to share knowledge that enables collaborative synergy towards equitable access of knowledge to all for the production, processing, storage, sales and consumption of food while improving nutrition.

They highlight the Unique Mappers Network in Nigeria and how this network is empowering women shareholders to improve their livelihood and present this example as a critical step toward producing adequate food to feed the vastly growing world population and to ending hunger, a challenge which the global pandemic has gravely highlighted.

In Chapter 15, "Learning and Leading Together to Transform the World: Jesuit Higher Education and Ignatian Leadership Formation at the Margins," Dung Q. Tran and Michael R. Carey explore leadership in global educational commons. Originally founded as "Jesuit Commons: Higher Education at the Margins" the "Jesuit Worldwide Learning: Higher Education at the Margins" (JWL) establishes self-organized educational commons in communities to provide education to marginalized groups and mentor them to become leaders. The authors introduce a differently nuanced notion of the commons as the

> collective and cooperative process of actualization of common... potentials [intellectual, spiritual, emotional, linguistic, and material, among others] that entails necessarily the mobilization of human-kind in its totality' to concretize collective strategies of solidarity among diverse individuals and communities to enact structural social change.

Based on the 500-year-old Ignatian spiritual and pedagogical tradition that undergirds this educational initiative, these commons currently provide education to 4,000 students in Afghanistan, the Central African Republic, the Democratic Republic of Congo, Guyana, India, Iraq, Italy, Jordan, Kenya, Malawi, Myanmar, Nepal, Philippines, Sri Lanka, Togo, and Zambia. Partner organizations allocate staff to the educational community volunteering, supporting, teaching, tutoring, and learning together. JWL has sixteen university partners throughout the world who make their contributions in kind "through the provision of volunteer faculty, academic and/or IT platforms and service" illustrating the power of self-organized, self-governed commons in which responsibility and care are the dominant values.

Chapter 16, "Traditional Leadership on the Commons: Main Challenges for Leaders of Community Organizations to Govern Rural Water in Ránquil, Chile," by Camila Alejandra Vargas Estay, Noelia Carrasco Henríquez, Victor Manuel Vargas Rojas, and Luis Gatica Mora, focuses on the local self-governance of water by local Water Committees in Chile. The chapter highlights the challenges leaders of these committees face. This chapter is especially important because it emphasizes the fact that leadership on the commons is especially vulnerable to a capitalistic system in which, as in Chile, water is considered an asset, subject to property rights, and is distributed by profit-making companies. Local communities often have to struggle to obtain access to safe, affordable water, which is necessary for life and provided freely by nature. The water wars in Cochabamba, Bolivia from 1999 to 2000 illustrated the result of communities being excluded from access to water because of the price. The citizens protested *en masse* until the government was forced to break the contract they had signed with a multinational water company. Citizens were then able to form local self-organized, self-governed water committees as a result of their uprising.

The authors of this chapter elaborate the main challenges local water committees have in effectively providing water to their communities as follows. Water outages continue to plague the community, often threatening their food production and livelihoods. Leaders need to have the ability to deal with an onslaught of complaints during these times. Water quality is also an issue the community has to deal with when it is contaminated by sediment and the leaders need to organize the community in order to clean the water. Dealing with the municipality and the state hydraulic works department causes the most problems for leaders since government procedures are slow. As Ostrom pointed out (1990), polycentric governance structures are necessary for commons to effectively function but obtaining the support of some of these higher-level structures can pose potential hurdles local communities need to cross.

As the authors conclude:

> *One of the main findings of this study shows that despite the regula-*
> *tion of the State and institutions, the community vision and sense*
> *of water as a common and a basic universal right prevails in them.*
> *In this interstice, leaders must face the challenges inside and outside*
> *their communities through constant interaction with public and*
> *private agents for the proper operation of local water systems.*

Edin Ibrahimefendic explores social movements, essential expressions of the commons that often lead not only to social change but also to the establishment of sustainable commons in Chapter 17, "Leadership of the Commons in Bosnia and Herzegovina: Protecting Natural Resources and Reclaiming Public Space." Commons, in this instance include the struggle against privatization and statization as their constitutive element. This more political definition of commons facilitates the exploration of "conflict over access and control of some specific resource, as well as to analyze various actors that engage in conflict and the discourse that they use." Ibrahimefendic explores two social movements in Bosnia and Herzegovina, a movement against the building of a dam as a prelude to building a hydropower station in Kruščica, a village in central Bosnia in the municipality of Vitez, and a movement to reopen the National Museum in Sarajevo.

Ibrahimefendic argues that leadership in the former social movement was collective whereas in the latter was elitist. After summarizing the war and its aftermath in his country which left a consocialist ethnically divided state with little sense of national identity, Ibrahimefendic argues that

> *leadership, in order to be truly effective, has to be exercised on*
> *important and commonly held causes above ethnic divisions and*
> *outside the politics of the government in order to maintain its legiti-*
> *macy in the eyes of the public.*

In the two cases he discusses, leadership was indeed exercised above divisions and outside politics. Leadership was exercised in Kruščica predominately by the women in the local community and in the case of the National Museum, by somewhat elite culturalists and international diplomats. Both groups demonstrated against the State and its ethnic politics and acted without reference to ethnicity. In fact, in Kruščica, one of the most violent and brutal localities during the civil war, ethnic divisions that persisted following the war were minimized as women of both the Bosniak and Croat ethnic groups – bitter enemies during the war – bonded together to save their river.

Ibrahimefendic characterized the leadership they employed to prevent the bulldozers from entering the river banks and in standing up against police brutality as collective.

The government of Bosnia and Herzegovina had closed the National Museum, a treasure trove of antiquity and the precious Jewish Haggadah from Spain because the sub-governments of the consocialist state could not agree on funding it. A social movement comprised of artists, art afficionados, historians, anthropologists, ambassadors and other diplomats, along with international donors began a movement "I am the Museum" to reopen the museum as the national home of the rich cultural history of the country. Museum employees worked in the museum without salaries in order to ensure that the artifacts were maintained and eventually the movement was able to reopen the museum and pressure the government to finance its maintenance. Ibrahimefendic called the leadership exercised by the movement as elitist since the participants stood apart from the emerging capitalist culture and valued history and art above profit. In both cases, the movements are still active and are continuing to pressure the government to protect the rivers from hydropower plants and the public space represented by the museum.

Katja Hleb, Miha Škerlavaj, and Domen Rozman assess the relationship between communal culture and responsible leadership in Chapter 18, "Hopping the Hoops or Building a Communal Culture as the Most Significant Pillar of Leadership of the Commons." Communal culture is the culture built and intertwined in the community, serving as its glue and pivotal axis. Responsible leadership is a leadership component of corporate social responsibility that focuses on the broad group of stakeholders instead of the narrow group of shareholders. Both communal culture and responsible leadership are relevant concepts for the commons. The authors employed grounded theory to explore these concepts in the Dunking Devils organization, an acrobatic basketball group who has earned several entries in the Guinness Book of Records. As they conclude, their findings

> establish responsibility on an individual and group level as a solid norm, strong presence of authenticity and international context, all elements of responsible leadership. These elements are intertwined with multiple evidence of community and communal culture, underlined in verbal, written, behavioral or group values expression.

In the final chapter of our book, Chapter 19 "Job Commons: The Overlooked Dimension of Commons Leadership and Global and Local Governance," Jan Hurst calls out commons scholars and activists for ignoring the importance of jobs and highlights the importance of establishing jobs commons. Instead of suggesting a leadership approach, Hurst provides an in-depth overview of the commons literature and its weakness in not confronting the need for everyone to have meaningful work in order to fulfill themselves and sustain everyday life. She requests that commons leaders everywhere recognize the importance of a job commons and move quickly to promote these globally.

Recognizing that capitalism purposefully rations jobs for profit and saving, Hurst contends that

> *commons conceptualization is a useful entry point to problematize jobs at a higher level of abstraction so that political and civic leaders, communities, policy-makers and institutions can link job struggle to the commons for personal and social survival.*

She argues that "shifting priorities requires an ethical awakening and transnational solidarity, similar to how recent civil rights protests are forcing leaders to disrupt the status quo and address structural racism." Hurst defines "job commons" as the commonization of jobs so that waged-labor can access local commons-protected jobs in addition to jobs in competitive job markets. A jobs commons would be self-organized and self-governed and would ensure that every person seeking employment could find a job. A key question is whether a job-centric commons can secure human dignity and incomes wherever worthwhile jobs are needed most and support multi-racial working classes to sustain livelihoods through work, not just wealth.

REFLECTIONS ON LEADERSHIP ON THE COMMONS

As is evidenced by these diverse chapters, leadership on the commons can play many different roles depending upon the stage of development of the commons and the type of commons. Trends are evident in the fact that leadership is built upon a relational rather than an individualistic paradigm and that leaders emerge throughout the commons rather than being identified positionally. Terms such as "collaborative," "horizontal," "distributive," "responsible," "sharing," occur, and indicate the cooperative nature of commons and their leadership approach. Table 1 summarizes most of leadership approaches and their role in the commons.

Table 1. Leadership Approaches on the Commons.

Author	Type of Leadership	Definition of Leadership	Role on Commons
Part I. Paradigm Shift			
Kathleen A. Curran	Responsible Leadership	Shifts the focus from shareholders to stakeholders and engenders social responsibility.	Transforms corporations into organizations focused also on sustainability and with a commons value system.
Kathleen E. Allen	Regenerative Leadership	Focus on whole open living system, evolution of whole system and adaptation to environment.	To reset our economy, education, and political systems and create a world designed as a regenerative system.
Elizabeth A. Castillo	Commons Leadership	Relational, mutually beneficial process of influence rooted in cooperation and reciprocity	Promotes autonomy, expands degrees of freedom, catalyzes participant capabilities, encourages pluralism and self-organization
Antonio Jimenez-Luque	Leadership as a relational process of meaning making through collective action	Leadership emerges in the 'in between' of relations and in the 'in between' of actions of people willing to achieve goals together.	Facilitates the commons identity.
Renato Souza, Thomaz Wood, Jr., and Brad Jackson	Relational Leadership	Leadership emerges in the shifting relationships between identified leaders and followers and subject to the "place" of the favelas.	Creates responsive leadership to challenges on the commons.
Catharyn Baird, Allison Dake, Jeannine M. Niacaris, and Nancy Sayer	Benevolent Leadership	Integrated Model of regenerative leadership with ethical sensitivity, spiritual depth, positive engagement, and community responsiveness.	Facilitates conscious conversations to develop commons values.
Randal Joy Thompson	Proleptic Leadership	Glimpses of the future commons-centric society and expanded consciousness invade the present and guide change.	Facilitates change toward a commons-centric society which manifests commons values.

Table 1. (Continued)

Author	Type of Leadership	Definition of Leadership	Role on Commons
Part II. Leadership on the commons lifecycle			
Robin Bisha	Initiating Leadership	"Stubborn optimism" that a commons is worth it and inspiring others by one's dedication and actions.	Initiates a commons and encourages/convinces individuals to join.
Patricia A. Clary	Convening Leadership	Convincing Stakeholders from different organizations to join together to solve complex challenge.	Brings in multiple perspectives and abilities to act and govern a complex commons challenge.
Gayla S. Napier and David Blake Willis	Distributed Leadership/Peer Governance	Leaders emerge when their perspectives and qualifications are required.	A commons group activity that works through and within relationships rather than individual action.
Patricia Greer	Shared Leadership	Members collaborate and form collective identity to solve commons problems.	Members from multiple organizations partake in actions to achieve a joint outcome without any formal hierarchy.
Angela Amayah, MD Haque and Wendolly A. Escobar	Catalytic Leadership	Works to convince organizations to collaborate and share resources.	Solves scarce resource issues with commons.
Part III. Leading Different Types of Commons			
Susan (Susie) J. Erenrich	Horizontal/collective Leadership	Everyone is a leader.	Take turns accomplishing the goals of the commons.
Éliane Ubalijoro, Victor N. Sunday, Foteini Zampati, Uchech Anaduaka, and Suchith Anand	Distributed, Inclusive, Diverse Leadership	Involves diverse experts and beneficiaries who converge on an open data system.	Facilitates experts and stakeholders forming relationship through data which catalyzes action.
Edin Ibrahimefendic	Collective Leadership Elite Leadership	Represent leadership approaches in social movements that evolve into commons.	Facilitate social action, social movements, and commons to achieve.
Katja Hleb, Miha Škerlavaj, and Domen Rozman	Responsible Leadership	Shifts the focus from shareholders to stakeholders and engenders social responsibility.	Transforms corporations into organizations focused also on sustainability and with a commons value system.

CARE AS THE FOUNDATIONAL ETHIC OF LEADERSHIP ON THE COMMONS

As stated earlier in this Introduction, the notion of the commons is etymologically comprised of the meanings of debt and gift, the notion both that we owe something to others and to the environment and hence have an obligation to them and that what we receive from others and the environment is given freely as a gift. Underlying these notions is a particular ethic based on the concept of "care." Care is what binds these Janus-faced concepts together. The ethic of care also underlies leadership on the commons as highlighted by Devin P. Singh, in his introduction Part II which follows.

NOTES

1. Some parts of this introduction have been adapted from my book *Proleptic Leadership on the Commons: Ushering in a New Global Order* (2020). Emerald Publishing.

2. This section on leadership within networks, systems, and nature is adapted from my book *Proleptic Leadership on the Commons: Ushering in a New Global Order* (2020). Emerald Publishing.

REFERENCES

Allen, K. (2019). *Leading from the roots: Nature-inspired leadership lessons fort today's world*. Morgan James Publishing.

Baker, M. N. (2014). *Peer-to-peer leadership: Why the network is the leader*. Berrett-Koehler Publishers.

Bauwens, M., Kostakis, V., & Pazaitis, A. (2019). Peer to peer. The commons manifesto. University of Westminister Press.

Benkler, Y. (2011). *The penguin and the leviathan: How cooperation triumphs over self-interest*. Random House.

Bollier, D. (2014). *Think like a commoner: A short introduction to the life of the commons*. New Society Publishers.

Bollier, D., & Helfrich, S. (2019). *Free, fair, and alive: The insurgent power of the commons*. New Society Publishers.

Dardot, P., & Laval, C. (2019). *Common: On revolution in the 21ˢᵗ century*. Bloomsbury Press.

DeAngelis, M. (2017). *Omnia sunt communia: On the commons and the transformation to postcapitalism*. Zed Books.

Edwards, A. E. (2005). *The sustainability revolution: Portrait of a paradigm shift.* New Society Publishers.

Gergen, K. (2006). *Relational being: Beyond self and community.* Cambridge University Press.

Hardin, G. (1968). The tragedy of the commons. *Science, 162,* 1243–1248.

Helfrich, S. (2013). Economics and commons: Toward a commons-creating peer economy. Presentation given at the conference Economics and the commons, From seed form to core paradigm. May 22–24, 2013. Berlin, Germany.

Ogden, C. (2018). What is network leadership? *Building Community.* Retrieved from https://www.nextgenlearning.org/articles/what-is-network-leadership

Ostrom, E. (1990). *Governing the commons: The evolution of institutions for common action.* Cambridge University Press.

Rifkin, J. (2014). *The zero marginal cost society: The internet of things, the collaborative commons, and the eclipse of capitalism.* Palgrave Macmillan.

Schreiber, C. & Carley, K. M. (2008). Network leaders: Leading for learning adaptability. In M. Uhl-Bien & R. Marion (Eds.), *Complexity leadership. Part I. Conceptual foundations* (pp. 291–332). Information Age Publishing.

Thompson, R. (2020). *Proleptic leadership on the commons: Ushering in a new global order.* Emerald Publishing.

Uhl-Bien, M., & Marion, R. (2008). Complexity leadership. Part I. Conceptual foundation. Information Age Publishing.

Uhl-Bien, M., Marion, R., & McKelvey. (2007). Complexity leadership theory: Shifting leadership from the industrial age to the knowledge era. *The Leadership Quarterly, 18,* 298–318.

Williams, R. (1983). *Keywords: A vocabulary of culture and society.* Fontana Press.

INTRODUCTION PART II:
DEBT, OBLIGATION, AND CARE
ON THE COMMONS

DEVIN P. SINGH

Discussions about the commons raise philosophical questions about what we owe to one another as members of communities and societies. They also invoke claims about what society or the larger whole owes to us as individual members. In a book such as this seeking practical and transformative visions for leadership on the commons, it is appropriate to step back and grapple briefly with some of the subtle conceptual issues at hand. Rights, duties, obligations – these are the kinds of terms used to map and legislate life together politically and economically. It strikes me that one of the sites of confusion and tension around mapping our responsibilities within a commons framework concerns the ways debt and indebtedness blur with broader notions of obligation. This is partly why economic considerations are (understandably) foregrounded since language of debt (correctly) invokes financial considerations. But it limits our analysis to reduce the scope of our social bonds to economic ones. Discussions about obligations on the commons are partly grasping at what exceeds or is simply different than the economic but still pertains to what we owe to one another in our common life together.

My research seeks to disambiguate debt from the many other types of obligations and bonds we might forge with one another. More clarity and delineation are necessary when we speak about various bonds along relational, affective, political, economic, and even spiritual or religious lines. I am not ultimately trying to purify social relations of debt completely. Not only do I think this may be impractical, but I suspect (radically chastened) debt agreements may indeed still have some place in social arrangements. Yet debt relations are a small subset of possible ways to form bonds, and yet they have crowded out these alternatives conceptually and structurally.

Conceptually, because we have allowed debt to overflow the banks of its proportionate and reasonable courses in our thinking about human life, letting it flood into other conceptual channels of bond and obligation. Debt has colonized our imagination, leading us to speak of many distinct forms of reciprocity under its banner in ways that have poisoned those relations and closed the horizons of possibility that other types of connections might allow. The fact that terms as diverse as debt, gift, duty, and guilt are regularly invoked together in ways that make them appear synonymous shows the failure of our conceptual discourse in adequately defining them (Godelier, 1999; Mauss, 1990). This fuzziness of speech reflects and can reinforce a fuzziness of practice and policy, further compounding potentially deleterious effects of letting the economic register of debt hold too much sway.

Structurally, because our economic systems have come to rely on debt as the central driving factor for growth. It is no secret that our market systems now center on debt as the generator of money (i.e., endogenous bank money), as fueling new enterprises and firms, and as the central financial instrument to generate new capital through speculation. The derivatives market and other forms of collateralized debt obligations that precipitated the 2008 financial crisis are one well-documented example of the instabilities brought on by a system saturated in debt. This preponderance of debt as a structural feature is partly due to a parallel invasion of debt into political arrangements, with debt forming the lifeblood of sovereignty in the modern, public debt-funded, nation state (MacDonald, 2003; Roos, 2019; Singh, 2018; Wray, 2003). This political transformation, coinciding with modernity and the rise of capitalism, has fueled extensive structural innovations in our economic and financial systems.

In a relationship far more ancient and longstanding than its role in funding the nation state, debt has also lent its conceptual devices to legal traditions and to theorizations of justice. As I will explore briefly below, debt is the background condition and assumption that makes notions of reciprocal justice, retribution, and punitive compensation intelligible. Visions of leadership and governance on the commons, such as the diverse array captured in this book, must grapple with how they fit into and deploy frameworks for justice and equity in the new communities we hope to construct or help emerge. Considering the links of debt to notions of justice and even civic obligation opens up to an assessment of care as an important element of life in common. As we will see, care proposes an alternative set of relational dynamics that may transcend the norms of debt-based obligation and reciprocity that justice assumes. Whether as complement to or replacement of justice as the governing normative framework, care offers important resources for arranging patterns of exchange and coordinating shared governance and resources on the commons.

BLURRED LINES

Discussions about the commons frequently (and understandably) explore the kinds of obligations and reciprocities that are called for in order to sustain common spaces, resources, and life orientations. One of the techniques is the etymological study of the term "commons" related to a variety of other terms such as "community" and "communion." The Latin background to such English terms, drawing on ancient Roman law and custom, reveals a cluster of associate terms with a range of application. "Commons," "community," and "communion" derive from Latin terms such as *communis* and *communitas*, composites containing the prefix *co-* ("with") and derivations of the substantive *munus*, which has a variety of possible senses ranging from "gift" to "duty" to "obligation."

Pierre Dardot and Christian Laval (2019), in their magisterial study of the commons, claim that *munus* is a term that blurs and binds together a variety of political and economic obligations: "What we find in the term's etymological meaning is thus the Janus-face of the debt and the gift, of obligation and recognition" (p. 10). Their analysis suggests and maintains the ambiguities of relation here captured in debt and gift, which for them are signaled by the dualities of obligation and recognition. While they go on to focus primarily on the notion of duty and civic responsibility here, what interests me is the duality of debt and gift that they highlight. They are right to suggest a proximity and even a possibility that debt and gift – as Janus-faced – may be two sides of the same coin. But they stop short of analysis and distinction.

Roberto Esposito (2010), in his significant work on the nature of community and immunity, also explores the relation of gift, debt, and obligation in the *munus*:

> the munus *that the* communitas *shares isn't a property or a possession. It isn't having, but on the contrary, is a debt, a pledge, a gift that is to be given, and that therefore will establish a lack.*

The subjects of community are united by an "obligation," in the
sense that we say "I owe you something," but not "you owe me
something." This is what makes them not less than the masters
of themselves, and that more precisely expropriates them of their
initial property (in part or completely), of the most proper property,
namely, their very subjectivity. (pp. 6–7)

Esposito here seeks to depict a posture of the self that is fundamental to life together in community. It is a posture of openness, giving, intentional lack, and response to obligation in the sense of relinquishing a part of oneself, giving up self-enclosure and self-sovereignty, so as to give of it to the common, the public, the whole. For Esposito, that position must be one of outward orientation, where obligation is to give but is not bent on reciprocity or return.

While there is much here to consider, much more than can be explored in this limited space, I want to highlight the swift ways that debt, gift, and obligation get blurred and woven together in this conversation. Esposito appears here to regard the distinctions as insignificant to designate the dynamics of the commons. Or perhaps instead it is their blurring and conceptual fuzziness that are generative, allowing these terms to capture a broad and vague swath of ways we might be bound together in mutuality and reciprocity.

Indeed, one might say that this blurring is necessary, that *munus* and concomitant notions of the commons and community require it. But I think otherwise. When gift dynamics are outlined and described, debt often figures in as a hazy background condition to explain the obligations and reciprocities we find in gifts. Certainly, overlap occurs but greater delineation and distinction are possible. While the realities of life together are always messy, and it may never be fully clear in practice where debt ends and gift begins, in the conceptual realm more clarity and delineation are called for and can be attempted. This is the purpose of abstraction and critical reflection, to give us distance and to attempt certain classifications and categorizations for the sake of clearer understanding and possibly more intentional forms of praxis.

There are a number of ways that gifts have been defined and I will not cover them here, but one of the primary characteristics often invoked is that gifts mark relationships. Gifts are often contrasted with money or commodities which focus on the exchange itself or the objects gained, while gifts supposedly put the relational bond front and center and put questions of the value of goods exchanged to the background. Costs are not openly discussed but the objects given are instead invested with symbolic power to signify the care, interest, or honor offered by the giver toward the receiver. While gifts may be celebrated as free, in the sense of not being required but being more spontaneous, they usually call for some kind of reciprocity, whether it is a simple word of thanks and acknowledgement, to a counter gift and return of something of value at a later point. In both cases, the recognition and reciprocation further solidify the relationship.

Much has been made of the fact that, in many contexts, gifts appear binding. In some non-market or so-called "primitive" societies studied by anthropologists, the exchange culture compels return or reciprocation, through offering counter gifts or through passing on the gift to others (Codere, 1950; Gregory, 1982; Malinowski, 1922; Mauss, 1990; Sahlins, 1972). The language often used is that of debt: the gift creates a debt that must be compensated for with a counter gift. And as we saw in both Dardot and Laval as well as Esposito, debt and gifts may be invoked in tandem in ways that convey if not synonymity then extreme proximity.

In addition to gifts, however, we also have a very different kind of reciprocal relationship that has been created in many human societies. In this relationship, a giver provides something of value to the recipient and the receiver acknowledges receipt. In this scenario, however, the value of what is given is openly discussed. More than that, its value is quantified and formally marked by the conventions of that society, according to its weights and measures. In addition, the giver states or otherwise is transparent about the fact that what is given is a kind of sacrifice, that it creates a loss to the giver. In addition to talk of price or value, this acknowledgement is typically something that would be shameful in gift exchange. Furthermore, the recipient also openly acknowledges the value of that which is received and recognizes the loss or sacrifice experienced by the giver. More than this, the receiver openly and transparently pledges to make up for and remediate the loss of the giver whether by returning what was given at a later time (usually with a little more of it) or by providing something else of comparable value in return. A clear timeframe of return is established. The recipient also agrees that if they fail to return the value to the giver, the giver may seize the value by force or, depending on the society, the recipient may serve as a slave to the giver in order to work off this value. This acknowledgement is formalized into an agreement, which is also attested to and recorded, whether in writing, witnesses, oaths, or contracts.

Clearly, we are in very different territory than gifts. Debt is the word typically used to describe this kind of exchange. It is distinct from gift in the open and acknowledged value given as well as the open and formalized terms of reciprocation as well as consequences for failure. The formalization of the exchange and quantification of value take it well out of the realm of what is typically described in gift exchange. The invocation of law or possibly forms of state violence as consequences for failure to repay also appears of a different order than the shame or communal sanction that may occur if one is a bad gift recipient who fails to offer an adequate counter gift. While we do have evidence of a kind of gift slavery in such archaic economies – in other words, the consequences of not reciprocating gifts could be severe and even lead to bondage and servitude – these implied and informal outcomes are also different than agreed upon terms in a debt contract.

My point is that to say that gifts create debts that must be repaid is to confuse the terms profoundly and cross registers in ways that risk incoherence and limit explanations of the logic of exchange and resultant patterns of community. Certainly, gifts create something that compels reciprocation, just as debts create and also formalize something that compels repayment, adding additional external consequences. To use debt to speak of gifts and to thus invoke this formal, quantified, economic exchange is unhelpful since it violates what is meant by gift. We need different terms. In my view, debt should remain relegated to this formal type of exchange. The category that both gifts and debts partake of, which captures this pressure to reciprocate, is obligation.

Just as it makes little sense to speak of the debt of the gift, it is unhelpful to use the term debt to speak of duties to parents or loved ones, senses of political fealty and loyalty, or other senses of having benefitted from gods, ancestors, or society at large, unless one intends to quantify this obligation, state it in formal terms, and delineate how one might repay it. My point is that, while all these dynamics certainly express and partake of a larger sense of obligation, debt remains a distinct subcategory. In using debt to describe these relations, we have allowed debt to colonize our imaginations and shape perceptions of this vast array of relational obligations. Debt, as one type of obligation, has been allowed to become a master category and lens through which other obligations are viewed. In doing so, we implicitly (or at times explicitly) insert a monetary sense of price, quantity, and payment into these interstices in ways that we may actually want to resist or at least question.

In discussion of the commons, we need to think about the place of gift (and it is a spectrum; there are some gift relations we may want to limit or exclude, others that we want to magnify as central), and the place of economic obligations we call debts. While the current trend in progressive circles is the elimination or eradication of most debt (for good reason given the abuses and excesses of a late capitalist system that runs on debt), it is not clear what it would take to move beyond any and all quantification of our economic obligations to one another coupled with requests to make good, pay back, or otherwise reciprocate in ways that are more specific and stipulated than gifts. We may decide that debt remains socially necessary in some sense and at some level, even if we want to reduce its scope and limit its reach. What we must do is resist and decolonize the imagination around obligation, conquered as it has been by debt and notions of economized and quantified reciprocities.

AMBIVALENT INTIMACIES

Mapping the potential networks of communal obligations takes us into discussions of trust, social capital, and social credit. Trust has recently dominated conversations about corporate governance (Kramer & Cook, 2004; Kramer & Pittinsky, 2012; Kramer & Tyler, 1996) and reconstructing civil society (Gambetta, 1988; Luhmann, 2017), and is sometimes invoked in discussions of the commons (Barnes, 2006). Trust is one label we have for navigating the ambiguities and ambivalences of exchange. Whatever spectrum we have in mind about more or less trust relates specifically to the capacities we have or obstacles we face to engage in some form of exchange. Exchanges are fraught with ambiguity and even tension. In the context of an exchange, much can apparently go awry. This causes us to seek out or create certain conditions to have in place to help us enter into exchanges with more ease and also leave open the possibility of future exchanges. These conditions fall under the rubric of trust. Trust is based on information, experience, and other external, material conditions, but also highlights a realm of emotion or affect.

Yet trust is also typically implicit. Because it is felt and partakes of the affective realm, trust does not enter into language or discourse unless it is troubled. Even expressions of trust – "I trust you" – signify that the boundaries of trust are being tested, that something has happened to put the bonds of trust at risk. While I write here with material, economic exchanges involving money, commodities, and other material resources primarily in mind, we can certainly think about trust and exchange in many areas. Within the context of intimate, interpersonal relationships, for instance, where we seek places to open up, become vulnerable, share of ourselves, and feel loved and accepted in return, the presence or absence of trust indicates our ability to engage in these kinds of interpersonal, emotional exchanges. We want to give of ourselves and have that offering accepted and honored. We want to experience reciprocity in having something of the other shared in return. In this sense, even when no commodities are involved, trust and exchange operate together.

When we approach potential exchanges, whether material or otherwise, things may not go as intended or desired. We might misrecognize the nature of the exchange. We might assume an exchange is happening or going to happen, in a way not assumed by the other party. The other party may do likewise, surprising us when we had no anticipation of an exchange. Even when both parties are on the same page that an exchange is taking place, they may be misaligned about the nature of it. Even if both agree on the nature of it, the terms and values of what are to be exchanged still need to be negotiated and worked out. With so many layers of ambiguity it is a wonder that humans have engaged in exchanges for as long as the species has been around and continue to do so (clearly, with varying degrees of success). This is why human societies have evolved so many varying ways to speak about exchanges: gifts, sacrifices, debts, money, commodities, etc. Each designation is in part a way to signal what is happening in an exchange, so that the various parties involved might have some commensurate level of information and expectation.

All of this assumes good intentions on the part of exchangers. But we know that exchanges can be duplicitous and manipulative. One can enter into an exchange with false pretenses. We have labels such as cheat, scam, or con, for instance, to designate such exchanges, where trust is taken advantage of and misused. This is further problematized when certain values or contexts may celebrate such duplicitous exchanges as somehow praiseworthy. Extracting the most value out of someone without their knowledge or consent, or under the pretense of providing equal value in return but actually not, may be seen as a great way to undertake exchanges. This is what the anthropologist Marshall Sahlins termed "negative reciprocity" (Sahlins, 1972).

Solutions to trust problems often take econometric directions by trying to save exchange relations through stabilization and measure. Tactics include attempting greater levels of explicitness and definition of roles and responsibilities, introducing metrics for behavior and execution, or providing cost-benefit analyses as tools for an incentive structure. What I want to highlight about these approaches to remediation is the reliance on a debt-based imagination and framework as the resource to redeem trust. It is debt-based (or, arguably, monetized, but they may amount to the same thing) because it seeks quantified, explicit, and formalized terms for exchange, relying on a history of debt contracts for assumptions about how to incentivize desired behaviors within a social network. Relations based on the care and trust glimpsed in informal reciprocities marked by gifts here give way to formal and measurable metrics of exchange characteristic of debt.

The discussion of trust has bearing on a related conversation about social capital. There are two dominant and slightly conflicting definitions of social capital circulating in the literature, differences that introduce some confusion. The first (both initial and primary) sense of social capital describes the benefits that accrue to members of certain groups (Bourdieu, 1986; Portes, 1998; Veblen, 1899). One has greater social capital when one is a member of a group that itself has greater capital, whether in resources or the capacity to access them, or in symbolic power and status in a society. Being a member of a certain group affords one privileges not afforded to outsiders. This notion of social capital highlights the necessarily exclusionary aspect of differential group membership. By its nature such capital is not and cannot be available to all, since part of its efficacy relies on difference and distinction. It must be sequestered and protected. This view also opens the door to considering so-called negative social capital, as in the costs of belonging to certain groups that lack resources or access or that have less status or symbolic power in a society (Portes & Landolt, 1996).

A second sense of social capital speaks instead to the level of social cohesion in a particular community (Putnam, 1993, 1995). Looking at indices such as civic engagement, trust, and the prevalence of informal arrangements and exchanges, this inquiry considers how communities gain and lose levels of proximity and closeness that may provide social benefit. This model is less differential – in other words it does not view capital as exclusionary and beneficial only to those in certain groups versus others. Capital in this sense is instead the wealth of community closeness and vague senses of "neighborliness." There may or may not be benefits to belonging in such groups vis-à-vis other groups in society except for the possible virtues and outcomes of living in close cohesion with other community members. It is important to keep these two senses of social capital conceptually distinct, even if they may at times overlap.

As should be clear, the aforementioned discussion of trust coincides with this latter conversation on social capital as cohesion and density of informal networks. Yet even conversations about social cohesion may become monetized and economized in ways reminiscent of debt relations. Putnam implies as much when he lauds social cohesion for its greater "efficiency" and strangely compares it to money economies: "A society that relies on generalized reciprocity is more efficient than a distrustful society, for the same reason that money is more efficient than barter. Trust lubricates social life" (1993, n.p.).

This is an odd statement on multiple levels. Putnam's use of "generalized reciprocity" misuses an anthropological term (see Sahlins, 1972) that actually speaks to informal exchange networks as well as gift reciprocities, which are decidedly inefficient according to modern economic principles – witness the way economists appear endlessly puzzled about the "irrationality" of gifts, evaluating their "deadweight loss" (Principe & Eisenhauer, 2009; Waldfogel, 1993; Wang & Van Der Lans, 2018). Putnam's elision of such generalized exchange networks with claims to efficiency appears to force economistic principles into the foreign territory of the gift as typically construed.

More significantly, Putnam sets up a parallelism between trustful generalized reciprocity and money. Lack of trust and barter form the second parallel couplet. For Putnam, then, money symbolizes trust and barter symbolizes distrust. Such a twist is odd given that money is typically understood to be precisely a replacement for social trust. What Putnam does not signal – and may not be aware of – is that money does indeed insert trust into the exchange but not in the way he implies. Money is in no way a marker of internal communal trust. Rather, money inserts trust in sovereignty as a replacement for social trust. Money works due to both parties' trust in its efficacy as a symbol of state power to undergird and guarantee it as a token of exchange value. Money operates in contexts where the exchangers know or need to know little about one another, since money serves as the state's underwriting of the exchange (Wray, 2003, 2012).

In barter and even more so in gift-like reciprocities, exchangers need to know more about the context of the exchange, their exchange partners, and the objects given. In barter, one needs to be sure that goods are of equivalent value and there is more haggling and idiosyncratic discussion about the exchange. Both exchangers must establish the trustworthiness of the objects offered as well as of their exchange partners. In short, such barter swaps appear more personal.

This is also why it is typical to associate monetization with erosion of social ties and trust (Marx, 1976; Simmel, 1978; Weber, 2011). The so-called "cash nexus" becomes the proxy of the relationship and mediates the interchange, making relational rapport less necessary. The trust that lubricates monetary exchange is not social trust or social capital but the power of sovereign oversight and with it whatever means of legal and violent coercion are called for to enforce a monetary system.

To be clear, barter is far from what is typically construed as an ideal form of reciprocity – and in reality, barter is a monetized form of exchange, one that occurs in societies that *already* have a concept of money and the categories to quantify value numerically and proportionally. Barter emerges in situations where cash has disappeared or a monetary system collapses but exchanges retain memory of money's accounting and valuation functions (Dillard, 1988; Graeber, 2010; Ingham, 2004). Yet barter certainly appears at least slightly further along the spectrum of social trust than money. Subjects who barter demonstrate a modicum higher level of trust in their neighbor than those who rely on money, particularly since they undertake exchanges based on abstract calculations of value that they must both agree on and express that each has products or services that the other needs.

These odd associations and parallels that Putnam constructs among reciprocity, trust, and money suggest again an overly monetized conception of trust, exchange, and social obligation, and hence one permeated by assumptions of debt. Perhaps this should be unsurprising given that his entire exploration occurs under the rubric of "social capital." In other words, the label implies that scholars have already agreed to view certain social relations in terms of capital and with it assumptions about money, property, and other assets. Social capital as a field thus arguably starts from the premise that such networks are calculable, quantifiable, and able to be formalized and made explicit. This critique can also be made about the aforementioned other category of social capital as differential and exclusionary benefits based on group membership. This is a criticism of Pierre Bourdieu's (1986, 1998) approach, which, although motivated by Marxian concerns of equity and justice, remains bound by an economistic framework and gives the preemptive win to economy over other forms of reciprocity. It is no wonder that Bourdieu is among the theorists of the gift that sees gifts as masked and dishonest barter exchanges: in other words, for Bourdieu, there is no true gift, just delays and misrecognitions of economically reciprocal barter swaps.

Endeavoring to advance a more qualitative approach to generalized reciprocity, the sociologist James Coleman (1988) proposes a notion of "credit slips" circulating in any given community:

> *If A does something for B and trusts B to reciprocate in the future, this establishes an expectation in A and an obligation on the part of B. This obligation can be conceived as a credit slip held by A for performance by B. If A holds a large number of these credit slips, for a number of persons with whom A has relations, then the analogy to financial capital is direct. These credit slips constitute a large body of credit that A can call in if necessary unless, of course, the placement of trust has been unwise, and these are bad debts that will not be repaid. In some social structures, it is said that "people are always doing things for each other." There are a large number of these credit slips outstanding, often on both sides of a relation (for these credit slips appear often not to be completely fungible across areas of activity, so that credit slips of B held by A and those of A held by B are not fully used to cancel each other out). In... social structures where individuals are more self-sufficient and depend on each other less, there are fewer of these credit slips outstanding at any time." (p. S102)*

This is a helpful way to schematize how obligations may form and circulate in a community, tying members together in webs of reciprocity and obligation. Here we can conceive of the obligations in a variety of ways that need not be quantified or formalized by contract and terms for repayment. A number of distinct time horizons, means of reciprocity, and priority levels for return may be imagined. As Coleman is careful to distinguish, only a subset of these types of credit slip relations need be analogized to financial capital: those wherein the holder (A) can go to associates of the obliged (B) to request reciprocation. This is the condition of *transferable* obligations that is recognized as necessary for modern money and finance. While it is not identical to money and debt (in other words, we can easily imagine archaic communal conditions where surrogates and substitutes are responsible for the obligations of others), this transferability is a precondition.

In the terms of my discussion, however, Coleman's mention of debt is misleading and risks financializing nonfinancialized reciprocal relations. Rather, we must take him to mean obligation in a broader sense. The other weakness of this schematic presentation is that with the clarity brought by simplification and reduction, important aspects of the social are left out. The reciprocities envisioned here are individualistic, contracted between two distinct agents. Yet we have no sense of the bounds of the community or terms of exchange within it, what makes their issuance of credit slips possible and intelligible (besides vagaries of "trust" and reliability). We cannot consider the role of a guarantor of last result such as a sovereign or state which may ground and make possible these circulating slips. Coleman risks replicating origin myths of spontaneously constituted exchange communities that naturally and immanently create their proportions for exchange and terms of return, whereas much of the historical record suggests the presence of forms of hierarchy and coercion in making standardized credit slip circulation possible.

The problem, then, with many discussions of trust, social capital, or forms of communal capital and credit, are undergirding assumptions about debt and monetization that render them intelligible. These include formalized weights and measures, explicit quantifications of value or the capacity to quantify if need be, coercive means of policing and enforcing exchanges and reciprocities, and the like. One of the concerns, then, with drawing on these resources to fund the imagination of the commons is that these tools may be flawed from the start. Silvia Federici (2012a) raises concerns about how the language of informal reciprocities has been appropriated by the interests of capital:

> Responding to different motivations, a revalorization of the commons has become trendy among mainstream economists and capitalist planners, witness the growing academic literature on the subject and its cognates: "social capital," "gift economies," "altruism"… [A] variety of economists and social theorists warned that the marketization of all spheres of life is detrimental to the market's well-functioning, for markets too – the argument goes – depend on the existence of nonmonetary relations like confidence, trust, and gift-giving. In brief, capital is learning about the virtues of the "common good"… We must be very careful, then, not to craft the discourse on the commons in such a way as to allow a crisis-ridden capitalist class to revive itself, posturing, for instance, as the guardian of the planet. (pp. 140–141)

Such concerns therefore raise the question of methods of enforcement and regulation to stave off and resist the encroachment of economistic indices and lenses that overtake other senses of bond, reciprocity and obligation. They also invoke calls for (re)distributive justice and mechanisms to ensure just distribution of resources and forms of communal oversight to ensure equity. In short, claims of justice and appeals to law and legality emerge as a potential aid here against the encroaching market sphere, cash nexus, and price mechanism. In what follows I explain why these moves, too, must be significantly problematized and adjusted.

FROM JUSTICE TO CARE

For theorist Jeffrey Di Leo (2018), Plato's portrayal of the death of Socrates captures the central role that debt plays in Western philosophy and morality. As Plato recounts, in his text *Phaedo*:

> *As his belly was getting cold, Socrates uncovered his head – he had covered it – and said – these were his last words – "Crito, we owe a cock to Asclepius; make this offering to him and do not forget." – "It shall be done," said Crito, "tell us if there is anything else." But there was no answer. Shortly afterwards Socrates made a movement; the man uncovered him and his eyes were fixed. Seeing this Crito closed [Socrates'] mouth and his eyes. (118a)*

The death of Socrates signals the birth of Western philosophy. Yet, at this symbolic inception, the importance of debt is made central. For Socrates, an ethical death could not proceed without making amends for this outstanding debt. Apparently, to be moral is to repay one's debts.

Di Leo proceeds to grapple with the fact that, not just for Socrates but for most of us in the West and arguably globally, debt appears to structure our inherited notions of morality. To complicate matters, Di Leo notes that it may be an ethical imperative today to question morality's own reliance on debt. For, as he notes:

> *It is one thing to ground morality on the repayment of debt when it is not a major source of oppression and domination over others; it is quite another thing to do so at a time when it is a major source of oppression and domination. (pp. 157–158)*

In our contemporary moment, when debt has become associated with predation, exploitation, and growing global inequality, does being moral today mean removing repayment of debt from our notions of morality? But in doing so, how does one not destroy morality itself in the process?

Matters of law, legality, and justice relate to morality as a broad and capacious term. While these matters shape and are shaped by morality as a diffuse social category, with notions of law we are in the realm of more formal institutionalizations, codes, and directives for life together in society. Inasmuch as our sense of morality may be infused with assumptions about debt and repayment, this is certainly the case with forms of law.

For millennia, debt has formed the basic category for measured, quantified, reciprocal justice. The foundation of "an eye for an eye" and so-called talionic law (from *lex talionis*) is debt and repayment. Removing your neighbor's eye deprives him of it; you incur a debt, just as if you have taken his property. As your creditor, he is owed repayment by you. The most equitable repayment of this debt is an act that accomplishes the same thing. Thus, your eye is removed. Violent acts are traded reciprocally, one for another. The second act is identical with the first. It is equated with it in order to achieve a notion of balance or parity, repaying the debt that was created. Alternatively, of course, some other form of compensation might be made. But this alternative payment follows the logic of substitution and is not identical or fundamentally equal. Compensation must be according to the proportions and measures established by the more basic, reciprocal economic logic of identical exchange – an eye for an eye.

All that distinguishes the second violent act from the first is the guise of legality, of creating law. This process sets the latter, reciprocal violence outside the law, for, of course, the second act of retaliatory punishment is not then condemned or punished, even though it is identical with the former. This second act, that of repayment and balancing the scales, is permitted in order to encode it within law itself. Laws of retribution and punishment are repetitions of original violence, justified and given exceptions because of the even more original "law" of debt and repayment that makes such responsive violence "just." We can see here that justice in this sense is simply an economic notion of balancing scales, of making up for a perceived lack through a form of return and repayment. While punitive and retributive law codes have evolved and complexified, this underlying logic remains the same and provides an enduring foundation (Singh, 2020).

Such formalized codes are based on more ancient practices called *wergild* that included pricing for insults and injuries, customs that imagined such offenses as able to be compensated for through symbolic substitution (Grierson, 1977; Ingham, 2004; Wray, 2004). One might be insulted or injured in comparable ways, or forced to provide resources of value to the injured party. These practices were eventually codified and enforced more universally, under weights, measures, and proportions determined by sovereign power seeking to consolidate territory and police bodies with the space it controlled. Law codes reflect this effort at standardization and stabilization across time and space, with local communal practices then reinterpreted, refracted, and enforced by some sovereign center of oversight and decision.

Certain ethical systems seek to move beyond justice based construals of what is moral or good. One reason for such moves is the centrality of retribution and punishment in many systems of justice. It is often also a reaction to the abstraction and distance insinuated in justice models, where right and the enforcement of right both center on assumptions of atomistic individuals making decisions when considering responsibility and duty. The problem is rarely understood in economic terms – after all, this is one of the blind spots of our legal tradition, that is, that we do not recognize that legal categories may be fundamentally economic. I suggest, however, that there is an inherent uneasiness with the reality of debt as the structuring framework for justice and legality that may also provoke this quest for alternatives.

These concerns typically apply to forms of punitive and retributive justice, notions of a perpetrator getting or "paying" their due, of providing compensation through their pain, suffering, deprivation, or actual assets. This economic, debt-based logic may or may not apply to (re)distributive justice or aspects of restorative justice. To the degree that these latter two categories include forms of punishment as well as compensation in the name of equality and fairness, they may also rely on debt logic.

While restorative justice appears the most relational and qualitative, (re)distributive justice continues to work within the confines of quantification, measure, and balance. Yet restorative justice may use redistribution as one of its methods. It need not exclude this. The point is that the overarching framework keeps debt and monetary economy in their place, as highly controlled and intentional tools in a broader aim of relational care and restoration. In the current penal logic that dominates globally, punitive and retributive justice are the main tools employed, and serve not the interests of care or restoration but the maintenance of sovereignty. Calls for more "law and order" seek to preserve status quo power arrangements, economic circuits, and hierarchies, using violence to police the surfaces of the regime and hold everything in place (Harcourt, 2011, 2018; Spade, 2015).

A reasonable critique of my presentation thus far is that I have collapsed justice, on the one hand, with law and legality, on the other. Theorists make critical distinctions between these nodes, and part of what is at stake is precisely concerns over the formalization, stabilization, calculability, and quantification that appear at work in law and legal codes that seems to truncate or otherwise violate some ideals of justice as qualitative, dynamic, contextual, and ultimately incalculable. In famously summing up this contrast, Jacques Derrida (2002) attempts to make "a difficult and unstable distinction between justice and law, between justice (infinite, incalculable, rebellious to rule and foreign to symmetry, heterogeneous and heterotropic) on the one hand, and, on the other, the exercise of justice as law, legitimacy or legality, a stabilizable, statutory and calculable apparatus [*dispositif*], a system of regulated and coded prescriptions" (p. 250). For Derrida, justice is always deferred, always arriving, never fully present, in part because of the ways it exceeds the capacity to be represented in law and fixed, locked, and ossified across time and space.

Engaging Derrida on this theme, Regina Schwartz (2011) echoes a sense of justice as exceeding law, as attentive and other focused, and as unmeasurable or unquantifiable. Justice is contrasted with legality, which shows forth in procedure and method. She notes the remarkable ways that, for some, the stabilization of formal procedure is what makes law superior to justice:

> *Much contemporary political theory takes refuge in the notion that it is law – and not justice – that can offer a true universal. After all, they say, substantive justice is particular, contingent, and culturally specific. Because one person's notion of justice is so different from another's, which emerges in another culture, they must adjudicate their differences through law. Thank goodness for law, for procedures, for offering them a formal universal. Stuart Hampshire has offered a clear expression of this: "fairness in procedure is an invariable value, a constant in human nature…. Because there will always be conflicts between conceptions of the good, moral conflicts, both in the soul and in the city, there is everywhere a well- recognized*

> *need for procedures of confliction resolution.... . This is the place of*
> *a common rationality of method." The contract is understood as a*
> *constraining effort to impose peace on this warring state of nature."*
> *(p. 211, citing Hampshire, 2000, pp. 4–5)*

Law and legality, by appealing to assumed universals of numerical and quantified standardization as well as assumptions about balance and parity, are what can establish actual fairness in any governed space. To a certain extent, this is true. This is why we have law and legal codes instead of justice, for the former are able to be administered and fit the patterns of sovereignty and governance. But it is one thing to admit their practicability and quite another to endorse them as superior or to claim that notions of compensation and repayment to balance scales are necessarily fundamental to human nature and society.

Rejecting the dead formalization of law, Schwartz seeks after justice, turning to Jewish traditions of divine law for a model. While there is much to laud and critique in Schwartz's analysis, what interests me here is the vision of justice that emerges for her. It is a unity of justice and law, an immediacy, that comes from "loving the source of law," which creates an "interiorized covenant, written on the heart" (pp. 208, 211). The focus on love, the heart, and internalization signals the organic, affective, relational, and communal aspects involved. Justice emerges from immanent individual and group impulses, desires, and decisions, not external, top-down, imposed frameworks. It is about being faithful to an agreement as opposed to an official contract. Justice-law in this approach is enacted within community, motivated internally, and emerges in the context of love and relationality. In fact, justice in this imagination begins to resemble something like care.

OBLIGATED LEADERSHIP AND A CARE ETHIC

A philosophy and an ethics of care turn attention to the obligations that emerge within concrete relationships and specific encounters with the other. Rather than the external compulsion brought through law or abstract notions of justice, care grapples with the internal and emergent impulses toward attending to the needs and vulnerabilities of those in our relational networks. Care is often contrasted or at least compared with justice as an alternative framework for understanding morality and patterns for life together. Thus, in problematizing justice as we have, we must consider care as an alternative.

Founding theorists of care (Gilligan, 1993, 2011; Held, 1993, 2006; Noddings, 2002, 2003) advanced it as a counterpart and complement to justice frameworks. Care is seen as interpersonal, relational, contextual, and responsive to concrete needs and vulnerabilities in ways that abstract, formal, and universal conceptions of justice miss. Early interventions also drew on presumed gender differences to assert notions of "feminine caring" over against "masculinist abstraction." These dichotomies have not aged well due to their gender essentialisms (despite early thinkers' caveats that such generalizations were rife with exceptions). Yet one can certainly retain the heuristic distinction between contextual care and detached abstraction without such essentialisms, even harmonizing the framework with social constructivist and performative understandings of gender and sexuality.

Other thinkers (Slote, 2007) view care as a direct challenge to certain versions of justice. They assert that care can be extended to those with whom we have no direct, personal relations. Through empathic imagination, care enables us to extend the kinds of concerns and responses we might offer to the concrete other in front of us to those on the other side of the world, for instance. In this respect something like a care-based framework could be constructed and would clash with and ideally replace a justice or legal framework that relies on punitive compensation or debt-based repayments of violence with violence. The possibility for constructing patterns, norms, and institutionalized practices around care offers promise for frameworks of interaction on the commons, ones that might sustain communal norms beyond the small scale, personal, and direct interactions and exchanges where care more spontaneously emerges.

Whether one sees care as complementary to or a disruptive replacement for abstract justice or legality, questions of gender and sexuality persist in important ways. They do so not only for the ways care and justice possibly map onto culturally based, fluid repertoires for femininity and masculinity, but more so because of the reality that women's bodies historically bear the brunt of care work in the form of affective labor and social reproduction. Women thus serve as the leadership and vanguard for care-based commoning:

If the house is the oikos *on which the economy is built, then it is women, historically the house-workers and house-prisoners, who must take the initiative to reclaim the house as a center of collective life, one traversed by multiple people and forms of cooperation,*

providing safety without isolation and fixation, allowing for the
sharing and circulation of community possessions, and above all
providing the foundation for collective forms of reproduction.
(Federici, 2012a, p. 147)

A reorientation to care has the possibility of redistributing divisions of labor, envisioning a commons where care work is made central and not peripheral or invisible, where all partake and undertake in explicit and self-conscious ways, rather than relegating such essential labor to the hidden undersides of a market that magically appears to reproduce itself (Bhattacharya, 2017; Federici, 2012b; Fraser, 2016; Marçal, 2015).

Care also pertains directly to questions of relationship, bond, and obligation already signaled in our exploration of gift and debt. Gifts are ideally meant to signal care, signify prioritizing the relationship over the objects of exchange (we know this is not necessarily the case in practice). Debts are often problematized as a perversion of care. While a loan could theoretically be made to ameliorate needs and care for one's neighbor, the history of debt reveals that it is more often a method of extraction and predation. Debt becomes a way to extract more through interest or to expropriate labor through debt slavery.

Thus, to speak of gifts, debts and obligations and to question debt-based formalizations in law and ideas of retributive justice is to bring us into the orbit of questions of care. Care emerges as one possible response to the ravages of debt in part because of this relation. Care may in fact be more able to address such concerns than justice, if justice itself assumes and requires debt. Clearly, with care we are still in the realm of obligation in the sense of something that compels us to respond to a perceived lack or deficit in the life of that other or in the experience of a community to which we are bound. While justice or law works with quantifications in the sense that calls for reciprocity and compensation in terms of amounts, values, or notions of balance, care appears much more qualitative.

These considerations help intervene in conversations about relations among leadership, power, and empathy, on one hand, and concerns over organizational and communal trust and cohesion, on the other. What role do leadership positions and dynamics play in the web of reciprocal exchanges that are necessary to sustain communities and organizations? How might leaders model and enter into reciprocal relations with those they lead, so as to manage power dynamics and nurture productive responses? What does it mean to lead organizations through the process of restoring trust, especially when such restoration includes consideration of the debts or reparations an organization owes, whether to its employees, clients, or the public? In other words, how does one lead through the best forms of reciprocal exchanges to demonstrate care? These and other concerns might be addressed through a more informed understanding of how human communities have approached reciprocal exchanges and how humans have negotiated the spectrum of debt, gift, and other mutual obligations.

While some literature naively asserts that what is needed is simply a return to gift as somehow emblematic of greater trust, care, and cohesion, gifts can also be implicated in problematic power dynamics. Not only can gifts be used to entrap and obligate in the context of informal exchanges and so-called primitive or non-market communities, but research on institutional corruption reveals that gifts may subvert trust and entrap agents in problematic exchanges that can corrode organizational bonds. The solution is not a choice of gift over debt, but a clearer understanding of the kinds of bonds and reciprocal relations that each attempts to map and engender. This can then be situated in a wider conversation about the kinds of bonds and obligations we might form as humans, and the best types of attachments necessary for effective and life-affirming organizational activity.

All of this has a bearing on questions of the commons. Whether we construe commons as a site and/or collection of goods or as an orientation, attitude, methodology, and/or set of practices, care must retain centrality as fundamental. Commoning is at root a search for ideal relations, ideal patterns of life together, many of which might be sustained outside of the violence of state enforcement or the rapacious self-interest of corporate charters and their shareholders. If we are to find the "stuff" of life together in ways that increase mutual aid (Spade, 2020) and sustainability, certainly care provides a key framework to consider. Beyond the abstractions of care it is to women that we must turn for leadership around what care means and how it should structure relations, exchanges, and obligations within the commons (Federici, 2019). Federici (2012a) reminds us that

> Arguing that women should take the lead in the collectivization of reproductive work and housing is not to naturalize housework as a female vocation. It is refusing to obliterate the collective experiences, knowledge, and struggles that women have accumulated concerning reproductive work, whose history has been an essential part of

*our resistance to capitalism. Reconnecting with this history is today
for women and men a crucial step, both for undoing the gendered
architecture of our lives and reconstructing our homes and lives as
commons. (p. 148)*

These are some components, principles, and values for any sense or notion
of commons-based leadership. Such leadership challenges the hierarchies,
centralizations, abstractions, and efficiency metrics that permeate current
discussions. Such leadership centers relationships, contexts, vulnerabilities,
and restorations. These leadership patterns are glimpsed in a diverse array, as
if refracted through a prism, in the rich, multifarious, and hopeful contributions of this volume.

REFERENCES

Barnes, P. (2006). *Capitalism 3.0: A guide to reclaiming the commons.*
Berrett-Koehler.

Bhattacharya, T. (2017). *Social reproduction theory: Remapping class, recentring
oppression.* Pluto Press.

Bourdieu, P. (1986). The forms of capital. In J. Richardson (Ed.), *Handbook of
theory and research for the sociology of education* (pp. 241–258). Greenwood.

Bourdieu, P. (1998). *Practical reason: On the theory of action.* Stanford University
Press.

Codere, H. (1950). *Fighting with property: A study of Kwakiutl Potlatching and
Warfare, 1792–1930.* J.J. Augustin.

Coleman, J. S. (1988). Social capital in the creation of human capital. *American
Journal of Sociology, 94,* S95–S120.

Dardot, P., & Laval, C. (2019). *Common: On revolution in the 21st century.*
London: Bloomsbury.

Derrida, J. (2002). Force of law: The "Mystical Foundation of Authority" (2001). In
J. Derrida & G. Anidjar (Eds.), *Acts of religion.* (pp. 228–298). Routledge.

Di Leo, J. R. (2018). On debt resistance. In J. R. Di Leo, P. Hitchcock, & S. A.
McClennen (Eds.), *The debt age* (pp. 157–175). Routledge.

Dillard, D. (1988). The Barter Illusion in classical and neoclassical economics.
Eastern Economic Journal, XIV(4), 299–318.

Esposito, R. (2010). *Communitas: The origin and destiny of community.* Stanford
University Press.

Federici, S. (2012a). Feminism and the politics of the common in an era of primitive accumulation (2010). In S. Federici (Ed.), *Revolution at point zero: Housework, reproduction, and feminist struggle* (pp. 138–148). PM Press.

Federici, S. (2012b). *Revolution at point zero: Housework, reproduction, and feminist struggle*. PM Press.

Federici, S. (2019). *Re-enchanting the world: Feminism and the politics of the commons*. PM Press.

Fraser, N. (2016). Contradictions of capital and care. *New Left Review, 100* (July–August), 99–117.

Gambetta, D. (Ed.) (1988). *Trust: Making and breaking cooperative relations*. Blackwell.

Gilligan, C. (1993). *In a different voice: Psychological theory and women's development*. Harvard University Press.

Gilligan, C. (2011). *Joining the resistance*. Polity.

Godelier, M. (1999). *The enigma of the gift*. University of Chicago Press.

Graeber, D. (2010). *Debt: The first 5,000 years*. Melville House.

Gregory, C. A. (1982). *Gifts and commodities*. Academic Press.

Grierson, P. (1977). *The origins of money*. Athlone Press.

Hampshire, S. (2000). *Justice is conflict*. Princeton University Press.

Harcourt, B. E. (2011). *The illusion of free markets: Punishment and the myth of natural order*. Harvard University Press.

Harcourt, B. E. (2018). Punishment, political economy, and the genealogy of morals. In R. Fredona & S. A. Reinert (Eds.), *New perspectives on the history of political economy* (pp. 375–392). Palgrave Macmillan.

Held, V. (1993). *Feminist morality: Transforming culture, society, and politics*. University of Chicago Press.

Held, V. (2006). *The ethics of care: Personal, political, and global*. Oxford University Press.

Ingham, G. K. (2004). *The nature of money*. Polity.

Kramer, R. M., & Cook, K. S. (Eds.) (2004). *Trust and distrust in organizations: Dilemmas and approaches*. Russell Sage Foundation.

Kramer, R. M., & Pittinsky, T. L. (Eds.) (2012). *Restoring trust in organizations and leaders: Enduring challenges and emerging answers*. Oxford University Press.

Kramer, R. M., & Tyler, T. R. (Eds.) (1996). *Trust in organizations: Frontiers of theory and research*. Sage.

Luhmann, N. (2017). *Trust and power*. Polity.

MacDonald, J. (2003). *A free nation deep in debt: The financial roots of democracy.* Farrar, Straus and Giroux.

Malinowski, B. (1922). *Argonauts of the Western Pacific.* Routledge.

Marçal, K. (2015). *Who Cooked Adam Smith's Dinner?: A story about women and economics.* Portobello Books.

Marx, K. (1976). *Capital: A critique of political economy.* Penguin Books.

Mauss, M. (1990). *The gift: The form and reason for exchange in archaic societies.* Routledge.

Noddings, N. (2002). *Starting at home: Caring and social policy.* University of California Press.

Noddings, N. (2003). *Caring: A feminine approach to ethics & moral education.* University of California Press.

Portes, A. (1998). Social capital: Its origins and applications in modern sociology. *Annual Review of Sociology, 24,* 1–24.

Portes, A., & Landolt, P. (1996). The downside of social capital. *The American Prospect, 26,* 18–22.

Principe, K. E., & Eisenhauer, J. G. (2009). Gift-giving and deadweight loss. *Journal of Socio-Economics, 38*(2), 215–220.

Putnam, R. D. (1995). Bowling alone: America's declining social capital. *Journal of Democracy, 6*(1), 65–78.

Putnam, R. D. (1993). The prosperous community: Social capital and public life. *The American Prospect,* (13). Retrieved from http://epn.org/prospect/13/13putn.html

Roos, J. (2019). *Why not default?: The political economy of sovereign debt.* Princeton University Press.

Sahlins, M. (1972). *Stone age economics.* Aldine-Atherton.

Schwartz, R. M. (2011). Law and the gift of justice. In M. E. Vatter (Ed.), *Crediting god: Sovereignty and religion in the age of global capitalism* (pp. 207–220). Fordham University Press.

Simmel, G. (1978). *The philosophy of money.* Routledge.

Singh, D. (2018). Sovereign debt. *Journal of Religious Ethics, 46*(2), 239–266.

Singh, D. (2020). Exceptional economy: Sovereign exchanges in Carl Schmitt and Giorgio Agamben. *Telos, 191*(Summer), 115–136.

Slote, M. (2007). *The ethics of care and empathy.* Routledge.

Spade, D. (2015). Normal *life*: Administrative *violence, critical trans politics, and the limits of law.* Duke University Press.

Spade, D. (2020). *Mutual aid: Building solidarity during this crisis (and the next).* Verso.

Veblen, T. (1899). *The theory of the leisure class: An economic study in the evolution of institutions*. Macmillan & Co.

Waldfogel, J. (1993). The deadweight loss of Christmas. *American Economic Review, 83*(5), 1328–1336.

Wang, S. S., & Van Der Lans, R. (2018). Modeling gift choice: The effect of uncertainty on price sensitivity. *Journal of Marketing Research, 55*(4), 524–540.

Weber, M. (2011). *The Protestant ethic and the spirit of capitalism*. Oxford University Press.

Wray, L. R. (Ed.) (2004). *Credit and state theories of money: The contributions of A. Mitchell Innes*. Edward Elgar.

Wray, L. R. (2003). *Understanding modern money: The key to full employment and price stability*. Edward Elgar.

Wray, L. R. (2012). *Modern money theory: A primer on macroeconomics for sovereign monetary systems*. Palgrave Macmillan.

PART I

THE PARADIGM SHIFT

1

LEADING REGENERATIVE SYSTEMS: EVOLVING THE WHOLE INSTEAD OF A PART

KATHLEEN E. ALLEN

WHY LEADERSHIP IS NEEDED FOR THE COMMONS

What is the purpose of leadership in this time and context? We are facing significant challenges today that require leadership to adapt to the growing complexity and dynamic interdependent systems in which we live (Allen, Stelzner, & Wielkiewicz, 1998). Complex issues like globalization, increasing stress on the environment, increasing speed and dissemination of information, technology, scientific and social change, including public health, racial justice, growing polarization demand a different purpose for leadership in the twenty-first century. The interactions of all these issues are creating the increasing need to have leaders hold the needs and perspective of the whole system front and center for the world. Along with holding the whole, leaders are now required to help create a generative rather than degenerative environment. As Allen, Bordas, Hickman, Matusak, Sorenson, and Whitmire (1998) wrote in *Leadership in the 21st Century*, the purpose of leadership is to:

- *Create a supportive environment where people can thrive, grow, and live in peace with one another,*

- *Promote harmony with nature and thereby provide sustainability for future generations; and*

- *Create communities of reciprocal care and shared responsibility – one where every person matters, and each person's welfare and dignity is respected and supported.* (Allen et. al., 1998)

If this were our purpose for leadership in this century, we would be leading in very different ways.

We are living in a time where all our major institutions, political, businesses, education, healthcare, religions, etc. are contributing to the diminishing vitality of the commons. In order to shift the default decision-making of these institutions to serve the strength, evolution, and vitality of the commons, we need leadership to help lead the shift in thinking and practice (Allen, 2018; Daloz et.al., 1996; Hutchins & Storm, 2019; Reed, 2007; Wahl, 2016). Without this concerted effort, the implications of conventional practice and thinking will continue to degenerate the commons.

REGENERATIVE VERSUS DEGENERATIVE SYSTEMS

Regenerative systems have more vitality, use less energy, are fully integrated with nature and its design principles, and assume a living systems framework (Allen, 2019). They are designed to work with life and nature instead of against it (Andracle & Pasini, 2015; Holliday, 2016). They are filled with resilience, self-organization, diversity, and cooperation. Nature is the longest running regenerative system and it provides a wonderful design model to use to rethink how we create systems in organizations, communities, countries, and the world (Benyus, 2002). It has experienced 3.8 billion years of "research and development" and has regenerated life after five mass extinctions. We are living proof that nature's design principles work. Nature's design purpose is to create conditions conducive to the life of future generations. Regenerative thinking focuses on the evolution of the whole system; it does not optimize a part of the system (like profit) over the health of the whole. Benefits and burdens are widely shared in a regenerative system. Regenerative systems adapt to changing conditions and their ability to continually learn and adapt makes them highly resilient.

In a degenerative system, there is less vitality, and the practices of extraction and exploitation are ubiquitous. All our inequalities are the result of the belief that some can exploit and extract resources from the planet or talent in their organization for their own profit or purpose. This belief is anchored in a short-term, self-interest orientation. And it sees the system and the people in it as objects that can be controlled and utilized by the "owner" of the company or country. Our mandate for the twenty-first century is to learn how to lead regenerative systems and let go of the conventional practices and theories of leadership that have contributed to the degenerating systems we have today.

WHAT IS HOLDING OUR DEGENERATIVE SYSTEM IN PLACE?

When we look at the state of our current system, we see all the signs of a degenerating system. The benefits and burdens are not widely shared, the rich and poor gap is widening, the climate crisis is getting worse, and COVID-19 has shown us the fragility of many of our systems. Education shifting to on-line exposed the lack of technology access and food stability of students in our school systems. The Black Lives Matter protests have exposed the racial inequities and the system of white privilege. The economic impact of the pandemic has hurt parts of the population much more than others. Our public health system has exposed more inequities. These are all signs of a degenerating system.

There is a specific mindset and worldview that causes us to lead and design organizations and systems that result in a degenerating system. Unfortunately, many of the conventional practices of leadership, management, economic theory, legal system, political system, and education have led to the current state we are experiencing in the world. Many of our leadership and management theories support focusing on a part of the system at the expense of the whole. The contrasts between key worldviews that hold a degenerative versus a regenerative system in place are laid out in Table 1.

A degenerating worldview creates an interactive impact on how we use energy and design solutions and products. A degenerative system uses consumptive design and requires more energy and resources to maintain the system. When we seek to control, optimize our separation, have a short-term view; we see solutions to problems through a self-interested lens. The external environment is seen as a problem that requires power, money, and resources to overcome. Solutions require ongoing resources to hold in place.

Table 1. Contrast Between Degenerative and Regenerative System Worldviews.

Degenerating System Worldview	Regenerating System Worldview
• Closed system where control is possible. This view leads people to pursue ownership. An ownership mentality means you can control others to serve your needs	• Open system where adaptation is the focus. The goal is to create the best fit with the external environment. This view leads people to seek mutualistic relationships with self and the environment. The goal is to learn and adapt
• Short-term thinking – focus on what works best for here and now without regard or knowledge of how decisions will impact future generations or the environment	• Long-term thinking – examine how a decision in the present will impact future generations. This is a version of seven generation thinking where leaders hold the needs and lives of unborn children seven generations in the future (Vecesy & Venables, 1980)
• Autonomous and separate from each other and focuses on self-interest. This causes leadership behavior that serves the individual and optimizes the part of the system instead of the whole	• Interdependent and connected that focuses leaders on how we care for the whole system. All systems are optimized when we serve the whole system and made less vital when we focus on only a part of the system (Meadows, 2008)
• Mechanistic and inert system – allows us to objectify others and exploit people and nature for our own ends. When we see our organization as a machine, it allows us to objectify it and the people in it. An object serves its owner reinforcing separation and self-interest	• Living system – aligns design and leadership with life principles; sees people as unique individuals that are in relationship to each other and the world (Allen, 2019; Holliday, 2016; Nxumalo, 2020). Living system perspectives help us see all the stakeholders in a system, people, planet, and other species. Relationships are key in living systems. To lead effectively we need to know the people individually and anchor leadership in the unique context of place
• Emotions of scarcity and fear are prevalent. When self-interest and separation are present and when we optimize profit over relationships, it engenders emotions of scarcity and fear. Leaders use fear as a way of attracting and controlling followers	• Emotions of trust and cooperation are prevalent. When we see our interdependence, we prioritize our relationships with each other. We respect differences because we are all part of a larger whole. This causes leaders to develop organizational cultures of trust and cooperation

A regenerative worldview creates a different approach and utilizes design to solve problems and find solutions. Regenerative design promotes a positive energy balance in the whole system (Andracle & Pasini, 2015). When we see our interdependence we adopt an adaptive orientation to the external environment. With this orientation, we design with the energy of the larger system. This alignment with the living principles of the system, causes us to seek solutions that work with the evolution and dynamics of the larger system (Allen, 2019, 2020; Holliday, 2016, Wahl, 2016).

These worldviews can be summarized in the following two continuums, one that is based on the approach of exploitative to sustainable approach (Fig. 1), and the other based on the degenerative to regenerative continuum (Fig. 2).

Fig. 1 shows that an exploitative approach is held in place by short-term thinking, separation, and self-interest. This is the perfect definition of a system that optimizes the parts of the system over the whole system. For example, when businesses optimize profit over the well-being of its employees, the planet, and the long-term health of the community, they will make decisions and implement strategies that work for them in the short-term, without regard to the consequences of their actions over time.

The sustainable approach anchors the other end of this continuum. A sustainable approach is held in place by long-term thinking, a deep appreciation and knowledge of interdependence and to focus on the whole system's capacity to thrive. This creates decisions and strategies that work for both the short and long-term. A short-term solution that ends in polluting the environment, or exploiting employees, does not work in a sustainable approach. The focus in the sustainable approach is to see all the stakeholders and make decisions that in combination will create a thriving world that uses less energy to accomplish their goals.

Fig. 2 shows the degenerative to regenerative worldview continuum. A degenerative system is characterized by less vitality and resilience. In a regenerative world, the "winner takes all" stance of the degenerative system is replaced by shared prosperity where benefits and burdens are widely shared.

Fig. 1.   Worldviews that Impact Sustainability.

Worldviews that impact sustainability

Exploitive approach -
Increases energy use

Sustainable approach –
decreases energy use

Worldview holding this
in place

Exploitive to
Sustainable
Continuum

Worldviews holding
this in place

- Short-term thinking
- Separation
- Self-interest

- Long-term
  thinking
- Interdependence
- Optimize the
  whole system's
  capacity to thrive

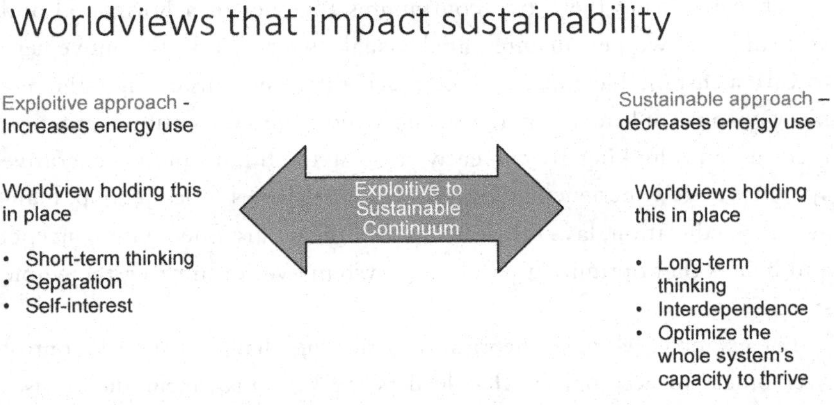

A regenerative system focuses on shared well-being and a healthy planet. Such a system is held in place by worldviews that individuals and leaders have about their perceived reality. The worldviews are held in place by seeing the world as an open system, where adaptation to the dynamic changing external environment is the focus. There is a recognition that one cannot control an open system. There is a strong integration with nature and individuals lead with a living system mindset. The result for people who lead from a regenerative system viewpoint is the experience of trust and transparency in their work environments and communities which creates a predisposition to cooperate with each other to create a world that works for all (Fig. 2).

Fig. 2. *Worldviews that Impact Regeneratively.*

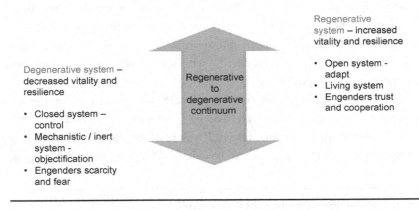

When we bring these two continuums together in a horizontal and vertical axis, we get an integrated visual and see how the movement toward a sustainable approach and regenerative systems changes the primary purpose of leadership. It also shows how our conventional practice, theories, and thinking are currently creating the fragile and degenerative system we are experiencing (Fig. 3). All our theories in leadership, management, education, law, religion, and healthcare are filled with concepts and beliefs that optimize a part of the system over optimizing the whole system.

For example, we have theories on managing change that seek control over others to accomplish what leaders think. Management theory uses terms like span of control, power, and structures that generate dependency in employees who seek to please their boss to remain employed. Our educational systems create a similar dynamic in the classroom, with students asking their teacher for direction because they will be evaluated by them. If our educational systems were regenerative, we would be focused on how to create a classroom or workplace where people would self-organize their own learning and work.

The right column in Fig. 3 shows that our goal is not just a sustainable approach; it is to move beyond this baseline and move toward restoration. Restoration redresses the unfairness of our social justice system and the damage we have done to the environment. We move from sustainability to restoration and then toward regenerative design and leadership. Our core purpose in regenerative leadership is to reset our economy, our education systems, our political system, and create a world that is designed as a regenerative system. To do this, we need to start with critical internal beliefs and worldviews and shift them to support a regenerative outcome.

The challenge is that we must develop an awareness of when we are being influenced by default thinking that leads to conventional (degenerative) practice and thinking. We need to become skilled at recognizing and consciously letting go of thinking that optimizes a part of the system instead of the whole.

Fig. 3. *Regenerative System Framework.*

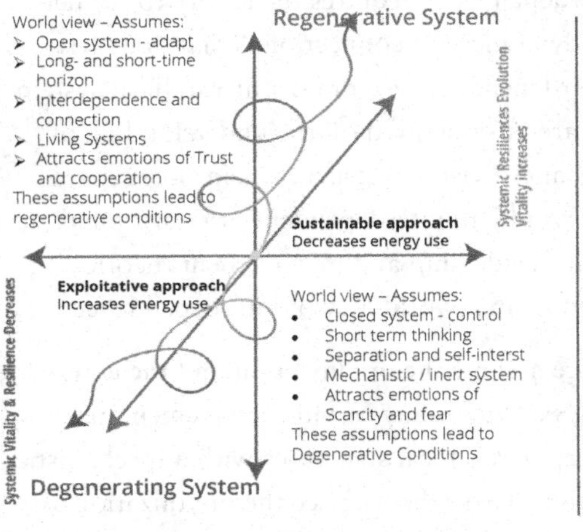

World view – Assumes:
➤ Open system - adapt
➤ Long- and short-time horizon
➤ Interdependence and connection
➤ Living Systems
➤ Attracts emotions of Trust and cooperation
These assumptions lead to regenerative conditions

Regenerative System

Systemic Resilience Evolution Vitality increases

Sustainable approach
Decreases energy use

Exploitative approach
Increases energy use

Systemic Vitality & Resilience Decreases

World view – Assumes:
• Closed system - control
• Short term thinking
• Separation and self-interst
• Mechanistic / inert system
• Attracts emotions of Scarcity and fear
These assumptions lead to Degenerative Conditions

Degenerating System

Regenerative - requires integration with nature
• Design as nature
• Lead with living systems mindset
• Optimizes self organization

Restorative
• Design for Rapid Recovery

Sustainable
• Do no harm to future generations

Conventional Practice & Thinking
• Embedded in leadership, management, education, politics, societal norms, and the law all contribute to a degenerating system

THE CHALLENGE FOR REGENERATIVE LEADERS

The key step in choosing to practice regenerative leadership is to become conscious and aware of the background assumptions of regenerative leaders' leadership practice or teaching. The worldviews that are anchoring degenerative leadership are widely dispersed in our literature and practice. How can we as individuals practice letting go of concepts, theories, and practices that lead to a degenerative outcome?

Here are some questions that leaders and teachers can ask themselves to examine if they are contributing to regenerative leadership.

1. **Is the focus to strengthen the whole system?** Our conventional practice that believes profit drives the economy and that profit and shareholder value takes priority over other stakeholders like the environment, employees, and community is pervasive. Leadership that looks at all stakeholders in the system is a first step toward regenerative leadership.

2. **Is the focus on long-term implications?** How do we teach understanding the implications of our decisions? Is long-term thinking being taught? Are criteria for long-term implications used in decision-making? Do we prioritize short-term gain over long-term costs in our decision-making? Does the management theory you teach have subtle or obvious statements about the importance of quarterly profits? What theories support seventh generation thinking?

3. **How is interdependence understood and apparent in leadership decisions or coursework?** Interdependence requires the ability to see networks, relationships, and dynamic interconnection. What does systems change look like in an interdependent system vs. a hierarchical system (Peat, 2008)? Hierarchies aren't structured on the understanding of interdependence. The silos and divisional structure reinforce separation and autonomy. What would an interdependent organizational structure look like? Do your leadership and management theories teach organizational design from a worldview of interdependence?

4. **Does the leadership practice assume the organization and the external environment is a living system?** Many of our management and leadership concepts support hierarchical structures with a mechanistic metaphor of the organization. These theories see the organization as an object that can be owned. Regenerative leadership requires leading

with a living system's framework. In a living system, decision-making rights are distributed to all entities impacted by the decision. For example, New Zealand's Whanganui River is a person under domestic law, and India's Ganges River was recently granted human rights. In Ecuador, the Constitution enshrines nature's "right to integral respect." Does your leadership practice and teaching introduce this practice?

5. **Does your leadership practice view the world as an open system that one must adapt to?** Leadership and management are often merged with establishing and maintaining control over the organization and its employees. Language like "span of control," and being able to control everyone below you on the organizational chart are just a few examples of implied control. Many of our human resources processes are designed to insure control and accountability. An open system can't be controlled, only influenced. Is your coursework supporting the myth of closed system and control, or open system focused on adaptation?

These are just a few of the key areas where we need to become conscious and aware of how what we teach, believe, and practice reflects defaults that have led to our current degenerating society. To become a regenerative leader, we must let go of the conventional thinking of the last one hundred years and replace it with new ways of thinking and worldviews that reflect regenerative leadership. This is a journey worth taking because we will no longer be complicit in creating a world that has diminishing vitality and resilience.

REGENERATIVE LEADERSHIP – ESSENTIAL FOR THE COMMON GOOD AND OUR FUTURE

Leading regenerative systems, by definition, serves the commons. They are filled with collaboration, interdependence, long-term time horizon, and resilient behaviors. To serve the commons, we need to reset our worldviews to perspectives that value the vitality of the whole system. We need to let go of our habit of prioritizing a part of the system. This is what will help us restore our planet, organizations, and community. Nature is designed to optimize the whole system. We can look to the one system that knows how to regenerate itself and learn from it.

We all have a role in making this happen.

REFERENCES

Allen, K. E. (2018). Critical internal shifts for sustainable leadership. In B. Redekop, D. R. Gallager, & R. Satterwhite (Eds.), *Innovation in environmental leadership: Critical perspectives* (pp. 213–224). Routledge.

Allen, K. E. (2019). *Leading from the roots: Nature-inspired leadership lessons for today's world.* Morgan James.

Allen, K. E. (2020, September 4). Jitterbugging as a metaphor for change. Retrieved from https://kathleenallen.net/jitterbugging-in-times-of-change/

Allen, K. E., Bordas, J., Hickman, G., Matusak, K. R., Sorenson, G., & Whitmine, K. (1998). Leadership in the 21st century. In G. R. Hickman (Ed.), *Leading organizations: Perspectives for a new era* (pp. 572–580). Sage.

Allen, K. E., Stelzner, S. P., & Wielkiewicz, R. M. (1998). The ecology of leadership: Adapting to the challenges of a changing world. *The Journal of Leadership Studies, 5*(2), 62–82.

Andracle, D., & Pasini, T. (2015, December 2). *Syntropic Agriculture.* YouTube. Retrieved from https://www.youtube.com/watch?v=gSPNRu4ZPvE

Benyus, J. M. (2002). *Biomimicry: Innovations inspired by nature.* Harper Collins.

Daloz, L. A., Keen, C. H., Keen, J. P., & Parks, S. (1996). *Common fire: Lives of commitment in a complex world.* Beacon Press.

Holliday, M. (2016). *The Age of Thrivability: Vital perspectives and practices for a better world.* Michelle Holliday.

Hutchins, G., & Storm, L. (2019). *Regenerative leadership: The DNA of life-affirming 21st century organizations.* Wordzworth Publishing. Retrieved from www.wordzworth.com

Meadows, D. H. (2008). *Thinking in systems: A primer.* Chelsea Green Publishing.

Nxumalo, M. (2020). *I am a Cross-pollinator.* Knowledge Connections (Pty).

Peat, F. D. (2008). *Gentle Action: Bringing creative change to a turbulent world.* Pari Publishing Sas.

Reed, B. (2007). Shifting from sustainability to regeneration. *Building Research & Information, 35*(6), 674–668.

Vecesy, C., & Venables, R. W. (1980). *American Indian Environmentalists: Ecological issues in Native American history.* Syracuse University Press.

Wahl, D. C. (2016). *Designing regenerative cultures.* Triarchy Press.

2

LEADING SO ALL CAN THRIVE: COMMONS LEADERSHIP FOR MUTUALISTIC SELF-ORGANIZATION

ELIZABETH A. CASTILLO

Leading systems change requires the development of new mental models and cultural narratives about leadership (Meadows, 1997; Waddock, 2020; Walker, Gunderson, Kinzig, Folke, Carpenter, & Schultz, 2006). Through the twentieth century, leadership has generally been thought of as asserting one's will onto others, imposing order, and prescriptively guiding followers to achieve a specified future state. Yet the past few decades, and the crises of 2020 in particular, make clear the urgent need for new thinking about leadership to untangle intractable problems like environmental degradation, racial injustice, growing inequality, and pandemics.

A key distinction between conventional leadership and COMMONS LEADERSHIP is their aims. Historically, leadership has sought *homeostasis* – creating stability at a moment in time by maintaining operational variables to stay within pre-established parameters via regulatory control. Yet what is needed to ensure adaptive capacity is *allostasis* – maintaining stability through dynamic change (cf, Sterling & Eyer, 1988). An analogy for understanding these differences is to think about leadership as a task to stabilize a marble in a gyrating bowl. Conventional leadership tries to solve this problem by putting a brick in the bowl to prevent it from moving. While this temporarily creates predictability and stability through forced control, it decouples components from the fluctuating environment, creating a build-up of energy that can ultimately cause the bowl to disintegrate. Instead, what is needed is dynamic stability – staying in tune with the dynamism through relational orientation, enabling the marble, bowl, and motion to remain coupled in reliable harmony over time.

Commons leadership is a way to achieve this dynamic stability. While governance of the commons (e.g., regulation, control, accountability) has been studied extensively, leadership of the commons has received much less attention (Thompson, 2020). Leadership entails functions such as providing direction, protection, and resources; developing adaptive capacity to learn, transform, and stay in tune with changing conditions; and mobilizing people to align through shared values to co-create a preferred, mutually beneficial future (Heifetz, Grashow, & Linsky, 2009). Leadership studies is interdisciplinary and a relatively young field, emerging in the last century by drawing from fields such as psychology, sociology, political science, and business. Yet these human-focused theories may be what is keeping us stuck in outdated mental models of leadership.

DIMENSIONS OF COMMONS LEADERSHIP

What can serve as a paradigm-shifting model for commons leadership? Nature offers 3.8 billion years of evidence-based sustainability strategies (Benyus, 2002). Using principles from ecology, relational biology, and complexity sciences as a guide, bioinspired thinking is a promising path to reorient conventional notions of leadership. Three important starting points are to develop new ways of thinking about relationships, power, and resources.

Relationships

We typically think about relationships as occurring between people. Commons leadership asks us to expand this framing by considering our relationship to nature, time, our values and aspirations, and the institutions and social systems in which we are embedded (Polanyi, 2001). These elements can be modeled as nested, interdependent systems (Castillo, 2016a), activated by processes that create flows of energy, information, and matter between them (Boulding, 1964). Fig. 1 illustrates embedded relations among the Earth, people, cultures, and financial systems.

Fig. 1.   Embeddedness (Castillo, 2016b).

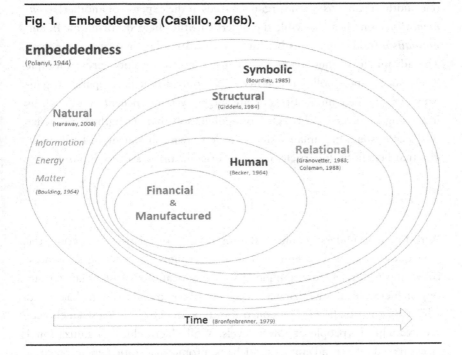

Modeling the system of relations completely is important because it illuminates interdependence, a relational ordering that circumvents randomness (Rosen, 1978). This ordering does not have to be static – it can be an ordered process of change, such as development and growth (Rosen, 1970). For example, pattern-recognizing algorithms (e.g., recurrent neural networks) create connections between nodes by mapping raw data to categories, creating multi-level relational structures that persist across temporal sequences (Schuster & Paliwal, 1997). Leadership can similarly be seen as a process that catalyzes the flow of energy, information, and matter through interdependent subsystems (categories), creating stabilizing connectivity and coherence. This relational process architecture promotes learning, adaptation, and dynamic coupling with the operating environment over time. Additionally, this network structuring fosters self-organization, enabling order to emerge spontaneously from individual actions rather than being imposed. An example of self-organization in nature is birds flocking. Common pool resource management is an example in communities (Ostrom, 2015).

How the relational exchanges take place across the subsystems is also important. Ecology describes three primary ways that organisms relate to one another: *parasitism* (one organism feeds at the expense of another), *commensalism* (one benefits while the other is neither helped nor harmed), and *mutualism* (both organisms benefit, while creating larger systemic benefits). The advantage of mutualism is that it can create benefits across multiple levels, such as bees pollinating flowers. Not only do the participating organisms benefit; their interactions create larger systemic benefits too, such as increasing biodiversity through cross-pollination that strengthens resilience of the ecosystem. In human systems, leaders create similar multi-level synergies that benefit both participants, their organizations, and communities.

Power

With this new understanding of the importance of relational ordering, the next question is, who is empowered to determine the ordering structures, rules, and processes, for example, resource allocation? Most organizations rely on hierarchical organizing, using chains of command to control how and where information flows. This constrains the system by limiting what choices are available to people at lower levels. While hierarchical organizational structures do have advantages, such as promoting static efficiency at a given moment in time in predictable environments, this functionality tends to break down in complex settings. In volatile and uncertain contexts, hierarchy can limit circulation and exchange of information within the organization and beyond, creating insularity and disconnect from the operating environment.

To prevent this loss of coupling and preserve information flows, commons leadership embraces a more expansive concept of power, such as shifting from notions of *power over* to *power to* (Allen 2018; Noddings, 1999; Nye, 2019). Rather than trying to control other actors, organizations, and the environment through *power over*, commons leadership develops capabilities and agency of system participants to preserve openness and exchange with the external environment. This empowering, catalytic approach to leadership enhances adaptive capacity by expanding degrees of freedom to act. Over time, this increases the number of options available for action. It also creates resonance, "… a general principle for governing self-organized processes" (Treffner & Turvey, 1993, p. 1234) that may provide better understanding of perception-action dynamics that a computational approach (Treffner & Turvey, 1993).

Resources

Conventional understanding of resources, such as bookkeeping and accounting, limits what gets valued – only physical and financial assets controlled by a firm are accounted for. Commons leadership recognizes there are many other types of resources, such as natural capital (e.g., ecosystem services), and social, reputational, intellectual, cultural, and political capital. COMMONS LEADERSHIP also values resources controlled by others or that emerge as collective properties, such as public infrastructure, social cohesion, and rule of law. Commons leadership intentionally develops these diverse resources to strengthen capacity at multiple levels (individual, organizational, networks, community, global). Frameworks such as community capitals (Emery & Flora, 2006), integrated reporting (IR) (International Integrated Reporting Council, 2013), and the multicapital scorecard (McElroy & Thomas, 2018) provide systematic approaches for understanding the various tangible and intangible resources that leaders can develop and deploy to create value for their stakeholders and society. These models also make visible the regenerative and recirculating properties of resource flows across multiple levels, similar to energy transfers across trophic levels in ecological food webs. Multiple capitals models also enable endogenous resource creation, for example, through development and emergence of higher qualities of energy (Odum, 2008), information (Hidalgo, 2015), and cooperative surplus (Koch, 1990).

COMMONS LEADERSHIP IN PRACTICE – A SYSTEM OF SYSTEMS ENGINEERING EXAMPLE

What does commons leadership look like in practice? The field of Systems Engineering offers some insights. Over the past few decades, Systems Engineering increasingly faced challenges of coordinating and integrating autonomous systems that had to work together cooperatively to produce a larger collective goal. Examples of these complex, interdependent systems include air traffic control, cyber security, military operations, enterprise systems management, and health care (Jamshidi, 2009). Each of these domains requires coordination of independent operating systems to work together to achieve a shared collective goal through participation in a metasystem. For example, in aviation, individual airlines pursue their own business strategies while collaborating to ensure efficient air travel and public safety. Conventional engineering principles based on control and homeostasis were incapable of guiding and controlling these complex systems.

To solve such coordination problems, an engineering approach called System of Systems (SoS) was conceptualized 50 years ago and developed practically over the past three decades (Gorod, Gandhi, Sauser, & Boardman, 2008). The goal of SoS is to create a more complex "supersystem" that can produce greater performance optimization and reliability than could be attained simply by combining individual capacities from the constituent organizations (Jamshidi, 2009, p. 4). SoS develops and maintains stability through allostasis, in contrast to traditional engineering strategies that seek stability through control and maintaining static, steady-state conditions (Tidball & Weinstein, 2011). A SoS approach is inherently interdisciplinary as it seeks to reconcile and coordinate disparate interests to achieve a collective goal (DeLaurentis, 2005).

SoS provides the structural and process architecture through which both certainty and uncertainty can be leveraged as strengths. SoS expands individual and collective degrees of freedom by channeling information and energy in ways that maintain the metasystem's and member systems' integrity while achieving shared goals (Gorod et al., 2008). Instead of relying on control, force, and uncertainty avoidance, a SoS approach provides dynamic stability through strategic design of the metasystem's architecture, relationships, and environment shaping (Tidball & Weinstein, 2011).

Architecture refers to designing the metasystem primarily in nonphysical ways to create interconnection among the member systems. These connections are usually accomplished through interface, a bridging process that enables sharing of information between member systems (Maier, 1996). Effective design facilitates autonomy of the members to activate and promote their agency (Boardman & Sauser, 2006), allowing for expansion and adaptation as conditions change, and for learning and other generative mechanisms to occur (Gorod et al., 2008). Rather than prescribing specific actions and outputs, a SoS design focuses on process structures (Maier, 1996; Malnight, 2001) that provide channels for communication, connection, and choice.

Well-designed architecture and interfaces foster relationship, the state of being interdependently connected to other members and the external environment. A growing body of literature suggests that relationships are a renewable resource that can be leveraged to produce other types of resources (e.g., psychological, reputational, and political capital), in turn enhancing the vitality of both the organization and the community (e.g., Bernardez & Kaufman, 2013; Coleman, 1993; Emery & Flora, 2006). This "spiraling up" (Emery & Flora, 2006, p. 28) is an example emergence, the sometimes surprising development of a macro-level phenomenon that is qualitatively different from simply aggregating its micro-level components (Stevens Institute of Technology, 2006; Waller, Okhuysen, & Saghafian, 2016).

Operating under resource constraints, institutions typically seek control through static efficiency to reduce transaction costs (Nemetz & Cameron, 2006). However, another way to reduce those costs is to build goal congruence through shared vision and values (Ouchi, 1980), and resonance, a syncing mechanism shown to maintain coordination under dynamic conditions (Peper, Beek, & van Wieringen, 1995).

SoS logic also suggests an additional alternative, reminiscent of Ghoshal and Moran's (1996) call for dynamic rather than static notions of efficiency. They observe that "the efficiency of a transaction is changed by actions that expand the available set of options" (Coleman, 1993; Ghoshal & Moran, 1996, p. 34; Milgrom & Roberts, 1992). Rather than relying on efficiency measures such minimizing overhead expenses, a SoS logic calls for investment in transactions that generate new options and produce benefits over multiple scales simultaneously (e.g., individual, department, university, academic field, community) and over time. However, resource allocation decisions in many institutions are frequently made by focusing on short time horizons, using a cost/benefit lens (Miller, 2007) or basing resource decisions on unequal power relations (Pfeffer & Salancik, 1974). The third SoS design principle is *environment shaping*, the process of proactively influencing the operating environment beyond simply adapting to it (Tidball & Weinstein, 2011). This shaping process should be participatory and include diverse internal and external stakeholders to consider problems and opportunities from many perspectives, in keeping with Ashby's law of requisite variety (Ashby, 1968). Environment shaping uses an iterative, asset-based approach to build from stakeholder strengths (e.g., what's working), rather than focusing on what's broken and needs fixing. This shaping process is recursive, incorporating physical and social feedback loops as subsequent planning rounds are developed (Tidball & Weinstein, 2011).

COMMONS LEADERSHIP PRINCIPLES

This chapter's bioinspired view of relationships, power, and resources, exemplified by SoS Engineering, suggests some guiding principles for leading commons systems. These principles include:

- Consider multiple temporal perspectives. Leaders must enact mechanisms to simultaneously assess a system's past performance, its current state, and its future capabilities for value creation. These mechanisms must also take into account intergenerational equity – the interests of future generations.

- Create a fractal architecture that enables self-organization and scaling across multiple levels (individual, organization, service delivery ecosystem, community, sector, national, global). This cross-level, relational ordering avoids reductionism and the loss of synergistic effects through decoupling. It also reduces likelihood of unintended consequences (e.g., negative externalities) and promotes synergistic goal alignment across levels.

- Be locally attunable. There is no one-size-fits-all template for leadership. Leaders must remain responsive, adaptable, and accountable to their communities and diverse contexts through communication feedbacks loops.

- Be inclusive. Strategy, planning, actions, and assessments are ideally co-created and monitored by diverse stakeholders.

- Include process measures to account for the vital role of catalytic processes such as leadership, communication, convening, and sharing.

CONCLUSION – MAKING COMMONS LEADERSHIP LEGIBLE

Articulating principles is an important step to understanding effective commons leadership practices. Yet, without values and intangible assets becoming visible in our metrics and accounting frameworks, it is unlikely that new mental models of leadership will take root. Adopting social accounting is an immediate leverage point to make values legible. Frameworks such as IR illuminate conventionally overlooked resources like relationships, knowledge, and nature that are fundamental to effective commons leadership. IR also calls attention to connectivity – the interdependence of various resources and how their synergistic actions can create cooperative surplus. IR makes visible the circular, recycling nature of resource flows and how mutualistic network structures enable these exchanges and conversions across multiple levels.

IR is a systematic communication tool to depict how an organization's strategy, governance, performance, and capabilities, in the context of its external environment, lead to sustainable value creation for stakeholders. It can be linked to commons governance models such as Ostrom's eight design principles (Ostrom, 1993; Wilson, Ostrom, & Cox, 2013).

Its multiple capitals approach provides a fractal architecture that works across varying scales, such as linking to organizational metrics, community well-being indicators, and the sustainable development goals (SDGs). Because it is principles-based, rather than standards-based, it is locally attunable for operating contexts. It also offers a framework to help shift economic thinking from reductionist, linear cause and effect to cyclical, bidirectional coaction found in complex adaptive systems.

The principles outlined in this chapter are a starting point for developing a theory of commons leadership. Using nature as a model to explain relational ordering, multi-level structuring and resource flows, and energy and information conversions provides a sound logic and vocabulary with which Commons leaders can explain why what they do works. Leading so all can thrive through mutualistic commons leadership is a way to effectively expand developmental capabilities of the system, its actors, and its embedded subsystems. This dynamic approach to stability expands collective potential for peace, prosperity, and progress.

REFERENCES

Allen, A. (2018). *The power of feminist theory*. Routledge.

Ashby, W. R. (1968). Variety, constraint, and the law of requisite variety. In W. Buckley (Ed.), *Modern systems research for the behavioral scientist*. Aldine Publishing Co.

Benyus, J. (2002). *Biomimicry: Innovation inspired by nature*. Harper Perennial.

Bernardez, M. L., & Kaufman, R. (2013). Turning social capital into social performance: Three case studies and a new framework for value creation. *Performance Improvement, 52*(5), 5–18.

Boulding, K. (1964). *The meaning of the twentieth century: The great transition.* Harper & Row.

Castillo, E. A. (2016a). Beyond the balance sheet: Teaching capacity building as capital building. *Journal of Nonprofit Education & Leadership, 6*(3), 287–303.

Castillo, E. A. (2016b, November 18). Spinning straw into gold: A study of resource creation, flow, and conversion in a nonprofit collaboration. Paper presented at Association of Research on Nonprofit Organizations and Voluntary Action.

Coleman, J. S. (1993). Properties of rational organizations. In S. M. Lindenberg & H. Schreuder (Eds.), *Interdisciplinary Perspectives on Organization Studies* (pp. 79–90). Pergamon Press.

DeLaurentis, D. (2005). Understanding transportation as a system-of-systems design problem. 43rd AIAA Aerospace Sciences Meeting and Exhibit. American Institute of Aeronautics and Astronautics. https://doi.org/10.2514/6.2005-123.

Emery, M. & Flora, C. (2006). Spiraling-up: Mapping community transformation with community capitals framework. *Community Development, 37*(1), 19–35.

Ghoshal, S., & Moran, P. (1996). Bad for practice: A critique of the transaction cost theory. *Academy of Management Review, 21*(1), 13–47.

Gorod, A., Gandhi, S. J., Sauser, B., & Boardman, J. (2008). Flexibility of System of Systems. *Global Journal of Flexible Systems Management, 9*(4), 21–31.

Heifetz, R., Grashow, A, & Linsky, M. (2009). *The practice of adaptive leadership: Tools and tactics for changing your organization and the world.* Harvard Business Press.

Hidalgo, C. (2015). *Why information grows: The evolution of order from atoms to economies.* Basic Books.

Hipel, K., Obeidi, A., Fang, L., & Kilgour, D. M. (2008). Sustainable environmental management from a system of systems engineering perspective. In M. Jamshidi (Ed.), *System of systems engineering-Innovations for the 21st century* (pp. 443–481). John Wiley & Sons.

International Integrated Reporting Council. (2013). Capitals background paper for <IR>. Retrieved from https://integratedreporting.org/wp-content/uploads/2013/03/IR-Background-Paper-Capitals.pdf

Jamshidi, M. (2009). *System of Systems engineering: Innovations for the twenty-first century.* John Wiley & Sons.

Koch, C. H. (1990). Cooperative surplus: The efficiency justification for active government. *William and Mary Law Review, 31*(2), 431–443.

Maier, M. W. (1996). Architecting principles for Systems-of-Systems. *INCOSE International Symposium, 6*(1), 565–573.

Malnight, T. W. (2001). Emerging structural patterns within multinational corporations: Toward process-based structures. *Academy of Management Journal, 44*(6), 1187–1210.

McElroy, M. W., & Thomas, M. P. (2015). The multicapital scorecard. *Sustainability Accounting, Management and Policy Journal, 6*(3), 425–438.

Meadows, D. (1997). Leverage points: Places to intervene in a system. *Whole Earth, 9*(1), 78–84.

Milgrom, P. & Roberts, J. (1992). *Economics, organization and management.* Prentice-Hall.

Miller, B. (2007). *Assessing organizational performance in higher education.* John Wiley & Sons.

Noddings, N. (2013). *Caring: A relational approach to ethics and moral education.* University of California Press.

Nye, A. (2019). *Words of power: A feminist reading of the history of logic.* Routledge.

Odum, H. T. (2008). *A prosperous way down: Principles and policies.* University Press of Colorado.

Ostrom, E. (2015). A framework for analysis of self-organizing and self-governing CPRs. *Governing the commons: The evolution of institutions for collective action* (Canto Classics, pp. 182–216).Cambridge University Press.

Ostrom, E. (1993). Design principles in long-enduring irrigation institutions. *Water Resources Research, 29*(7), 1907–1912.

Peper, C. L. E., Beek, P. J., & van Wieringen, P. C. W. (1995). Multifrequency coordination in bimanual tapping: Asymmetrical coupling and signs of supercriticality. *Journal of Experimental Psychology: Human Perception and Performance, 21*, 1117–1138.

Pfeffer, J., & Salancik, G. R. (1974). Organizational decision making as a political process: The case of a university budget. *Administrative Science Quarterly, 19*(2), 135–151.

Polanyi, K. (2001). *The great transformation: The political and economic origins of our time* (2nd ed.). Beacon Press.

Rosen, R. (1970). *Dynamical system theory in biology: Stability theory and its applications* (Vol. 1). John Wiley & Sons.

Rosen, R. (1978). *Fundamentals of measurement and representation of natural systems.* Elsevier North-Holland.

Schuster, M., & Paliwal, K. K. (1997). Bidirectional recurrent neural networks. *IEEE Transactions on Signal Processing, 45*(11), 2673–2681.

Sterling, P., & Eyer, J. (1988). Allostasis: A new paradigm to explain arousal pathology. In S. Fisher & J. T. Reason (Eds.), *Handbook of life stress, cognition, and health* (pp. 629–649). Wiley.

Thompson, R. J. (2020). Reclaiming leadership on the commons. In *Proleptic leadership on the Commons: Ushering in a new global order* (pp. 141–159). Emerald Publishing Limited.

Tidball, K. G., & Weinstein, E. D. (2011). Applying the environment shaping methodology: conceptual and practical challenges. *Journal of Intervention and Statebuilding*, *5*(4), 369–394.

Treffner, P. J., & Turvey, M. T. (1993). Resonance constraints on rhythmic movement. *Journal of Experimental Psychology: Human Perception and Performance*, *19*, 1221–1237.

Waddock, S. (2020). Thinking transformational system change. *Journal of Change Management*, *20*(3), 1–13.

Walker, B., Gunderson, L., Kinzig, A., Folke, C., Carpenter, S., & Schultz, L. (2006). A handful of heuristics and some propositions for understanding resilience in social-ecological systems. *Ecology and Society*, *11*(1), article 13.

Wilson, D. S., Ostrom, E., & Cox, M. E. (2013). Generalizing the core design principles for the efficacy of groups. *Journal of Economic Behavior & Organization*, *90*, S21–S32.

3

REDEFINING LEADERSHIP THROUGH THE COMMONS: AN OVERVIEW OF TWO PROCESSES OF MEANING-MAKING AND COLLECTIVE ACTION IN BARCELONA

ANTONIO JIMENEZ-LUQUE

INTRODUCTION

Leadership can be understood as transformation (Burns, 1978), mobilization (Heifetz & Sinder, 1988), and 'the process by which "social order" is constructed and changed' (Hosking & Morley, 1988, p. 90). Overall, in the leadership literature, when it comes to analyzing how these processes of transformation, mobilization, and construction of social orders unfold, scholars and practitioners have adopted a hierarchical approach based on the leader. This top-down and individualistic perspective of analyzing and practicing leadership results from the dominance of the charismatic leadership paradigm that still embeds the field of leadership studies (Spoelstra, 2018) and legitimizes the accumulation of power in a few hands (Tourish, 2013). However, in the last decades, leadership theories such as contingency, cultural, or power and influence theories have started to lay the groundwork for examining leadership as a process, and gradually the emphasis has been taken away from an individual and put on more distributed forms of leadership (Horner, 1997; Spillane, 2006). According to Horner (1997), "the focus of leadership research cannot be a specific person, even if that person is designated as the team leader, if a comprehensive understanding of the leadership process is expected" (p. 280).

Today, despite charismatic and heroic-centered perspectives of leadership still being the mainstream approaches to understanding and analyzing the phenomenon of leadership, it is getting more accepted that, although leaders influence followers, culture, and the context involved in the process of leadership, followers, culture, and context contribute to shaping leaders (Jimenez-Luque, 2020). This alternative approach of understanding leadership as a more relational and collective process redefines classic notions and assumptions regarding the phenomenon of leadership and its emergence. For example, Drath and Palus (1994) view leadership as a social process where people of a community of practice interact and make sense of the world by creating frameworks within which their actions have meaning. According to this definition, leadership emerges when people act together and make sense of those actions. It is a process of framing, or meaning-making of collective actions, that aims to achieve a specific goal.

The study of the commons represents an excellent opportunity to broaden knowledge regarding the phenomenon of leadership and redefine its conceptualization from a hierarchical, individualistic, and leader-centered perspective where power is accumulated in a few hands to a more collective, relational, and participatory approach of distributed power. According to Basu, Jongerden, and Ruivenkamp (2017), "the concept of commons is often understood to refer to resources shared among a group of people" (p. 144). The idea of commons does not depend on the state or the private sector/ market and emphasizes social relations and a collaborative community to self-govern resources through organizations and institutions that they create (Ostrom, 1990). More specifically, when it comes to the commons' collaborative economy, the overall philosophy is that the citizens must have a central role as producers and decision-makers. Commons' collaborative economy is supported by digital platforms for collaborative processes of consumption, production, sharing, and exchange among distributed groups of peers in horizontal conditions that empower them and society (Fuster, 2019).

This chapter aims to redefine mainstream conceptualizations of leadership through an overview of two specific processes of the commons in Barcelona: (1) *Som Energia*, a renewable energy coop that resells energy bought from the market and develops its own renewable energy projects to produce energy for its members; and (2) *Guifi.net*, a broadband telecommunications network that is managed as a commons for the benefit of ordinary internet users and small businesses. More specifically, in order to redefine leadership through the analysis of these two examples of commons, this chapter will focus on two particular elements: (1) how the collective frameworks to make sense and meaning of the organization as a commons are designed; and (2) how the collective practices to achieve its goals are developed.

With an overview of these two particular cases of commons such as *Som Energia* and *Guifi.net*, this chapter aims to shed light on how leadership processes emerge. Additionally, this chapter contributes to debunking the myth that leadership is only about a person, the leader, and through a lens of process philosophy, provides a more in-depth and relational understanding of leadership through the combination of framing for meaning-making and collective action to advance a task or goal.

PROCESS PHILOSOPHY AND LEADERSHIP

From a mainstream perspective of vertical and heroic/leader-centered leadership, the commons might not be a very appealing setting for study. Even more, some may say that there is no leadership emerging in those spaces. Conversely, in this chapter, the commons are viewed as an opportunity for an ontological challenge of the leadership field and to approach the phenomenon of leadership as a relational process through a lens of process philosophy.

According to process philosophy, concepts such as leaders, followers, and organizations are "simple appearances we employ to give substantiality to our experience, but under whose supposed 'naturalness' the fundamentally processual nature of the real is neglected" (Wood, 2005, p. 1104). The key issue in process studies is how an actor "condenses within itself … a multitude of social dimensions and meanings" (Cooper, 1983, p. 204), because leadership is not situated in "the autonomous, self-determining individual with a secure unitary identity [at] the centre of the social universe" (Alvesson & Deetz, 2000, p. 98).

Therefore, leadership is "the point of difference" (Cooper, 1983, p. 204), and 'is already a "complete" relation, where the relation is the thing itself and each part necessarily refers to another, but without "completion" in a straightforward way' (Wood, 2005, p. 1105). In other words, viewing the phenomenon of leadership as a process 'is the unlocalizable "in" of the "between" of each, a freely interpenetrating process, whose "identity" is consistently self-differing' (Wood, 2005, p. 1105).

As a result of the particular characteristics of the commons, such as being collectively self-organized, self-governed, and autonomous, these emerging organizational practices around the world offer an excellent case for studying in-depth leadership as a "systematic complex of mutual relatedness" (Whitehead, 1967, p. 161) where conceptual interpretations are always "an incompletion in the process of production" (Whitehead, 1978, p. 327).

FRAMING FOR MEANING-MAKING AND COLLECTIVE ACTION

In the organizational sciences, there is varied research regarding framing, including reframing for organizational change (Bartunek, 1984; Weick, 1979); problem framing and its impact on decision-making processes (Kahneman & Tversky, 1979; Tversky & Kahneman, 1981); and political actors using framing to promote a particular definition, interpretation, and treatment of a problem (Entman, 1993). Although the ways of approaching framing vary, "one commonality is the casting of framing as both a cognitive device and a communicative activity defined by selection, emphasis, interpretation, and exclusion" (Fairhurst, 2005, p. 167).

According to Fairhurst and Sarr (1996), framing can be defined as the ability to shape the meaning of a subject, to judge its character and significance. To hold the frame of a subject is to choose one particular meaning (or set of meanings) over another. When we share our frames with others (the process of framing), we manage meaning because we assert that our interpretations should be taken as real over other possible interpretations (p. 3). When it comes to the idea of collective action from a perspective of the literature of social movements, Melucci (1995a) defines such movements as social construction with purpose and meaning. This purpose and meaning emerge from framing to legitimize the actions of actors in these movements (Snow & Benford, 1992). However, framing is also defined through collective action transforming elements of the dominant culture, bridging, amplifying, or transforming other frames (Snow, Rochford, Worden, & Benford, 1986). Therefore, framing influences action, but action influences framing when preexisting beliefs or oppositional values that emerge during the struggle are incorporated within the groups' frames (Taylor & Whittier, 1995).

In what follows, I provide a brief overview of different assumptions and definitions regarding the phenomenon of commons. I then introduce and analyze two specific processes of the commons in Barcelona: *Som Energia*, a renewable energy coop, and *Guifi.net*, a broadband telecommunications network managed as a common. Finally, I discuss the implications for theory and practice in the leadership field and present some conclusions.

FROM THE "TRAGEDY OF THE COMMONS" TO "GOVERNING THE COMMONS": A LEADERSHIP STRUGGLE OF CONCEPTUALIZATIONS AND DEFINITIONS

While leadership is a process that builds and transforms social orders (Hosking & Morley, 1988), mainstream leadership theories offer ideological support for the existing social order (Gemmill & Oakley, 1992). Moreover, in mainstream conceptualizations of leadership, there is an assumption that leaders and hierarchies are needed for the functioning of organizations (Gemmill & Oakley, 1992). These conceptualizations of leadership and images of leaders can have negative consequences when it comes to exercising leadership such as accumulation of power at the top, lack of participatory approaches, and noninclusive processes of decision-making.

Today, to support the capitalist system and the neoliberal social order, mainstream leadership theories emphasize individualism, top-down decision-making, and power concentration, which for mainstream perspectives are considered effective leadership. Although defenders of neoliberalism talk about free market and deregulation, they do not acknowledge the asymmetries of power in society that exist as a result of processes of accumulation of capital originating with colonialism that were key to developing the industrial revolution and the current global social order. In other words, today's discourses of free market and deregulation are functional to legitimize a system where those with the most capital remain at the top (they are the market), and mainstream discourses of leadership justify that leading is an action reserved for a those chosen ones (they are the leaders). For example, when American biologist and philosopher Garrett Hardin coined the concept of the "tragedy of the commons" in 1968, he argued that people could not work together to benefit from common resources because they would look for their own profit and the system would inevitably collapse. Hardin's work was based on assumptions of individualism and competition between people functional to the capitalist system.

However, a few years later, Nobel Prize in Economics Winner Elinor Ostrom proved that although common resource systems have been known to collapse due to overuse, many examples have existed and still do exist where members of a community with access to a common resource cooperate or regulate their behavior in order to use those resources prudently without collapse. Through the concept of "governing the commons" instead of "the tragedy of the commons," Ostrom showed how local communities could organize themselves together through collective action without top-down regulations or privatization. In other words, these communities veered away from mainstream conceptualizations and practices of individualistic and competitive leadership and embraced collective processes of power-sharing leadership.

These nonmainstream views of leadership represent not just a challenge to dominant theories of leadership, but also to the entire socio-economic system that these theories support. However, since Hardin's article in *Science* (1968), the expression "the tragedy of the commons" has become very popular, and the assumption that the degradation of the environment is always expected whenever many individuals use a scarce resource in common has been the hegemonic view regarding shared resources (Ostrom, 1990). According to Dawes (1975), Hardin's model has been formalized as a prisoner's dilemma game and has fascinated many scholars who have reproduced it and contributed to creating the "myth" of the impossibility of organizing the commons collaboratively.

The paradox that individually rational strategies lead to collectively irrational outcomes seems to challenge a fundamental faith that rational human beings can achieve rational results. As Campbell (1985) argues regarding the "attraction" of the prisoner's dilemma:

> *Quite simply, these paradoxes cast in doubt our understanding of rationality and, in the case of the Prisoner's Dilemma, suggest that it is impossible for rational creatures to cooperate. Thus, they bear directly on fundamental issues in ethics and political philosophy and threaten the foundations of the social sciences. It is the scope of these consequences that explains why these paradoxes have drawn so much attention and why they command a central place in philosophical discussion. (pp. 3–5)*

At the heart of this model and others that consider the cooperation between people impossible is the "free-rider problem." As Ostrom (1990) explained, this particular problem argues that

> *Whenever one person cannot be excluded from the benefits that*
> *others provide, each person is motivated not to contribute to the*
> *joint effort, but to free-ride on the efforts of others. If all participants*
> *choose to free-ride, the collective benefit will not be produced. (p. 6)*

Also, by referring to natural settings as "tragedies of the commons," the "prisoner's dilemma" and so on, "the observer frequently wishes to invoke an image of helpless individuals caught in an inexorable process of destroying their own resources" (Ostrom, 1990, p. 8).

It is necessary to deconstruct this assumption that originated with the "tragedy of the commons" and, rather than taking for granted that a group of individuals sharing a commons are inevitably caught up in a trap without escape, it is critical to consider that the capacity of individuals "to extricate themselves from various types of dilemma situations varies from situation to situation" (Ostrom, 1990, p. 14). Additionally, it is a key to acknowledge that it is possible, in fact, for people to successfully extricate themselves and successfully govern and share resources when certain conditions exist. In essence, it is critical to deconstruct conceptualizations and definitions of the commons providing new frameworks where people can make sense and meaning of new ways of understanding processes of collective leadership and contributing to create more horizontal social orders. The following two cases can shed some light regarding how the collective frameworks are designed to make sense and meaning of *Som Energia* and *Guifi.net* as commons and how collective practices to achieve their goals are developed.

SOM ENERGIA AND GUIFI.NET: TWO SUCCESSFUL COMMONS IN THE CITY OF BARCELONA

Som Energia is Catalonia's first renewable energy cooperative that offers thousands of people who support the idea of powering their homes with locally generated, clean, sustainable electricity the chance to come together to make the concept a reality. As a nonprofit cooperative *Som Energia* started selling green energy from existing sources in 2011. This energy is bought from the market and sold to its members. Moreover, the cooperative develops its own cost-effective renewable energy projects to produce energy for members who can use affordable eco-electricity in their homes – while playing a part in transforming the country into a sustainable and environmentally friendly place to live.

Guifi.net was created in 2008 by a group of *Guifi.net* users who decided to organize themselves as a foundation to promote and develop the network as an infrastructure with equal conditions for all. This foundation advocates for the "human right to access the Internet" through a social and collaborative economic model and believes that people are the engine of transformation and change. Since 2009, the *Guifi.net* network has created systems oriented to the transparency, maintenance, and improvement of the infrastructure and its management as a "common good." The foundation promotes coordination mechanisms in collaboration with local administrations, entities, and companies that offer Internet access services to *Guifi.net* network users.

Commons are characterized by shared resources; a collaborative community; citizens who, besides being producers and consumers, are also decision-makers; and access for everybody to diverse platforms for production, consumption, sharing practices, and knowledge exchanges. Based on the study of documents and communication artifacts of *Som Energia* and *Guifi.net* (official documents, websites, pictures, audios, and videos), I highlight patterns in communication in both organizations regarding issues of framing and collective action. The main findings are organized in the following two main sections: (1) framing through language and artifacts and (2) creating spaces to unfold collective practices and build collective agency.

FRAMING THROUGH LANGUAGE AND ARTIFACTS

Using framing as both a cognitive device and a communicative activity, *Som Energia* includes in all their documents, websites, and meetings a sustainable energy model to address climate change where resources are shared in a collaborative and participatory way. Every member of the organization invests money to produce sustainable energy collectively, and this amount of money is eventually returned. Also, the need to share resources for future generations and the importance of taking control of a sustainable energy model rather than leave it to private corporations looking for their economic interests are emphasized. Concepts like "sustainable energy in the hands of the citizenship," "social and solidarity economy," "breaking the oligopoly," "transparency," or "a transformative social movement" are present in official documents, websites, videos, and audios.

When it comes to issues of a collaborative community, the organization highlights collaboration and cooperation throughout their documents and videos, which talk about "a model centered in the people," "leadership that enhances autonomy empowering other leaders," "coordination," "co-responsibility," and "horizontal participation." Moreover, in every document, there is an important space reserved for motivating people to share knowledge and good practices with comments like "you can do it" or "share what you are thinking." Additionally, the organization suggests that everybody can contribute regardless of their knowledge about sustainable energy production because everyone is needed in their local groups to participate in organizing events or spreading the word.

Guifi.net emphasizes in its official documents and videos the concept of self-organization of neighbors collaborating to provide an infrastructure with equal conditions for all people. For the organization, access to the Internet is a human right and hence it proposes a system based on "transparency" and the "common good" rather than private interests to benefit those who have resources to pay for the Internet. The words highlighted throughout the documents are "collaborative economy," "people as the engine of transformation and change," "open and free network of Internet," or "no discrimination."

Moreover, the organization emphasizes a collaborative community, highlighting that access to the Internet is a human right as recognized by the United Nations in 2011. It advocates for a solidarity Internet against the corporate monopolies, promoting a collaborative economy within the commons' network. The organization also argues that everybody must have access to the Internet regardless of socio-economic, cultural, or territorial status. Besides, it advocates for collaboration between civic society, the public sector, and the private sector to establish relationships and collaborations while participating in common projects.

Guifi.net highlights the idea of an open and inclusive project in which everybody can take part. Like *Som Energia*, *Guifi.net* reserves important spaces in its documents and videos to encourage people to participate using sentences like "We are waiting for you!" "You are *Guifi.net*," "It is not about we can... we just do!" or "Get involved." Also, they provide many examples of what one person can do like "Extending the network" by making donations; doing research on *Guifi.net*; developing network managing website applications, multimedia applications, map servers, and so on; setting up collaboration agreements between your work and the *Guifi.net* Foundation, etc.

CREATING SPACES TO UNFOLD COLLECTIVE PRACTICES
AND BUILD COLLECTIVE AGENCY

Collective action is a social construction with purpose and meaning (Melucci, 1995), and this purpose and meaning emerge from framing to legitimize the actions of the collective (Snow & Benford, 1992). *Som Energia* emphasizes that citizens are not just producers and consumers but also decision-makers and that everybody needs to be involved in the process. They talk about self-organization and the self-production of energy. The main organ for decision-making is the Assembly, and every member is part of the Assembly and has a vote. In the Assembly, members elect the Council, which is in charge of implementing the organization's principles and respecting its values. From there, there are "work groups" and "local groups." Besides the Assembly, there are virtual spaces and platforms for processes of accessible and quick decision-making.

Moreover, *Som Energia*, creates spaces where members of the organization can share good practices and exchange knowledge and ideas. Local groups are central for offering spaces where participating, sharing practices and experiences, and learning from each other take place. Additionally, *Som Energia* offers a virtual space where the organization's members can share information, debate, and make decisions. There is also the option of creating groups based on studying themes that share some of their findings, conclusions, or proposals with the rest of the organization. Participation and sharing ideas and giving one's opinion are encouraged throughout *Som Energia* documents. The decisions of the organization need to be based on broad and collective feedback. Another space for sharing and exchanging is the "September's school." The format of this space is similar to the Assembly but in a more relaxed way and more focused on sharing ideas and developing relationships.

Guifi.net emphasizes the idea of enhancing the collective agency of its members. The organization tries to empower members' collective agency with the idea that "People are the engine of transformation and change." With the intention of building collective agency, it is a key to reserve important spaces in their documents and videos that encourage people to participate in as many spaces provided for the Foundation as they can. It is a different approach than mainstream leadership perspectives which defend the idea that leadership is just for a few chosen ones.

The idea of platforms for developing collective action and agency through sharing and exchanging is present in the commons' structures. As in *Som Energia*, the Assembly is the main space for decision-making in *Guifi.net* where every member of the Foundation has a vote. In the Assembly, they vote for the Board of Trustees, the structure that implements the organization's principles. Moreover, as in *Som Energia*, at *Guifi.net*, various spaces where members of the organization can share good practices and exchange knowledge and ideas are provided. However, in this case, the Foundation focuses more on developing collaborative research projects to unfold collective actions. Thus, they organize many courses and seminars to raise awareness about the goals of the organization where everybody is welcome to present their research. They also participate in European projects of research, development, and innovation focused on telecommunications, networks, sustainable development, and participatory democracy.

Besides creating spaces for unfolding processes of collective action that eventually enhance collective agency, *Guifi.net's* work aims to distribute power by empowering each one of its members. The foundation is an open and inclusive project that highlights that "everybody can take part," "We are waiting for you!" "Do-it-Yourself!" "You are *guifi.net!*," or "You will be part of a network belonging to all of us!" It is a shared-power approach that overcomes the accumulation of power in a few hands that dominant discourses of leadership legitimize.

IMPLICATIONS FOR THE LEADERSHIP FIELD AND CONCLUSIONS

This chapter argues that deconstructing mainstream conceptualizations and assumptions of individualistic leadership and leaders is central to unfolding processes of collective action required for governing the commons. These collective action processes will challenge mainstream approaches where there is a leader at the top exercising leadership in a hierarchical way, and power is concentrated. Additionally, my main argument is that for breaking out of the trap of mainstream leadership and assumptions of the "tragedy of the commons," it is critical to design collective frameworks (1) to make sense and meaning of an organization as a common; and from there (2) to develop the collective practices needed to achieve the organization's goals.

At both *Som Energia* and *Guifi.net*, the process of sense and meaning-making of the organization as a common requires the type of leadership that starts with language and artifacts. Language in organizations is central to create frameworks where people can make sense of reality. Thus, using inclusive and empowering language, it is critical to develop a sense of belonging and motivating people to participate. This language needs to be present in every document, picture, video, and even the logo of the organization.

Moreover, at *Some Energia* and *Guifi.net*, the work is enhanced through the creation of spaces where practices of collective action can take place to empower the collective agency of the members of the organization. Through these processes, the members of each organization make sense of their organization as a common or space to share resources, participate in a collaborative community, be involved in sharing practices and exchanging knowledge, and act as decision-makers. Organizations need to provide spaces where people can participate collectively, and their voices are heard. Spaces for collective processes of decision-making are critical to empower people and to benefit from different perspectives and approaches when it comes to achieve goals. These spaces can be physical, virtual, or even symbolic, but they have a big impact in enhancing the emergence of effective leadership.

As a result of the particular characteristics of the commons, such as their collective self-organization and being self-governed and autonomous, the analysis of these organizational practices at *Som Energia* and *Guifi.net* contribute to redefine mainstream leadership practices centered on a leader at the top who is not influenced by followers or the context. Leadership is not situated in "the autonomous, self-determining individual with a secure unitary identity [at] the centre of the social universe" (Alvesson & Deetz, 2000, p. 98). Leadership is a relational process that emerges in a context to achieve a particular goal. Thus, analyzing these two examples of commons from a lens of process philosophy shows that leadership emerges in the "in between" of relations and in the "in between" of actions of people willing to achieve goals together.

Moreover, dominant views of leadership imply the idea that leadership is reserved for a few chosen ones or an elite with the expertise rather than a process where everybody can participate. The example of the commons in general, and in the cases of *Som Energia* and *Guifi.net* in particular, prove that leadership can be implemented in a more collaborative way, power can be distributed more equitably, and collective processes from bottom up where everybody is valued and heard are possible. Additionally, implementing more collective leadership or public leadership from below (Jimenez-Luque, 2020) will contribute to democratizing dominant practices that have resulted in inefficient and, in many cases, unethical consequences.

Further research is needed in the field of leadership to theorize about the commons type of organizations and their ways of leadership. The study of the commons is critical not just to redefine definitions of leadership and practices of leading and following but, at a broader level, to redesign the distribution of wealth and resources, working across differences, and essentially, building healthier and stronger democracies.

REFERENCES

Alvesson, M., & Deetz, S. (2000). *Doing critical management research*. Sage.

Bartunek, J. M. (1984). Changing interpretive schemes and organizational restructuring: The example of a religious order. *Administrative Science Quarterly, 29*, 355–372.

Basu, S., Jongerden, J., & Ruivenkamp, G. (2017). Development of the drought tolerant variety Sahbhagi Dhan: Exploring the concepts commons and community building. *International Journal of the Commons, 11*(1), 144.

Burns, J. M. (1978). *Leadership*. Harper and Row.

Campbell, R. (1985). Background for the uninitiated. In R. Campbell & L. Sowden (Eds.), *Paradoxes of rationality and cooperation* (pp. 3–41). University of British Columbia Press.

Cooper, R. (1983). The other: A model of human structuring. In G. Morgan (Ed.), *Beyond method: Strategies for social research* (pp. 202–218). Sage.

Dawes, R. M. (1975). Formal models of dilemmas in social decision making. In M. F. Kaplan & S. Schwartz (Eds.), *Human judgement and decision processes: Formal and mathematical approaches* (pp. 87–108). Academic Press.

Drath, W. H., & Palus, C. J. (1994). *Making common sense: Leadership as meaning-making in a community of practice*. Center for Creative Leadership.

Entman, R. (1993). Framing: Toward clarification of a fractured paradigm. *Journal of Communication,43*(4), 51–58.

Fairhurst, G. T. (2005). Reframing the art of framing: Problems and prospects for leadership. *Leadership, 1*(2), 165–185.

Fairhurst, G. T., & Sarr, R. A. (1996). *The art of framing: Managing the language of leadership*. Jossey-Bass.

Fuster, M. (2019). Procomuns: City policies for the commons collaborative economy. Shareable. (5/28/2018). Retrieved from https://www.shareable.net/procomuns-city-policies-for-the-commons-collaborative-economy/. Accessed on December 12, 2020.

Gemmill, G., & Oakley, J. (1992). Leadership: An alienating social myth? *Human Relations*, 45(2), 113–129.

Heifetz, R. A., & Sinder, R. M. (1988). Political leadership: Managing the public's problem solving. In R. B. Reich (Ed.), *The power of public ideas* (pp. 179–203). Ballinger.

Horner, M. (1997). Leadership theory: Past, present and future. *Team Performance Management*, 3(4), 270–287.

Hosking, D. M., & Morley, I. E. (1988). The skills of leadership. In J. G. Hunt, B. R. Baliga, H. P. Dachler, & C. A. Schriesheim (Eds.), *Emerging leadership vistas* (pp. 89–106). Lexington Books.

Jimenez-Luque, A. (2020). Exercising public leadership from below: An empirical research on a Native American health clinic. *Journal of Leadership Studies*, 14(1), 74–79.

Kahneman, D., & Tversky, A. (1979). Prospect theory: An analysis of decision under risk. *Econometrica*, 47(2), 263–291.

Melucci, A. (1995). The process of collective identity. In H. Johnston & B. Klandermans (Eds.), *Social movements and culture* (pp. 41–63). University of Minnesota Press.

Ostrom, E. (1990). *Governing the Commons: The evolution of institutions for collective action.* Cambridge University Press.

Snow, D. A., & Benford, R. D. (1992). Master frames and cycles of protest. In A. Morris & C. McClurg Mueller (Eds.), *Frontiers in social movement theory* (pp. 133–155). Yale University Press.

Snow, D., Rochford, E. B., Jr, Worden, S. K., & Benford, R. D. (1986). Frame alignment processes, micromobilization and movement participation. *American Sociological Review*, 51, 456–481.

Spillane, J. P. (2006). *Distributed leadership.* Jossey-Bass.

Spoelstra, S. (2018). *Leadership and organization: A philosophical introduction.* Routledge.

Taylor, V., & Whittier, N. (1995). Analytical approaches to social movement culture: The culture of the women's movement. In H. Johnston, & B. Klandermans (Eds.), *Social movements and culture* (pp. 163–187). University of Minnesota Press.

Tourish, D. (2013). *The dark side of transformational leadership: A critical perspective.* Routledge.

Tversky, A., & Kahneman, D. (1981). The framing of decisions and the psychology of choice. *Science*, 211(4481), 453–458.

Weick, K. E. (1979). *The social psychology of organizing.* Addison-Wesley.

Whitehead, A. N. (1967 [1925]). *Science and modern world*. Cambridge University Press.

Whitehead, A. N. (1978 [1929]). Process and reality. In D. R. Griffin & D. W. Sherburne (Eds.), *Process and reality: An essay in cosmology*. Free Press.

Wood, M. (2005). The fallacy of misplaced leadership. *Journal of Management Studies, 42*(6), 1101–1121.

4

RESPONSIBLE, RELATIONAL, AND INTENTIONAL: A RE-IMAGINED CONSTRUCT OF CORPORATE-COMMONS LEADERSHIP

KATHLEEN A. CURRAN

Aboriginal ontology believes in the interconnectedness of everything on earth – every rock, tree, waterfall, grain of sand, animal, and human are interconnected stakeholders. From its inception, therefore, every idea considered and action resulting are made with the planet and all its stakeholders in mind, inclusive of impact on their lives in the present and in the future – in other words, the ontology is a model for what matters.

This chapter explores leadership in a new light and supports a model for what matters, an intentional model that is premised on the merger of attitudes toward beliefs, desires, and agency and value placed on those elements that matter such as truth, beauty, and purpose (Turner, 2017). The principle of causality explains the sense of agency, for example, which can generally be considered the driving force as well as rationale behind corporate strategies as they seek to increase profit and shareholder value. The elements that matter, based on intentionality, can be categorized as those that provide the impetus behind the initiatives of the commons, the self-organized groups who work to protect what they believe to be commonly shared natural resources and the right of access for all.

Unfortunately, state and capitalist corporate bodies have frequently expanded their rights to resources, for example, by establishing legal ownership and charging for use of those common resources that include natural, human, and intellectual resources; they have functioned according to what matters to them alone. As corporate power exploited citizens' access to resources usurped their rights, the commons' movement toward *what matters* fueled efforts to resist the corporate resource grab. In broad brush strokes, a picture of the hundreds of years old tendency for corporations and commons to share an adversarial relationship, neither agreeing on what matters is painted.

Yet, what if corporations and the commons were on the same side, aligned in their model of what matters? What would it look like if they joined forces? Who would their adversaries be then? Re-imagining the corporate and commons relationship provokes a re-imagining of the leadership that would best serve such a hybrid. While a corporate-commons hybrid may seem a paradox at first glance, upon closer investigation, the notion may pique possibilities. In fact, the time for leadership to tap the spirit of the commons and leverage the engines of the corporation, rather than self-limit or dichotomize by context, may have arrived.

In this chapter, I will first cursorily review the paradigm of capitalism as the economic structure generally adopted by for-profit corporations, and the contrasting paradigm of the commons, illuminating four key contrasts that require alignment for a proposed hybrid to be successful: (1) Purpose of entity – profit extraction from resources or protection of resources; (2) Rights of resource ownership – individually controlled or collectively shepherded; (3) Responsibility to shareholders or collective responsibility to stakeholders, that is an egocentric attitude of dominance or an ecocentric concern for the whole interconnected planet; and (4) Time orientation – short term with an emphasis on shareholder value or long term with an emphasis on sustainable care of shared resources. Secondly, based on a review of selected leadership models, responsible leadership will be suggested as a construct on which both commons and corporations can foster a shared ecocentric core. A hybrid model for what matters will then be proposed, and a self-proclaimed imperfect model, Patagonia, Inc., will be considered as a hopeful example on which to build. Finally, in this chapter that provides questions much more than answers, I will identify areas for future thought leadership and research.

CAPITALISM, CORPORATIONS, AND THE COMMONS AT ODDS

Beinhocker and Hanauer (2014) declare that "capitalism is under attack" (p. 1). Myriad crises and inequities exposed at the time of their publication,

Table 1. Capitalism and the Commons: Contrasting Paradigms.

	Capitalism	The Commons
Purpose	Profit extraction; resource exploitation	Protect planet and resources
Rights of ownership	Individually/privately controlled	Shared collective/public access
Responsibility to…	Private shareholders	Public stakeholders
Time orientation	Short-term focus measured by shareholder profit	Long-term focus measured by shared care & sustainability of planet

and amplified in 2020, have led to the present need to challenge taken-for-granted beliefs concerning how, why, and for whom businesses exist. Many corporations may believe that they know why, for whom they exist, and how they operate, but these questions are now aptly demanding attention and challenging their thinking. Cracks revealed in social and economic systems have also pointed to this being the time for recognizing and acting on the signs that assess how the capitalist system is actually performing today.

The assumption underpinning the position that capitalism, the economic paradigm upon which market-driven corporations operate, and the paradigm of the commons differ is derived from a comparison of four key elements that address the how, why, and for whom questions (Table 1).

In practice, paradigms widely differ. Capitalism follows a mechanistic view of business, based on an efficient allocation of societies' resources. Self-interested firms thus work to maximize profits by maximizing perceived usefulness to consumers. Based on the exchange between supply and demand, prices are set, and resources are distributed in what the market determines to be fair. Capitalist paradigm advocates declare the system optimal for solving human problems and making the solutions as efficient and widely accessible as possible, which brings immediate gratification, and enhances their construct of prosperity (Beinhocker & Hanauer, 2014). The Commons paradigm, in contrast, addresses the four key elements simply and comprehensively as "a shared heritage of all global citizens … and a commitment to future generations, to communities beyond our local sphere, to working for both the local and the global common good" (Hess, 2008, p. 34).

On August 19, 2019, the Business Roundtable (McKinsey and Company, 2020) issued its latest statement on the purpose of a corporation, which illustrates a slight shift to longer-term value creation and the position that businesses can and should take into account the interests of all *stakeholders*, (which includes shareholders).

> *Businesses play a vital role in the economy by creating jobs, foster-ing innovation and providing essential goods and services. Busi-nesses make and sell consumer products; manufacture equipment and vehicles; support the national defense; grow and produce food; provide health care; generate and deliver energy; and offer finan-cial, communications and other services that underpin economic growth. While each of our individual companies serves its own corporate purpose, we share a fundamental commitment to all of our stakeholders.*

Prosperity *for whom*, asks commons' advocates. Who are *all stakeholders*? From an ecocentric perspective, the corporate response to *for whom* has myopically neglected nonhumans, dis-including resources on whom life itself depends. According to commoners, who believe that ownership of resources is the right of individual firms is tantamount to holding the planet in bond-age, shrinks the orientation toward time to short-term milestones, and meas-ures profits by narrowly defined, self-centered gains. Resources also sit at the center of the clashing perspectives. Ironically, the capitalist paradigm that focuses on return-on-investment to stakeholder/shareholders assumes that capital is a major limited resource that must be protected and for which strat-egies, systems, and operations must be designed, while it is open knowledge, creativity, and wisdom that are the scarcer resources – the very resources that are crucial for problem solving and the planet's prosperity. The commons paradigm inclusively fights for all.

Clearly, the questions concerning *resources, for whom* reveal the crux of the matter and the core or heart from which differences have grown. Capi-talism takes an egocentric approach to why their businesses entity exists. It is noteworthy that the etymological Greek root from which *ego* is derived means "one," while *ecos* means "home," thus by extension, "all." The com-mons has been birthed from an ecocentric perspective, thus seek to protect the prosperity of the planet for generations to come.

It is also clear that the re-orientations that firms are currently professing do not go far enough in its consideration of all stakeholders, especially to be able to find common ground with the commons. While their statement infers a possible shift in leadership to one that includes boundary spanning skills for managing multiple stakeholders with conflicting pulls and priorities, it is time to re-imagine how intentions may differ if seen through an ecocentric lens? Beinhocker and Hanauer (2014) created the image of a party scene in which attendees held a new view on business as planet-inclusive problem solvers. They astutely wonder how the conversation might change if, rather than *what do you do,* one was asked *what problems do you solve, and for whom?* (p. 10).

LEADERSHIP: A MODEL FOR WHAT MATTERS

The previous section pointed out that the capitalist and commons paradigms are dichotomized in fundamental ways and driven by polarized values. Corporations are presumed to be based on the capitalist paradigm, while commons on a planet-inclusive philosophy. Varied leadership models similarly expose a contrast in values, beliefs, intention, and desired outcomes as their development have tended to focus on particular contexts and considered parameters; therefore, distinctive strategies, structures, and behavioral practices have been examined in terms of how the philosophies, strategies and objectives of each paradigm are carried out.

In this chapter, I suggest that the increasingly interconnected world is calling forth a re-imagined form of leadership that equitably includes, inspires, engages, and facilitates change for the good of *all* stakeholders, human and nonhuman, not just shareholders, for the prosperity of the planet. Leadership is a practice, not a role or position; the goal, therefore, the purpose, strategy, and practices that may produce a community that benefits all is sought over identification of characteristics of an individual leader. Only then can the kind of leadership be exercised that creates the conditions for stakeholders to co-manage resources and align for shared outcomes.

This section, therefore, continues to question the possibility of a corporate-commons leadership hybrid as a potential solution for marrying the *heartfulness* of the commons (Murphy-Shigematsu, 2018) with positive economic power that a corporation could contribute. The quest for a corporate-commons hybrid guides the suggestion of critical components. Concurring with Fuller, "You never change things by fighting the existing reality. To change something, build a new model that makes the existing model obsolete" (Thompson, 2020, p. 113) and creates the path to a better future.

Conventional leadership. Conventional leadership models tended to narrow attention to the individual as the unit of analysis in the corporate context and to identify traits, behaviors and competencies of the leader as they affected the one-dimensional interaction between leader and subordinate (Yukl, 2002). The nature of communication and relationship that result from this interaction were examined according to the aspects of character and capability that the individual leader has at present and could develop for more effective performance in a particular context. Ethical leadership (Brown, Treviño, & Harrison, 2005) and servant leadership (Greenleaf, 2002), are two examples that highlight noteworthy features from conventional models which view the individual as the leader who influences others through ethical behavior, and the leader who is driven by a calling to serve the needs and interests of others. An internal focus appears to be the domain of interest to such leader models as the actions demonstrated generally work to bring together service and meaning for the good of the organization.

Conventional leadership models also tend to seek to elevate the *single heroic leader* within the corporation *and to target short-term financial results. If responsible leadership is to be integrated within a corporation a much wider perspective is needed, leadership theories* must reframe a *single strong man* viewpoint to a *strong group viewpoint* (Keränen, 2019; Lämsä & Keränen, 2020), which encourages more long-term oriented goals, team, and distributed leadership.

Responsible Leadership

The concept of responsible leadership (Maak, 2007; Maak & Pless, 2006; Keränan, 2019; Lynham, 1998; Pless & Maak, 2011; Miska & Mendenhall, 2018; Voegtlin, 2016) has gained attention as a more inclusive, relational, and integrated approach to leading as it is "based on the concept of leaders who are not isolated from the environment, who critically evaluate prevailing norms, are forward looking, share responsibility, and aim to solve problems collectively" (Voegtlin, 2016, p. 581).

Maak and Pless (2006) include ethical citizen and servant as two of the roles comprising a model of responsible leadership, as well as visionary, steward, change agent, storyteller and meaning enabler, architect, and coach (p. 107). Despite the inclusiveness of the roles suggested, their orientation and approach to responsible leadership revealed a cultural influence. A study comparing a U.S. and German managers' views found that the U.S. view was based on utilitarianism and emphasized the moral responsibility of the individual, while the German view emphasized social partnerships and companies as social entities that carried ethical dimensions. Given the global context in which leadership functions, cultural perspectives are fundamental to effectiveness.

Equally if not more important, responsible leadership is solidly situated in the social constructionist perspective on meaning making, thus (1) considers leadership a shared practice and responsibility of all stakeholders, and (2) stakeholders include internal and external parties. Expanding the sense of service and meaning, important elements of conventional models, to include external stakeholders, the construct of responsible leadership (Maak & Pless, 2006; Pless & Maak, 2011) suggests a more relational perspective on leadership. Not only practically can the single leader not be in full control of the complexity of data, trends, or the full scope of the interconnected global environment, philosophically, it is even more meaningful that strong relations co-create and accomplish goals together. Uhl-Bien and Arena (2017) call the bias toward order as preferred by conventional leadership the "enemy of adaptability…Ordered responses stifle out the interactive dynamics needed by organizations to respond effectively to complexity" (p. 10), certainly requisite for co-creating new ways to get things done together.

Clearly not about the individual leader's attitude or behavior, responsible leadership as a distinctive model is defined as

> *a values-based and ethical principles-driven relationship between leaders and stakeholders who are connected through a shared sense of meaning and purpose through which they raise one another to higher levels of motivation and commitment for achieving sustainable values creation and social change…(and provides) a multi-level response to complexities and challenges*

which other models of leadership do not have (Maak, 2007, p. 438). Responsible leadership "takes place in interaction with a multitude of followers as stakeholders inside and outside the corporation" (Maak & Pless, 2006, p. 99), and are "sensitive to the world in which they operate" (p. 101). Overall, relevant to a corporate-commons hybrid, responsible leadership engages in "coordinating responsible action to achieve a meaningful, commonly shared business vision" (Maak, 2007, p. 334).

Despite such institutional and contextual differences, the model is comprehensive in elaborating the roles of responsible leadership in the context of stakeholder theory. Unfortunately, the model to this point stops short of including nonhuman stakeholders, a critical aspect of what a hybrid model must include in order to consistently address the tensions posed by ownership of resources, sustainability, and consistent intent toward prosperity for the planet.

Commoning

The seminal work of Thompson (2020) found that the commons is less of a static entity than a fluid process of leadership. A model of a self-organized, self-managed, responsible collective, aligned on shared intent and concerns, commoning leadership is distributed among all stakeholders; each member practices commoning beliefs, values, and behaviors. Commoners as leaders create commons that facilitate the processes of democratizing, collaborating, sharing, localizing, and trans-localizing.

In summary, when reviewing comparisons and contrasts among conventional leadership, responsible leadership, and commoning leadership, the perspectives differ by degree, as if on a continuum with conventional leadership on one pole, responsible leadership midway, and commoning on the other. The most salient points concern:

1. Purpose

The purpose of conventional leaders' activities is typically internally focused and aimed at increasing shareholder profits. The shareholder model affects the goal, operational decisions, and definition of success. Expanding the purpose, Responsible leadership is defined as

> the art and ability involved in building, cultivating and sustaining
> trustful relationships to different stakeholders, both inside and outside
> the organization, and coordinating responsible action to achieve a
> meaningful, commonly shared business vision. (Maak, 2007, p. 334)

Responsible leadership also rests on a bed of strong relationships, which builds social capital; the social capital can grow into even broader and firmer value networks. Basically, social capital works to leverage the potential energy of stakeholders, mobilizing them to contribute to business sustainability.

Social capital, however, carries the connotation of investments made for mutual benefit and mutual advantage. *For whom?* If we believe in a responsible leadership stakeholder configuration, we are moving away from talking solely about profit; we now speak to ecological balance and reciprocity. Responsible leadership may function for the good of the organization and society, as compared to the strategy of for-profit corporations; however, to a person well versed in environmental justice, this stops well short of the goal of protecting what is considered to be the property of the people, not corporations or governments. Again, this stops short of the property of the planet (Personal conversation, Peter Nerothin, January 2021).

Commoning strives to be a force of good for the many, not just particular shareholders. Commoning, therefore, replaces competition with cooperation as the driving force of social production and acts on the foundations of community as opposed to individual choice. Committed to an ethical life, social justice, and values that place the well-being of the people of the world and of the planet above price, commoners aim to build a society where people can fully participate in developing policies and taking actions that impact their lives, thereby effecting intentional macro and micro social change (Thompson, 2020).

2. Rights of Resource Ownership

Conventional leadership models do not speak to ownership in the parameters of leadership; the focus is directed to the individual leader's impact within a task and organizational context. Responsible leadership views the rights of ownership as a systemic responsibility shared by multiple stakeholders, predominantly still within the scope of an organization's portfolio.

The concept of ownership itself must be called out. In the context of this chapter, ownership is a western construct that lies at the heart of the corporate economic growth model to which conventional leadership subscribes, a very different heart in contrast to the commoning self-managed model of shared leadership.

Commoning, in contrast, extends both rights of ownership and responsibility to include human and nonhuman stakeholders, and most importantly, believes in freedom of access to resources and

> *a collective performativity that cultivates civic we-ness...[a transformational process that offers] new ways of conceptualizing and performing social roles, of mutual support, negotiation, conflict resolution, and experimentation to create systems to manage shared resources. (Zhang & Barr, 2018, p. 78)*

The process dramatically shifts the power differential at the base of owner-ship from human is greater than nature, to human and nature are equal partners in terms of rights of ownership and responsibility.

3. Scarcity or Abundance – Orientation to Time

The for-profit corporate mindset, self-defining their role as problem solv-ers, prioritize efficiency and short-term metrics in support of tracking what is perceived as scarce resources. Unfortunately, across the globe, the value-extraction perspective reinforces the sense of urgency and need for control of time as a resource, and what it can produce for the corpo-ration. A comparison between Indian and U.S. business leaders' alloca-tion of time, for example, illustrated a different priority structure across diverse cultures yet a similar perspective. U.S. corporate leaders spent more time on regulatory and compliance issues, reporting to the board and managing shareholder relations than did Indian leaders by signifi-cant percentages. Of eight leadership tasks, Indian leaders spent more time on setting strategy and customer relations. Despite the difference in the recipients of their attention and circles of concern, both sets of lead-ers functioned with time as a scarce resource (Cappelli, Singh, Singh, & Useem, 2010).

Responsible leadership, geared toward concerns of collective stakehold-ers, tends to consider factors from cultural contexts, such as the influence of power differentials and the impact on various system mechanisms (Pless & Maak, 2011); the time orientation is more inclusively circular. Followers inside and outside of the organization contribute to social change and a sus-tainable future.

Commoning takes a long-term perspective on present term activities; cyclically, one serves the other. Individual goals are subsumed to community goals, in service to resource protection and access. Paradoxically, resources may be perceived as abundant, but the access to the resources such as land, water, knowledge and data continues to be a short-term concern.

The range of perspectives contribute aspects to a proposed hybrid model of leadership that have the potential to bring the optimal spirit, heart, and hands to the work that doesn't extract value from resources for profit but shares resources for profit for the planet that all have equitable access to for generations to come.

THE ECOCENTRIC MODEL FOR WHAT MATTERS

It is clear that purpose and strategy are the foundation of a corporate-commons ecocentric entity from which systems, operations, culture, within and outside of the organization are designed and fulfilled. Fig. 1 shows the intersectionality of three pillars of a leadership model for what matters that combine the corporate structure and economic prowess with the Commoning heart and soul and intention. Together they merge their strength, sustainability, and caring persistence for the hard work of jointly producing prosperity for the planet. The merger is built on intention, responsibility, and relationality. The *core* of this hybrid model is the Ecocentric identity and spirit. (NB: *core* is derived from the Latin root meaning *heart*).

Responsible. Responsible, the adjectival form that describes the capacity and capabilities of responsible leadership has been effectively operationalized by Lynham (1998, p. 211) as

1. Being legally or ethically accountable for the welfare or care of another

2. Involving personal accountability or ability to act free from guidance or higher authority

3. Being a source or cause

4. Capable of making moral or rational decisions on one's own, thereby being answerable for one's behavior

Fig. 1. Ecocentric Leadership Model for What Matters.

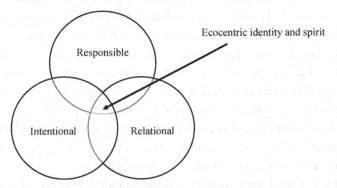

5. Capable of being trusted or depended on: reliable

6. Based on or marked by good judgment

7. Having the means to pay dept or obligations

8. Required to render account: answerable.

In light of an ecocentric corporate-commons hybrid model of leadership, the listed capacity and capabilities provide a strong foundation for direction and growth, as well as a blueprint for leadership metrics at every resource level, for example, individual, team, organizational, external stakeholder, and nonhuman. The comprehensive template would enable the hybrid to exceed just meeting short-term economic goals. Most importantly, the biased questions regarding ownership of resources and *for whom* work is done are moot.

Applied within the proposed hybrid, the performance-based conventional models of leadership and corporate focus are inclusively addressed using this list. Each of these points can be framed in terms of measured performance, development opportunities, growth, and overall comparative advantage. A new basis for inter-organizational competition would also hold the potential to produce broader, and exceptionally positive impact at exponential levels.

Relational. A social constructionist model, responsible leadership is based on relationships that reflect patterns of communication (Bateson, 1972). Relationality, therefore, is the notion that all who are stakeholders are interconnected, and that relationships are the only way shared goals can be accomplished. Not only interconnected, a nonlinear ecocentric system of comprehensive elements infers that both humans and nonhumans are also interdependent in purpose, strategy, processes, and desired ongoing outcomes of prosperity. We both shape and are shaped by our social experience in everyday interactions and conversations (Berger & Luckman, 1966; Gergen, 1991). In other words, the relational element of leadership in the model for what matters, that is, in the frame of postheroic leadership, "requires a relational ontology, which means going back to the fundamental philosophical issue of understanding social experience as intersubjective and leadership as a way of being-in-relation-to-others" (Cunliffe & Eriksen, 2011, p. 1430). Importantly, *others* in the hybrid model includes every human and nonhuman element.

Intentional. The principle of intentionality (Turner, 2017), expanded from the Dennettian model of intention, is described simply as a stance (Dennett, 1987) or a relation between a meaning and to whatever the meaning is about (Brentano, 1973), that is "I intend it" as an "I-it" subject-object relation (Turner, 2017, p. 3). "I-cause-it" is a principle of causality common to both corporate commoning mindsets; both interpret the sense of agency positively. Yet, I-intend-it, a more potent force, according to the principle of intentionality, suggests that

> *actions are guided by what the subject (the agent) intends to accom-*
> *plish, given what she understands of her interests, the situation and*
> *the likely consequences of available choices that come to mind. (p. 4)*

Thus, the subject is in charge, and choices of action and degree of motivation reflect the mental model of *intent*.

In the ecocentric hybrid model, the responsible leadership *intent* leverages the merged collective to collaborate using (a) interdependent forces and resources, (b) among internal and external, (c) human and nonhuman stakeholders. The intent, therefore, *is the heart, core, and drive* toward prosperity for the inclusive planet. "The principle of intentionality not only guides all voluntary thought and behavior, but is also implicated in all meaning, value and purpose" (Turner, 2017, p. 2). Greatly influencing the development of the intentions, therefore, are elements such as beliefs and desires, and what matters, that is, truth, purpose, and the protection of shared resources for the long term. In other words, the application of the ecocentric perspective extends from a community to an individual, that is, "to a community of minds in addition to an individual mind" (p. 8), bringing a multiplier effect to the merger.

Various approaches have questioned the model of intentionality, denying that intent is governed by values and beliefs (Carruthers, 2013), and that there is no law-like behavior to explain intentionality (Gauker, 2005), as might be found in a model of causality. Yet, the model of intentionality provides a valuable vector to the hybrid model for what matters. "Whereas a causal model traces behavior to external and past influences, an intentional model traces it to interpretations of the environment and to the imagined desirable future" (Turner, 2017, p. 7). Intention, therefore, is crucial for the spirit that sustains the challenging work at which a corporate-commons hybrid must persist.

The ecocentric hybrid model for what matters may not be as far-fetched or difficult to develop as it may appear, given the systemic changes that even businesses have indicated they hope to become. According to Bollier and Helfrich (2019) and Bauwens, Kostakis, and Pazaitis (2019), allies within the market and the state are essential to prosper the commons; more than allies;

a hybrid model may even more effectively increase the interdependency among the elements as well as the stakeholders. Similar to yet different from boundary commoning, the structural coupling of continuous interrelations among commons systems to create an enlarged, internally interdependent commons (Thompson, 2020), a hybrid infuses the mindset, spirit, and energy of the commons with the levers of the corporate entity for the intention of sustainable prosperity for the planet.

The proposed corporate-commons hybrid model of leadership also includes multiple inflection points where choices for change will frequently occur and as a result, multiple opportunities for observation to see both selves and approaches to change. Not only us/them, either/or, my way or your way, responsible, relational, intentional leadership calls on all to look inward, not only outward at what we wish to change.

Finally, and fittingly, *prosperity*, etymologically a concept found in Old French in circa 1500, refers to a "flourishing or thriving condition, good fortune, wealth, success in anything good or desirable (Online Etymology Dictionary, 2001-2021)." The varied associations with the conception itself offers yet one more way, a semantic way, in which corporation and commons can find powerful existential reasons to merge forces and resources for the greater good.

LEADING FROM A COMMONS MINDSET IN A CORPORATE BODY: PATAGONIA INC.

This chapter posed the question, how could a marriage between a for-profit corporation and the spirit and mindset of the commons produce a successful model for what matters and create a leadership model that facilitates the strategy and structure of the ecocentric core of a hybrid? The spirit of commoning is clear; the business prowess is crucial. Such an enterprise imagined would support the long-term profit for the planet and require an ecocentric identity and responsible, relational, and intentional leadership; the core elements would be grounded on

- Conscious awareness of actions and their impact on every aspect of their business and concomitant initiatives

- Interconnectivity and interdependency among all human and nonhuman stakeholders

- A proactive, open invitation to belong to the corporate-commons purpose through actions

- A conviction for advocacy.

Patagonia is a corporation that offers an example of this re-imagined corporate-commons possibility. Founded in 1973 by Yvon Chouinard, Patagonia as of 2018 is a corporation valued at one billion dollars. Fully committed to the first priority of social and environmental change, along the way, they sell a wide array of sports clothes, equipment, and provisions. Never in business to serve shareholders, Patagonia has remained privately held. Summarily, Chinouinard declared in an interview with Herring (2018), "We're in business to save our home planet." For over 40 years and counting, Patagonia Inc. (Patagonia Inc. (https://www.patagonia.com/business-unusual/) and Patagonia Works (Patagonia Works, 2013) have used their resources – voice, business, platform, and the Patagonia community – to be part of a movement for change.

Fig. 2 illustrates what, in Patagonia terms and words, responsible, relational, and intentional leadership may look like in action.

As a snapshot, Fig. 2 captures Patagonia's identity and way of being as well as way of working. The clarity and strength of purpose

Fig. 2.   Patagonia: An Example of a Corporate-commons Hybrid Model for What Matters.

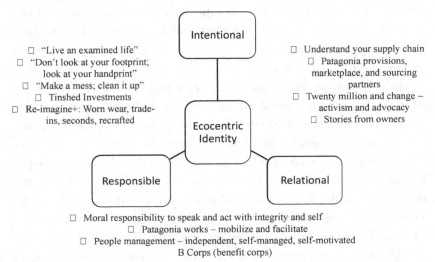

provides a powerful assurance that making profit for the planet is possible. Notably, the model illuminates the leadership of the individual and the corporation as an individual.

Ecocentric identity. Patagonia embodies an ecocentric identity. For example, operationalizing their purpose for existence, they name four stakeholders to which they are responsible and for whom they work: employees, customers, community, and nature. When all decisions are based on saving the planet and prosperity for all stakeholders, it is clear to see the heart that drives the business. As a self-proclaimed imperfect example of their ecocentric identity in action, the full network of stakeholders "take one step toward responsibility, learn something, take another step, and let examination build on itself" (Chouinard & Stanley, 2013, p. 47).

Responsible and intentional. The intention behind the embodied purpose is fully and consistently demonstrated through the Patagonia philosophy: *Live an examined life*. The simple phrase represents a conscious awareness of the impact of every thought, word, and action – applied to the burgeoning company decades ago as well as to the present-day commitment to the nonharmful materials sources and production, the philosophy guides thinking and practice. Chouinard cited his mother as the source of this lesson learned early in life, "If you make a mess, you clean it up" (Herring, 2018). An avid mountain climber, Chouinard realized the impact of metal pitons on the mountain; not wanting to leave a mess on the mountain he climbed, he established a business that found a way to leave no harm on the environment. Later on, he discovered the harmful ways cotton was grown and fabric produced; the commitment to understanding the source of all products Patagonia sells and ensuring the least harmful process possible became the unquestioned way of working.

The examined life of Patagonia includes a deep investigation into everything touched in their business processes. A visit to the Patagonia website is like an educational tour of the farms, factories, and forests from which Patagonia acquires components of products – from fiber to fish to seeds and spices. Furthermore, the intimacy of the stories from suppliers and producers enables Patagonia to self-assess according to the handprint or impact they have had on the lives and livelihoods of providers and partners as well as the planet. They specifically do not just assess their footprint, as that is limited to what has been depleted or worse, destroyed in their wake. Tinshed Investments, the socially and environmentally conscious venture capital arm, and reimagine, the multiple methods Patagonia uses repurposing and reselling worn products, trade-ins, seconds, and new items recrafted from old likewise demonstrate Patagonia's belief in taking no more from nature than what it can replace.

Intentional and relational. "As your company is responsible for everything done in its name, so are your partners responsible for your part of their social and ecological footprint" (Chouinard & Stanley, 2013, p. 14). According to Chouinard, a group aligned, all believing in going the same direction, gives incredible power to accomplish more and better outcomes. Patagonia's intimacy with their supply chains and support of activism manifest in both activist networking and financial initiatives.

Firstly, the Patagonia website's navigating tabs give a clue; there are just four headings: Shop, Activism, Sports, and Stories. Activism (https://www.patagonia.com/activism) takes a visitor to two options: Get funded and Get Involved. Patagonia financially supports local community activities and connects website visitors to projects in their own communities as well as organizes opportunities into areas of interest with which users can connect and become involved. Secondly, the Patagonia website gives a platform for their value network of Patagonia product owners and advocates to express their local experiences stories and benefit from the opportunity to belong and share with a community in whose purpose and methods they believe. The commons that Patagonia creates and facilitates illustrate their and their leadership's intention toward purpose and belief in continually broadening the community with a shared spirit.

Responsible and relational. Responsible refers to stakeholder inclusion, while relational refers to the power of the collective. Patagonia not only exercises a moral responsibility to speak and act with integrity and self-constancy, through Patagonia Works, they work to mobilize and facilitate the activist efforts at the community level. Chouinard and family also personally launched $20 Million and Change, an internal fund to help like-minded, responsible start-up companies bring about positive benefit to the environment. Lastly Patagonia was one of the first B Corporations, the values of which have become an explicit part of their own legal corporate charter.

Thus far, many efforts described seem externally focused; yet the responsible and relational perspective is practiced in internal people management, too. The attitude from Chouinard and the corporation's management methods have created the conditions for an exceedingly creative and capable cadre of highly independent, self-managed, and self-motivated employees.

As a result, similar to the Native American belief that the chief is not the strongest but is the best orator, Patagonia and employees together invest the time and heart to achieve consensus among independent people who share a common purpose, a profound ecocentric identity that does not thrive on conquering but on leaving no trace while doing good.

In conclusion and important to the discussion of Patagonia as an example of the re-imagined corporate-commons leadership possibility, this company illustrates the realistic success from expanding and redefining the concept of profit. The battle between profits from value extraction and shared profit for sustainable value creation has clearly been shown to be a fabricated division that does not need to persist. In Chouinard's words,

> *Those who watch the forest be cut and raise their voice against it cannot be heard when the company that did the cutting does not belong to the community....When local politics becomes subservient to distant economic power, the concept of citizenship, of its duties and possibilities, loses its meaning. The human commons loses its value; it too can become a desert. (2013, p. 18)*

In the corporate-commons hybrid, community becomes a strong fabric woven by and for the whole planet.

WHAT'S NEXT?

The corporate-commons hybrid model of leadership was proposed in an attempt to reimagine what leadership on the commons could evolve to become, especially given that the climate crisis is increasing in urgency at a rapid pace. While commoning is a process dedicated to protecting what is believed to be resources owning to every stakeholder, human and nonhuman, on the planet, it is traditionally clashing with private industry whose purpose narrows the definition of profit. A hybrid, innovatively comprised of both, may prove to be possible, as per the example of Patagonia, a highly successful and competitive-by-quality-and-spirit corporation.

In this chapter, I have offered a model of capacities and capabilities, salient to a meaningful hybrid. Clearly, not all concepts have been elaborated or explored fully. Future conceptual explorations may augment ideas triggered here. For example, some researchers have called the hybrid proposal "compassionate capitalism" (Benioff & Southwick, 2004); "moral capitalism" (Young, 2003); or "inclusive capitalism" (Hart, 2005). Yet, if capitalism is defined as an economic and political system in which a country's trade and industry are controlled by private owners for profit, rather than by the state, then the proposed leadership hybrid contradicts the fundamental premise and cannot be called capitalism. It intriguingly seems that an industry described using this hybrid corporate/commons construct would not be solely or wholly controlled by private owners for purpose of profit alone. An economic or political perspective on this ecocentric model could take the challenge of legitimacy to the audience who would most question the actualization. Furthermore, an approach to shared resources for mutual benefit, not to monopolize or dominate them for sole profit would ask for a present-day look at the "Tragedy of the Commons" (Meadows, 2006, p. 116).

In a theoretical perspective, examining the hybrid model as a complex adaptive system would possibly shed light on how elements within the system impact and are impacted by the system, and uncover adaptive ways the system may positively evolve, especially given that both Patagonia as an illustrative model and that of the commons mirror each other in many ways. Ecosystem identity and intentionality, in particular, are conceptual constructs that call for more reflection and nurturing to bloom.

Finally, and practically, it would be valuable to examine other corporations, privately owned or publicly traded, to understand similarities and differences between Patagonia and others' work in sustainability and corporate social responsibility initiatives. There appear to be a qualitative difference among them; the specific revelations may be a compass for the future.

CONCLUSION AND IMPLICATIONS

Chouinard and Stanley (2013) provides the most succinct and powerful conclusion to this chapter and suggests implications most passionately. Many companies are doing something to behave more responsibly toward the earth and toward the commons. And every company that learns to take a responsible step without faltering gains confidence to take the next.

> *"Responsible seems to us the apt, more modest word to use while*
> *we walk the path that, we hope, leads to a place where business*
> *takes no more from nature than what it can replace (p. 15)...that we*

can illustrate how any group of people going about their business can come to realize their environmental and social responsibilities, then begin to act on them, see how their realization is progressive and how action build on one another" (p. 7).

REFERENCES

Bateson, G. (1972). *Steps to an ecology of mind.* University of Chicago Press.

Bauwens, M., Kostakis, V., & Pazaitis, A. (2019). *Peer to peer: The commons manifesto.* University of Westminster Press.

Beinhocker, E., & Hanauer, N. (2014). Redefining capitalism, McKinsey Quarterly, September, 1–10. Retrieved from https://www.mckinsey.com/featured-insights/long-term-capitalism/redefining-capitalism

Benioff, M., & Southwick, K. (2004). *Compassionate capitalism: How corporations can make doing good an integral part of doing well.* Career Press.

Berger, P. L., & Luckmann, T. (1966). *The social construction of reality.* Doubleday.

Bollier, D., & Helfrich, S. (2019). *Free, fair, and alive: The insurgent power of the commons.* New Society Publishers.

Brentano, F. (1973). *Psychology from an empirical standpoint.* Routledge.

Brown, M. E., Treviño, L. K., & Harrison, D. A. (2005). Ethical leadership: A social learning perspective for construct development and testing. *Organizational Behavior and Human Decision Processes, 97*(2), 117–134.

Cappelli, P., Singh, H., Singh, J., & Useem, M. (2010). *The India way: How India's top business leaders are revolutionizing management.* Harvard Business Press.

Carruthers, P. (2013). On knowing your own beliefs. In N. Nottleman (Ed.), *New essays on belief: Structure, constitution, and content* (pp. 144–165). Palgrave MacMillan.

Chouinard, Y., & Stanley, V. (2013). *The responsible company: What we've learned from Patagonia's first 40 years.* Patagonia Publishers. Kindle edition.

Cunliffe, A. L., & Eriksen, M. (2011). Relational leadership. *Human Relations, 64*(11), 1425–1449.

Dennett, D. (1987). *The intentional stance.* MIT Press.

Gauker, C. (2005). The belief-desire law. *Facta philos, 7,* 121–144.

Gergen, K. J. (1991). *The saturated self: Dilemmas of identity in contemporary life.* Basic Books.

Greenleaf, R. K. (2002). *Servant leadership: A journey into the nature of legitimate power and greatness* (25th Anniversary ed.). Paulist Press.

Hart, S. L. (2005). *Capitalism at the crossroads*. Wharton School Publishing.

Herring, H. (2018). Backcountry Hunters & Anglers, Interview with Patagonia founder Yvon Chouinard, April 24, 2018. Retrieved from https://www.backcountry-hunters.org/bha_podcast_blast_episode_21

Hess, C. (2008). Mapping the new commons. *12th Biennial Conference of the International Association for the Study of the Commons*. Retrieved from http://dlc.dlib.indiana.edu/dlc/bitstream/handle/10535/384/iascp2000.pdf?sequence=1

Keränen, A. (2019, 22 August). Exploring a new understanding of responsible leadership. Globally Responsible Leadership Initiative. https://responsibility.global/exploring-a-new-understanding-of-responsible-leadership-part-1-830df82ce108

Lämsä, A.-M., & Keränen, A. (2020). Responsible leadership in the manager–employee relationship. *South Asian Journal of Business and Management Cases*, 9(3), 422–432.

Lynham, S. A. (1998). The development and evaluation of a model of responsible leadership for performance. *Human Resource Development International, 1*(2), 207–220.

Maak, T. (2007). Responsible leadership, stakeholder engagement, and the emergence of social capital. *Journal of Business Ethics, 74*, 329–343.

Maak, T., & Pless, N. M. (2006). Responsible leadership in a stakeholder society – A relational perspective. *Journal of Business Ethics, 66*, 99–115.

McKinsey and Company. (2020). From there to here: Fifty years of thinking on the social responsibility of business. Retrieved from https://www.mckinsey.com/%7E/media/McKinsey/Featured%20Insights/Corporate%20Purpose/From%20there%20to%20here%2050%20years%20of%20thinking%20on%20the%20social%20responsibility%20of%20business/From-there-to-here-50-years-of-thinking-on-the-social-responsibility-of-business.pdf?shouldIndex=false

Meadows, D. H. (2008). *Thinking in systems: A primer*. Chelsea Green Publishing.

Miska, C., & Mendenhall, M. E. (2018). Responsible leadership: A mapping of extant research and future directions. *Journal of Business Ethics, 148*, 117–134.

Murphy-Shigematsu, S. (2018). *From mindfulness to heartfulness: Transforming self and society with compassion*. Berrett-Koehler.

Patagonia – Business Unusual. (n.d.). https://www.patagonia.com/home/

Patagonia Activism. (n.d.). https://www.patagonia.com/activism/

Patagonia Works. (2013). https://www.patagoniaworks.com/#index; https://patagoniaworks.com/faq.

Pless, N. M., & Maak, T. (2011). Responsible leadership: Pathways to the future. *Journal of Business Ethics, 98*, 3–13.

Prosperity. (2001–2021). https://www.etymonline.com/word/prosperity

Thompson, R. J. (2020). *Proleptic leadership on the commons: Ushering in a new global order*. Emerald.

Thompson, E., & Stapleton, M. (2009). Making sense of sense-making: Reflections on enactive and extended mind theories. *Topoi, 28*, 23–30.

Turner, C. K. (2017). A principle of intentionality. *Frontiers in Psychology, 8*(137), 1–10.

Uhl-Bien, M., & Arena, M. (2017). Complexity leadership: Enabling people and organizations for adaptability. *Organizational Dynamics, 46*, 9–20.

Voegtlin, C. (2016). What does it mean to be responsible? Addressing the missing responsibility dimension in ethical leadership research. *Leadership, 12*(5), 581–608.

Young, S. (2003). *Moral capitalism: Reconciling private interest with the public good*. Berritt-Koehler.

Yukl, G. (2002). *Leadership in organizations* (5th ed.). Prentice-Hall.

Zhang, J. Y., & Barr, M. (2018). The transformative power of commoning and alternative food networks. *Environmental Politics, 28*(4), 771–789.

5

WHAT FAVELAS CAN TEACH ABOUT LEADERSHIP: THE IMPORTANCE OF SHARED-PURPOSE AND PLACE-BASED LEADERSHIP

RENATO SOUZA, THOMAZ WOOD AND
BRAD JACKSON

The aim of this chapter is to examine the leadership practices in the favelas of São Paulo, Brazil. According to the United Nations Report (2014), one in eight people live in slums. In total, around one billion people live in slum conditions today around the world. Favelas have been portrayed as spaces of exclusion that are commonly associated with marginality and segregation (Imas & Weston, 2012), or the geographical spaces that epitomize the great socioeconomic divide in Brazilian society (Hughes, 2012). Yet, favela residents have engaged in "try[ing] to appropriate the mechanisms of producing their own representations of themselves and the world" (Hamburger, 2008, p. 201), from a periphery that produces not only culture, but also a critical discourse on racism, police violence, and poverty to rival that of mainstream media (Holmes, 2016).

Favela leaders are residents of the favela that either act as informal leaders who engage with favela residents as "informal organizers" that residents rely on to deal with specific issues (e.g., housing, education, and environment) or can be elected by members of the community to hold positions in local grassroots organizations or as spokespersons of social movements (Pandolfi & Grynszpan, 2003; Savell, 2015). The emergence of (in)formal leaders among residents is a response to the need to manage services, activities, or resources that are not provided by the state but rather depend on self-organization and on individuals coming together as a collaborative community to tackle situations of social vulnerability. This is the reason to consider a favela to be a commons. In this place, leadership emerges from these situated relational dynamics as a collective construction process (Crevani, Lindgren, & Packendorff, 2007) since leadership needs to be constantly created in the face of significant odds.

This chapter analyzes the production of collective leadership practices in the context of urban slums using the concept of the "leadership moment," which theorizes leadership as "an event which occurs when context, purpose, followers and leaders align" (Ladkin, 2017, p. 393). Specifically, we examine how leadership occurs through a process of mutual influence between favela leaders and residents, connected by a shared purpose, which produces collective direction, alignment, and commitment in this distinctive place (Drath et al., 2008). Moreover, we argue that by viewing leadership in the favelas as a collective construction process, we are able to see new patterns in how leadership is exercised in practice (Crevani et al., 2007), and how the interconnections between place, purpose and leaders/residents combine to create collective leadership as leadership needs to be constantly created in the face of the significant challenge of securing infrastructural necessities for sustaining everyday life (Das & Walton, 2015).

METHOD

We draw on a two-year qualitative study that has taken place in three slum districts in São Paulo, Brazil, with favela leaders and residents, which explored the ways in which communities trying to reduce social and economic vulnerability engage in leadership practices. These neighborhoods are largely comprised of precarious, low-quality housing and lacking in basic sanitation, medical services, quality education, and work opportunities. They commonly face the social stigma of marginality and exclusion (Lara, 2013), and are synonymous with violence, inequality, and poverty (Koster & de Vries, 2012). Furthermore, they are often positioned as not being part of the city (Holmes, 2016). In the last decades of the twentieth century, urban slums have become a landmark of all major Brazilian cities. By 2010, roughly 6% of the Brazilian population (11.4 million) lived in vulnerable communities such as urban slums, the majority of them being located in São Paulo (Pasternak, 2016).

In these places, neighborhood associations and nonprofit organizations are commonly sites of social mobilization and resistance (Savell, 2015). In these spaces, favela leaders and residents organize collective action aimed at making communities more resilient and sustainable (Moulaert, Martinelli, Swyngedouw, & Gonzalez, 2010). They engage in a self-representational reframing by positioning themselves and the favela as a rightful part of the city and combating exclusionary and marginalizing perspectives on favelas (Holmes, 2016).

In District A, there is a community project created in 1999 that 10 years later became a local NGO using sport as a tool to promote social inclusion, health, self-esteem and the quality of life of children, young adults and women from the local community. It is based in a neighborhood where 26% of its area is made of conglomerates of slums, largely comprised of precarious, low-quality housing lacking in basic sanitation. In the late 1990s, the São Paulo Civil Police considered this district as part of the "Triangle of Death" (Izzo, 2012) due to high levels of homicides. This social project was created as a response to the conditions in this place. The leader is a woman whose son was killed by criminals. Community residents took the initiative to ask her to do something for the community's children. The consequent social project was collectively created and aimed at rescuing the children of the neighborhood and preventing them from becoming criminals or being used by criminals in the drug trade.

In District B, an NGO organization was created in 1987 by a group of residents, dedicated to providing support and protection to women in situations of domestic and gender violence. This support and protection are carried out through psychosocial care, legal support, income generation, and a local microcredit program. The NGO is based in a neighborhood known by its social division and exclusion, where low-income people live in slums (27%) next to residences of low standard and popular housing estates that are near to middle- and high-class condominiums. In the 1980s, this neighborhood had one of the highest levels of violence against women. This reality triggered the creation of this NGO dedicated to fighting violence against women in this district as well as to claiming women's rights. In the 1970s, the leader and some members of this organization were part of social movements to fight oppression, poverty and social exclusion in the community. As a consequence of this prior social involvement, this NGO was created with the aim of promoting female emancipation and gender equality.

District C comprises several local community initiatives (i.e., not necessarily as formal projects or organizations) as well as individual community leaders and residents working together or separately in different projects related to housing, youth education, culture, environment, and social inclusion. In 1996, the United Nations declared this neighborhood as one of the most dangerous places on earth (Manso, 2016). Currently, this district has one of the lowest family income averages in São Paulo (below US $350 per family, per month). It also shows one of the worst housing conditions as 31% of the households are classified as slum households. At the same time, this neighborhood registers a population with a relatively high number of young people from 15 to 29 years old, namely 27% of the city, living in such conditions. These conditions triggered the work of community leaders and residents in promoting social change aiming to tackle these problems.

In all cases, leaders are members of the community who started social projects in response to a "call to action" from residents or as self-engaged, informal organizers of local initiatives that responded to a specific need of the place. Therefore, formal relationships of authority are not necessarily present in these grassroots initiatives as leadership is rooted in interactions between favela leaders and residents attempting to organize collective action to generate solutions for more resilient and sustainable communities.

Leadership in Favelas as a Collective Process

Leaders are seen as a key element to social organization in urban slums in a way similar to the role they play in social movements (Morris & Staggenborg, 2004). They are known for making efforts for the community and creating social networks inside the community and beyond its borders. Leaders are seen as those who inspire commitment, mobilize resources, articulate demands, create opportunities and develop strategies (Eichler, 1977; Schwartz, Rosenthal, & Schwartz, 1981). However, the available theory on leadership in urban slums seems to be inadequate due to the reductionist view on what constitutes the "leader" in a favela (DeCesare, 2013). The social basis of favela leaders does not lie in formal positions of authority but in the complex sets of social relations and cultural representations that constitute life in slums (Koster & de Vries, 2012).

A focus on the formal role of favela leaders has thus neglected the social context and how collective action is created from within the social interactions between leaders and residents. An emphasis on leaders tends to relegate favela residents to the category of "followers," which does not take into account the complex mechanisms by which favela residents attribute a leadership identity to a favela leader. Favela-based organizations and actions are made possible only because of the voluntary commitment of individuals, and the legitimacy of a leader exists solely on the basis of that commitment. Therefore, favela residents demand action and grant leadership identity of favela leaders (DeRue & Ashford, 2010). Furthermore, the dynamics between favela leaders and residents varies according to the congruence, or lack thereof, of their interests, which may or may not limit leaders' actions (Schwartz et al., 1981). However, to favor the "agency" of favela leaders may neglect the role played by residents of the favela in the emergence and construction of these leaders (Pandolfi & Grynszpan, 2003). For example, the living conditions in District A (e.g., high levels of criminality) triggered the relations between a future leader and community residents. The emergence of this leader occurred as a response to residents who took the initiative to ask her to work with them to initiate a collective effort aimed at creating a social project (granting leader identity) to rescue children from the streets. According to her...

> I'm not the one who conceived this organization... all this was born from a need of the community... they saw in me the person who could lead the cause; and that's how it all happened, I am just the one who had the idea to follow up the dreams of this community. (Favela leader, District A)

Therefore, it is relevant to identify situations in which collective leadership is mobilized in the favela context (Raelin, 2016). Collaborative agency thrives in such complex relational settings since it requires coordination across a range of diverse social actors. A favela is characterized by a plurality of agencies and authorities corresponding, as a consequence, to a diversity of purposes and methods, which may lead to different processes of construction of leaders and leadership (Raelin, 2011).

The Leadership Moment Concept

The notion of the "leadership moment" proposed by Ladkin (2013) is particularly useful in this case as it proposes leadership as an event which occurs when context, purpose, followers, and leaders align.

The "leadership moment," therefore, theorizes leadership as a collectively produced phenomenon (Ladkin, 2010), building on accounts of relational leadership theory (Cunliffe & Eriksen, 2011; Uhl-Bien, 2006). Uhl-Bien (2006) defines leadership as a "social influencing process through which emergent coordination and change are constructed and produced" (p. 655). This relational perspective attempts to redefine leadership as a property of the collective, be it a group, an organization or a social system (Raelin, 2016).

Additionally, the "leadership moment" proposes that followers' perception of context and leaders determines who is accepted in the leader role. The context within which leader–follower relations are embedded encompasses both the space "between" leaders and followers and the "around" space which influences how leaders and followers perceive one another (Ladkin, 2017). The author also argues that affective perception of the context by followers, which is subjectively determined, is the mechanism which facilitates leader-follower relations. Furthermore, the purposes to which leaders direct their efforts play a key role in achieving leadership since it holds people together and keeps them aligned as they move toward common purposes (Ladkin, 2013).

We find this proposition particularly useful to describe the leadership phenomenon that takes place in the favela context. It foregrounds a complex web of relationships, practices, and structures. By shifting perspective from viewing leadership as a leader-centric activity to viewing it as a collective construction process which involves followers, context and purpose, we see new patterns in how leadership is exercised in practice (Crevani et al., 2007). In the favelas, this complexity is intensified in situations where several individuals share the leadership space and distributed leadership roles (Chreim, 2015).

However, we argue that the "leadership moment" framework with its emphasis on the "affective perception" of followers about leaders and context misses some important elements of leadership practices in favela settings. Firstly, the role of "shared purpose" in followers' perception is only partially theorized. We argue that in the favela context, purpose plays a key role in situations where collective leadership is mobilized. Secondly, although we agree that "between spaces" and "around space" affect follower's perceptions, we argue that "place" rather than "context" acts as both an enabler and a constraint of leadership, mainly in the favela context. Place actively shapes leadership and vice versa (Jackson, Nicoll, & Roy, 2018). It provides the basis for forging a common identity, purpose and direction. By the same token, place is shaped by leadership (Jackson & Parry, 2018). Leadership processes are created in order for groups to respond to particular challenges posed by the place in which they are located.

THE LEADERSHIP MOMENT IN THE FAVELA

Ladkin (2010) argues that

> *leadership cannot exist without those who would enact it, the context from which it arises, as well as the socially constructed appreciation of it as a particular kind of interaction between human beings. (p. 31)*

In the context of favelas, it implies the involvement of favela leaders and favela residents who interact in a distinct place. As a result of these daily interactions, at times leaders may be following and favela residents may be leading. This is not to say that leaders do not bring any contribution to the leadership process; they have a role in helping to create vision and lead change in the favela context. However, vision and change are not simply accepted by passive "followers." Sometimes, favela residents assume the leaders' roles depending on the relations they have with place or a specific problem being tackled (e.g., housing, gender inequality, social inclusion) in the context of the urban slum. This is exemplified in the quote below, from a favela-based organization member:

> *Sometimes we are leading, sometimes we are following depending on the situation...in every leadership moment some people take the lead and you follow... We rely on our values, if you always work from a perspective that you are not the leader but just a reference, you are not alone; it is not a role but the principle of self-manage-ment. I know it is a bit utopic but the group needs to be autono-mous so in a moment that I need to follow and not to lead they are ready to take the lead and make the decisions. (Favela-based organization member, District B)*

On the one hand, *place* foregrounds both the "between spaces" and "around space" proposed by Ladkin (2017). This may involve relations that leaders and residents have with government, political parties, church representatives, members of social movements located in the favelas, and trafficking gangs. Furthermore, favela residents have different personal and historical backgrounds related to economic and social inequalities, gender issues and political engagement. These relations with place influence favela leaders and residents, their expectations toward leadership, level of involvement and commitment regarding favela problems. On the other hand, *purpose* is the anchor which enables favela residents to understand how their work contributes to social change in the favela environment. The way favela leaders and residents are able to create a common purpose will define the quality of their relations and the leadership practices in place in the favelas.

A practice-oriented leadership in the favelas involves, in our view, mechanisms that "makes things happen" (Huxham & Vangen, 2000) toward social change. This outcome-oriented approach influences the leadership process and the nature of the collaborative effort of favela residents. The way residents of a favela tackle activities may or may not concur with traditional notions of leadership. Some residents may prefer a person to lead the collaborative agenda, assuming the role of the "leader," while others may favor a "nobody in charge" approach. In this scenario, collective leadership is enacted not because of favela leaders, but because of the collaborative dynamics embedded in the interactions of residents of the favela, considering both place and purpose.

This means that favela leaders' and residents' identities are co-constructed through their interactions and the leadership practices in place (DeRue & Ashford, 2010). The process of leading-following produces emergent leader–follower identities (DeRue, 2011), which are situated, fluid and dynamic. When a favela leader engages in a leadership act, the influence of that act on the leadership process and favela residents is contingent on the response of these residents. Therefore, favela residents engaging in the leadership process are both leading and following (Hackman & Wageman, 2007) which means that the "claiming" and "granting" of leadership identity is always in flux, temporary and changes over time (DeRue & Ashford, 2010). Leaders and residents talk about the need for a collective effort and, therefore, collective leadership, but some may find it hard to build the necessary relations that will result in greater involvement of the community residents in all types of mobilization.

[...] they come after me, sometimes they do not know how to raise a complaint, others are a bit shy and think they will not be received at the City Hall, think that their problem will not be solved... and they think that I can help, and I do help... but when I feel overwhelmed, I start delegating tasks because I cannot do everything... everyone needs to take responsibility. (Community leader, District C)

Favela Leaders–Residents and Place Relations

Place enables the development of multiple forms of relations among favela leaders, residents, and organizations dedicated to address the high level of inequality and social vulnerability in these neighborhoods. Each organization or favela leader has her/his own history and relation with the neighborhood, and their actions tackle different issues like housing, environment, violence, and social inclusion. Leaders are sometimes described as "bridges" between the favela and other areas of the city. Residents describe themselves as living on one side of the bridge (named "Ponte do Socorro"), an area excluded by the government, and lacking public policies. The notion of "bridge" plays a pivotal role in the emergence of relational leadership in these districts. The idea of a "bridge" means a relational role with the favela and favela leaders are perceived as such in the moment they help connect the favela with other areas of the city, for example, the city hall and city council.

In this bridge, collectivism is a form of political action for some favela residents, who feel that action represents resistance and opposition to social exclusion. These views are grounded in their notion of leadership as a collective construction, not a single person's ability. Therefore, they see collective process as the *only* form of organization, as stated by an organization member:

[...] our approach is based on solidary economy, which means cooperativism and self-management... we need to decide collectively how we should proceed with the women we receive here...nobody is supposed to decide alone, we are going to do this together. (Organization member, District B)

By shifting perspective from viewing leadership as a leader-centered activity to viewing it as a collective construction process that involves leaders, followers, place and purpose, we see new patterns in how leadership is exercised in practice (Crevani et al., 2007). In the favelas, this complexity is intensified in situations where several individuals share the leadership space and distributed leadership roles (Chreim, 2015).

In addition, due to the unpredictability and complexity of the situations residents may face on a daily basis, the nature of the problems they deal with also creates the parameters for this collective action. This is exemplified by the following quote:

> *Here we have a very complex work process. Each woman that arrives here brings in common domestic and gender violence. But each one brings a life history with very particular elements. So, the answer that we are going to provide to one woman does not apply to the other…. (Favela leader, District B)*

This is well reinforced by a resident who observes: "what was right in the morning does not mean that it will be right in the afternoon, the answers are not the same because each situation is unique." Overall, residents and leaders share the idea of leadership as a collective process, since they do not believe in the idea that a single person is able to solve problems and bring the solutions to the favela.

Shared Purpose

Shared purpose acts as an anchor for the relations between favela leaders and residents in these specific places. There is a shared perception held by favela residents that other social actors (e.g., government) are unable to help them and, therefore, they need to provide their own response to the conditions imposed by place. A shared purpose is born from a perception of not being part of the society, of not being counted, and of being excluded from governmental politics. To address this problem by creating social projects aimed at promoting social inclusion is commonly the first step to give voice to residents of the favela. The collective stories of favela residents, who once perceived themselves helpless, sandwiched between an absent state and dominant criminals, are united under a shared purpose which was triggered by dramatic stories of residents willing to change the course of events in their lives. According to one favela leader, a shared purpose

*was born from the need of this community, since the government
did not look after them, it was created as both leader and residents
experienced adverse conditions under high levels of criminality. To
address this problem by creating a social project aimed at promoting social inclusion was a first step to do many other things in this
community that had no voice. (Favela leader, District A)*

However, different perceptions or needs of a group of people in a favela
about the living conditions in this place may facilitate the emergence of
multiple purposes and leadership spaces. Indeed, in a favela it is possible to
identify the emergence of not a single but multiple purposes in response to
the diversity and complexity of problems faced by favela residents. Consequently, many leadership spaces have been created, also fostered by different
social, religious, and political backgrounds. It is worth noting how the presence of multiple purposes in this place may hinder the creation of collective
leadership and can even slow down transformational actions, as leaders perceive that it is difficult to combine all purposes in one single purpose, as one
resident stated...

*There are many people disputing this leadership space...it is very
dispersed, one does not strengthen the other because everyone wants
to be a leader here, and this ends up weakening our strength... we
have lost the power of bringing people together around a common,
shared proposal, which is to improve this neighborhood; we all are
looking for the same thing.... (Favela resident, District C)*

Each group or organization may pursue its own purpose and at some
point these purposes may meet and they start doing things together. Along
with place, purpose bonds favela leaders, residents, and organizations.
Despite the different approaches and backgrounds, they are connected by
the same stories of social vulnerability that makes people want to be a leader
in the favela, in territory where they live because they see the favela's wounds
and they feel impelled to act and transform place.

The sheer magnitude of community problems (e.g., sanitation, education, violence, housing and transportation), dispersed geography, and distinct worldviews due to personal, political and religious backgrounds have
resulted in different approaches to tackle local problems. There is, however,
an overarching purpose of transforming the neighborhood, to reduce the

economic and social vulnerability in this place. Distinct actions like signing petitions, creating spaces for dialogue with the state and private sector, or attending forums for group discussions, are ways that leaders and residents have fostered collective action and ensured mobilization.

In our view, purpose precedes the emergence of collective leadership practices and acts as an anchor or facilitator of the creation of a collective effort. Purpose differentiates leadership from other activities, despite the results that may originate from it (Grint, Jones, & Holt, 2017). Purpose has a role to play in leader–follower relationships that are forged in a place as "leadership is more than a person; it is a sense of purpose, a force that gives peoples a common direction" (Drath, 1998, p. 406).

FINAL CONSIDERATIONS AND CONCLUSIONS

The chapter raises several considerations concerning the challenge of developing leadership on the commons to tackle social problems, as those faced by favelas' residents. It reinforces the notions of shared and distributed perspectives on leadership (Pearce & Conger, 2003), emphasizing leadership as a collective activity rather than an activity of a single leader (Yammarino, Salas, Serban, Shirreffs, & Shuffler, 2012). It shows leadership practices are embedded in a system of interdependencies (Koivunen, 2007). The notion of "leadership moment" is useful for analyzing how collective leadership practices emerge through the purposeful, place-based interactions of "leaders" and residents in favelas. Our chapter attempts to build on Ladkin's model by revealing the dynamic leadership practices in the favela context that can be analyzed and developed through interconnections between community leaders and residents, place, and purpose.

First, the chapter provided instances of the moments between favela leaders, residents, and place, and how leadership is created in response to place. The creation of leadership in the commons is associated with the ability of a group of people to meaningfully define a sense of place that can be compellingly shared by members of a community. As individuals engage in relationships in a distinctive place, a leading and following process unfolds and can assume different configurations (Gronn, 2015). The chapter showed the collective and collaborative agency of people who coordinate their actions and activities to be effective in achieving substantive impact in the specific place within which they act.

Second, the chapter highlighted important elements of the role of purpose in leadership. Favela residents hold a shared perception that other social actors (e.g., government) are unable to help them and, therefore, they need to provide their own response to the conditions imposed by place. Additionally, some of residents also share a view about the unequal relations between members of a society (e.g., women) with other members (e.g., men), which drives the creation of a common purpose toward fighting domestic and gender violence. Furthermore, different perceptions or needs of a group of people in a community about the living conditions in that place may facilitate the emergence of multiple purposes and leadership spaces. The chapter revealed the idea that leadership is a set of activities which generate outcomes that involve mutually important purpose and direction within a specific place (Drath et al., 2008). The construction of a shared direction is connected to the construction of shared purposes, which changes moment by moment (Carson, Tesluk, & Marrone, 2007). In addition, achieving a shared purpose may require resolving conflicts and the capability to bridge differences within an interconnected web of actors (Ospina & Foldy, 2010). Therefore, direction may not mean "one direction" all the time, but may evolve along with the interactions of favela residents and individuals or collective interests, all of which depend on the specific problems faced by different actors of the favela. The perspective of leadership as practice is to look for leadership as a "cooperative effort among participants who choose through their own rules to achieve distinctive outcomes" (Raelin, 2011, p. 196).

Finally, conceiving leadership as a collective process that unfolds over time and is enacted by a number of actors connected within a social context where formal relationships of authority are not necessarily present brings to the fore an issue about boundaries. Favelas pose the question of where leadership activity begins and ends and how it is recognized by actors who may or may not be labeled as leaders (Denis et al., 2012; Sergi, Denis, & Langley, 2012). In collaborative efforts, members of a community may find it difficult to identify themselves as leaders (Huxham & Vangen, 2000). In our view, leadership does not lie in the people of the favela studied but in their relations and recurrent interactions. Collective leadership is a practical solution devised by members of these urban slums to cope with social and economic vulnerability present in these places. This reinforces the notion that place leadership development should focus on developing emerging and established leaders to tackle place-based problems and opportunities (Jackson, 2019). As Sergi et al. (2012) argue, in such contexts "plural leadership is needed because no single individual alone could conceivably bridge the sources of influence, expertise and legitimacy needed to move a complex social system forward constructively" (p. 406). Favela leaders and residents work on issues such as housing, education, violence, and gender inequality using "combinations of advocacy, organizing, community development and service delivery to address these key problems, engaging their constituents in the work" (Ospina & Foldy, 2010, p. 295). Their work in small, grassroots, nonprofit organizations is defined as a typical work of social change organizations that "aim to address systemic problems in a way that will increase the power of marginalized groups, communities or interests" (Chetkovich & Kunreuther, 2006, p. 2) promoting leadership among groups that have been disadvantaged.

One of the key learnings from the favela-based organizations that could be taken to other organizational settings is the recognition that leadership is co-created in the situated relational interactions between people as a dynamic process that develops over time. This view locates leadership in the ways that actors engage, interact, and negotiate with one another to influence organizational understandings and to produce outcomes. It reinforces the primacy of relations in the creation of leadership that is a hallmark of collective leadership. The dialogic nature of these relations serves to highlight the fact that leadership should be seen as preferably a collaborative and collective responsibility where the responsibilities, competencies, and decision-making need to be distributed to several individuals rather than to one. Because leadership is essentially a social activity, a relational view recognizes leadership not as a trait or the behavior attributed to an individual leader but as a phenomenon generated in the interactions among people, that needs to be more holistically appreciated in a more systemic manner. This is a challenge that leadership development needs to embrace wholeheartedly.

REFERENCES

Carson, J., Tesluk, P., & Marrone, J. (2007). Shared leadership in teams: An investigation of antecedent conditions and performance. *Academy of Management Journal, 50*, 1217–1234.

Chetkovich, C. A., & Kunreuther, F. (2006). *From the ground up: Grassroots organizations making social change.* Cornell University Press.

Chreim, S. (2015). The (non)distribution of leadership roles: Considering leadership practices and configurations. *Human Relations, 68*(4), 517–543.

Crevani, L., Lindgren, M., & Packendorff, J. (2007). Shared leadership: A post-heroic perspective on leadership as a collective construction. *International Journal of Leadership Studies*, 3(1), 40–67.

Cunliffe, A., & Eriksen, M. (2011). Relational leadership. *Human Relations*, 64(11), 1425–1449.

Das, V., & Walton, M. (2015). Political Leadership and the Urban Poor. *Current Anthropology*, 56(11), S44–S54.

DeCesare, M. (2013). Toward an interpretive approach to social movement leadership. *International Review of Modern Sociology*, 39(2), 239–257.

Denis, J., Langley, A., & Sergi, V. (2012). Leadership in the plural. *Academy of Management Annals*, 6(1), 211–283.

DeRue, S. (2011). Adaptive leadership theory: Leading and following as a complex adaptive process. *Research in Organizational Behavior*, 31, 125–150.

DeRue, S., & Ashford, S. (2010). Who will lead and who will follow? A social process of leadership identity construction in organizations. *Academy of Management Review*, 35(4), 627–647.

Drath, W. (1998). Approaching the future of leadership development. In C. McCauley, R. S. Moxley, & E. Van Velsor (Eds.), *Handbook of leadership development* (pp. 403–432). Jossey-Bass.

Drath, W., McCauley, C., Paulus, C. J., Van Velsor, E., O'Connor, P., & McGuire, J. B. (2008). Direction, alignment, commitment: Toward a more integrative ontology of leadership. *Leadership Quarterly*, 19, 635–653.

Eichler, M. (1977). Leadership in social movements. *Sociological Inquiry*, 47(2), 99–107.

Grint, K., Jones, O. S., & Holt, C. (2017). What is leadership: Person, result, position or process, or all or none of these? In J. Storey, J. Hartley, J. Denis, P. Hart, & D. Ulrich (Eds.), *The Routledge companion to leadership* (pp. 3–20). Routledge Taylor & Francis Group.

Gronn, P. (2015). The view from inside leadership configurations. *Human Relations*, 68(4), 545–560.

Hackman, J. R., & Wageman, R. (2007). Asking the right questions about leadership. *American Psychologist*, 62, 43–47.

Hamburger, E. (2008). Wired up to the world: Performance and media in Contemporary Brazil. In P. Birle, S. Costa, & H. Nitschak (Eds.), *Brazil and the Americas: Convergences and perspectives* (pp. 199–222). Iberoamericana/Frankfurt am Main: Vervuert.

Holmes, T. (2016). Reframing the Favela, Remapping the City: Territorial Embeddedness and (Trans) Locality in 'Framing Content' on Brazilian Favela Blogs. *Journal of Latin American Cultural Studies*, 25(2), 297–319.

Hughes, A. (2012). Re-creating the Favela in O Homem que Copiava by Jorge Furtado. *Latin American Research Review*, *47*(1), 64–77.

Huxham, C., & Vangen, S. (2000). Leadership in the shaping and implementation of collaboration agendas: How things happen in a (not quite) joined-up world. *Academy of Management Journal*, *43*(6), 1159–1175.

Imas, J., & Weston, A. (2012). From Harare to Rio de Janeiro: Kukiya-Favela Organization of Excluded. *Organization*, *19*(2), 205–227.

Izzo, J. (2012). *Stepping up*. Berret-Koehler Publishers.

Jackson, B. (2019). The power of place in public leadership development. *International Journal of Public Leadership*, *15*(4), 209–223.

Jackson, B., Nicoll, M., & Roy, M. (2018). The distinctive challenges and opportunities for creating leadership within social enterprises. *Social Enterprise Journal*, *14*(1), 71–91.

Jackson, B. & Parry, K. (2018). *A very short, fairly interesting and reasonably cheap book about studying leadership* (3rd ed.). Sage Publications Ltd.

Koivunen, N. (2007). The processual nature of leadership discourses. *Scandinavian Journal of Management*, *23*, 285–305.

Koster, M., & de Vries, P. (2012). Slum politics: Community leaders, everyday needs, and utopian aspirations in Recife, Brazil. *Journal of Global and Historical Anthropology*, *62*, 83–98.

Ladkin, D. (2010). *Rethinking leadership: A new look at old leadership questions*. Edward Elgar.

Ladkin, D. (2013). From perception to flesh: A phenomenological account of the felt experience of leadership. *Leadership*, *9*(3), 320–334.

Ladkin, D. (2017). How did that happen? Making sense of the 2016 US presidential election result through the lens of the 'leadership moment'. *Leadership*, *13*(4), 393–412.

Lara, F. L. (2013). Favela Upgrade in Brazil: A reverse of participatory processes. *Journal of Urban Design*, *18*(4), 553–564.

Manso, B. (2016). *Homicide in São Paulo: An examination of the trends from 1960–2010*. Springer.

Morris, A., & Staggenborg, S. (2004). Leadership in social movements. In D. Snow, S. Soule, & H. Kriesi (Eds.), *The Blackwell companion to social movements* (pp. 172–196). Blackwell Publishing.

Moulaert, F., Martinelli, F., Swyngedouw, E., & Gonzalez, S. (2010). *Can neighborhoods save the city? Community development and social innovation*. Routledge.

Ospina, S., & Foldy, E. (2010). Building bridges from the margins: The work of leadership in social change organizations. *The Leadership Quarterly*, *21*, 292–307.

Pandolfi, D., & Grynszpan, M. (2003). *A Favela Fala*. Editora FGV.

Pasternak, S. (2016). Favelas: fatos e boatos. In L. Kowarick & H. Frugoli (Orgs.), *Pluralidade Urbana em São Paulo*. Editora 34 Ltda.

Pearce, C. L., & Conger, J. A. (2003). *Shared leadership: Reframing the hows and whys of leadership*. Sage.

Raelin, J. (2011). From leadership-as-practice to leaderful practice. *Leadership*, 7(3), 195–211.

Raelin, J. (2016). Imagine there are no leaders: Reframing leadership as collaborative agency. *Leadership*, 12(2), 131–158.

Savell, S. (2015). I'm not a leader: Cynicism and good citizenship in a Brazilian Favela. *Political and Legal Anthropology Review*, 38(2), 300–317.

Schwartz, M., Rosenthal, N., & Schwartz, L. (1981). Leader-member conflict in protest organizations: The Case of Southern Farmers' Alliance. *Social Problems*, 29(1), 22–36.

Sergi, V., Denis, J.-L., & Langley, A. (2012). Opening up perspectives on plural leadership. *Industrial and Organizational Psychology*, 5(4), 403–407.

Uhl-Bien, M. (2006). Relational leadership theory: Exploring the social processes of leadership and organizing. *The Leadership Quarterly*, 17, 654–676.

United Nations. (2014). *World urbanization prospects*. Author.

Yammarino, F., Salas, E., Serban, A., Shirreffs K., & Shuffler M. (2012). Collectivistic leadership approaches: Putting the "we" in leadership science and practice. *Industrial and Organizational Psychology*, 5(4), 382–402.

6

FROM GOVERNANCE TO LEADERSHIP: ETHICAL FOUNDATIONS FOR VALUE-INFUSED LEADERSHIP OF THE COMMONS

CATHARYN BAIRD, NANCY SAYER, JEANNINE NIACARIS AND ALLISON DAKE

Today we see a burgeoning global movement of the commons in response to the degradation of the earth and inappropriate cordoning of resources without a corresponding responsibility for the care or sharing of those assets. As people come together and share resources outside of the usual market or regulatory environment to create a specific instance of the commons, they are committed to self-governance and often find themselves outside of the normal constraints of either traditional organizational policies or the expectations or protections of the law (Bollier, 2014). Furthermore, as organizers create new common activities, they will need to create appropriate statements of values, rules, and policies to navigate the ever-changing landscape. Elinor Ostrom explored this problem in her seminal work, *Governing the Commons*, as she laid out seven design principles required for effective governance (Ostrom, 1990, p. 90). However, she did not explore the ethical foundations deeply informing the value priorities of the community as reflected in the participants' ethical assumptions nor a methodology for establishing the community's norms. Thus, we present an approach to ethics open enough to encourage people to express differences in value priorities without moving into ethical relativism – where people use their own value priorities as the ethical yardstick rather than engage in the work of harmonizing the divergent values and interests necessary for a community to flourish.

FROM AN ETHIC OF CERTAINTY TO AN ETHIC OF CREATIVITY

Ethics is the study of right relationships (Arvidsson, Bauwens, & Peitersen, 2008; Baird, 2011). Over the sweep of history, the focus of ethics – understandings about how to build right relationships within communities – has moved between highlighting the responsibilities of the community and those of the individual. While early agrarian ages demonstrated a concern for community, during the Age of Reason (1685–1815 CE) the emphasis moved toward making individuals responsible for identifying personal values resulting in ethical frameworks highlighting personal responsibility. As the scientific method gained ascendency, the philosophers applied the methodology of testing hypotheses to ethics as they sought to identify universal ethical principles governing the behavior of individuals and members of the community. This quest resulted in ethical models privileging humans over the rest of creation, independence over interdependence, and certainty over an unfolding and indeterminate existence (Henning, 2005). Over the past 300 years, leaders translated ethical constructs touted as universal individual norms into policies, regulations, and laws. Then, as people applied the metaphors of science to the practices of governance, the narrow vision of ethics as personal responses to one's environment instead of a harmonization of values in tension became ensconced into organizations while administrators created systems to monitor people, track accountability, and balance power (Johnson, 2018, p. 330).

Two scientific advances in the early 1900s disrupted the project of finding universal ethical norms. The first was Darwin's theory of evolution, advancing the proposition that all of life was in a state of continual change. As foundational work in evolution matured into systems theory, those studying ethics grappled with how to have both aspirational goals for persons-in-community (Daly & Cobb, Jr, 1994) while acknowledging that, except at a very abstract level, no ethical norms would ever be absolute for all people at all times (de los Reyes, 2020). For example, while every community prohibits the taking of human life, the variations about whose lives are protected and the circumstances counting for justifiable homicide are legion. The second advance was Einstein's theory of relativity, forwarding the proposition that people's observations of the natural world are not really open to consensus, because the questions people ask and the perspectives they take inform what they see (Wilson, 1998).

As the quest for universal ethical norms faltered during the mid-twentieth century, researchers engaged in three strands of study concerning the formation of moral identity to better understand the variations in ethical norms. The first explored the relationship of biology to ethics to examine how much of a person's ethical disposition is inherited. Jonathan Haidt, a leader in behavioral ethics, posits that about 30% of a person's ethical responses are instinctual and coded in their DNA (Haidt, 2012). The remaining 70% of one's ethical identity comes from socialization and psychology. One's socialization, the implied and explicit expectations for acceptable behaviors forwarded by parents and respected elders, deeply informs and conditions a person's understanding of their place in the community (Niemeyer, Franks, & Turner, 2013).

Finally, the balance of one's ethical identity is psychological, which is the individual's use of reason to make sense of their experiences in the world informing their values and actions. Behavioral psychologists describe how the working of a person's mind shapes their ethical identity as they blend reason and experience to make sense of how they fit into various communities (Stets, 2011). This discernment helps individuals determine which values and behaviors will allow them to be accepted, recognized, and included by those who matter to them (Aquino & Reed, II, 2002). While these strands of research aid people in understanding the variety of values and behaviors exhibited by humans, they do not help one harmonize all those diverse values and understandings of how to be a person-in-community into a set of shared norms, values, and behaviors essential for the work of creating and sustaining the commons.

Thomas Donaldson and Thomas Dunfee's Integrative Social Contract Theory (ISCT), which explores how to establish guiding principles while acknowledging the diversity of approaches to living and working in community, provides one path forward (Donaldson & Dunfee, 1999). ISCT introduced the notion of micro-social norms, those agreements made by people in local communities about what kinds of behaviors will count as ethical in the context of that community. Those negotiations set expectations and harmonize the inherent tensions between the desires and prerogatives of individuals and the communities in which they live and work. Exploring micro-social norms is one of Ostrom's primary design principles, as those establishing rules for the collective need to ensure "congruence between appropriation and provisional rules and local conditions" (Ostrom, 1990, p. 92).

While Donaldson and Dunfee posited the importance of hypernorms, those universal expectations transcending local expressions of ethical action, ongoing research acknowledging the futility of seeking universal principles has led to reframing absolute hypernorms into a nuanced concept called justifiable hypernorms. In this process, members of a community describe their individual and shared core values. Then through conversation, those impacted by the decision agree on what behaviors flowing from those values will be accepted as ethical (Scholz, de los Reyes, & Smith, 2019). By using "discursive engagement" to explore and define the limits of acceptable behavior through "hypothetical reasoning," a community, such as one created in the commons, can develop its own provisional code of ethics, a set of values and behaviors tailored to the goals and specific organizational models appropriate for that particular enterprise.

A small example of this process comes from a set of families in Oakland, California, who upon disruption of their children's schooling with the onset of COVID-19 in 2020 had to find a new way to provide education. The solution was to create a "pod," an agreement among six families who agreed to co-schooling. This venture required thoughtfully harmonizing the values of the parents, the children, as well as the school district with its expectations for learning. Not only did they have to find school supplies and furniture, but they had to decide what they would require in terms of social distancing, testing for the illness, and the various contours of the educational experience.

One parent sent out an invitation. Several other parents responded, and the first layer of details was worked out over a series of emails. Then the parents and children visited the garage transformed into a classroom and made additional adjustments to the anticipated learning experience. Finally, as new situations came up – such as children being exposed to COVID-19 and deciding what kind of quarantining was required – the parents worked together to adjust the expectations. The evolving process involved continuously discerning the values and expected shared behaviors of the stakeholders – identifying the evolving micro-social norms – and then harmonizing those expectations over time into an educational experience that persisted much longer than anyone had expected (T. Lambert & M. Haning, personal communication, September 5, 2020).

The above process may not seem earth-shattering, but many do not consider the importance of listening to all stakeholders to determine the micro-social norms flowing from shared values and embodied in specific practices before embarking on new action. When the community is homogenous, the process is invisible. However, when applying the practice to diverse communities, those engaged in leadership would be well advised to be open to the various ways that core commitments can be expressed. The importance of the process of discursive reasoning will become starkly apparent as we consider the second case study later in this chapter.

The next question becomes what ethical framework to use for the hypothetical reasoning. If traditional ethical models cannot answer the question of how people should best live in community, what framework or combination of frameworks can be used by those creating new communities in the commons to establish their ethical expectations of how to be persons-in-community?

IDENTIFYING VALUES IN TENSION

Each major ethical family explores two universal overarching sets of values in tension (Baird, 2011). The first is the perennial tension between individuals and the larger communities where they live and work. When do individuals get to choose how to live their lives? What agreements will they honor while expecting the community to provide some modicum of safety, access to resources, and companionship? When does the community get to determine what individual behaviors will be accepted? What individual contributions are expected in exchange for community protection? The second overarching tension is the perennial tension between reason and experience, colloquially known as the tension between the head and heart or justice and mercy. When do agreed upon ethical principles grounded in provisional knowledge – justifiable hypernorms – take priority over lived experience leading to nuanced ethical norms based on individual needs and preferences?

After analysis, each traditional ethical theory is necessary but none is sufficient to enable members of a community to translate justifiable hypernorms into micro-social norms so participants can create and live into the ethics of the commons. Within an evolving worldview, rather than privileging one or another combination of value priorities with a favorite ethical lens, a leader needs to see the enterprise as a whole to identify and harmonize shared core values, as well as to name and resolve conflicting interests of the members (Allen, 2019).

Responding to that challenge and drawing on the work of Alfred North Whitehead, Brian Henning put forward the Ethics of Creativity, an ethical theory using an organic worldview as a framework for identifying and harmonizing core values and then resolving conflict (Henning, 2005). Henning placed his theory within a processive worldview, where knowledge is never static. He notes individuals and communities dance together as they notice a conflict, imagine solutions to resolve the conflict, and then take action to live into a new worldview. Henning is very clear that this method of discerning ethical action is to include all of creation – humans, animals, plants, air, water, and earth (Henning, 2005). Next, the worldview presumes interdependence rather than independence. Lastly, this approach embraces fallibility, where one seeks to act from truth while understanding truth is provisional and one must always be open to new and deeper understandings of those truths (Fig. 1).

Henning (2015) then demonstrates how to turn the search for ethical absolutes into embracing obligations that can maximize the ethical intensity of a life, as people become comfortable with engaging in reflexive discourse to harmonize ever more complicated ethical issues. First, rather than choosing critical goals to help one live into their meaning and purpose for life (consequentialism), Henning posits an obligation to maximize "the intensity and harmony of one's own experience (self-respect)" (Location 1562) that changes the focus to living into an individualized mission to serve.

Next, rather than seeking absolute principles by which to live (deontology), humans are encouraged to "strive continually to expand the depth and breadth of one's aesthetic horizons (education)" (Location 1562). Then, rather than focusing on developing virtues demonstrating ethical excellence in the

Fig. 1.   Evolving Ethical Obligations.

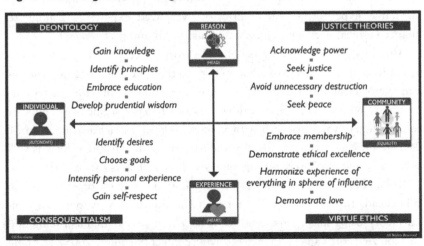

Source: Baird & Niacaris, 2016.

community (virtue ethics), humans can embrace the "obligation to maximize the harmony and intensity of experience of everything within one's sphere of influence (love)" (Location 1562). And finally rather than focusing on developing fair systems and ensuring appropriate use of power (justice theories), people can endeavor to "avoid the destruction (or maiming) of any [part of creation], unless not doing so threatens the achievement of the greatest harmony and intensity possible in each situation (peace)" (Location 1574).

These obligations provide the ethical content for a leader facilitating a conversation to establish micro-social norms for an emerging community striving to live into the values of the commons. As leaders embrace their responsibilities in a time of complexity and focus on the common good, they can mindfully engage a community in discursive reasoning through conscious conversations. These conversations create space for people to share their vision for the enterprise as well as the resulting organization, agree upon their core values, and establish expectations for behavior. These skills support the creation of spirals of positive change generating a progression of behaviors tending to create the most value for all within the circle of concern.

While those using different leadership styles may successfully engage in conscious conversations, leaders embracing benevolent leadership practices are particularly well-suited for the project of identifying and then facilitating the establishment of shared micro-social norms. Benevolent leadership is an integrated model of regenerative leadership. Emphasizing qualities and behaviors contributing to the common good, four key processes anchor this approach: (1) ethical sensitivity, the process of moral reflection and ethical decision-making; (2) spiritual depth, the search for deep meaning and purpose; (3) positive engagement, an emphasis on care and concern for the stakeholders of an organization, instilling hope and courage; and (4) community responsiveness, where the leader and members of the organization together solve "social problems...enabling social innovation to contribute to society" (Karakas & Sarigöllü, 2012; Sayer, 2018, p. 10).

CONSCIOUS CONVERSATIONS

The obstacles blocking engagement in life-affirming conversations have never been greater. Currently every segment of public discourse (political, racial, gender-equality, climate, economic, etc.) is becoming increasingly toxic (Pew Research, 2019). The divisiveness among people and communities is at an all-time high (Dean & Gramlich, 2020). People's willingness to listen to different viewpoints is becoming increasingly unthinkable. And, in this time of polarization, many have a marked indifference to seeking the truth – fiercely defending "my truth" as "the truth" (Glendon, 1991; Haidt, 2012). Defending their position, people align with those who share the same opinion as they intractably identify with their "tribe." With identification and interaction with those who are more like-minded strengthening over time, people become unwilling to critique the tribe mindset, and their ability to approach issues through critical thinking diminishes significantly (Lynch, 2013).

Those committed to creating governance models within the commons must go against the cultural grain described above to engage participants in the reflective discourse needed to establish a set of shared ethical values, norms, and behaviors. Those involved in the project must increase their self- and other-awareness, or consciousness, and seek a place of understanding serving a higher purpose, or greater good, beyond themselves and their tribe. Developing the skill to engage in and facilitate conscious conversations increases both self- and other-awareness, communicates inclusivity, respect, and dignity, maintains integrity, and opens the space for dialogue to support transformational agreements and organizational structure (Fig. 2).

Fig. 2.   Engaging Conscious Conversations.

CONSCIOUS LISTENING WITH OPENNESS, EMPATHY, AND COMPASSION

Ask Conscious Questions:
Practice Curiosity
Be Intelligent:
What do we know?

Orchestrate Conscious Contention:
Practice Harmonizing Values in Tension
Be Reasonable:
How do we use power?

Cultivate Conscious Wisdom:
Practice Reflection
Be Reflective:
What have we learned?

Create Conscious Space:
Practice Courageous Covenant
Be Attentive:
What is the context?

Co-Create Conscious Action:
Practice Discernment
Be Responsible:
How can we serve?

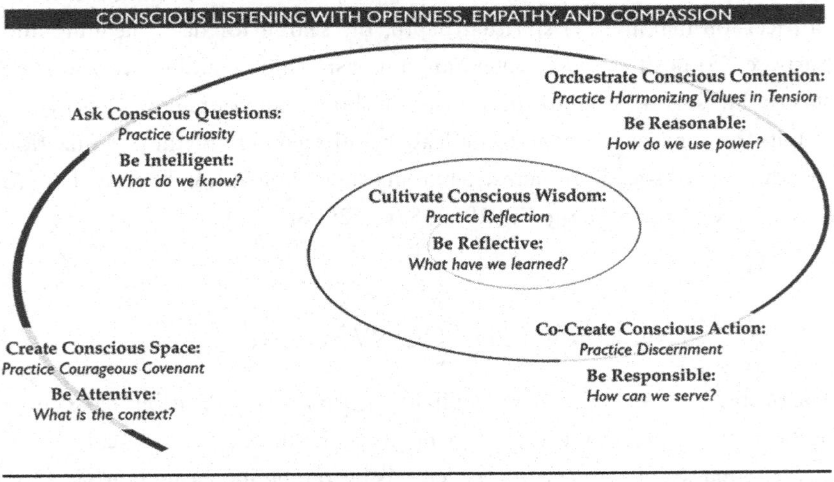

Sources: Sayer, 2018; Baird & Niacaris, 2016.

Conscious conversations™ are a form of deliberative dialogue where the participants discuss and resolve issues of importance to individuals and the group. The conversations require mindful attunement to one's own values-based worldview in addition to awareness of the value priorities of other individuals, the group, and stakeholders outside of the group. Developing the skill of participating in conscious conversations enhances the ability of all participants to function as persons-in-community. As skilled facilitators and participants embrace both the heightened awareness of self and others' values and the dynamic, interactional tension between them, they create the space for resolution of the tension into harmony.

Facilitating conscious conversations requires a leader to master six critical practices to create a virtuous cycle of encouraging and initiating positive change in organizations – practices needed to navigate the ethical life cycle of the commons. By using the practices listed below to engage in ethical decision-making, create a sense of purpose and meaning, and foster hope and courage for positive action, the leader and their community participating in conscious conversations can positively impact the larger community (Karakas & Sarigöllü, 2012).

To demonstrate the principles in action, we'll be highlighting the story of Chloé Jackson of Minneapolis, one of the primary tenants in a complex called the Corcoran Five who had the audacious idea of buying their apartment complex from the owner who had let the property fall to pieces. This initiative was a small part of the work of a tenants' rights organization, Inquilinxs Unidxs por Justicia (United Renters for Justice/IX). The larger vision of IX is defined as "commoning," the process of decommodifyng housing by

> the creation of democratically controlled affordable housing. "We want to transition from this extractive model that takes away people's wages and forces them to live paycheck to paycheck to a model that's regenerative," says Davin Cárdenas, of the Right to the City Alliance. (Desmond, 2020, p. 12)

1. Engaging in Conscious Listening – The Practice of Empathy and Compassion

The grounding space for any conscious conversation is conscious listening which involves hearing and understanding at three different levels. The first is the visceral level: This *reactive* listening happens in one's body, the somatic experience where the body is fully engaged and sending wordless messages. The next is the cognitive level: This *reflective* listening engages one's mind as one interprets the feelings within their bodies and evaluates the situation based on known facts, beliefs, previous experiences, opinions, and assumptions. The final is the emotional level: This *responsive* listening is where one meets the shared human experience through empathy and compassion.

Conscious listening is foundational to the process and integral to each layer of the conversation. Implicit in this listening is the willingness to have one's heart and mind changed through the encounters.

> *The co-director of the Minneapolis chapter of IX, Roberto de la Riva, worked tirelessly with the renters in Corcoran Five. As Jackson tells the story, de la Riva visited with tenants individually and as a group over many years, engaging them and helping them dream first of having their apartments repaired, then having fair rents, and finally owning the properties. Throughout the process, each listened to the other as they worked together to identify and then reach their goals. (Desmond, 2020)*

2. Creating Conscious Space – The Practice of Courageous Covenant

For conscious conversations to take place, the leader must create a safe, inviting environment where people can courageously engage in conversation. The leader guides the participants in gaining clarity around the purpose of the conversation, establishing agreement and accountability around confidentiality, committing to be in conversation, and pledging to include all and treat all with respect and dignity.

> *As de la Riva and the tenants met, they were able to share their experiences, document their efforts for getting their apartments repaired, and over months come up with a plan of action. Over the course of years, the tenants went to city council meetings, sharing with them their frustrations and demands for action. A team of lawyers supported the initiative by relentlessly pursuing actions against the building owner, Stephen Frenz, who stated that he was just trying to get a fair return on his investment. (Desmond, 2020)*

3. Asking Conscious Questions – The Practice of Curiosity

Humans are naturally curious. Questioning facilitates satisfying implicit and explicit curiosity. Questions help people get information, allowing them to expand their own understanding and taking them to places of deep personal exploration.

> * Each new discovery led to more questions. The overarching quest was to find where Frenz was vulnerable. Through poring over legal documents, they discovered he had lied to the city about the habitability of the building. They found the mortgage was held by someone prohibited from owning rental units in Minneapolis because of his own fraudulent dealings. When the building operation was turned over to a court administrator, the group began dreaming of buying the property. IX identified a mortgage company, "Land Bank Twin Cities, a collection of real estate speculators whose goal is not to maximize profit but to preserve affordable housing" (Desmond, 2020, p. 8) where the question was determining the appropriate price-point for the property as well as the tenants ability to pay the mortgage and keep up the properties.

4. Orchestrating Conscious Contention – The Practice of Harmonizing Values in Tension

Those participating in conscious conversations must agree to value and respect all voices and perspectives around the table. Because of differences in experience and value commitments, people voice competing ideas, which can lead to tension. As the leader is conscious and aware of these tensions and keeps the space open and safe for differing thoughts, perspectives, and feelings to be voiced, the members of the group develop trust as they move into a space of deeper wisdom.

> *Perhaps the most audacious action of the Corcoran Five tenants was staging a vigil at Steven Frenz's church, Our Lady of Peace. The negotiations for purchase had come to a standstill. The tenants decided to organize a march; Jackson was the MC. The tenants descended on the church's annual feast and mingled with the parishioners, telling

them that one of their members was going to evict people of color from his apartment complex. The action held a mirror up to the parishioners who had a professed ethic of care for the marginalized and invited them to consider how they would hold one of their own accountable for living into their ostensibly shared values, the micro-social norm of the church community. (Desmond, 2020)

5. Co-Creating Conscious Action – The Practice of Discernment

Co-creating conscious action invokes the process of discernment as the group harmonizes the tensions to reach an agreement on appropriate action – or inaction. Conscious valuing, consideration, and integration of all perspectives voiced during the conversation strengthens the buy-in of the stakeholders and increases the likelihood of participants' successfully implementing and following through with the decisions.

*The tenants celebrated when Frenz accepted an offer to sell them the Corcoran Five – a goal that took many years to reach. Over the years, the group met repeatedly. At each step of discernment, the spiral of conscious conversation was repeated as the group under the leadership of IX discerned what action was next needed to reach their goal of living in habitable buildings.

6. Cultivating Conscious Wisdom – The Practice of Reflection

Cultivating conscious wisdom invites participants into an active practice of reflection where the core work of transformation resides. Taking time and using guiding questions to deeply reflect enables participants to sit with their own thoughts, feelings, and conscience – their own ethical self – to reflect on the experience of the conversation and the decisions made by the group.

*Chloé Jackson reports she did not set out to be an activist – she only wanted good housing for herself and her son. However, as the community came together, led by thoughtful and skilled leaders

committed to the practice of regenerative benevolent leadership within a vision of the commons, spirals of positive change occurred and she was equipped to be a voice for action and change leading to transformation!

CREATING SPIRALS OF POSITIVE CHANGE

The practices of benevolent leadership have a positive ripple effect throughout organizations in four significant ways: (1) attracting other benevolent leaders; (2) shaping behaviors of direct reports and other employees; (3) establishing normative behavior; and (4) creating a benevolent organizational culture (Sayer, 2018). The synergy of these behaviors creates upward spirals of positivity in six key areas: The spirals of generosity, human connectivity, organizational performance, flourishing, capacity building, and emulation (Fig. 3).

As the benevolent leader and members of the commons engage in conscious conversations to create, nurture, and enforce ethical norms, they facilitate the likelihood of these upward spirals emerging within the organization.

The interconnected nature of the spirals results in an overall spiral of generativity for the common good. This type of spiraling has the transcendent

Fig. 3. Upward Spirals of Benevolent Leadership (Sayer, 2018).

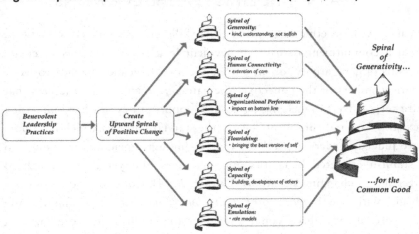

effect of moving awareness from the individual, to the team, to the organization, and then to the greater society. The spiraling also embodies Ehrenfeld's definition of sustainability: "the possibility that humans and life will *flourish* forever on earth" (Ehrenfeld, 2008, p. 49). Ehrenfeld goes on to claim all are interconnected:

> *Flourishing also consists of other distinctions of human origin that relate to the collective state. Justice, fairness, and equity come from our historical sense that flourishing has to do with more than our own self-attainments. We accept, but fail to act accordingly, that there is a social dimension to living that recognizes in some way that all humans are interconnected and that the state of our individual lives is tied to the states of others with whom we share our only world. (Ehrenfeld, p. 51)*

The inherent nature of benevolent leadership practices puts the impact for the common good at the center of the entire enterprise – inspiring others to do the same as they transcend the desire to only serve themselves while seeking the higher purpose of preserving the commons. Imagine a world where benevolent leaders embed these behaviors into the very culture of their organizations, creating generative and regenerative entities (Dake, 2018).

CREATING THE ETHICS OF THE COMMONS

Armed with an ethic of creativity, the skills of conscious conversations, and a commitment to using benevolent leadership strategies to create spirals of generativity for the common good, the leader is ready to work with members of the collective to create agreements and structures that are responsive to emerging needs and opportunities. Rather than using existing law and current policies as the standard against which behaviors are judged, leaders are able to craft living agreements clear enough to establish expected behaviors and outcomes and yet open enough to respond to changing situations (Laloux, 2014). Conscious conversations begin with the *Practice of Courageous Covenant*, exploring the life purpose of individuals coming together to establish their organization within the commons (Fig. 4).

Fig. 4.   Creating the Ethics of the Commons.

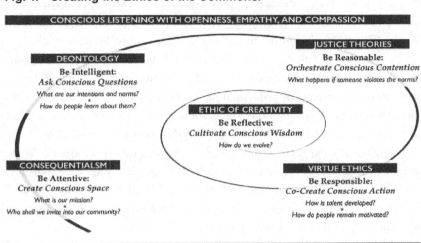

Sources: Sayer, 2018; Baird and Niacaris 2016.

As members become attentive and create conscious space, they explore the value priorities of consequentialism (Mill, 2002): (1) recognizing the desires people have for their work together; (2) identifying their personal goals; (3) then discerning how an individual's meaning and purpose fits within the articulated mission and vision of the collective purpose (Baird & Niacaris, 2016). As the group explores their mission and determines who should be invited into the community, typical questions each individual must explore are: (1) What would be a good outcome; (2) what consequences am I willing to tolerate; (3) what actions will show that I respect myself and others; (4) what actions will help me and others make a positive impact on our communities and the world?

Next, to explore the purpose and structure of the organization, the group becomes reasonable and orchestrates conscious contention to address the value priorities of justice theories (Rawls, 1971): (1) identifying sources of power; (2) designing the structures for an organization to achieve the greatest harmony and intensity possible; (3) then creating systems resulting in productive peace (Baird & Niacaris, 2016). As they put processes in place to resolve differences of direction and address violations of the norms they ask: (1) What are fair processes for distribution of resources and resolution of conflict; (2) what is needed to get to a fair result for all; (3) whose voice needs to be heard; (4) what actions will support and sustain a healthy, interconnected web of life?

Then as individuals are intelligent and the organization comes into focus, they ask conscious questions to test the organizational structure against their own principles by addressing the value priorities of deontology (Kant & Wood, 1785): (1) committing to lifelong learning and willingness to change; (2) exploring how value commitments and behaviors expected by the community square with individual values and principles; and (3) then exhibiting wisdom in the exercise of prudential judgment (Baird & Niacaris, 2016). As members clarify their intentions and commit to the shared norms as well as put structures in place so that members of the community can learn about and agree to the expectations of the group, typical questions are: (1) What are my intentions, my reasons for action; (2) what principles are important; (3) what agreements must I keep; (4) how can I live into my principles and fulfill my duties while caring for others; (5) what actions will help me act with integrity and support ideal results?

And then, being responsible, the group returns to the collective and explores value priorities through the lens of virtue ethics (MacIntyre, 1984): (1) identifying salient memberships; (2) discerning what behaviors count for ethical excellence within various roles; (3) then showing respect and appreciation for everything within their sphere of influence (Baird & Niacaris, 2016). During this step, influencers and leaders take conscious action to develop talent within the group and help people remain motivated to do their best work. They also consider how to have people able to leave with integrity and grace. Clarifying questions are: (1) Given our roles, what action would set a good example; (2) what virtues – qualities of being – are required by the various roles; (3) what actions will allow each of us to be a benevolent leader in this situation; (4) what actions will allow those within our sphere of influence to thrive; (5) how can we show personal courage?

The cycle ends and begins by being reflective and cultivating creative wisdom. As members of the community embrace an ethic of creativity, even in the face of ambiguity and an uncertain future, they commit to evolving as individuals and as a community and changing their norms – their expression of beliefs, values, and behaviors – when conditions change?

By engaging salient questions in the *Practice of Harmonizing Values in Tension*, leaders learn to live with the intensity of dissonance emerging through the exploration of values applied to behaviors until they find a resolution synthesizing the value priorities and laying out strategies for implementation. Included in those strategies is an awareness that each person and organization might express its shadow side, a concern seen in Ostrom's design principles regarding monitoring, putting graduated sanctions in place, and providing for conflict-resolution strategies (Ostrom, 1990, p. 90). When one believes their needs are in jeopardy, they engage their shadow side, triggering destructive behaviors to protect core needs for survival, security, affection, esteem, approval, power, and control (Niemeyer et al., 2013). As the shadow side moves into play, these behaviors can create a downward spiral, thwarting positive change. The *Practice of Harmonizing Values in Tension* assists the leader in identifying and responding to inappropriate behaviors through a mutual reaffirmation of shared values and a renegotiation of core agreements.

The *Practice of Discernment* allows the leader to note the responses and shepherd the decision process toward a harmonization of the value priorities. From this practice, instead of a top-down directive, the wisdom of the collective emerges to determine the course of action. Using the practices of conscious conversations requires more time than individual decision-making, but the results are nuanced and better harmonize the various value priorities – to say nothing of the membership's greater ownership of micro-social norms and behavior commitments. The process is iterative because the agreed-upon micro-social norms will not address emerging problems or opportunities not covered or anticipated in the initial conversation. As changes are needed, individuals and the community can again work through all four sets of questions to ensure they consider and harmonize each of the core values in tension.

CONCLUSION

Creating a governance system to support an ethical community has three elements. First, those within the community must identify and agree upon the ethical norms by which they will live. An Ethic of Creativity provides a framework by which to identify values in tension enabling the creation of maximum value for all within the circle of concern. Next, those in leadership can help members establish a process for harmonizing those value commitments and expected behaviors. As the benevolent leader and members of the community engage in the practices of conscious conversations to create spirals of generativity, those value priorities will come to life. Finally, those doing the work must identify the context, in this case within the construct of the commons as they are transforming usual ways of understanding how people can live and work together. Whether as small of an instance of the commons such as creating a learning pod to cope with educational disruption, or a multi-year effort as seen in the case study of Chloé Jackson, the tenants at Corcoran Five, and the co-organizers of IX who demonstrated the value of patiently creating regenerative organizational systems, the process of creating an ethics of the commons supports the organizational lifecycle of new and evolving organizations. Those participating in these ever-evolving systems grounded in a commitment to the commons become co-creators of the shared values, organizational solutions, and flourishing systems required for equitable, healthy, and prosperous relationships within a thriving community (Dake, 2018).

REFERENCES

Allen, K. E. (2019). *Leading from the roots: Nature-inspired leadership lessons for today's world*. Morgan James Publishing. Kindle Edition.

Aquino, K., & Reed, A., II (2002). The self-importance moral identity. *Journal of Personality and Social Psychology, 83*(6), 1423–1440. doi:10.1037//0022-3514.83.6.1423

Arvidsson, A., Bauwens, M., & Peitersen, N. (2008). The crisis of value and the ethical economy. *Journal of Futures Studies, 12*(4), 9–20.

Baird, C. A. (2011). *Everyday ethics: Making wise choices in a complex world* (2nd ed.). EthicsGame Press.

Baird, C. A., & Niacaris, J. M. (2016). *The ethical self: Using the ethical lens inventory to journey toward ethical maturity*. EthicsGame Press.

Bollier, D. (2014). The commons as a growing global movement. News and Perspective on the Commons. Retrieved from www.bollier.org/blog/commons-growing-global-movement

Dake, A. (2018). *Thriving beyond surviving: A regenerative business framework to co-create significant economic, social, and environmental value for the world*. Unpublished Dissertation.

Daly, H. E., & Cobb, J. B., Jr (1994). *For the common good: Redirecting the economy toward community, the environment, and a sustainable future* (2nd ed.). Boston, MA: Beacon Press.

Dean, Claudia and John Gramlich. (2020, November 6). *2020 election reveals two broad voting coalitions fundamentally at odds*. Pew Research Center. Retrieved from https://www.pewresearch.org/fact-tank/2020/11/06/2020-election-reveals-two-broad-voting-coalitions-fundamentally-at-odds/

Dean, C., & Gramlich, J. (2020, November 6). *2020 election reveals two broad voting coalitions fundamentally at odds*. Pew Research Center. https://www.pewresearch.org/fact-tank/2020/11/06/2020-election-reveals-two-broad-voting-coalitions-fundamentally-at-odds/

de los Reyes, G., Jr. (2020, August 2-7). *Organic corporate purpose*. Academy of Legal Studies in Business, Annual Meeting, Virtual Conference.

Desmond, M. (2020, October 13). The tenants who evicted their landlord. *New York Times Magazine*. Retrieved from https://nyti.ms/3lKEbTd

Dolnick, E. (2011). *The clockwork universe: Isaac Newton, the Royal Society, and the birth of the modern world*. HarperCollins e-books. Kindle Edition.

Donaldson, T., & Dunfee, T. W. (1999). *Ties that bind: A social contracts approach to business ethics*. Harvard Business School Press.

Ehrenfeld, J. R. (2008). *Sustainability by design: A subversive strategy for transforming our consumer culture*. Yale University Press.

Glendon, M. A. (1991). *Rights talk: The impoverishment of political discourse*. Simon & Schuster.

Haidt, J. (2012). *The Righteous mind: Why good people are divided by politics and religions*. Pantheon Books.

Henning, B. (2005). *The Ethics of creativity: Beauty, morality, and nature in a processive cosmos*. University of Pittsburgh Press.

Johnson, C. E. (2018). *Meeting the ethical challenges of leadership: Casting light or shadow* (6th ed.). SAGE Publications.

Jurkowitz, M., Mitchell, A., Shearer, E., & Walker, M. (2020, January 24). *U.S. media polarization and the 2020 election: A nation divided*. Pew Research Center. Retrieved from https://www.journalism.org/2020/01/24/u-s-media-polarization-and-the-2020-election-a-nation-divided/

Kant, I., & Wood, A. W. Tr. (1785). *Groundwork for the metaphysics of morals*. Yale University Press.

Karakas, F. (2009). *Benevolent leadership*. Unpublished Doctoral Dissertation. McGill University, Montreal, CAN.

Karakas, F., & Sarigöllü, E. (2012). Benevolent leadership: Conceptualization and construct development. *Journal of Business Ethics, 108*, 537–553. doi:10.1007/s10551-011-1109-1

Laloux, F. (2014). *Reinventing organizations: A guide to creating organizations inspired by the next stage of human consciousness*. Nelson Parker. Kindle Edition.

Lambert, T., & Haning, M. (2020, September 5). Creating a Learning Pod [Personal communication].

MacIntyre, A. (1984). *After virtue: A study in moral theory* (2nd ed.). University of Notre Dame Press.

Mill, J. S. (2002). *The basic writings of John Stuart Mill: On liberty, the subjection of women and utilitarianism*. Modern Library.

Niemeyer, R.E. (2013). What are the neurological foundations of identities and identity-related processes? In D. D. Franks & J. H. Turner (Eds.), *Handbook of neurosociology* (pp. 146–165). Springer Netherlands.

Ostrom, E. (1990). *Governing the commons: The evolution of institutions for collective action.* Cambridge University Press.

Pew Research Center. (2019, January 24). *Public's 2019 priorities: Economy, health care, education and security all near top of list.* Retrieved from https://ww.pewresearch.org/politics/2019/01/24/publics-2019-priorities-economy-health-care-education-and-security-all-near-top-of-list/. Accessed on June 1, 2021.

Rawls, J. (1971). *A theory of justice.* Belknap Press of Harvard University.

Sayer, N. E. (2018). *Benevolent leadership and upward spirals of positive change: A mixed methods study* (Publication No. 10936523) [Doctoral Dissertation, Benedictine University]. ProQuest Dissertations Publishing.

Scholz, M., de los Reyes, G., Jr, & Smith, N. C. (2019). The enduring potential of justified hypernorms. *Business Ethics Quarterly,* 29(3), 317–342. doi: 10.1017/beq.2018.42

Stets, J. E. (2011). The moral self: Applying identity theory. *Social Psychology Quarterly,* 74(2), 192–215. doi:10.1177/0190272511407621

Wilson, E. O. (1998). *Consilience: The unity of knowledge.* Vintage Books.

7

LEADING PROLEPTICALLY ON THE COMMONS

RANDAL JOY THOMPSON

Participating in commons means being an agent of social transformation. The commons stand for a different way of seeing the world, of organizing, and of valuing than the current way manifested in the state and private sector. As made clear in the chapters in this book, commons are based on a relational ontology that includes the human and more-than-human. They are self-organized, self-governed, autonomous, and based on values of responsibility, care, compassion, justice, equality, and love. Commoners are intent on remaking the world in accordance with these values and hence live these values in the present.

Several authors in this volume have examined leadership from the perspective of adaptive open systems. Others have looked at how leadership manifests from relationships and the in-between relations. Yet others have looked at leadership as a function of different processes on the commons. Still others have looked at types of leadership. In this chapter, I pursue leading from the individual leader's perspective, employing a human action framework. The human action framework assumes that different levels of organization impact the leader and the leader in turn impacts these. These levels include the individual or micro, the collective, or meso, the social, or macro, and the universal, or meta. Leadership is a bridging process between all these levels and is a process of engendering change. Hence, the values that flow from these levels as well as the values imparted by the leader impact the quality of that change. Leading proleptically implies that glimpses of the perfect future invade the present and motivate leaders to live in the present in order to help bring into being that future, catalyzed by the hope that the future is possible. This hope, as George Por wrote, derives from a deep-seated longing of the human heart for a just, peaceful society in which everyone has enough to live at a universally established standard. This longing has been driving humankind since its inception and will continue to drive humankind until this utopian vision becomes the imaginary of a new socioeconomic order (Por, 2012).

PROLEPTICISM AND LEADING PROLEPTICALLY[1]

"Prolepsis" is a literary, rhetorical, and theological term, etymologically derived from the Latin prolepsis and the Greek prolepsis meaning "an anticipating," a "taking beforehand," from prolambanein "to take before," from pro "before."

American Heritage Dictionary defines prolepsis as "the representation of a thing as existing before it actually does." Prolepsis is "the representation of a future act or development as if presently existing or accomplished" according to the Merriam-Webster Dictionary. Prolepticism conveys the

> *fundamental idea that the future has priority over the past and [present, and that we can see some of the future in the prolepsis, where the future invades the present in advance of itself. (Jantii, 2017, p. 17)*

Leading proleptically is allowing that future to pull one forward, to guide one's path, and to be reflected in leading oneself, leading others, and leading society. Leading proleptically is leading with awareness, with mindfulness that one is being impacted by values emanating from all four levels of human action, the micro, meso, macro, and meta, and that one is also impacting these four levels. Such awareness should serve to make one more conscious of the importance of leading carefully and consciously.

Senge (2015) contended that the best definition of leadership is "the capacity of a human community to shape its future, how we bring into being things we really care about" (n.p.). Leadership thus has a future orientation. Proleptic leadership shapes the future in the prefigurative commons by glimpses of that future invading the present. No matter what other leadership role a particular commoner may play, they should also practice proleptic leadership because it is a value-based, future-oriented creative leadership approach. The vision of a commons-based society is the future that pulls the proleptic leader forward. In order to unleash the proleptic leader's creative power and to connect with an evolving social and even universal order, the proleptic leader needs to prepare oneself to lead, to possess and practice presence, and several key qualities of leading oneself, leading with others, and leading community, as will be discussed. Furthermore, through leading, the proleptic leader is infusing society with the values of commoning and serving as a model of care and compassion.

In leading proleptically, the future invades the present at all four levels, the universal, social, collective, and individual and through proleptic leadership, the future is realized through all four levels, as illustrated in Fig. 1. Furthermore, while leading the proleptic leader needs to be cognizant and mindful of all four levels and how they are influencing and being influenced by their leadership and events in the world.

Fig. 1. Inter-relationship Between Future and Proleptic Leadership.

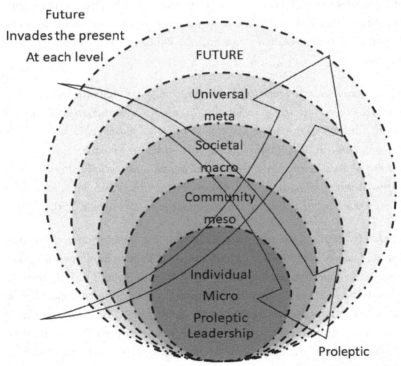

Future
Invades the present
At each level

FUTURE

Universal
meta

Societal
macro

Community
meso

Individual
Micro
Proleptic
Leadership

Proleptic
Leadership helps realize the
future through all levels

HUMAN ACTION FRAMEWORK FOR LEADING PROLEPTICALLY

The schemata of human action in organizations proposed by Schwandt (2008) provide a framework within which to observe the interactions of the meta, macro, meso, and micro levels and the influence of individuals on systems and leadership and visa-versa. Schwandt (2008) defined action as

> *normatively expended energy in a situation that is goal oriented [and] includes the means and conditions that enable the act to occur ... such as resources, signal, formation, resources, information, and the time and space to act. (n.p.)*

Such action is future goal-oriented and conscribed by individual and collective norms and values that provide meaning to the relationship between the situation and the end goal. Action within a social system, defined as "a set of categories for the analysis of the relations of one or more actors to, and in, a situation" (Schwandt, 2008, n.p.) entails human structuring interactions both related to the individual actor and the collective. Human structuring interactions

> *are composed of agents' explicit actions (e.g., setting boundaries, physical interaction, organization of work, social status, rules, leadership) and implicit guiding social patterns (e.g., norms, values, traditions, culture). When individual agents interact with each other, or with objects in their environment, each action potentially alters both the context and nature of the proceeding actions. These interactions, over time, create collective structural patterns. (Schwandt, 2008, n.p.)*

Schwandt (2008) contended that leadership is a structuring activity and process and can occur anywhere within a system. Leadership in process contributes to the collective intelligence of the system, Schwandt (2008) argued. As Schwandt pointed out, given that the micro, meso, macro, and meta levels are all complex adaptive systems, they are characterized by emergence, and also schemata, nonlinearity, and self-organization. Individuals' behavior is based on individual schemas, cognitive structures, such as values, meanings, relationships which may change through learning and personality development. Schemas at the meso and meta levels include routines, rules, normal and shared cultural values, all of which can also change. The fact that these systems are non-linear means that they can self-generate and self-organize and create new opportunities for interaction. As Schwandt (2008) maintained:

> *The triadic reciprocal relationship among agent actions, organizational environment, and personal cognitive, emotional, and efficacy factors regulate motivational, affective, and cognitive functioning of the actor, and over time and space simultaneously influence other actors and enable them to create beneficial organizational environments. (n.p.)*

Schwandt (2008) argued that the individuals' personality and understanding of self co-evolves as they interact with other individuals in the context of the collective's social structure. These interactions provide information and feedback for personal cognitive and emotional evolution. Individuals are changed by these interactions by learning and growing self-efficacy. As a consequence, individuals can act as causal agents and help shape the environments they act within.

Schwandt's schema provides a framework within which to examine some of the key values, level of consciousness, and other qualities of commoners as they act at the individual micro level, the meso commoning level, and as influenced by and influencing the macro social and meta universal levels.

Proleptic leadership must remain resilient and agile, open to new possibilities and surprises as it seeks to grasp that ideal future and manifest it partially in the present. Such leading can open the vista for higher levels of awareness and consciousness for individuals and societies. According to integral theorists and developmentalists, the movement to higher levels of consciousness is not automatic but requires certain types of experiences as well as an openness to confronting oneself and one's beliefs and being open to changing, even if uncomfortable or terrifying. Society is also evolving along the same path toward higher levels of consciousness, although as society moves, not all of the people in society move.

In addition, there are disruptive futures that shatter the status quo, such as new technologies, several of which may be created by commoners, crises such as the coronavirus pandemic, and global disasters such as climate change. Such disruptive futures serve as futures which demand sudden and deep-seated changes in human action and leadership.

Leading proleptically is allowing the future to lead us, being open to higher levels of consciousness, being available to be pulled into the future, which in terms of expanded consciousness, cognitive abilities, sense-making is either known or disruptive. Leading proleptically is also leading with the values of a commons-centric society and modeling these values to the world. The potential future narratives of philosophers and religions can serve as inspirations. Commoners can create a common vision by drawing on philosophical and religious sources to sketch a picture of the future, which then pulls them forward. Overall, the future is depicted as ideal, as utopian, a world of equanimity, equality, goodness, and other positive descriptors. As the theologian, Wolfhart Pannenberg believed, humankind

> *noetically anticipated the future through [their] plans, hopes, and*
> *expectations, [and] that the whole of reality is anticipatorily structured*
> *in [their] very being; that is, [their] very substance is anticipation of the*
> *very outstanding future end of history. (Pasquariello, 1976, p. 339)*

PREPARING ONESELF TO LEAD PROLEPTICALLY

Proleptic leadership calls for intentional preparation. One is typically not automatically or naturally predisposed to an openness toward the future and its radical possibilities in the present. Otto Scharmer, for example credited Bill O'Brien, CEO of Hanover Insurance, for helping him realize that

> *what counts is not only what leaders do and how they do it but*
> *their "interior condition," the inner place from which they operate*
> *or the source from which all of their actions originate. (2016, p. 7)*

In her study of efforts to create sustainability in rural development communities, Horlings (2011) identified leaders, not as those who hold positional authority, but rather,

> *all those, who follow their inner consciousness and inner values, take*
> *responsibility for sustainability in their own communities, localities,*
> *and regions. Passion and commitment and the capability to mobilize*
> *others are essential in this process ... as is a shift of will and heart. (p. 2)*

Furthermore, as Buddhist teacher Chogyam Trungpa (2015) pointed out, our attitude toward ourselves is projected in our interactions with others. Without gentleness toward ourselves, we cannot experience harmony or peace, and instead project a spirit of confusion and inharmoniousness toward others, which militates against forming relationships required for well-functioning commons (Trungpa, 2015, p. 13). The wisdom traditions of Tibetan Buddhism stressed the importance of lifelong training of the mind and the heart as a way of aligning people toward compassionate action

(Schuyler, 2012). Since care is the foundational attitude in the commons, proleptic leaders need to prepare themselves to manifest care in all their relations. A leader needs to understand that one's perceptions of the world begin in their inner values and attitudes. It is necessary to be cognizant of these and to challenge them in order to lead proleptically.

OPENING ONESELF TO THE FUTURE

In order to lead proleptically, it is also necessary to open oneself up to the future and to perceive that future from a deep state of knowing. Several leadership scholars and practitioners have posited approaches to opening oneself to a changed perception of oneself, others, and to the world and to an opening of awareness and consciousness and to the "whole." This also includes being receptive to the leadership of the future. Kathryn Schuyler (2014) wrote that

> *mindfulness or awareness intrinsically means connecting simultaneously with oneself as an embodied being and with the vastness and interconnected quality of life developing a view of impermanence and the constructed nature of human society. (p. xxiii)*

This opening of self to a deeper level of mindfulness and awareness is the first critical step to leading proleptically after self-preparation.

In their now classic book *Presence: An exploration of profound change in people, organizations, and society*, Peter Senge, Otto Scharmer, Joseph Jaworski, and Betty Flowers (2004) discovered an approach to connecting self with the whole universal level and to evolve with this level which is also evolving. Scharmer more fully developed this approach in *Theory U: Leading from the Future as it Emerges* (Scharmer, 2016; Scharmer & Kaufer, 2013).

By following Theory U, one accesses one's blind spot and learns to access one's authentic self from which one acquires knowledge and inspiration and connects to the emerging future. By listening with an open mind, heart, and will, one moves down the "U" through: (1) "suspending" old patterns of perceiving and understanding to; (2) "seeing" with fresh eyes and redirecting to: (3) "sensing" from the field and letting go to; (4) "presencing," and connecting to the whole where one interrogates the identity of one's self and one's work and letting the emergent self and emergent future come to; (5) "crystallizing" vision and intention and enacting to; (6) "prototyping" the new and connecting it to head, heart, and hand to; (7) "performing" by operating from the whole.

Meditation and journaling are methods that help one achieve presencing and connection with the "whole."

Jaworski (2011, 2012) employed a similar process to tap into the underlying intelligence, or source, within the universe to guide and prepare one for futures to be created at the same time that the future invades the present. In his introduction to Jaworski's book *Synchronicity: The Inner Path of Leadership*, Senge wrote that leadership

> *is about creating a domain in which human beings continually*
> *deepen their understanding of reality and become more capable of*
> *participating in the unfolding of the world. Ultimately, leadership is*
> *about creating new realities, (Jaworski, 2011, p. 3)*

a conception Jaworski shared. Jaworski meditated to connect with this source and employed meditation in his organizational consultancies in order to help organizations develop collective intelligence to guide them to make effective decisions. Through facilitating groups' connection with the "whole" after individuals have instilled the practice of meditation, Jaworski helped these individuals bridge the individual (micro) with the community (meso) levels and helped them create "collective intelligence" to guide their organizational decisions.

Religious traditions achieve connection with God through meditating on scripture, prayer, and contemplation. These traditions often seek to hear the voice of God for guidance about what actions to take in the present. Proleptic leaders, if coming from a religious tradition, can employ these approaches to open themselves up to God's unfolding plan and co-create with Him.

Integral theorists also offer approaches to opening up to the universal unfolding of the world and to develop an "evolutionary relationship to life" (Hamilton, 2020). Like the other approaches discussed above, the integral approach employs meditation to link into the universal spiritual level for guidance, to live and lead in love and connection, and to rid oneself of the more vile traits of human nature (Hamilton, 2020) which many feel are incarnated in neoliberal capitalism, and are the same values rejected by commoners.

EXPANSION OF CONSCIOUSNESS

Being mindful of one's stage of consciousness and opening up to a higher stage of consciousness can also foster leading proleptically by expanding awareness and developing the cognitive skills necessary to cope with a more complex future. Each successive level of consciousness represents a vision of a future in some sense. Each level pulls one upward if one is open to expanding one's awareness and if the social conditions require more sophisticated cognitive and sense-making abilities.

Higher levels of consciousness help leaders master two competences required by leaders in complex environments, according to Turner (2017). These include: "contextual thinking" and "decision-making processes." Contextual thinking allows leaders to understand the various contributions of individuals in the solution of complex problems. Successful decision-making requires taking all the perspectives in a complex problem into account in the solution (Turner, 2017). Whereas those at the postmodern level of consciousness seek community and harmony and equality, those at the post-postmodern level seek new knowledge and autonomy, traits appropriate for open networks.

LEADING ONESELF, LEADING WITH OTHERS LEADING COMMUNITY PROLEPTICALLY

No matter what specific leadership role an individual plays in a commons, leadership must begin with leading oneself. In actuality, all members of a commons are leaders as well as followers, especially when they lead with the intention of creating a commons-based society.

LEADING ONESELF THROUGH THE VALUES OF COMMONING

Commoners lead themselves with particular values through commoning. These include "we-ing," understanding that their identity is not individualistic but is relational; "caring" as the foundational value of their being and relating; "reverencing," as their stance vis-à-vis the world, nature, and others; "eco-synergizing" as living as part of nature, the world, and the cosmos, and not apart; "de-commodifying" themselves from the value of the market; and valuing autonomy and hence "self-provisioning" as a way of not having to depend upon others and not being at the mercy of others to provide their basic needs. Manifesting these values in commons (the meso level) and to the world (the macro level) accompanies and enriches the prefiguration of living in commons.

CRITICAL ABILITIES OF LEADING ONESELF

Self-leadership has become popular in the management literature in recent years. The concept of "leading oneself" as conceived by peace scholars Ebben van Zyl and Andrew Campbell (Van Zyl & Campbell, 2019; Campbell & Van Zyl, 2020) reflects the values and purpose of commons. These authors contended that leading oneself, or even self-transformation, is the first necessary step to achieving peace in the world, followed by leading with others and leading community. Instead of focusing on leading oneself for performance, the authors proposed leading oneself with emotional intelligence, wisdom, spirituality, morality, consciousness, and sense-making maturity. Leading for peace requires a mammoth social transformation just as does transforming to a commons-centric society. Hence it is an apt model to consider. Leading proleptically, thus, includes leading oneself, leading with others, and leading community and society.

Individuals need self-awareness, self-management, social awareness, and relationship management (Goleman, 2005) in order to be able to coordinate leadership roles and create synergies. Goleman (2006) argued that social intelligence is also critical. Based on the recognition that humankind is fundamentally social, social intelligence operates with the understanding that people "create" each other to a large extent and hence need to understand how to live and work harmoniously in community, understanding the impact they have on each other and how their emotional and cognitive bonds impact their behavior.

Contextual intelligence is also critical (Kellerman, 2012) since the cultural, social, political, and economic context in which the commons works impacts the approach the leaders take. Khanna (2014) defined contextual intelligence as "the ability to understand the limits of our knowledge and to adapt that knowledge to an environment different from the one in which it was developed" (para. 4). Commoners need to adjust their mental models when participating in commons, since many if not most of them were raised in the market system with clashing values and approaches. The process of commoning itself helps to change mental models by creating new subjectivities.

Closely related to emotional intelligence is spiritual intelligence, which Vaughn defined as "the ability to create meaning based on a deep understanding of existential questions and the awareness of and ability to use multiple levels of consciousness to solve problems" (quoted in Nullens, 2019). Blencowe (2016) contended that spirituality on the commons

> *is the movement of a soul beyond the boundaries of its own identity, the movement of perception beyond the perceptive capacities – the worlded realities – of the perceiver. It is the recognition of the existence of somethings radically other, the sure knowledge of unknowability. Spirituality decentres the self; it is calling to think, feel and act interestedness in others. (p. 186)*

Spirituality involves the continual search for meaning and is inextricably linked to ethical and moral behavior "with a focus on sustainability and credibility, rooted in self-knowledge and in the desire for growth and development" (Nullens, 2019, n.p.). The experience of transcendence "may help one to cope with difficulties and to experience higher feelings of purpose and meaning" (Castellon, 2019, p. 96).

Leading with spiritual intelligence requires continued spiritual practice. Nullens (2019) pointed out that the practice of Ignatian spirituality, for example, can help leaders become sensitive to interior movements or motions of the soul such as "desires, feelings, thoughts, imaginings, emotions, repulsions, and attractions" (n.p.) and thereby become more open and mindful leaders. Being spiritual

> *may also help one be more focused on human dignity....[and] can foster environmental awareness and pro-social behavior, possibly through a process of enhanced identification with the surrounding world and a strong feeling of interconnectedness. (Castellon, 2019, p. 97)*

Spiritual discernment is especially important in leading proleptically because the leader needs to discern glimpses of the future, needs to connect to the universal to the extent possible, and needs to be mindful of the four levels of the micro, meso, macro, and meta (Kok & van den Heuvel, 2019).

LEADING WITH OTHERS PROLEPTICALLY

The foundation of leading and following with others in a commons is a commoner's intent and ability to build relationships of care, trust, and authenticity and to "connect" with one's fellow commoners. Kathleen Curran's concept of global resonance is a useful model to employ to guide the building of such relationships (Curran, 2018). Global resonance is the mutual and subliminal non-cognitive connection between people that arises from: (1) sincere intent to connect with each other; (2) respecting, honoring, and caring for each other; and (3) expecting brilliance from each other. Global resonance creates "being" a leader, a state that reflects an emotional and even spiritual connection with others, rather than "doing" leadership.

Through global resonance, individuals develop connections in interests, values, and objectives. Global resonance is an inside-out approach to leadership derived from one's inner sense of self vis-à-vis the world and the desire to shift the "I-you" relationship to a "we" relationship. Such "we" relationships establish shared understanding and communal intelligence (Van Zyl & Campbell, 2019) and facilitate the co-creation of the commons as well as the co-creation of the transformation to a commons-centric society (Figs. 2 and 3).

Close relationships build trust which is important in commons. Trust building depends on one's ability, integrity, and benevolence (Jordaan, 2019). As Jordaan (2019) explained:

> Ability refers to an assessment of the other's knowledge, skill, or competency … as adequate…. Integrity is the degree to which we perceive that the other person adheres to principles and norms that are acceptable to us. Benevolence is our assessment that the other person is concerned enough about our welfare to either advance our interests, or at least not impede them. (n.p.)

As a "we" identity, commoners co-activate the communal values of commoning through self-organizing, self-governing, collaborating, sharing democratizing, localizing, and translocalizing, values and actions that manifested in the grounded theory of the commons. Commoners lead proleptically these values and actions as they would exist in a commons-centric society. Together, commoners build a commons and through commoning these values and actions, autopoiesis maintains and reproduces the commons and expands these values into the broader society, modeling a prefigurative society. The individual values of commoners discussed above co-evolve with these communal values and together they bridge to the societal macro level, influencing the social imaginary. Proleptic leaders incorporate aspects of transformational leadership by becoming a collective that inspires itself to participate in a significant societal change.

Communal intelligence and collective intelligence emerge from this close trustworthy relationship and comprise important abilities in proleptic leadership. Van Zyl (2019) defined communal intelligence as

> *a shared way of awareness, thinking, understanding and acting within a community in order to solve problems and carry out tasks for the well-being, welfare and benefit of the community as a whole and for its individual members. (p. 41)*

Collective intelligence or the shift from individual to community intelligence emerges from deep relationships and from communal tapping into the universal (meta) level of awareness (Dyer, 2020).

Collective, proleptic leadership includes enabling a rich and compelling vision of the future to come into being, as an early and necessary stage in allowing others to be drawn forward. Through a process of co-creation or, better, communal midwifery, leaders facilitate and help the vision from the future to be born in the present. In other words, leadership should not see itself as creating the future vision itself out of its own present resources. Rather, leadership involves the openness, seeking, debate, discussion, reflection, and meditation required to enable this future vision to come into view in the present. This slight change in key ensures that leaders are not dictating the future through their own goals and desires, but allowing a shared and common vision of the future to reveal itself. Enabling as rich and complex a future vision as possible to come into view is a powerful step in motivating and inspiring the commons to be pulled forward toward that future reality.

LEADING COMMUNITY AND SOCIETY

Commoners lead proleptically by visioning and then prototyping a way of living derived from a future somewhat utopian vision, a future which commoners are prefiguring and co-creating. Commoners are living purposefully, mindful that they are creating a society reflecting their values and that their commons will serve as an example to society writ large. Commoners also lead proleptically to help create a commons-based society by transforming the current society through protesting, prefiguring, languaging, federalizing the commons and lobbying government, and making deals with the market to support the commons way of life.

Leading at the macro societal level connects commoners with the overarching socioeconomic changes. Here commoners contribute to these changes, are impacted by them, and ideally help to ensure that the changes give rise to a society with the same values the commoners hold dear. Indeed, many commoners are providing open-access plans for building one's own home-based 3D printer, as well as open-access plans for building automobiles, farm equipment, homes, and many other products that consumers previously depended upon the market to produce. Other commoners are running businesses in which they produce products made by 3D printers and a many businesses run as commons that are contributing to the prosumer trend.

The steps of leading proleptically are illustrated in Fig. 2.

The values being manifested through proleptic leadership at the individual, communal, and societal levels are visualized in Fig. 3.

Fig. 2. Steps of Leading Proleptically.

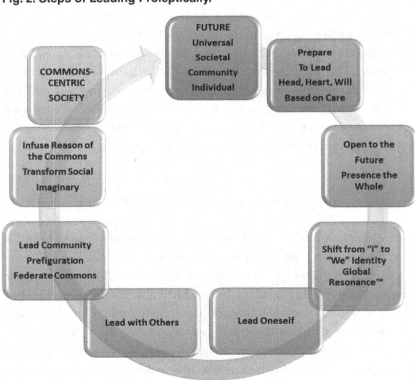

Fig. 3.   Values Manifested by Proleptic Leadership.

Future values
invading the
Present

WE-ing, caring, reverencing, eco-
synergizing, de-commodifying,
self-provisioning

Self-organizing, self-governing,
collaborating, sharing, democratizing,
localizing, translocalizing

Prefiguring, co-creating, protesting,
federalizing, languaging, dealing

Federating, infusing commons reason,
lobbying for supportive state, creating
new social imaginary

Commons centric
society

Future realized

CONCLUSION

As argued in this chapter, leading proleptically is leading with glimpses of the future that manifests all the best that the commons has to offer and leading mindfully of the impact that the four levels of human action have on one's leading as well as the impact that one's leading has on these four levels. Leading proleptically requires leading to manifest the values of a commons-centric society in the present. Leading proleptically also requires leading oneself, leading with others, and leading society with emotional, social, and spiritual intelligence, with close and resilient relationships, and with great hope and expectation that we can in fact create a world far more ethical, equitable, and just than the one we live in today.

NOTE

1. Sections of this chapter are adapted from my book *Proleptic Leadership on the Commons: Ushering in a New Global Order* (2020). Bingley: Emerald Publishing.

REFERENCES

Blencowe, C. (2016). The matter of spirituality and the commons. In S. Kirwan, L. Dawney, & J. Brigstoke (Eds.), *Space, power, and the commons: The struggle for alternative futures* (pp. 185–203). Routledge.

Campbell, A., & Van Zyl, E. (Eds.) (2020). *Chaos is a gift? Leading oneself in uncertain and complex environments*. K.R. Publishers.

Castellon, A. (2019). The role of wisdom and spirituality in leading self and others. In E. Van Zyl & A. Campbell (Eds.), *Peace leadership: Self-transformation to peace* (Chapter 5, pp. 87–102). K Publishing.

Curran, K. (2018). Global resonance. In R. J. Thompson & J. Storberg-Walker (Eds.), *Leadership and power in international development: Navigating the intersections of gender, culture, context, and sustainability* (pp. 311–329).

Dyer, D. (2020). *The return of collective intelligence: Ancient wisdom for a world out of balance*. Rchester, VT: Bear & Company Publishers.

Goleman, D. (2005). *Emotional intelligence: Why it can matter more than IQ*. Bantam Books.

Goleman, D. (2006). *Social intelligence: The revolutionary new science of human relationships*. Bantam Books.

Hamilton, C. (2020). *Integral enlightenment: Awakening to an evolutionary relationship to life*. Integral Institute Online Course.

Horlings, I. G. (2011). Value-oriented leadership in the Netherlands. Paper presented at RSA Annual Conference, Newcastle Upon Tyne, April 20.

Jantii, L. T. (2017). *Prolepticism: The futurist theology of Ted Peters*. Schriften der Luther-Agricola-Gesellschaft.

Jordaan, B. (2019). Leading organisations in turbulent times: Towards a different mental model. In J. Kok & van den Heuval (Eds.), *Leading in a VUCA world: Integrating leadership, discernment, and spirituality* (pp. 59–76). Springer Open Publishers.

Jaworski, J. (2011). *Synchronicity: The inner path of leadership*. Berrett-Koehler Publishers.

Jaworski, J. (2012). *Source: The inner path of knowledge creation*. Berrett-Koehler Publishers.

Kellerman, B. (2012). *The end of leadership*. Harper Collins Publishing.

Khanna, T. (2014). Contextual intelligence. *Harvard Business Review*, 92(9), 58–68.

Kok, J., & van den Heuvel, J. (2019). *Leading in a VUCA world: Integrating leadership, discernment, and spirituality (Kindle edition)*. Springer Open Publishers.

Nullens, P. (2019). From spirituality to responsible leadership: Ignatian self-discernment and theory-u. Chapter 11. In J. Kok & J. van den Heuvel (Eds.), *Leading in a VUCA world: Integrating leadership, discernment, and spirituality* (pp. 185–199). Springer Open Pubishers.

Pasquariello, R. D. (1976). Pannenberg's philosophical foundations. *The Journal of Religion*, 56(4), 338–347.

Por, G. (2012). School of commoning. In D. Bollier & S. Helfrich (Eds.), *The wealth of the commons: A world beyond market and state* (Part III, n.p.). Levellers Press.

Schwandt, D. R. (2008). Individual and collective coevolution: Leadership as emergent social structuring. In M. Uhl-Bien & R. Marion (Eds.), *Complexity leadership. Part I. Conceptual foundations* (pp. 101–128). Information Age Publishers.

Scharmer, O. (2016). *Theory U*. Berrett-Koehler Publishers.

Scharmer, O., & Kaufer, K. (2013). *Leading from the emerging future: From ego-system to ecosystem economies*. Berrett-Koehler Publishers.

Schuyler, K. G. (2012). *Inner peace global impact*. Information Age Publishing.

Schuyler, K. G. (2014). Introduction. In K. Schuyler, J. E. Baugher, & K. Jironet (Eds.), *Leading with spirit, presence, and authenticity* (pp. xiv–xxix). Jossey Bass.

Senge, P., Scharmer, C. O., Jaworski, J., & Flowers, B. S. (2004). *Presence: An exploration of profound change in people, organizations, and society*. Currency Doubleday.

Senge. P. (2015). What makes a good leader? [video] YouTube. https://www.youtube.com/watch?v=1aYaj2-GZqk

Trungpa, C. (2015). *Shambala: The sacred path of the warrior*. Shambala.

Turner, M. D. (2017). Political ecology III: The commons and commoning. *Progress in Human Geography*, 4(6), 795–802.

Van Zyl, E. (2019). A peace-leadership-in-action model: Self-transformation to the creation of peace. Chapter 3. In Van Zyl & A. Campbell (Eds.), *Peace leadership: Self transformation to peace* (pp. 49–64). K.R. Publishers.

Van Zyl, E., & Campbell, A. (Eds.). (2019). *Peace leadership: Self transformation to peace*. K.R. Publishers.

PART II

LEADERSHIP ON THE COMMONS
LIFECYCLE

8

DEVELOPING LEADERSHIP ON THE COMMONS: ANIMAL RESCUE

ROBIN BISHA

In this essay, I tell my story of leading the creation of a commons in animal rescue in my town. Through this recounting and analysis of my experiences, I reveal the process by which my care for animals developed into leadership for a town poised to adopt shared responsibility and collaboration in managing the relationship of the human community and unowned animals in the city. My reflections on this process show how an individual modeling a humane approach to unowned animals and advocating for shared responsibility can instigate change that creates a sustainable shared space for compassion and collaboration. This focus on narrative of experience coupled with analysis is called autoethnography. Autoethnography allows me to capture the experience of animal rescue work to study how one or a handful of community members adopting practices of the commons can invite other members of a community to commoning.

Autoethnography is an appropriate method for a study of leadership in animal rescue for several reasons. The work of animal rescue is not widely studied. I not only participate in animal rescue but also am a historian and journalist with experience in the use of qualitative methods for social research. I view my work in the animal rescue field as a text that reveals much about the thoughts, motivations, and actions of a leader in a local animal rescue movement. As such, I consider my narrative to be a sound source for the study of the process by which a person becomes a leader in this sphere and in the global commons movement.

The connection to the global commons movement occurred to me in the process of rescue work when I learned of wild ponies that have been held in common in villages in the United Kingdom since the Middle Ages. The historical model of the commons struck me in its similarity to what my fellow rescuers and I were doing. Commoning in the New Forest maintains the wild ponies and the land in common ownership and care while leaving them to roam the forest freely (Go New Forest, 2020). Animal rescue is a commons in the contemporary sense as well, including both humans and animals in its vision of sustainability, equity, and interdependence. This essay will discuss how core beliefs in interdependence with humans and animals and a desire for sustainable animal welfare practices in my community drew me into vocal leadership advocating better treatment for both animals and humans.

Unowned animals sharing urban spaces with humans are best managed from the perspective of shared responsibility, duty of care, and collaboration of public and private actors. In this, the animal rescue commons draws on the historical idea of the commons as well as the newer usage of the communal governance of a shared resource. Animals in rescue become a resource to care for and to distribute as pets, service animals, search and rescue workers, pest removers, and other jobs animals can do as well as or better than most humans. Adopters may or may not pay a fee for animals. A fee rarely covers the expense of veterinary care for animals that have been living on their own or in conditions of neglect. Animal rescue work itself provides opportunities for humans to deepen and exercise empathy and compassion.

Most sustainable strategies for managing populations of dogs rely on taking them out of public spaces and into care in shelters and homes. However, successful management of domestic cats that have returned to wild living bring humans and cats together in urban wild spaces, making these spaces safer for both cats and humans. Humans and animals in the community became partners in transforming public space from wastelands inhabited by neglected homeless animals, thereby enhancing both public and quasi-public (parking lots and vacant land, for example) spaces.

WORKING ALONE

Seguin, Texas, in 2002, was a small city that devoted few of its resources to the wellbeing of cats and dogs. When my cats and I moved to the town for me to take a teaching position at Texas Lutheran University, I saw scraggly stray dogs regularly and bedraggled cats congregated around dumpsters and parking lots. My heart broke every time I went into the commercial areas. My neighbor's dogs greeted their owner when he came home from work, but he ignored them. When one got hit by a car, he shot the dog rather than getting vet care. My heart broke a little more every day. I felt helpless to do anything and convinced that no one who had the power to change the situation cared. I could not ignore the dogs that strayed to my house or the cats that came looking for food.

Cats kept coming. First a big, gray Tom we called Gray Kitty. Then an old guy with an awful respiratory infection that we euthanized. Then a calico Manx made our yard her home. Then a pregnant feral cat had her babies at our house. The humane society didn't (and still doesn't) work with feral cats. Taking a cat to the city animal control was generally believed to be a death sentence. Someone suggested I call a woman named Barbara who could help. She told me to get the mom and babies spayed and neutered and put them back in my yard. We let Mama Kitty teach the two kittens who made it their cat skills and over the years taught the kittens they could trust us. And only us.

The path to leadership for me started by developing courage to step out on my own to address the needs of some individual animals (mostly cats but a few dogs). I accepted responsibility and the potential sacrifices that came with it. The town had allocated few resources to help those who cared for community animals. The Guadalupe County Humane Society, a nonprofit animal shelter, would take stray dogs if I got a vet exam and paid a surrender fee (Guadalupe County Humane Society, n.d.). When strays stayed around our house, we would take them there in spite of the expense. Pepito was an exception. While the neighbors claimed to be looking for his owners, there were no posters, and meanwhile the puppy spent most of his time in the street. When he came up on our porch, we took him in and found a home for him with a lovely family (where he still lives as I write).

Leading for animals on the commons requires one to act as if the care we are showing to cats, dogs, horses, and other animals, is just as important as our attention to human family and friends. Leading on behalf of animals requires humans to act as if animals deserve the regard and care we offer them, even when human society does not generally extend that regard to them. It demands that we embody our assertion of dignity and care for animals, sometimes by taking actions that might be considered extreme by people who don't share our mindset, for example, taking in a larger than average number of cats, remodeling a job to center on animal welfare, paying for veterinary services and food to help others keep their cats, gathering dozens of cats for vaccination and spay/neuter surgery. Sometimes, offering an animal that has suffered neglect or abuse love in the last days or moments of life and a humane death. These, and other similar actions, make an argument for a shared compassion.

CONNECTING WITH COLLABORATORS

I fed cats. I blogged about cats. I learned about managed community cat colonies. And then I asked a sobbing woman walking out of the vet clinic if I could help her. She told me her kitten had been taken and tortured. In an unusual turn of events, the police actually did manage to identify the abusers. One did some jail time while the other fled to Mexico because he did not have immigration papers (Maloney, 2010, 2011).

By this time, I had started a blog in the voice of another of my cats, a mostly feral guy who showed up alone at my house at about one month old. Online I met dozens of people who were active in animal rescue and welfare around the world. I wrote a post asking for donations to pay the kitten's vet bills and received money, toys, and other things a kitten would need. It turned out Barbara had started a nonprofit organization that was taking responsibility for the kitten's vet bills. I finally met her when I made the donation on behalf of my online community.

I was actively raising funds online for organizations around the world and meeting people who were doing great work with cats, dogs, and small pets around the world. But I still believed I couldn't make a difference locally beyond my own yard.

Meanwhile, a friend of mine opened a dog grooming and training boutique in the center of the town. The police opposed it and told her they would shut her down if dogs strayed from her shop. People gave her free advice that Seguin wasn't ready for humane training. She would never make it in business. Although I believed in my friend and her work with dogs, I lacked faith in the community. What I saw of the way people kept dogs in the city – let alone the rural county surrounding us – didn't give me hope she would find people for her positive reinforcement training classes. Thunderpaws Canine Solutions opened in 2006 and right away attracted local dog lovers (Thunderpaws Canine Solutions, LLC, n.d.) My friend immediately began fundraising for the humane society. She brought humor and showmanship to the events and made supporting dogs fun.

The city animal control department still had the reputation as a death trap for both dogs and cats. Stray animals still wandered the streets and parking lots. My heart still broke, and I still felt like I couldn't make a difference in my own town. I thought my dog trainer friend had special magic to be able to bring the best out in dog lovers in Seguin.

I met people who were rescuing dogs and working to hold the municipal animal control authorities accountable. (In the early 2000s, neither city nor county authorities publicized data on the fate of animals taken in by animal control. This is common across the country and is a stumbling block to the study of animal rescue. Later, when data were shared with rescuers, we discovered what we suspected: almost all dogs and cats taken in were put down. Now, data are more freely shared by local authorities and the collaboration between government agencies and animal rescue organizations ensures the vast majority of animals taken in are adopted or moved to rescue.) I became active in leading people by supporting these local efforts. Little by little, I revised my courses at TLU to include content and projects dealing with the relationship between humans and animals. The most notable of these projects for commoning is teaching positive reinforcement dog training in my leadership for social change course and engaging students with volunteer rescuers to support collaborative efforts in rescue.

Collaboration with others working in adjacent spaces led to collaborations with veterinarians and city authorities on behalf of unowned companion animals in general. As the local authorities began to trust animal rescuers, we invited broader participation from community members to the work. The move from a management model based on animal control – the approach codified in state law – to an adoption-based model was a voluntary turn on the part of public officials and police authorities initiated by engagement with community volunteers. In the developing collaborative space, I sought new avenues to help cats. I reevaluated what success would look like in care for community cats and learned that a person leading in the thick of things may not recognize that necessary changes are already taking place.

COLLABORATIONS

A handful of community members asserted that the needs of animals for food, water, and safety, at the very least, must be considered part of the wellbeing of the entire community. We pitched in to the work of finding and making suitable homes, mostly for dogs, even as many people in the community remained oblivious to the suffering of animals or actively promoted a mindset in which the animals were not considered to have value. In asserting a moral obligation to change the way we treat animals, we embodied a vision of a shared compassion as well as a shared responsibility.

Barbara started a campaign to harness the energy of the dog lovers that Thunderpaws had unleashed (so to speak!) to spread the kindness to more dogs. I found myself a bit player in a drama that resulted in the founding of a dog park administered by a nonprofit organization on land leased from the city.

With the momentum from the dog park, Barbara expanded into rescuing dogs from the city shelter and getting them adopted. She and a shifting cast of board members and volunteers of the Animal Rescue Foundation (ARF) started holding adoption events in the central square of the city (Animal Rescue Foundation, n.d.). A local B&B proprietor started a dachshund rescue in her inn. Other people worked with them and on their own to pull dogs from the city shelter and foster them till they found homes. Barbara picked up dogs at the shelter and took them to people she "knew" needed a dog, thus saving numerous dogs' lives.

When I decided to include positive reinforcement dog training as a component of my annual leadership course at Texas Lutheran University, I learned how to train from Thunderpaws with a rescue dachshund named Tiko. My students and I went to the B&B for training classes. Later, we went to a location that allowed us to train with dogs from more than one rescue and added in dogs from ARF. My students volunteered at adoption events. I did the groundwork on campus for a friendly dog visit at the end of each semester. Community members responded by bringing their dogs twice a year to play with TLU students.

By this point in my leadership story, I had come to believe that I had a little of the magic I recognized in my dog trainer friend. I believed that a handful of individuals could lead a whole community in a new direction. I was both leading and following.

While I saw fewer dogs living at large and better outcomes for shelter dogs, I still felt hopeless that we could make changes for cats when I still seemed to be the only one in town who cared enough about cats who were not my pets to work on their behalf. I kept trying to find ways to change what I saw as an impossible situation.

Some people started to believe that cats should be treated well, but they either couldn't or didn't want to do the work themselves. The B&B dog rescuer took in a pregnant cat but couldn't care for her because of the number of dogs in the facility and her allergy to cats. The cat had her babies in an antiques auction warehouse. After the kittens were old enough to be weaned, one of my neighbors agreed to let them live with her while I cared for them and looked for homes. I did flea baths and combing daily, feeding, cleaning for the five kittens. Three went to the Humane Society and two stayed with the temporary foster (still temporarily, it turned out).

I continued to support cat welfare and rescue efforts through my social media community. I was thrilled to be invited to join the board of ARF to bring in a focus on work with cats. I hoped to activate advocacy for cats in Seguin. Barbara, the ARF president, suggested I write a letter to the editor informing the community that ARF was able to assist people who were trying to care for cats who were not theirs.

I was overwhelmed with phone calls! Most of the people wanted me to take the cats away from their property, although almost no one wanted assistance to spay or neuter and vaccinate the cat before they were returned to their yards or farms. The humane society still didn't take in feral cats or kittens. The small room for cats at Animal Services was always full. Few people fostered cats. Cat adoption was daunting, given that local adoption events were all about dogs.

I spearheaded a community trap, spay/neuter, vaccinate event. We sterilized 27 cats. I was joined by Barbara, a retired veterinarian and a cat lover who let us use her garage for a recovery room for cats who were going to be returned to colony caregivers after they recovered from sedation.

REACTION

The story of my work shows that timing is vital in the creation of a mindset for work on a common. Patience is of utmost importance, as the work may be taking hold underneath a loud reaction. When we ask a community to take on a common responsibility, we must expect resistance. We are lucky if anyone wants to share the burdens with us. We must forge on in spite of the feeling that we are alone in a wasteland. I watched those I served with in the rescue movement in Seguin practice what Christiana Figueres, Executive

Secretary of the United Nations Framework Convention on Climate Change from 2010 to 2016, and Rivett-Carnac (2020) call stubborn optimism. What felt like hopeless despair was really the beginning of my willingness to forge ahead toward a goal that seemed impossible to reach.

I was vilified in the letters to the editor and comments on the online article reporting on the community cat spay/neuter event (There are better answers, 2012). One letter writer wrote in great detail how I was breaking state animal cruelty law by "abandoning" sterilized cats although all the cats went back to properties they had permission to live on with people who fed them daily (Cat plan irresponsible, 2012). A commenter on my blog stated that he would leave dead cats on my porch until I stopped advocating for feral cats (Bisha, 2009–2018). The next year, I donated $400 for the spay/neuter event. That year we gave vouchers to low-income seniors to visit the veterinarian.

I resigned from the board of ARF because I couldn't manage the dog rescue responsibilities and spearhead cat-related projects. The vitriol eventually dissipated. ARF kept trying to help cats, even including them in foster and adoption programs until it became apparent that this was not getting cats adopted in Seguin. The community didn't see cats living at large as a resource that needed attention. How to get cats adopted has been an item of concern nationally, so much so that Betsy Saul, the founder of Petfinder.com said in 2012 that the rescue community had completely failed cats (Saul, 2012).

Cats kept showing up at my house. I kept getting them spayed and neutered. Occasionally, I found people to adopt them. I participated in a nationwide network of volunteers to transport cats to distant adopters. I provided rescue to a family of kittens that couldn't find a shelter on the East Coast and their rescuer couldn't keep them. (Yes, the family still lives with me.)

DOGS OWN OUR COMMONS

I participated in a citizen effort to get the city to build a new building for the animal services department. Spoke in council meetings. Rejoiced when the city hired an adoption-oriented deputy chief of police to spearhead the planning and construction of a new shelter. Rejoiced even more when the city council voted to appropriate $4 million for a state-of-the-art shelter that opened in 2017 (McCormack, 2017). Signed up as a volunteer in the new shelter volunteer program and sent my students to do volunteer service at *the shelter. The staff are adoption-focused and collaborate with volunteer rescues. They cooperate with shelters and rescues in other towns to get animals (dogs and cats) to the place where they are most likely to get adopted into a home.*

We made amazing changes in the way people view unowned dogs in Seguin: they act together to care for lost dogs, help animal services staff find owners of lost dogs. People now trust city animal services as a partner in dog welfare and adoption. They take in a dog, post a picture on social media, network to find dogs homes, support ordinances that raise the bar for dog welfare. It started with an active dog trainer and a citizen-led effort to build a dog park. It's cool to rescue a dog. It's cool to adopt. Dogs found at large are considered a resource for adoption into families.

Fifteen years of advocacy have established that dogs are the responsibility of the community. During those years, an informal group of volunteer leaders in animal advocacy forged ahead with little or no support from the local population or the elected and appointed leaders of the town and county. Sometimes, we faced active interference from public officials.

Seguin now buzzes with dog rescue activity, with at least four volunteer dog rescues and a well-run city animal services department that collaborates with private rescues and involves volunteers. Acceptance of a shared duty to care for the animals and understanding that collaboration is necessary to safeguard them are important elements of leadership on this commons. Leadership here includes redefining the space from one of animal control – essentially a view of unowned animals as disposable – to a common sphere of care for and adoption of animals into the guardianship of specific humans. The duty of care in the animal rescue commons extends beyond the legal ownership. Reputable rescuers and rescue organizations pledge to support animals if their care becomes a burden for their legal owners. Rescuers regularly safeguard and care for animals that have become evidence in criminal cases. Management of colonies of community cats requires commitment to feed and provide veterinary care throughout their lives.

Seguin is not the only town in the United States to move toward a model of common responsibility for animal welfare in this period. From the time I moved to Seguin in 2002 to the present, more and more people adopt dogs from shelters or rescues and proudly announce that they rescued their dog. Similar efforts nationally are taking place with livestock, primarily equines, and cats.

CAT COMMONING IN THE SHADOWS

Dogs are now treated as a common resource, but I thought I had failed to move the lever much from a view that cats are vermin. The flow of cats from a couple of places around my house in Seguin was never ending. New cats needed help every year. Neither volunteers nor animal services staff were able to persuade some of my neighbors to spay and neuter their cats.

Finally, I moved out of Seguin to five acres in the country. When I left with my animal family, I felt like we had created a more compassionate, humane, and collaboratively managed space for dogs in the city, but that I had failed to make much of a change for cats.

Personally, I had gained in confidence and hope. I could lead a community to embrace its shared responsibility for the creatures that live within it (as long as they were dogs). Yet, I was exhausted. I wanted to disengage from advocacy for cats in Seguin. My efforts did not seem to be leading the community in general to view the cats with compassion or feel a responsibility to care for them.

I thought I had failed, but in fact, my ideas were taking hold and had become appealing to other members of the community. At the time I moved to the country, I was thinking the measure of my leadership toward humane and collaborative management of cats in the community was in counts of the percentage of cats that had been neutered and a detectable leveling of the cat population. I had not achieved this concrete outcome for cats, but unbeknownst to me at the time, I had planted the seeds for others to follow my example.

Something had changed in Seguin following our efforts to spay and neuter community cats, and maybe even because of the negative attention the project received in the local press. I heard a hint a few years ago that at least the diatribes in the press got people thinking. A colleague's "good ole boy" neighbor saw a cat in his yard and said, "Maybe that girl who wants to help them is right." A prominent local attorney undertook to spay/neuter, vaccinate and return the cats who hung around her office.

I have started to see evidence that more people are taking up responsibility for cats. This summer a former neighbor asked for my advice and moral support as she trapped a family of cats in her yard for vaccination and sterilization before coming home to live in her yard. An acquaintance started feeding cats at a couple of sites in town. She messages me for advice. People in the park greet her and thank her for her care for the local cats.

She encounters helpful groundspeople where I saw cats removed and disposed of. She recently reported that she and a small group of collaborators have official approval to care for cats on the university campus.

I may have decided prematurely that I was fighting a battle I couldn't win. I suspect that stepping away actually amounted to an act of leadership. Without me to either upset people or act as a lightning rod on cat issues, the cat rescue commons has actually expanded. Looking back, I see evidence in my own story that stepping into leadership takes a long time. Why would my potential allies not have needed time to make the choice to go against the community's grain? A funny thing is, the "grain" had actually changed direction under the surface.

People who care for colonies of community cats (in cat welfare work there's a strict distinction between those cats that are truly feral and those that are friendly to humans) try to fly under the radar. There's good reason for this. The neighboring community of New Braunfels has had a number of cases of large fines and other legal action taken against people who feed community cats (Jones, 2006). A person attempting to treat community cats as a community responsibility, a resource of the commons, was punished for acting on the idea. Many states and towns have laws that criminalize caring for community cats (Alley Cat Rescue, n.d.). Seguin has an ordinance limiting the number of cats per household to four, thus, when I cared for the cats of my neighborhood, I violated that ordinance. Animal Services could have confiscated the cats if a neighbor chose to complain.

ENCOURAGING OTHERS

I look for moments in leadership class when students look at a dog they will never own and feel the deliciousness of caring for animals that do not belong to them. It feels a bit like falling in love. Maybe it is falling in love. Love that doesn't possess, but that nurtures all beings toward a life that fulfills their potential.

Love is necessary to commoning. In the case of animal rescue, commoning involves working in the wasteland where no one seems to care. A leader sacrifices a sense that the community is whole and well. An animal rescuer working alone or with only a few compatriots can be exhausted by doing the work of animal care and advocacy. This can mean sacrifice of physical and mental health. Yet, the rescuer keeps on loving and caring for the animals.

Only when the work of rescue becomes valuable to the community as a way to fill human needs, and the animals gain value as pets and therapy or service animals, does the rescuer begin to feel the community come into balance. Before the scales tip toward the commons, love and stubborn optimism keep rescuers going.

David Bollier said something similar in a 2014 interview about his book *Think Like A Commoner*:

> *It's partly about recovering our humanity. Simply put, the market culture – in which we assume the role of selfish, utility-maximizing individuals – is incredibly alienating and makes us unhappy. It also has some profoundly harmful consequences for the planet and our social lives and democracy.*
>
> *We need to relearn and reeducate ourselves about what it means to be in relationship to one another and to the world. The commons helps us do that – while providing a framework for new policy and technology that will enable those essential social relationships to flourish again. (P2P Foundation, 2014)*

In the case of animal rescue, we begin to see the flourishing of nature and human society in healthy animals living among the humans in our communities. This is particularly true in the work of caring for community cats. Animal welfare workers, both professional and volunteer, are finding that a particularly fruitful path to managing the welfare of domestic cats that have become wild in our towns and cities is to trap them, see to their health issues, vaccinate them, and neuter them before returning them to their wild homes. This serves the cats well because it returns them to the place where they are comfortable. Successful cohabitation of urban humans and wild kitties requires continuing management of cat colonies to maintain health, neuter newcomers, remove and socialize friendly cats and kittens from colonies, and ensure the animals are monitored and fed daily. This work is best accomplished by volunteers sharing the care in partnership with property owners and managers who view cats as an asset, either for the emotional wellbeing of people who visit the cats' home or because cats help control rodents, reptiles, and insects. This is now taking place in Seguin. The university facility managers, for example, have given their blessing to community groups to feed and care for campus cats (they wouldn't even talk to the group I worked with earlier about establishing a presence in cat care on campus).

CONCLUSIONS

Commoning in animal rescue requires a community to abandon an animal control approach centered on municipal government and embrace collaboration and redefinition of unowned animals. My actions in support of community cats remaining in place under community care directly challenged that paradigm, eliciting fear and anger. As a leader at the center of the storm I was unable to help opponents of a new approach find an accommodation with it. It is likely that long-held and strong beliefs will be tied to any nascent commons. Leaders need to be ready to both cope with vitriol directed at them and to develop strategies to facilitate community conversations on the heated issues.

To see beyond the idea that either there is no solution for a problem or that the solution must be found by government professionals, community members are likely to be inspired to take action by watching a neighbor. My experience in Seguin shows that the contours of a nascent commons are not always visible. Leaders may think they have done little, but other people in the community have been watching their example. Modeling commoning can provide the path out of the wasteland to sustainable collaboration based on shared responsibility.

In the case of animal rescue, the challenge of managing all the unowned animals in a community in the U.S. South is too large for a small government department to handle well. The animals of the community cannot be cared for without community participation. When government workers can accept the collaboration of community members acting on their commitment, they do not have to resort to killing large numbers of healthy dogs and cats to perform the animal control functions. When public servants and community members work together to manage dog and cat population growth, care for neglected animals, move adoptable animals from towns that cannot handle the numbers to other towns that want more potential pets, the animals are no longer costly burdens, but a resource for the flourishment of the community. Humans are well served by the opportunity to engage their hearts through witnessing the struggles of unowned animals, to act on their compassionate impulses, to care for animals, and to adopt pets.

REFERENCES

Alley Cat Rescue. (n.d.). "Feral Cats and the Law." Retrieved from http://www.saveacat.org/feral-cats-and-the-law.html

Animal Rescue Foundation. (n.d.). Retrieved from http://arf-texas.org/

Bisha, R. (2009–2018). "Cheshire Loves Karma." Retrieved from http://cheshire-loveskarma.wordpress.com

Cat plan irresponsible. (2012). Seguin Gazette-Enterprise, The (TX), sec. Letters To Editor, 30 October 2012. *NewsBank: America's News*. Retrieved from infoweb.newsbank.com/apps/news/document-view?p=NewsBank&docref=news/142414BDF2972FE8

Figueres, C., & Rivett-Carnac, T. (2020). The future we choose: Surviving the climate crisis. Alfred A. Knopf.

Go New Forest. (2020). "Commoning." Retrieved from https://www.thenewforest.co.uk/explore/new-forest-heritage/commoning

Guadalupe County Humane Society. (n.d.). Retrieved from https://www.gchshumane.com/. Accessed on August 30, 2020.

Jones, L. (2006). "No purr-fect solution." New Braunfels Herald-Zeitung (TX), sec. News, 14 September2006. *NewsBank: America's News*. Retrieved from infoweb.newsbank.com/apps/news/document-view?p=NewsBank&docref=news/126DB68FCE0F3670

Maloney, R. (2010). "1 jailed, 1 wanted in cat mutilation," *The Seguin Gazette*, September 24. Retrieved from http://seguingazette.com/news/article_c4abd1bc-61f6-5bee-91e4-1e91ecda10f7.html

Maloney, R. (2011). "Two indicted in cat torture case," *The Seguin Gazette*, January 21. Retrieved from http://seguingazette.com/news/article_6fde77a6-24ec-11e0-85ae-001cc4c03286.html. Accessed on August 30, 2020.

McCormack, Z. (2017). Seguin preparing to open 'top of the line' animal shelter. *San Antonio Express News*, June 21. Retrieved from https://www.expressnews.com/news/local/article/Seguin-preparing-to-open-top-of-the-line-11236749.php

P2P Foundation. (2014). *Think Like a Commoner*. Retrieved from https://wiki.p2pfoundation.net/Think_Like_a_Commoner

Saul, B. (2012). Blogpaws 2012. Retrieved from https://www.slideshare.net/BlogPaws/betsy-saul-keynote-top-issues-for-pet-bloggers

Seguin, Texas. Code of ordinances, sec. 14-54. Retrieved from https://library.municode.com/tx/seguin/codes/code_of_ordinances?nodeId=PTIICOOR_CH14AN_ARTIIIDOCA_DIV1GE_S14-54MANU

There are better answers. (2012). Seguin Gazette-Enterprise, The (TX), sec. Letters To Editor, 30 October2012. *America's News*. Retrieved from infoweb.newsbank.com/apps/news/document-view?p=NewsBank&docref=news/142414BDF2972FE8

Thunderpaws Canine Solutions, LLC, (n.d.). Retrieved from http://thunderpaws-dogs.com/

Time to drop no-feeding-stray-cats ordinance. (2013). *New Braunfels Herald-Zeitung (TX)*, sec. Opinion, 6 March2013. *America's News*. Retrieved from infoweb.newsbank.com/apps/news/document-view?p=NewsBank&docref=news/144DF6C8D46CD220

9

CONVENING LEADERSHIP ON THE COMMONS: INITIATING STAKEHOLDER NETWORKS TO SOLVE COMPLEX GLOBAL ISSUES

PATRICIA A. CLARY

Globalization has made it obvious that most of the issues facing the world are "complex, interacting systems of problems that affect multiple parts of a social or ecological system...[and whose] impacts are not localized or linear" (Svendsen & Laberge, 2005, p. 93). Uncertainty regarding their root causes and solutions compound the complexity of such issues, while their interconnectedness to many countries, organizations, institutions, and other issues makes it clear that they can only be solved by collaboration between countries and the many stakeholders that work at the different levels of society within these countries. Furthermore, some of these issues, such as climate change, sustainability, and hunger are being tackled largely by local commons who are addressing these issues outside of the state and the private sector. To have a global impact, however, these local commons need to collaborate and negotiate with organizations and institutions within both the state and private sector, as well as with international organizations such as the United Nations who are tackling such problems through their Sustainability Development Goals (Thompson, 2020). As Nobel Peace Prize Winner Elinor Ostrom and her colleagues J. Burger, C. B. Field, R. B. Norgaard, and D. Policansky (1999) contended,

> *Although the number and importance of commons problems at*
> *local or regional scales will not decrease, the need for effective*
> *approaches to commons problems that are global in scale will*
> *certainly increase. (p. 278)*

Moreover, in an article in Science (2003), Dietz, Ostrom, and Stern argued that flexible and adaptive management between a multitude of stakeholders was required to effectively cope with such complex global challenges.

Although adaptive management may be the most effective approach to managing such challenges, a particular kind of leadership is required in order to bring stakeholders together to develop adaptive management systems. The commons literature is silent about such leadership. I argue that "convening leadership" is the leadership required to bring multiple stakeholders to the table to develop a stakeholder network, solutions, and systems that can effectively manage these challenges adaptively. In this chapter, I introduce the concept of convening leadership and "the convenor" and illustrate how such a leader can initiate the type of collaboration required to solve global issues, especially those heretofore addressed locally by commons. The knowledge and abilities such a leader needs to possess to convene stakeholders to address governance issues on the commons will also be elaborated.

THE CONVENOR

As defined by the collaborative leadership network (Colburn, n.d.), a convenor is:

> *an individual or group responsible for bringing people together to*
> *address an issue, problem, or opportunity. In the context of collabo-*
> *rative leadership, it usually involves convening representatives from*
> *multiple sectors for a multi-meeting process, typically on complex*
> *issues. A convenor, or group of convenors working together, might*
> *invite public officials, business professionals, or leaders of commu-*
> *nity or nonprofit organizations to participate. Convenors use their*
> *influence and authority to call people together to collaborate.*

According to Svendsen and Laberge (2005), convenors help build interdependent relationships to create a "stakeholders' network," which they define "as a web of groups, organizations and/or individuals who come together to address a complex and shared cross-boundary problem, issue or opportunity" (p. 92). The role of the convenor, then is "to help [this] multi-stakeholder network tap its latent energy, resources and intelligence to generate novel solutions and whole-system innovations that no one member could achieve on their own" (Svendsen & Laberge, 2005, p. 92).

Several other authors highlighted the importance of the convenor in various contexts. Clark, Lowitt, Levkoe, and Andree (2020), in their study of organizations involved in food movements, argued that successes in governance processes are related to the "power to convene, a process-oriented approach that increases movements capacity to mobilize; leverage different types of power; and integrate, coordinate, and build a systems-oriented vision" (p. 1). In an editorial in *The American Journal of Public Health,* Erwin (2020) called on the National Academy of Medicine to "convene" a new future of public health (p. 1161). Mair and Hehenberger (2014) studied frontstage and backstage convening in organizational philanthropy.

The word "convene" originated in the fifteenth century as a derivative of the Latin word *convenire,* meaning come (e.g., *venire*) together (e.g., *con*). As a verb without an object, convene means to come together or assemble, usually for some public purpose. To convene as a verb used with an object means to cause to assemble or convoke. Words synonymous with the act of convening are to assemble, gather, congregate, meet, muster, unite, draw together, or come together (March & March, 1902, 1958, 1968). A significant role for the convenor is to cause to assemble. In that space, a second consideration of importance is their leadership style. Ansell and Gash (2012) stated that a convenor should "adopt a contingency approach to convening, recognizing there is no best way [to convene], rather the process is situational (p. 3)."

Convening

Dorado (2005) distinguished the process of convening from leverage and accumulation as a form of agency employed in creating new institutional arrangements. Convening, according to Dorado (2005) describes institutional change that begins with the creation of collaborative arrangements that may be necessary to generate change in problem domains, which are "organizational fields defined by problems too many-sided and complex for any one single individual or organization to handle" (p. 391). Convening is more likely to be practiced when a potential convenor perceives that change is required but the solution is not known. This is certainly true in the case of the most pressing global issues that involve the commons.

Convening derives from scholarship that focused on how to organize to solve complex social problems. Scholars such as Emery and Trist (1965) and Trist (1983) conceived of convening as necessary to establish cooperative interorganizational links to "jumpstart a process of change" by convincing stakeholders to collaborate. Convenors are, to a large extent, catalytic agents who help create bridges between actors to explore cooperation. According to Dorado (2005), the effectiveness of convenors depends on: "(1) the credibility they have among the parties involved, (2) their familiarity with the problem being addressed, and (3) their position as a balanced or unbiased party" (p. 391).

Convenors Way of Thinking, Being, and Acting

Convenors build stakeholder networks and hence think in terms of systems rather than in uni-directional relationships. Networks are systems of inter-relationships where the totality of these relationships creates something bigger than the parts. All the stakeholders in such a network understand that they are interdependent with each other, that they belong to a larger system, and that they have a distinctive relationship to nature and the environment. Stakeholders need to develop trustworthy and respectful relationships with each other to effectively collaborate and find solutions to complex problems that are beneficial to everyone in the network rather than the most powerful or wealthiest. As Svendsen and Laberge (2005) pointed out:

> Network convenors know that trust and mutual understanding are necessary for members to take action together. Creating opportunities for learning about the history and points of view of other members, developing shared language, vocabulary, interpretations, and mental models are all important aspects of building networks. (p. 97)

On occasion a convenor arises out of pressure exerted by other stakeholders in a complex system. Such was the case that compelled the logging company in British Colombia, McMillan Bloedel to become a convenor of stakeholders called the Solutions Group, consisting of the company, local environmental groups, Green Peace, and home supply chain companies. A massive protest consisting of Clayoquot Sound Peace Camp, blockades of logging companies, and agreements with home supply chain companies to boycott wood from McMillan Bloedel had forced the logging company to change its approach to logging and to form a network of stakeholders who could find solutions to logging that were environmentally sound (Svendsen & Laberge, 2005). The company switched from a war-metaphor to one of an eco-system in which collective intelligence was generated to collaborate to produce solutions beneficial to the entire network.

Svendsen and Laberge (2005) characterized the identity of convenors as "warriors" and "midwives." Warriors are dedicated and courageous and are trained to protect their groups. They have the courage "to openly enquire into the deeper systemic forces and pressures behind an issue and to take a stand for a systems approach to change" (p. 99). Convenors, in this sense, work hard to maintain the stakeholder network they catalyzed and to help ensure that it endures. As midwives, they help "birth" the network and continue to hold stakeholders accountable to maintain relationships and meet regularly to pursue their joint solution. Midwives "see power as a boundless force that springs up between people when they act together" (p. 99). In a sense, Nike served as a midwife in convening a multilateral stakeholder network to form the nongovernmental organization Organic Cotton Exchange after they made a commitment to use organic cotton in their products. The global organic cotton production was inadequate for the level of production required and the stakeholder network had to seek ways to expand the production and the market for organic cotton.

Convening a network is a co-creative process comprising three steps: outreach, collective learning, and joint action-innovation (Svendsen & Laberge, 2005). Outreach typically requires that the convenor is capable of framing an issue and determining that a complex issue requires a stakeholder network in order to solve; can identify who the key stakeholders are; has the ability to convince them to join a network to maximize the benefit of the entire network; can help them define the goals of the network, facilitate their discussion to share background information, articulate and agree on guiding principles and network norms, establish effective communication, and clarify roles and responsibilities (Svendsen & Laberge, 2005).

The stakeholder group is involved in a collective learning process as together they explore the challenge by sharing and developing knowledge and exploring the system within which the challenge exists; define different solution scenarios; construct shared meanings; and clarify their different perspectives and interests (Svendsen & Laberge, 2005). The convenor facilitates this process. From outreach and collective learning, the network crafts a shared solution and joint action.

Convenors Come from All Sectors

In both the Nike and McMillan Bloedel cases mentioned above, private companies were virtually forced to become convenors because of the pressure exerted on them by environmental groups fighting for a more sustainable environment and less toxic products for human use. Many of these environmental groups are commons in the sense that they are self-organized, self-governed organizations working outside the state and the private sector.

In another case, *Mere et Enfant* a local nongovernmental organization working in Palestine to improve child nutrition served as a convenor. After initially identifying academia as a key stakeholder, they approached the government and several other nongovernmental organizations, and collaboratively they developed a strategy to solve the problem. As Dorado (2005) pointed out, the socio-political framework in Gaza and the West Bank

> *created an environment too uncertain for any single organization to establish means-ends connections. The problem of child malnutrition, then, could not be solved strategically by any one single organization. Convening – establishing connections with other organizations to frame and make sense of the situation – was, if not the only, the most likely way to produce a solution to this problem. (p. 408)*

CONVENING ON THE COMMONS

Ostrom (1990) developed principles for effectively governing commons which are designed especially for common-pool resources (CPRs), that is, natural and human resources which are difficult if not impossible to keep people from accessing them. Her governance principles, based on scores of studies of commons around the world, include the following: (1) boundaries of users and resource are clear; (2) congruence exists between benefits and costs; (3) users have procedures for making their own rules; (4) regular monitoring of users and resource conditions occurs; (5) graduated sanctions for members who abuse the rules are defined and implemented; (6) effective conflict resolution mechanisms are practiced; (7) there is at least minimal recognition of the commoners rights by government; and (8) commons are governed in nested or polycentric enterprises consisting of outside stakeholders.

Ostrom designed her principles to facilitate collective action and cooperation. Cooperation, building trust and social capital, and continuous communication overcome "the tragedy of the commons" without privatization or government intervention, Ostrom claimed (1990). Ostrom's research also focused on how the above eight principles helped to form stronger communities and how then such communities strengthened the governance of the commons. Ostrom also focused on the design of institutions that would pressure firms to more effectively ensure environmental sustainability. The example discussed previously of the logging company being pressured to more sustainably log is an example of how such pressure yields positive results. Furthermore, Ostrom and her colleagues extended the eight principles into a model of complex socio-ecological systems which illustrate the complexity of systems that need to find a common ground and work toward an agreed upon objective in order to effectively govern CPRs.

As cited by Albareda and Sison (2020), commons organizing underscores the need to support communities of people working together at the lowest possible level to deal with societal challenges, exploring the principle of subsidiarity in novel ways (Sison & Fontrodona, 2012). These initiatives also connect to larger networks that are able to mutually interact without any central authority and maintain their autonomy while searching for broad common goals and instilling shared organizing principles that is polycentricity (Aligica & Tarko, 2013).

Although Ostrom and other commons scholars have successfully focused on defining governance principles, they have not discussed the catalytic process necessary to initiate governance nor the need for leadership. In fact, leadership is rarely discussed in the commons literature. There is little mention of how the challenges of forming an effective stakeholder group could be met. As Sugden, Ash, Hanson, and Smith (2003) pointed out,

disparities in the perceptions, knowledge, and beliefs of different
stakeholders present barriers to effective communication between
stakeholders in the management of common-pool resources, and
that recognition of this problem by all protagonists is an important
step on the road to policy-making. (p. 1906)

Consequently, in order for a commons to govern resources on a local or global level, a leader is required who can discern that a governance challenge is sufficiently complex and that a solution is not readily apparent, and that therefore a network of stakeholders from a variety of organizations is necessary to collaborate on a solution. Furthermore, a leader is required who can help build the trust and positive communication between these organizations required for effective collaboration. That leader needs to be skilled in identifying the necessary stakeholders and in convincing them to collaborate and in helping the stakeholder network maintain the process of governance. A convenor is the leader required in order to fulfill this function.

A convenor needs to be able to identify stakeholders for local or global level commons and a convenor needs to be savvy enough to determine which stakeholders are key to the success of the commons and convince them to form a collaborative network. Stakeholders may come from governmental entities; partnerships; funders; nongovernment organizations; community-based organizations; social enterprise organizations; community members; researchers; educational institutions; political parties; informal influencers; external influencers; supply chain organizations; lobbyists; global communities – like the United Nations; media outlets/social media; collaborations; venture capitalists; political parties, or other groups. The success of a commons often depends on selecting the most influential and committed stakeholders who will agree to collaborate to ensure that the resources are effectively and efficiently governed at all levels. Stakeholders need to believe in the concept of the commons, namely that communities have the right to govern their resources themselves, outside of the control of the state or private sector. A convenor is a key in helping stakeholders understand the need for self-organized and self-governed commons and why building a collaborative network will result in benefits to all.

Adaptive Management

Because each resource exists within a unique system with particular characteristics, adaptive management is required in order to develop the principles and governance practices appropriate to specific commons challenges. Furthermore, the governance system needs to be responsive and flexible enough to adapt to changes in the environment and within the stakeholder community. Again, the role of the convenor is highlighted as the leader who can help signal the need for adaptation and help stakeholders make the necessary changes to continue on their path to a joint solution.

Convenors need to be sensitive to changes in the external and internal environment in order to signal to the stakeholder group that adaptation is required. Convenors need to monitor factors such as the motivating force of invisible leadership (Hickman & Sorenson, 2013), risks, system design, operationalization, holding environments, and other adaptive management considerations that may impact the governing arrangements and rules.

Moreover, as social demand for trusted governance of shared resources is growing (Frischmann et al., 2019) convenors should also understand how aggregated information is important in identifying problems and developing solutions (Dietz, Ostom, & Stern, 2003), there are no assurances that repetitiveness in processes will work one year to the next (Berge & van Laerhoven, 2011), and that problem solving is integrated into adaptive management processes (Miles, 2013), where adaptive management is a process for learning through experimentation (Walters, 1997).

Challenges Typically Encountered in Governing Commons

In a Science's Compass Review, *Revisiting the Commons: Local Lessons, Global Challenges* by Ostrom and colleagues J. Burger, C. B. Field, R. B. Norgaard, and D. Policansky (1999), identified five challenges in governing CPRs on the commons:

1. *Scaling Up*. Scaling up refers to the increased difficulty of organizing and agreeing on governance principles as the number of stakeholders increases. Certainly, as resource governance challenges extend from the local to the global level, it will be necessary to include more and more stakeholders. Convenors will necessarily have to learn how to facilitate collaboration of larger stakeholder networks.

2. *Cultural Diversity Challenge*. Even local commons include stakeholder networks with different cultural beliefs and practices. As commons

governance is scaled up to deal with global challenges, the magnitude of cultural diversity will increase. As Ostrom, Burger, Field, Norgaard, and Policansky (1999) contended, 'cultural diversity can decrease the likelihood of finding shared interests and understandings. The problem of cultural diversity is exacerbated by "north-south" conflicts stemming from economic differences between industrialized and less-industrialized countries' (p. 281). Convenors will need to develop a keen understanding of cultural differences, develop a global mindset, and be able to facilitate collaboration by highlighting diversity as a positive trait.

3. *Complications of Interlinked CPRs.* The linkages between systems at the local level create complexity that needs to be understood in order to craft workable solutions. As the challenges become increasingly global, the complexity between interdependent systems will become even greater, complicating the collaborative process. Ostrom et al. (1999) warned that: 'As we address global issues, we face greater interactions between global systems. Similarly, with increased specialization, people have become more interdependent. Thus, we all share one another's common interests, but in more complex ways than the users of a forest or grassland. While we have become more complexly interrelated, we have also become more "distant" from each other and our environmental problems. From our increasingly specialized understandings and particular points on the globe, it is difficult to comprehend the significance of global CPRs and how we need to work together to govern these resources successfully. And given these complexities, finding fair solutions is even more challenging' (p. 281). Convenors will want to understand how the beliefs, values, and attitudes of all stakeholder's factor into the operationalization of commons governance.

4. *Accelerating Rates of Change.* The rapid rate of technological change and changes in the political, social, and environmental factors means that tried-and-true solutions are rarely applicable to commons governance. Hence, a convenor needs to facilitate a creative co-learning and co-creating environment to assist the stakeholders to think outside of the box and derive a new approach to a major challenge.

5. *Requirement of Unanimous Agreement as a Collective-Choice Rule.* For local commons, it may be possible to obtain agreement on a course of action.

The possibility of obtaining unanimity on an agreed upon course of action is extremely difficult for global commons. According to collective-choice models, all stakeholders should voluntarily assent to agreements. However, on a global level, when the course of action requires a negotiated treaty, some national government stakeholders might hold out and attempt to negotiate privileges before they will agree to sign or follow the treaty. Such a situation creates an enormous challenge for convenors to attempt to negotiate with such stakeholders.

CONCLUSION

As illustrated in this chapter, the role of the convenor is both an extremely important and challenging leadership role. I argued that "convening leadership" and "convening" are required to bring multiple stakeholders to the table to build a stakeholder network, identify solutions, and develop adaptive management systems to address complex global challenges. Additionally, the chapter introduced the knowledge and skills a leader requires for collaboration, convening, and adaptive management on the commons.

The power of convening illustrated in a study of food movement organizations is reliant on capacity mobilization, leveraging types of power, integrating, coordinating, and building a systems-oriented vision (Clark et al., 2020). The convenor is presented as the catalytic agent who helps to create bridges between actors to explore cooperation.

As such, the convenor needs to develop enormous perception, negotiation, and facilitation skills and become highly knowledgeable about how complex systems function and what internal and external environmental factors influence such systems. A convenor must also become a highly effective negotiator and facilitator of collaboration.

In review of Ostrom's (1990) principles for effectively governing commons and underscored through the work of leading scholars in commons work, as introduced in this chapter, "convening leadership" is required to help build trust and positive communication between the organizations for effective collaboration and commons governance, to signal the need for adaptation, and to help stakeholders make changes on their path to joint solutions. To address the challenges typically encountered in commons governances, Ostrom et al. (1999) identified five challenges. To address these challenges, convenors will: (1) necessarily have to learn how to facilitate collaboration of larger stakeholder networks; (2) need to develop a keen understanding of cultural differences, develop a global mindset, and be able to facilitate collaboration by highlighting diversity as a positive trait; (3) want to understand how the beliefs, values, and attitudes of all stakeholders factor into a flexible adaptive management model of commons governance; (4) need to facilitate a creative co-learning and co-creating environment in order to assist the stakeholders to think outside of the box and derive a new approach to a major challenge and; (5) need strong negotiation skills to meet challenges associated with collaborative stakeholder networks.

As presented previously, Ostrom et al. (1999) contended,

> *Although the number and importance of commons problems at local or regional scales will not decrease, the need for effective approaches to commons problems that are global in scale will certainly increase. (p. 278)*

The concept of "convening leadership" and the "convenor" is more critical now than ever before in solving complex global challenges.

REFERENCES

Albareda, L., & Sison, A. J. G. (2020). Commons organizing: Embedding common good and institutions for collective action. Insights from ethics and economics. *Journal of Business Ethics, 166*(4), 727–743.

Aligica, P. D., & Tarko, V. (2013). Co-production, polycentricity and value heterogeneity: The Ostrom's public choice, institutionalism revisited. *American Political Science Review, 107*(4), 726–741.

Ansell, C., & Gash, A. (2012). Collaborative governance in theory and practice. *Journal of Public Administration Research and Theory, 18*(4), 543–571.

Berge, E., & van Laerhoven, F. (2011). Governing the commons for two decades: A complex story. *International Journal of the Commons, 5*(2), 160–187.

Clark, J. K., Lowitt, K., Levkoe, C. Z., & Andree, P. (2020). The power to convene: Making sense of the power of food movement organizations in governance processes in the Global North. *Agriculture and Human Values.* doi:10.1007/s10460-020-10146-1

Colburn, L. (n.d.). *Strategy Overview.* Collaborative Leaders Network. Retrieved from https://collaborativeleadersnetwork.org/strategies/community-transformation/

Dietz, T., Ostom, E., & Stern, P. C. (2003). The struggle to govern the commons. *Science, 302*(5652), 1907–1912.

Dorado, S. (2005). Institutional entrepreneurship, partaking, and convening. *Organization Studies, 26*(3), 385–414.

Emery, F., & Trist, E., (1965). The causal texture of organizational environments. *Human Relations, 18*(1), 21–35.

Erwin, P. C. (2020). The National Academy of Medicine should convene a new "Future of public health". *American Journal of Public Health,110,* 1611–1612. doi:10.2105/AJPH.2020.305899

Frischmann, B. M., Marciano, A., & Ramello, G. B. (2019). Tragedy of the Commons after 50 years. *Journal of Economic Perspectives, 33*(4), 211–289.

Hickman, G. R., & Sorenson, G. J. (2013). *The power of invisible leadership: How a compelling common purpose inspires exceptional leadership.* Sage Publications.

Mair, J., & Hehenberger, L. (2014). Front-stage and backstage convening: The transition from opposition to mutualistic coexistence in organizational philanthropy. *Academy of Management Journal, 57*(4), 1174-1200.

March, F. A., & March, F. A. Jr. (1902, 1958, 1968). *March's thesaurus and dictionary of the English language.* Doubleday & Company, Inc.

Miles, J. D. (2013). Designing collaborative processes for adaptive management: Four structures for multistakeholder collaboration. *Ecology and Society, 18*(4), 5. doi:10.5751/ES-05709-180405

Ostrom, E. (1990). *Governing the commons: The evolution of institutions for collective action.* Cambridge University Press.

Ostrom, E., Burger, J., Field, C. B., Norgaard, R. B., & Policansky, D. (1999). Revisiting the commons: local lessons, global challenges. *Science, 284*(5412), 278–282.

Sison, A. J. G., & Fontrodona, J. (2012). The common good of the firm in the Aristotelian-Thomistic tradition. *Business Ethics Quarterly, 22*(2), 211–246.

Sugden, A., Ash, C., Hanson, B., & Smith, J. (2003). Where do we go from here? *Science, 302*(5652), 1906.

Svendsen, A. C., & Laberge, M. (2005). Convening stakeholder networks. *Journal of Corporate Citizenship, 19*(91104), 1–18.

Thompson, R. (2020). *Proleptic leadership on the commons: Ushering in a new global order.* Bingley, UK: Emerald Publishing.

Trist, E. (1983). Referent organizations and the development of interorganizational domains. *Human Relations, 36*(3), 269–284.

Walters, C. (1997). Challenges in adaptive management of riparian and costal ecosystems. *Conservation Ecology, 1*(2), 1–20.

10

COLLABORATING AND CO-CREATING LEADERSHIP IN THE VIRTUAL AND NOT-SO-VIRTUAL COMMONS: ROAD WARRIORS, COMMUNITAS, AND CULTURE

GAYLA S. NAPIER AND DAVID BLAKE WILLIS

Living in the Borderlands (is)...a numinous experience.
It is always a path/state to something else.
– Gloria Anzaldúa (2012, p. 95)

INTRODUCTION

Since COVID-19, everything has changed. With the world changing around us, recalibration of how we lead and negotiations about how people work are only the beginning. A movement for distributed work that was slowly building has now catapulted leaders into new forms of collaboration and communication. Projections for 2020 that mobile workers would account for nearly three-quarters of the total U.S. workforce were far exceeded as the COVID-19 pandemic spread across the globe. Global mobile workforce projections of 1.87 billion mobile workers by 2022 now speak for 42.5% of the total global workforce as businesses choose to embrace this new distributed way of working (Market Research, 2015–2020). As the nature of work shifts to remote work for many and continues to evolve for both essential workers and nonessential workers, how will we as leaders rise to the challenge of supporting and sustaining community, connection, and widely distributed, liminal employee networks? How will we create belonging in shared, collaborative spaces that are more open and distributed as the workforce becomes more nomadic? How will we ensure the inclusion of others from different cultures as virtual teams become global? How will we create *communitas*? How will we lead? The new nature of work, like the old, will refashion us. For as the poet David Whyte (1994) wrote,

> *Work is the very fire where we are baked to perfection and like the master of the fire itself, we add the essential ingredient and fulfillment when we walk into the flames ourselves and fuel the transformation of ordinary, everyday forms into the exquisite and the rare.*

The recognition of the shifting workplace and the need to create working and learning communities for an increasingly diverse workforce has attuned us to the need for an open discourse on how we work, how we lead, and how we create inclusion of "the other," those from different races, cultures, and ethnic groups.[1] As part of this discourse, we argue that we should embrace a new culture of work in the commons. As a commons, workers in distributed spaces will be required to self-organize, to establish rules and processes of self-governance, to work more autonomously, to lead more collaboratively, and to create a sense of belonging, of communitas, based on mutuality and care.

PURPOSE

This chapter explores how workers in distributed spaces create and function as commons based on a study of 21 Road Warriors, people who live on the borderlands of organizations and work in reflexive environments of mobile liminality (Napier, 2016). The chapter focuses primarily on how Road Warriors create *communitas* and how leadership is distributed in their virtual or near virtual communities. Road Warriors are consulting professionals who frequently travel for work, moving between projects, clients, and often organizations, co-creating and redefining their work again and again. For Road Warriors, negotiations, reproduction, and reinterpretation of notions of *communitas* are constantly challenged and co-created. New meanings, forms, and practices then emerge. As leaders they are no longer the stereotype of lone wolves or rugged individuals, but frequently, quiet, collaborative, mutually supportive, and inspiring leaders. The lessons drawn from the study of Road Warriors can be applied to all workers who work in distributed spaces, both within and outside their organizations. The lessons may also apply to self-organized unstructured online communities and even social movements whose participants interact virtually or in urban streets, but do not form defined organizations.

After providing a brief introduction to the commons, we address the liminal nature of work as it has become increasingly remote and how we as workers must shift to accommodate the new landscape. We then look at the work of Road Warriors and how liminality impacts them and their creation of *communitas* and how ritual is employed, and group identity is formed. We next examine the "virtual third places" where Road Warriors meet and work and how these places help create *communitas*. The peer governance or distributed leadership that emerges in these places is then discussed. Finally, we look ahead at work in the future and how the experience of Road Warriors and their work on the commons forecasts an increasingly typical model of work in the twenty-first Century.

THE COMMONS

Commons are living social systems through which people address their shared problems in self-organized ways (Bollier & Helfrich, 2015). The commons are living social organisms that embody a relational ontology expressed through recurrent behavioral patterns such as the ritualizing of togetherness and trust in situated knowing (Bollier & Helfrich, 2019).

Commoning is a verb that suggests aspects of participation and caretaking (Nikolić & Skinner, 2020). The commons, and its verb form commoning offer us an opportunity to explore the creation of *communitas* among our mobile workforce, which require people to move in and out of their everyday life to a liminal work. It also brings us closer to thinking about community beyond geographical proximity.

Commoning allows us to create value together, and in the process, create meaning for ourselves, potentially changing the way we conceive of leadership. By creating communities of mutual commitment, we may be changing the value chains of work. Thinking about community formation and the intrinsic need for employees to belong affords us space to creatively explore the definitions, boundaries, and character of this co-created experience.

In the commons, communitas is formed, creating a deep sense of belonging that may reflect on how leaders emerge and may negate the importance of traditional leadership. In the commons, meaning and leadership are fluid, emergent, and based on need. When experiencing liminality, or ever-changing states of rebalancing and reordering, the social order is renegotiated. In these moments, before established structures assert themselves, actions, behaviors, and relationships are governed by *communitas*. *Communitas* is that exquisite and rare occurrence of human connection. We all recognize when it happens, how a bond is created, and we are willing to go beyond participation to engage in situational leadership and co-creation. Let us ask ourselves: Who is "we" and how are we creating the commons where we reside, work, lead, and co-create?

LIMINALITY

The concept of liminality was first used in the social sciences by anthropologists to denote the transition from one social status to another, such as the passage between childhood and adulthood and can be traced to ethnographer-folklorist Arnold van Gennep's *Les Rites de Passage* (1960), an analysis of ritual, and later the work of Victor Turner (1977, 1979), Homi Bhabha (1994, 1997a, 1997b; Benhabib, 2002; Breckenridge, Pollock, Bhabha, & Chakrabarty, 2002), and Audre Lorde (2020, 2007). Bhabha speaks about "minority maneuvers and unsettled negotiations" taking place at what he calls "frontline/border posts" (1997a), which we would argue have come into the center of many of our lives now. They are represented by hybrids, which imply multiple futures and a rapidly spreading cultural form. This new mixing of newer and older cultural forms may actually be the "normal" state of affairs. As Homi Bhabha states, "The borderline work of culture demands an encounter with 'newness' that is not part of a continuum of past and present. It creates a sense of the new as an insurgent act of cultural translation" (Benhabib, 2002, p. 23).

Liminality thus describes the transition experiences involved in the process of separating from one state of being and incorporating into another. In organizational research, the term is used to denote the position of individuals for whom organizational boundaries are unclear (Garsten, 1999; Tempest & Starkey, 2004; Zabusky & Barley, 1997). This term is also used in discussions about the consulting experience since consultants move in and out of their assignments, from one reality to another (Czarniawska & Mazza, 2003; Wagner, Newell, & Kay, 2012).

Liminality refers to "betwixt and between" conditions, an understanding that opens space for possible uses of the concept beyond that which Victor Turner originally suggested. Liminality can be applied to an individual or a group. As a concept, liminality applies to both space and time. Temporally, liminality can exist as a single moment, as more prolonged periods, or even as whole epochs (Thomassen, 2009). Spatially, liminal spaces can be crossed into via precise thresholds or they can represent an expansive area like a borderland or country (Anzaldúa, 2012; Thomassen, 2009).

ROAD WARRIORS: *COMMUNITAS*, LIMINALITY, RITUAL, IDENTITY, AND BOUNDARIES

Road Warriors' working conditions blur boundaries among client organizations, professional services firms, and co-workers. Finding themselves in-between organizations, Road Warriors are in a liminal state with social status or role often nonexistent or secondary (Napier, 2014; Shields, 1991; Turner, 1977, 1979, 2012). The work they perform is primarily project-based and has often required the Road Warriors to travel extensively. An important aspect of this work is being "on" all the time: evenings and sometimes weekends participating in practice calls, performing administrative tasks, and catching up on work not completed during the workweek. The effect of performing remote project-based work speaks to the impact of time, stress levels, and their relationships, both personal and professional.

COMMUNITAS

Communitas is usually understood to refer to an unstructured community where people are equal and have a sense of sharing and intimacy that develops as they experience liminality as a group (Letkemann, 2002; Olaveson, 2001; Ryan, 2012; Shields, 1991; Turner, 1979, 2008, 2012). Victor Turner's description of communitas as a sense of common purpose and communion (1979, 2008) is like the collective human connection that is the existential basis of the idyllic notion of "community." *Communitas* and commoning have also featured in the Italian autonomist tradition of Roberto Esposito (2010) and others, representing the primacy of the concept of community by drawing on its original etymology. Similar to the Road Warriors reported here, this conception of community is not about property or territory but an alternate way of seeing the world. Esposito suggests, "community is nothing other than the limit that separates or joins" people, which suggest the structure of boundaries (Esposito, 2010, p. 149). Additionally, we might argue that structure emerges through enacted rituals and is symbolically defined by those who experience it.

When *communitas* exists, it involves that part of the community expressed in unity. Boundaries may be invisible but are known to those in the group. Lines of inclusion are drawn, and there exists an "us" and "them" mentality (Napier, 2016). Those who belong to the group know that they belong, and belonging becomes a marker for someone who is "in." The experience of *communitas* is intricately tangled in the symbology of community. Nevertheless, *communitas* is more than community. *Communitas* is about journeying together through something, where the journey or experience brings people together (Napier, 2016).

Communitas is similar to community in that there is a feeling of fellowship or belonging with others. This feeling results from sharing common attitudes, interests, and goals. *Communitas* typically occurs within a liminal state. Thus, while *communitas* bears similarities to community, it is a concept distinct from structured sociological systems like the family or neighborhoods that govern social life and give us communities. For instance, a community is a broad classification and can include almost any gathering of people. *Communitas* is a definitive grouping and only applies where there is a felt sense of close connection. Communitas also connects the unstructured elements of our social interactions. When experiencing liminality, or states of shifting, rebalancing, and reordering, the social order negotiates itself. In these moments, before established structures assert themselves, actions, behaviors, and relationships are governed by *communitas*.

The experience of *communitas* more closely represents what Road Warriors experience. If we understand *communitas* to be symbolically constructed, we can perceive how members create a sense of group identity based on a system of values, norms, and moral codes. These, in turn, provide a sense of identity within a bounded whole. Symbols, here, are objects, words, or gestures that are understood and interpreted through the cultural lens of a Road Warrior. Rituals and symbols may represent the boundaries created by Road Warriors when defining themselves. Symbols do more than merely represent something, too – they also allow those who employ them to supply part of their meaning. By looking at how both community and *communitas* are symbolically constructed, we can see how Road Warriors might create meaning about their experience.

The professional services firms that Road Warriors work with are often liminal in structure. They may exist as brick-and-mortar companies but with flexible boundaries, retaining anti-organizational attributes to remain more flexible (Lindsay, 2010). Examples of these attributes may include a flattened organizational structure, employees that are dispersed both geographically and organizationally, and an increase in strategic alliances to maximize flexibility. As a group, Road Warriors work in the ambiguous condition of being in "a between state" where new structures are continuously emerging beyond the existing social structure of their organization (Garsten, 1999; Turner, 1982).

RITUALS AND SYMBOLS

In anthropological work, ritual is commonly associated with ceremonies, both secular and religious. However, rituals can also be represented by everyday activities. Michel de Certeau refers to these sites as "common places" where "making do" can be seen as specific forms of operations taking place in them that can even be poetic or mythic. This is "another spatiality," as Certeau notes (1984, p. 93). For Road Warriors symbolic activities may well include everyday events such as frequent flying, eating in restaurants and staying in hotels. Symbolic objects might include suitcases, laptop bags and even travel attire. Even language becomes symbolic when it is used to define or identify themselves as members of a group.

For liminal or dispersed members, daily rituals like dinner, drinks, or the sharing of stories may provide an occasion for reconstituting the community (Cohen, 1985). Symbols and rituals that give the community significance may be rich with meaning. Turner (1967) argued that some rituals can create *communitas* by providing identification among members. Take travel rituals, for example. It is easy to spot a frequent traveler in the security line at an airport. While others are fumbling with baskets and security lines, the frequent traveler has the process down to a few concise steps and moves through the line quickly. In this way, rituals and symbols may reveal group values at their deepest levels. Social relationships often include rites of passage, not only as what Durkheim (1964) called a projected expression of social cohesion and unity, but suggest complex social tensions mediated and negotiated through ritual. Ritual is thus a mechanism to continuously re-create social equilibrium and unity (Bell, 2009; Gluckman & Gluckman, 1977).

The meanings inherent in rituals are informed by dialectical processes where groups, individuals, and place all contribute to the ways that rituals are considered, performed, and understood. Shared rituals help us recognize others as members of our social group or network. Rituals are an important means of establishing *communitas*, providing us with visible signals of connection. Rituals are how we perform and confirm our affiliation with social groups. War stories, for example, are a way for participants to create a shared history, to engage and build trust with one another. The war stories told by participants create and sustain a shared history. The stories also set Road Warriors apart from others who do not have those experiences, creating a boundary for their community.

The term *mediated ritual interaction* was introduced by Richard Ling (2010) and is defined as the way we greet one another, communicate, and relate stories using technology. The use of mediated communications, phone, text, and social media gives participants a sense of being connected to something larger. It provides a frequent confirmation of their position within the Road Warrior community. Mediated interactions transcend a situation or environment, allowing Road Warriors to connect to their community wherever they may be geographically. Mediated ritual interactions are the threads that weave the social fabrics of distributed community. Rituals give the workforce order and meaning. Good rituals create a story which helps employees make sense of their belonging. They bring the abstract into their daily work. Integrating rituals is a way for leaders to bring in underlying values and beliefs, reinforcing the culture we want to create.

SHARED IDENTITY

If we consider how individuals within a group talk about community, we can identify two aspects of their shared identity: (a) they have something in common with each other and (b) this commonality distinguishes them in a significant way from the members of other groups (Cohen, 1985). Aspects of virtual communities of practice may come into play, such as shared beliefs, group values, shared history, and shared experiences. Frequently, studies of professional communities are juxtaposed as either online or offline. The online community is virtual, and members engage through technology, and the offline community is face-to-face. Workplace boundaries for Road Warriors are unclear: The place of their community can be either virtual or face-to-face and may shift frequently.

The construct of togetherness is therefore intricately connected to liminality through the concept of *communitas*. Turner further developed van Gennep (1960) ideas on liminality to highlight liminal spaces in other aspects of societal change. He expanded on the significance of the social bonding that occurs during the liminal separation.

> *It is in this liminality that* communitas *emerges, if not as a spontaneous expression of sociability, at least in a cultural and normative form – stressing equality and comradeship as norms rather than generating spontaneous and existential* communitas. *(Turner, 1975, p. 96)*

For Road Warriors, being in a liminal state and participating in everyday rituals contributes to a strong collective identity. As shown in Fig. 1, their work ecosystem is highly interconnected and complex. Rituals serve to promote feelings of connectivity, a sense of belonging and of belonging to a group (Durkheim, Cosman, & Cladis, 2001). Through ritual interaction – either mediated or co-present – Road Warriors build a sense of social cohesion similar to Arlie Hochschild's (2000) global care chain.

COMMUNITAS AND CULTURE: COLLABORATING AND CO-CREATING LEADERSHIP

When considering "place," this study goes beyond typical categorizations of community. It suggests that Road Warriors intermingle in a kind of "virtual third place" or "virtual commons" where they experience *communitas*. Third places, as public spaces on neutral ground where people gather and interact (Oldenburg, 1998), have been extended in recent years to "virtual third places" (Hickman, 2013; Köhl & Götzenbrucker, 2014; Moore, Hankinson Gathman, & Ducheneaut, 2009; Soukup, 2006; Spence, 2008).

Fig. 1.   Work Ecosystem.

Work Ecosystem. Data for this figure licensed and adapted from Shutterstock from gkatz; schiva; Artex67; Astarina; Susann Schroeter; Daniela Barreto; Burunduk's; alex74; Mila Basenki; Loseva Marina; NikVector; and VasilkovS.

Employees come together in virtual third places on neutral ground where status is not as essential as the conversation and what can be accomplished together. These places are levelers that are accessible and accommodating to everyone. Regulars set the mood for others, and new people are accepted from all walks of life. These spaces are places where feelings of warmth and belonging exist. Virtual third places represent a place where people can come together, be renewed, and transformed by *communitas*.

Remote leadership, or leading from a distance, is not new. However, the developments of the last several years, and more recently, the forced shift to remote work in the year 2020, require us to give remote leadership more attention. Fig. 2 illustrates just some of the complexity leaders are being challenged with as they face the new ecosystem of work. Leadership as a term suggests one leader with multiple followers. While intentional work communities may have a designated leader, virtual third places or the commons may shift toward *peer governance* and *distributed leadership*. Peer governance in the commons is governance that ensures needs are met, common use-value produced, and relationships have a chance to deepen. This distributed leadership can be a quiet leadership that enables a new landscape, acknowledging and supporting local movements as they struggle to "recover the commons" (Reid & Taylor, 2010). It can be described as a collective social process that emerges through the interactions of multiple actors (Bolden, 2011).

Distributed leadership is not leadership by a single person; it is a group activity that works through and within relationships, rather than individual action (Woods, Bennett, Harvey, & Wise, 2004). Sharing leadership roles is not a new concept (Hoy & Miskel, 2012). Where a traditional hierarchical organization might have one leader much like a conductor in an orchestra, distributed or shared leadership might resemble a jazz ensemble led by one of the musicians based on the rhythm of the moment (Schlechty, 2001). As the workforce becomes more distributed and work becomes increasingly virtual, at least part of the time, it becomes vital to understand how it affects our sense of belonging, the factors which influence performance, and the way that we approach leadership.

CROSSING BORDERS TO THE COMMONS: IMAGINING THE FUTURE, NEW IDENTITIES, AND NEW CONSCIOUSNESS

The borders are our natural sites of creation: the places where we invent, transgress, and create.

— Toni Morrison (2007)

Fig. 2. An Ecosystem of Work.

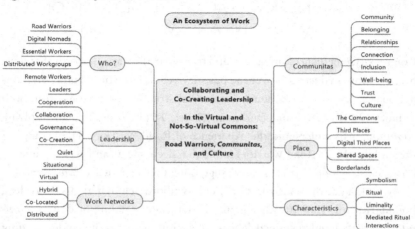

Crossing borders to a "new commons" for the world is needed now more than ever. Quiet leadership emerges based on need and allows for a different way of thinking about people and organizations, for effective action and taking on challenges. Road Warriors and their quiet leadership help us to understand this need. Their experience with *communitas* and collaboration has created new pathways for all of us. With Road Warriors and their experiences, we see how the world is now open in ways unimaginable even a few years ago. Peter Drucker (2001) saw three main characteristics of the knowledge society that were emerging and that are very much related to this discussion of new paths and a new consciousness: (1) *Borderlessness*, (2) *Upward Mobility*, and (3) *The Potential for Failure as Well as Success*.

Will the new knowledge workers that Drucker calls for be socially sensitive and ready for newcomers? The most striking growth in terms of jobs will be for those Drucker calls "Knowledge Technologists": IT people, teachers, lawyers, accountants, and engineers. These jobs require a certain degree of formal training: apprenticeship alone will no longer suffice. Learning is now taking place in what we might call "Learning Circles," a term being used more and more frequently by educators. Learning circles can be seen as "sacred hoops" where we honor an intentional education for liberation that brings this vision to life. How can we as educators, leaders, and citizens transform the centers of power and privilege by reimagining our societies in the Americas, China, Japan, Europe, India, Southeast Asia, Africa, and elsewhere?

WHO IS LIVING AND LEADING IN THE COMMONS? CONCLUSIONS AND IMPLICATIONS

Complexity, emergence, ambiguity, and transformation are all words that have become more mainstream over the past few years. This study builds on foundational concepts of community as a social structure originating from both Tönnies (2001, 1887) and Durkheim (1964, 1893). It does so by applying *communitas* to understand the experience of Road Warriors. The findings of the study of the 21 Road Warriors found that deep, social, and even communal bonds exist among Road Warriors, suggesting they experience *communitas*.

By looking at the constructs of ritual, symbols, belonging, place, borders, boundaries, and liminality, we gain a better understanding of how *communitas* is created and sustained. This exploration increases our understanding of the work–life challenges inherent in project-based work. It helps leaders understand how to hold space for the emergence of *communitas* in the commons. Leaders can imaginatively rethink how we look at boundaries and opportunities to co-construct community in a way that supports the emergence of *communitas*.

From this research, we realize the significance of rituals as they symbolically create community. The symbolic creation of community helps to replace what we have lost by losing our office spaces. The office was not just a place: it was a collection of artifacts, surrounded by and woven into rituals. Rituals created social cohesion and effect. Our badges provided entry, our coffee cups made the office "ours," and the patterns of greeting, the in-jokes, and the lunchtime routines provided a framework and structure to our days. By going remote, we lost more than just a place to work. We should consider what new artifacts we will create and the meaning we will weave into them. We should reflect on what our new rituals should be.

The COVID-19 crisis resulted in a forced shift to remote work, throwing our notion of belonging and place off balance. Working in the commons may imply a shift in identity that requires both employees and leaders to evolve into different roles and adopt different perspectives perpetually. We are thus seeing the emergence of a new way of working. Where, when, and how people work will become more flexible. We can expect a significant increase in remote work after the COVID-19 crisis that will have implications for how we use office space and flex our time. The commons are hybridized open spaces of knowledge and culture sharing, where the individual (a Road Warrior, remote worker, virtual team member, teleworker, or distance leader) finds his or her place of belonging. These are places for learning, work, process dissemination, and knowledge sharing. The commons (virtual or in-person) are emerging, growing, and reorganizing as fluid workplaces where employees with differing interests and talents come together to co-create and lead. We may need to reassess what matters in our organizations and how essential work gets done. We have been given an extraordinary opportunity to learn from this sudden shift in the landscape of work.

In summary, leaders must look for ways to work differently in the future. People across cultures and companies will come together on the commons or in other liminal spaces to create new ways of working. The commons offer us the potential to organize work in new ways, and another way to come together in *communitas*. The commons, virtual or otherwise, will be where people thrive through this interaction and experience *communitas*. As workers and leaders, we must:

- Hold space, creating an environment where *communitas* can develop, where we can promote mindful interrelating and strong emotional belonging.

- Develop meaningful rituals that promote belonging and support group identification.

- Promote social activity that brings people together for networking, development, and that accommodates time for socializing as well.

- Encourage collaboration hubs and innovation centers where people can come together.

- Develop structures and processes that are fluid and allow for the emergence of situational or distributed leadership.

- Consider place: the acknowledgement of it and the need to intentionally create and tend to place for and between the people who share that place.

The commons, virtual or otherwise, will be where people thrive through this interaction and experience *communitas*.

As we consider the iterative entanglement of community, *communitas*, belonging, and inclusion, we must again ask ourselves: Who is "we" and how are we creating the commons where we reside, work, lead, and co-create? As we seek to understand how we are living and working in the commons, we recognize that we open many new paths of further inquiry that cannot be answered here. Only by engaging in this conversation collectively can we begin to explore our coming together in *communitas* within the commons.

NOTE

1. For two examples of possible new ways of perceiving totalized, monolithic representations of society, see Willis and Rappleye (2011) and Willis and Murphy-Shigematsu (2009).

REFERENCES

Anzaldúa, G. (2012). *Borderlands: La frontera; The new mestiza* (4th ed.). Aunt Lute Books.

Bell, C. (2009). *Ritual: Perspectives and dimensions* [Kindle Paperwhite version]. doi: D01-9880836-6464216

Benhabib, S. (2002). *The claims of culture: Equality and diversity in the global era.* Princeton University Press.

Bhabha, H. (1994). *The location of culture.* London: Routledge.

Bhabha, H. (Guest Editor) (1997a). Front lines/border posts. *Critical Inquiry*, Spring, 23(3).

Bhabha, H. (1997b). Life at the border: Hybrid identities of the present. *New Perspectives Quarterly*, 14(1).

Bolden, R. (2011). Distributed leadership in organizations: A review of theory and research. *International Journal of Management Reviews*, (13), 251–269. doi: 10.1111/j.1468-2370.2011.00306.x

Bollier, D., & Helfrich, S. (Eds.). (2015). *Patterns of commoning.* Common Strategies Group, Retrieved from http://patternsofcommoning.org

Bollier, D., & Helfrich, S. (2019). *Free, fair, and alive: The insurgent power of the Commons.* New Society Publishers.

Breckenridge, C. A., Pollock, S., Bhabha, H., & Chakrabarty, D. (Eds.). (2002). *Cosmopolitanism.* Duke University Press.

Certeau, M. de. (2011). *The practice of everyday life* (S. F. Rendall, Trans.; 3rd ed.). University of California Press.

Cohen, A. P. (1985). *The symbolic construction of community.* Tavistock.

Czarniawska, B., & Mazza, C. (2003). Consulting as a liminal space. *Human Relations*, 56(3), 267–290. doi: 10.1177/0018726703056003612

Drucker, P. (2001). The next society. *The Economist.* Retrieved from https://www.economist.com/special-report/2001/11/03/the-next-society

Durkheim, E. (1964, 1893). *The division of labor in society.* Free Press of Glencoe.

Durkheim, E., Cosman, C., & Cladis, M. S. (2001). *The elementary forms of religious life.* Oxford University Press.

Esposito, R. (2010). *Communitas: The origin and destiny of community.* Stanford University Press.

Garsten, C. (1999). Betwixt and between: Temporary employees as liminal subjects in flexible organizations. *Organization Studies*, 20(4), 601–617. doi: 10.1177/0170840699204004

Gay, R. (Ed.). (2020). *The selected works of Audre Lorde.* W.W. Norton & Company.

Gluckman, M., & Gluckman, M. (1977). On drama and games and athletic contests. In S. F. Moore & B. G. Myerhoff (Eds.), *Secular ritual* (pp. 227–243). Van Gorcum.

Hickman, P. (2013). "Third places" and social interaction in deprived neighbour-hoods in Great Britain. *Journal of Housing and the Built Environment, 28,* 221–236. doi: 10.1007/s10901-012-9306-5

Hochschild, A. (2000). Global care chains and emotional surplus value. In T. Giddens & W. Hutton (Eds.), *On the edge: Globalization and the new millennium* (pp. 130–146). Sage.

Hoy, W., & Miskel, C. (2012). *Educational administration: Theory, research, and practice* (9th ed.). McGraw-Hill Higher Education.

Köhl, M. M., & Götzenbrucker, G. (2014). Networked technologies as emotional resources? Exploring emerging emotional cultures on social network sites such as Facebook and Hi5: A trans-cultural study. *Media, Culture & Society, 36,* 508–525. doi: 10.1177/0163443714523813

Letkemann, P. G. (2002). The office workplace: Communitas and hierarchical social structures. *Anthropologica, 44,* 257–269. Retrieved from http://www.jstor.org/stable/25606085

Lindsay, D. M. (2010). Organizational liminality and interstitial creativity: The fellowship of power. *Social Forces, 89*(1), 163–184.

Ling, R. (2010). New tech, new ties: How mobile communication is reshaping social cohesion (pp. 240). Retrieved from www.amazon.com database. doi: D01-6209744-9246617

Lorde, A. (2007). *Sister outsider: Essays and speeches.* Crossing Press.

Market Research. (2015–2020). *U.S. mobile worker forecast. Report IDC5713418.* Retrieved from Market Research database.

Moore, R., Hankinson Gathman, E., & Ducheneaut, N. (2009). From 3d space to third place: The social life of small virtual spaces. *Human Organization, 68,* 230–240. doi: 10.17730/humo.68.2.q673k16185u68v15

Morrison, T. (2007). Unpublished speech. Delivered at Radcliff Institute for Advanced Studies, June 8, 2007.

Napier, G. S. (2014). An exploratory study of road warrior communitas in a profes-sional services firm. In G. D. Sardana & T. Thatchenkery (Eds.), *Organizational transformation: Change management perspectives* (pp. 143–155). Bloomsbury Publishing.

Napier, G. S. (2016). *Beyond community: Understanding the experience of commu-nitas among information technology road warriors.* Doctoral dissertation. Retrieved from ProQuest Dissertations & Theses Global database (Accession No. 1024428).

Nikolić, M., & Skinner, S. (2020). Community. *Philosophy Today, 63*(4), 887–901.

Olaveson, T. (2001). Collective effervescence and communitas: Processual models of ritual and society in Emile Durkheim and Victor Turner. *Dialectical Anthropology, 26,* 89–124. doi: 10.1023/A:1020447706406

Oldenburg, R. (1998). *The great good place: Cafés, coffee shops, bookstores, bars, hair salons, and other hangouts at the heart of a community.* Marlowe.

Reid, H., & Taylor, B. (2010). *Recovering the commons: Democracy, place, and global justice.* University of Illinois Press.

Ryan, A. (2012, October). Ritual, liminality and communitas in business relationship dynamics. Paper presented at the 7th Nordic Workshop on Relationship Dynamics, Umeå, Sweden.

Schlechty, P. C. (2001). *Shaking up the schoolhouse: How to support and sustain educational innovation.* Wiley.

Shields, R. (1991). *Places on the margin: Alternative geographies of modernity.* Routledge.

Soukup, C. (2006). Computer-mediated communication as a virtual third place: Building Oldenburg's great good places on the World Wide Web. *New Media & Society, 8,* 421–440. doi: 10.1177/1461444806061953

Spence, J. (2008). Demographics of virtual worlds. *Journal for Virtual Worlds Research, 1*(2). doi: 10.4101/jvwr.v1i2.360

Tempest, S., & Starkey, K. (2004). The effects of liminality on individual and organizational learning. *Organization Studies, 25*(4), 507–527. doi: 10.1177/0170840604040674

Thomassen, B. (2009). The uses and meanings of liminality. *International Political Anthropology, 2,* 5–27. Retrieved from http://www.politicalanthropology.org/

Tönnies, F. (2001, 1887). *Tönnies: Community and civil society* [Kindle Paperwhite version]. doi: D01-3832934-0761816

Turner, E. (2012). *Communitas: The anthropology of collective joy* [Kindle Paperwhite edition]. doi: D01-9564110-1899433

Turner, V. (1967). *The forest of symbols: Aspects of Ndembu ritual.* Cornell University.

Turner, V. (1975). *Revelation and divination in Ndembu ritual.* Cornell University.

Turner, V. (1977). Variations on a theme of liminality. In S. F. Moore & B. Myerhoff (Eds.), *Secular ritual* (pp. 36–52). Van Gorcum.

Turner, V. (1979). *Process, performance, and pilgrimage: A study in comparative symbology.* Concept.

Turner, V. (1982). *From ritual to theatre: The human seriousness of play.* Performing Arts Journal.

Turner, V. (2008). *The ritual process: Structure and anti-structure* (Lewis Henry Morgan lectures 1966) (2nd ed.). Aldine Transaction.

van Gennep, A. (1960). *The rites of passage* (M. B. Vizedon & G. L. Caffee, Trans.). University of Chicago.

Wagner, E. L., Newell, S., & Kay, W. (2012). Enterprise systems projects: The role of liminal space in enterprise systems implementation. *Journal of Information Technology*, 27(4), 259–269. doi: 10.1057/jit.2012.22

Whyte, D. (1994). *The heart aroused: Poetry and the preservation of the soul in corporate America*. Doubleday.

Willis, D. B., & Murphy-Shigematsu, S. (2009). *Transcultural Japan: At the borderlands of race, gender, and identity*. Routledge.

Willis, D. B., & Rappleye, J. (2011). *Reimagining Japanese education: Borders, transfers, circulations, and the comparative*. Oxford Series in Comparative Education. Symposium Books.

Woods, P. A., Bennett, N., Harvey, J. A., & Wise, C. (2004). Variabilities and dualities in distributed leadership: Findings from a systematic literature review. *Educational Management Administration & Leadership*, 32(4), 439–457. doi: 10.1177/1741143204046497

Zabusky, S. E., & Barley, S. R. (1997). "You can't be a stone if you're cement": Reevaluating the emic identities of scientists in organizations. *Research in Organizational Behavior*, 19, 361–404.

11

USING INTERORGANIZATIONAL COLLABORATION TO CREATE SHARED LEADERSHIP THROUGH COLLECTIVE IDENTITY DEVELOPMENT

PATRICIA GREER

INTRODUCTION

Interorganizational collaboration (collaboration) is an example of a shared leadership process, where members from multiple organizations partake in actions to achieve a joint outcome without any formal hierarchy (Endres & Weibler, 2020). Shared leadership requires a shared goal, an internally supported process, and a high level of voice and involvement (Carson, Tesluk, & Marrone, 2007; Endres & Weibler, 2020). Collaboration is one available tool to solve "messy" or complex issues within a problem domain. Successful collaboration requires the existence of several key elements, including committed members, resources, time, communication, trust, shared goal, defined process, and collective identity. Collective identity is an outcome of this process that nourishes shared leadership. Information, voice, power, and motivations are shared within the group resulting in a feeling of shared identity and being one with the group (Endres & Weibler, 2020). This chapter validates initial and emergent (co-constructed) factors of collaboration, identifies the most important dimensions of success, and offers a new model for developing collective identity as part of shared leadership. Through interviews, survey results and focus groups of collaboration experts who submitted 46 collaborations to the Colorado Collaboration Award competition in 2013 and 2014, collective identity, the development of relationships that bring value to communities, and despite challenges and differences, the building of something wonderful together were identified as the most important dimensions of success.

THE ELEMENTS OF COLLABORATION

Based on interviews, surveys, and focus groups as part of a mixed method study, the elements of successful collaboration are identified with specific consideration of time, collective identity as shared leadership, and the multiple definitions of success in collaboration. Each element adds value to the process, and without each of them, the probability of success decreases. This section begins by identifying the essential elements required to start collaboration, namely, committed members, time, and resources. Emergent or elements created within the socially constructed boundaries of the collaboration are then discussed. Such elements are developed by members inside the collaboration framework and include trust, shared goal, defined process, and communication. Finally, the surfacing of collective identity and its development conclude the discussion.

Two of the elements require an additional note. First, although time can be reviewed as a resource or standalone element, for purposes of this chapter, time is considered independently because of its role in relationship development and for the collaborative process. Second, communication is required to start the informal and formal conversations at the beginning of collaboration but then transforms as relationships grow. Communication gains in importance as the collaboration process continues.

The initial elements of collaboration set the context for the development of elements which emerge during the process. Through the development of these elements as an iterative process, collective identity is formed. Collective identity is recognized by the behavior changes of the members when the members identify as a group. Once collective identity exists, members develop shared commitment to each other and the goal and mission, thus increasing the probability of perceived success. With collective identity, the conversations become fluid, and the members create outcomes together, each taking responsibility for collective decisions (Endres & Weibler, 2020). Each of the identified elements is described below, beginning with the initial elements, followed by the emergent elements, and concluding with collective identity as the central construct of this chapter.

Initial elements provided for collaboration. Successful collaboration requires the development of constructs within the boundary or space. The required initial elements include committed members, time, and resources.

Committed members. The identification and inclusion of committed members are critical for effective collaboration. Emerson, Nabatchi, and Balogh (2011) reflected that the importance of membership is the combination of commitment, the expertise of each member, and the access to information and resources provided by each organization. Huxham and Vangen (2005) posited critical membership considerations, including who the member is as a person, how the member is involved in the problem domain, and how the member will be participating in the collaboration. Two concerns exist about member selection: (1) Will potential members be overlooked because of concerns about their organization, relative position in the community, or stated or public position on the problem or issue? and (2) Will potential members be included for the same reasons, regardless of their concerns or knowledge in the problem domain? There is a practical need that members reflect a relevant diversity, yet too many members may influence the outcome of successful collaboration. Available resources, ideas, and diversity are limited if the number of members is low. There is no optimal number of members. Consideration for membership includes the ability to implement outcomes or provide needed resources.

Commitment to the group affects the motivation to contribute energy, ideas, and resources. Members need to have both the interest and the capacity to participate in collaboration (Ivery, 2007). When committed members already understand the interconnected quality of the problem or issue, they are likely to collaborate because they address the problem instead of people (Thomson & Perry, 2006). When there are several people to consider for membership, the people having the capability to be committed members should be selected first.

Time. Successful collaboration takes time. The lack of time presents a challenge since establishing communication practices and developing relationships is not easy and is a process which evolves over time. If there are imposed time constraints, it may not be practical or possible for relationships to develop. If there is a deadline or the process or a timeline is driven by outside agencies or organizations, there may not be enough time to succeed. Large amounts of time are necessary to develop effective relationships and build trust (Thomson & Perry, 2006). In fact, the biggest cost for an effective collaboration is the time and member energy to discuss, define, build, and implement all the elements addressed in this chapter (Thomson & Perry, 2006).

There may be real or imagined barriers to ultimate outcomes, especially time. Inadequate time for the collaborative process creates a real barrier and may interfere with members' trust building, communication, and development of the collective identity (M. Kramer & Crespy, 2011). Because collaborations are fragile and operate in a temporary structure, time pressures result in ineffective or collapsed collaborations (Thomson & Perry, 2006). Purdy (2012) determined that a longer length of the collaborative process enhances effectiveness due to greater participation. Erakovich and Anderson (2013) found the benefits increase when enough time is provided to overcome the inefficiencies present in beginning the process. Thomson and Perry (2006) considered the need for enough time to be a critical element due to the nonlinear nature of the process, the understanding that grows through interaction and relationships, and the evolution of collaboration. Time is built into many of the steps and is necessary for successful outcomes.

Resources. One of the strengths of collaboration is the ability to leverage existing resources from many organizations or members to resolve an issue or problem. The members invest resources (time, expertise, and materials) to develop outcomes (Thomson & Perry, 2006). Coordination among the members is fundamental, particularly with respect to first providing and then maintaining the flow of resources (Durugbo, Hutabaret, Tiwari, & Alcock, 2011). Emerson et al. (2011) stated required resources may include funding, time, support from home organizations, skills, and expertise to support outcomes. Through collaboration, the resources may be identified, leveraged, and distributed as shared resources. This sharing of resources may be instrumental in providing legitimacy and equitable outcomes (Emerson et al., 2011)

Greater funding, as a resource, is linked to improvement and sustainability of the collaboration (Harper, Kupermine, Weaver, Emshoff, & Erickson, 2014). Ales, Rodrigues, Snyder, and Conklin (2011) contended that collaboration includes significant costs, human and financial. These costs include the funding required during the process, in-kind contributions, salaries and the loss of employee time, and cost for the implementation of the outcome. Even though members identify options to use scarce resources effectively, there are required resources and costs connected to the outcomes. Resources, a critical element in effective collaboration, include available time for each committed member, and move to money, commitment, and other identified costs for the outcome.

Emergent elements developed during collaboration. With the assets of committed members, resources, and time, with the initial communication, assimilated into the collaboration, elements emerge and are co-constructed through the development of relationships among members within the socially constructed boundary (Fayard & DeSanctis, 2010). These elements include communication, trust, shared vision or goal, defined process, and collective identity.

Communication. At the beginning and during the life of collaboration, communication is a fundamental element for successful outcomes. Communication begins as the members come together, whether in person, via email or some other mechanism (Hamilton, 2010). By initiating a reason for people to sit down together, communication occurs, and collaboration transforms over time as the members become more familiar with each other.

Communication is necessary to construct the relationships among a shared understanding, defined process, trust, and creation of a collective identity between the members (Mulder, Swaak, & Kessels, 2004). Perrault, McClelland, Austin, and Sieppert (2011) considered the initial emphasis and attention paid to developing the informal connections to be a requisite for a successful collaboration. As the result of communication and conversation, an open relationship is created where trust and understanding occur naturally (M. Kramer & Crespy, 2011). Members provide different knowledge, views, perspectives, and experience. To generate the ideas and learning, members build their capacities through conversations in order to arrive at a shared understanding within the scope of the goal (Mulder et al., 2004).

At its core, collaboration is a social process where members build a group through communication, thoughtful actions, and inclusion of ideas, resources, and experiences (Vila-Henninger, 2015). Creative tension exists within a nonorganizational structure that holds the members within its sphere, yet is permeable so communication, ideas, and actions can flow between the group and outside of the boundary. Through communication, socially sustained boundaries are created, and allow members to communicate, make decisions, and act, while defining the norms and rituals (Watson & Foster-Fishman, 2012). The strength of the socially sustained boundary is dependent on the depth of commitment to the group by the members (Vila-Henninger, 2015). Co-created communication performs many functions. It creates understanding, builds relationships, creates social boundaries, and starts the act of building trust. Without communication, collaboration is impossible.

Trust. Trust is a necessary element for effective collaboration and develops over time (Perrault et al., 2011; Vangen & Huxham, 2003). Trust expands when there is a consistent demonstration of respect and understanding by members (Perrault et al., 2011). The actions of the members establish trust, and no single action is more critical than humanizing and respecting other members. Building trust is foundational in building the social capital of group cohesion and is of practical importance in collaboration, where it is not held together by one organizational hierarchy (Gupta, Huang, & Yayla, 2011).

Trust grows over time and is an outcome of members' demonstrated reliability, predictability, and engagement (Emerson et al., 2011). Trust is necessary to provide members an opportunity to provide input and participate in productive conflict so better solutions can be developed. When trust exists, open discussions, active listening, and deliberations occur, with equal rights and responsibilities for all members (Endres & Weibler, 2020). This open environment occurs when members know the conflict will not escalate or damage the relationships because there is trust. Social capital built inside the structure creates opportunities outside the structure by extending the trust and relationships to other organizations and community members.

Members of successful collaborations denote building trust as an important aspect of managing difficult conversations and conflicting ideas during the process (Vangen & Huxham, 2003). Trust emerges through member interactions, adapting and strengthening over time. By developing trust through consistency of actions, the creation of a group culture of mutual respect and trust adds strength to the collaboration and increases the strength of the collective identity. The foundation of trust generates the platform for the member discussion of the shared goal.

Shared goal. The creation and role of a shared goal in collaboration is important, as members work together to achieve an overarching purpose, as a shared leadership process (Endres & Weibler, 2020). Although the collaboration is typically formed around a problem with a preliminary goal, the members need to internally validate or approve it. The idea of a shared goal is rarely achievable until communication has started, with time provided to develop relationships and available resources. The goal needs to be so compelling that members will continue its pursuit despite the challenges to achieve it. "Creating a shared vision of the future is a powerful vehicle" (Austin, 2000, p. 74), one that assists the committed members to visualize, mobilize, and act.

Developing the shared goal by members of the collaboration is a critical element for successful outcomes due to member contributions. The design of the collaboration provides a space for members from multiple organizations to jointly create solutions to a problem (Endres & Weibler, 2020). While the shared goal may have a positive outcome in the problem domain, there may provide differing benefits for members and their organizations. The shared goal provides energy to the process and supersedes competition among the members or their organizations. The creation generates a deeper collective identity by going through the process of deciding and defining the shared goal. The element of shared goal moves the collaboration forward to action.

Defined process. Another element constructed within the collaboration is the defined process, which offers a framework for the members to operate within. Petri (2010) stated, "First and foremost, interdisciplinary collaboration is described as a process" (p. 75). The defined process provides the structure of governance for the members: communication frequency and modes, sharing of responsibility, and the methods for making decisions (Vangen, Hayes, & Cornforth, 2014). When the next steps toward the shared goal are unclear, when conflict arises, or outside pressure is applied to the members, the defined process provides the structure to move the collaboration forward. Because the members usually do not belong to the same organization or entity, the process provides the structure to address the problem without an organizational hierarchy (Gray, 1989).

The defined process allows the members to move forward even when differences are not resolved. Perrault et al. (2011) discussed the challenge of bringing together members from separate organizations to create a new structure bound by a member-defined process and to use pooled resources. Because the work of the members supports a shared goal, the process can proceed organically, due to the motivation to complete the collaboration, through the shared leadership structure (Endres & Weibler, 2020). The defined process promotes collaboration without a formal structure or organizational hierarchy (Vangen et al., 2014). Because the members have developed a process together to support a shared goal, the collective identity deepens with a positive outcome of their efforts. The identity shifts to the collective group results in behavior change and produces a product or artifact, the defined process.

Collective identity. Collective identity is a social identity construct that plays a role in how people behave, how they demonstrate their commitment to the other members and the goal, how they interpret connections to others, and how they choose correct behaviors during the collaboration. De Cremer and van Knippenberg (2005) asserted that when collective identity forms, individuals move from self-interest to the collective interest of the group. Individual and collective identities occur simultaneously and cause a transformation in how the member perceives himself or herself. Collective identity relates to willingness to participate in the member-created collective behavior, the level of commitment to the mission, and willingness to take part in meeting the shared goal (R. Kramer, 2006).

Collective identity formation begins with informal and formal communication, carried through to group rituals, followed by the development of group norms, and solidified by the creation of the shared process and goals. At the cognitive level, collective identity is reinforced and strengthened through increased commitment to the group processes, completion of the shared goal and defined process, and continual informal conversations and formal dialogue. After the formation of collective identity, the probability of solving the problem and completing the shared goal increases in the collaboration (Bunniss, Gray, & Kelly, 2011). When collective identity is attained, communication among members of the group changes and becomes more fluid. A benefit of this significant change is the new space that is created where the members can listen and learn from each other (Oborn & Dawson, 2010). With the importance of collective identity in collaboration, it becomes pivotal to understand how it develops.

Collective identity development begins with conversations before any defined process develops within the group. At this point, the role of group rituals becomes critical. Group rituals include simple practices such as specific start times, greetings and closing practices, the length of the meetings, and location of the meetings (Fayard & DeSanctis, 2010). Group rituals are part of celebrating small and significant successes that bolster member commitment, energy, and connection to the other members and the purpose.

After the formation of collective identity, the holding space for difficult conversations exists. Members discuss and settle differences in viewpoints and resolve conflicts that would otherwise threaten effective collaboration (Hardy, Lawrence, & Grant, 2005). Collective identity increases individual engagement in collective behavior and decreases the likelihood of conflicts due to differences (R. Kramer, 2006). When collective identity is present, conversations are held about those differences because of the equal voice, shared purpose, and crafted support, demonstrating the shared leadership among the members (Carson et al., 2007). With the foundation of collective identity, members contribute time, energy, leadership, and emotional involvement (Hardy et al., 2005). Members receive emotional benefits from working in the framework by receiving respect and support from the other members (Stümer, Simon, & Loewy, 2008). The more benefits received because of the contributions, the more members are willing to participate over the longer periods often needed to develop options and recommend outcomes (Mizrahi, Rosenthal, & Ivery, 2013).

Collective identity is built within a socially sustained boundary and strengthened iteratively by using group rituals and norms, informal and formal communication, defining a process and sharing a goal (Fayard & DeSanctis, 2010). Time and resources are added as critical antecedents alongside committed members. Building relationships over time formed and maintained the socially sustained boundary. Breaking down traditional boundaries navigated outside and inside the collaboration builds something wonderful. The "why" centers a collaboration, by creating the authentic need for the work, and validating the shared goal. Norms and rituals begin the defined process, which acts as both a temporary governance structure and a reminder of the commitment to the goal. The aspects of communication, respect and honesty, conflict resolution and civility, both consistently and continually, are captured by the informal and formal practices of the group. The model for collective identity development is shared in Fig. 1.

Summary of elements created within the collaboration.

There are numerous critical aspects of collaboration contained in the development of collective identity. Collective identity occurs after other elements of collaboration have taken place and, in general, continues to develop and strengthen during the time of the collaboration, where the emphasis remains on the united actions of the members (Endres & Weibler, 2020). The foundations for the creation of collective identity include the initial elements of communication, committed members, time, and resources, which lead to the development of emergent communication, defined process, trust, and a shared goal. Collective identity becomes critical for the successful outcome of collaboration because the committed members now look internally to identify the options, held together by the member created shared leadership (Endres & Weibler, 2020). This internal focus provides the basis for frank discussion, innovation, idea generation, shared leadership, respect, diversity of thought,

Fig. 1.   Model of Collective Identity Development (Greer, 2017).

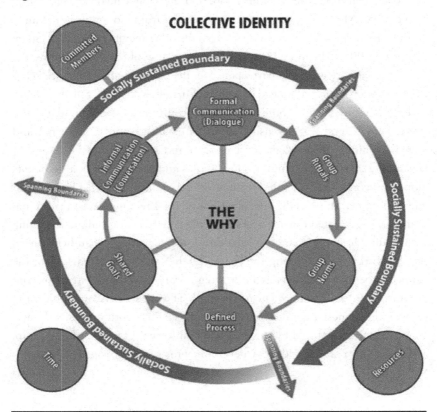

and commitment to each other, while working toward the resolution or solution. Collective identity is a critical element and may distinguish collaboration from a cooperative effort within the problem domain. Cooperative efforts are reasonable approaches; however, collaboration contains the co-creation of knowledge, development of collective identity, and the designing of options, resolutions, and solutions.

Collective identity continues to emerge throughout the life of the collaboration. The development of collective identity is iterative and requires time. The strength of the collective identity comes from the members and the strength of identification with the collective group. Collective identity, as a form of shared leadership, is difficult to construct, yet is influential in the outcomes of a collaboration. Collective identity is a critical element that leads to successful collaboration.

FINDINGS AND IMPLICATIONS FROM THE STUDY

Collaboration is a complex process, situated in a specific context, with adaptive practices utilized for success. The adaptive processes include the elements identified in this review. The essential elements that are needed at the beginning of the collaboration include committed members, time, and resources, with initial communication practices. Elements also appear within the socially sustained boundary as an outcome of interactions. These elements are trust, shared goal, defined process, effective group communication, and collective identity. Members create collective identity through engaging in informal conversations and formal dialogue, participating in the development of rituals, and internalizing norms. Collective identity strengthens when the members increase trust and successfully conceive a shared goal and defined process. Adjustments are made to continue movement toward the outcome. The employment of adjustments, retreating, resolving, reconfiguring, or restructuring, used as specific strategies allows the collaboration to continue (Dibble & Gibson, 2013). The model for successful collaboration is dependent on the interactions of all elements within the socially created and sustained boundary.

Fig. 2 illustrates a model for the process of successful collaboration, showing the initial elements, emergent elements, and the adjustment strategies. This model shows the complexity and the process required for successful outcomes and demonstrates the interactions of all elements within the socially sustained boundary.

Collaboration is complex, and a complex system needs precise direction and the ability to adapt to new information and ideas added to the system (Fenwick, 2012). The elements of effective collaboration provide the direction and adaptability that, when present, allow options to be generated and an outcome and solution achieved. What constitutes success is discussed in the next section.

OUTCOMES OF SUCCESSFUL COLLABORATIONS

It would be simple to state the outcome of a successful collaboration is the solution of the problem or issue, or success equaled completing the goal. The participants in the research described success in a far more complex and

Fig. 2. Process of Successful Collaboration (Greer, 2017).

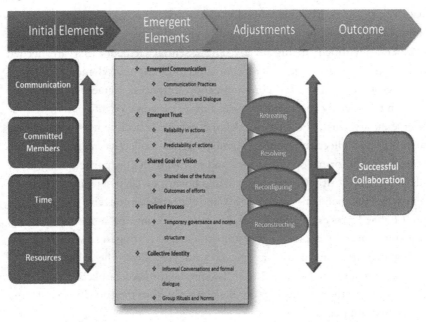

adaptive manner than was found in the literature. Based on analysis of the application and interview narratives, these four measures of success arose:

1. Our collaboration was successful.

2. Our collaboration successfully achieved our goals.

3. We built strong successful relationships that brought positive benefit to our community.

4. In spite of our differences, we built something wonderful together.

   Each of these measures are discussed.

Our collaboration was successful.

Most members viewed their collaboration as successful, more than those who felt their goals were achieved. Success was perceived as being accomplished through many different measures such as gaining legislative support, small wins, increased funding, and success for the larger community. Members shared increases in the number of people using services, growth in programming, increased outreach, and better utilization of available funding as illustrations of success. Like the findings of Innes and Booher (1999), the most important outcome was for members to build capacity and a problem-based focus in the local community. Others provided insight about contributions to their communities and to other members as indicative of success. The creation of a social infrastructure to continue the sharing of resources, ideas, and support were also viewed as success.

Other members reflected on the long-time horizon for success, and the story telling and small wins necessary to keep members going and focused. These examples show how success looks, feels, and are accomplished in different ways, based on the individual nature and the uniqueness of the collaboration. Each of the 46 collaborations had stated their goals. Some of the goals were lofty and long term, such as implementing outdoor water conservation for users in Colorado. One sought to eliminate a food desert in a Denver community. The overall success is predicated on contribution to the community, based on the formed links and relationships. Fig. 3 shows many different measures of collaboration success, in addition to goal attainment.

Fig. 3. Ways Success Manifests in Collaboration (Greer, 2017).

Our collaboration successfully achieved our goals.

A slight majority of members agreed their goals were achieved, the achievement of small goals, or the interim goals which supported the mission or purpose. This finding of solving complex problems through the efforts of different organizations working together is supported by Vangen et al. (2014).

Success includes having a benefit to the community. Three themes were derived from the findings: commitment, engagement, and teamwork. Commitment describes the feeling toward the goal, other members, and the community. Engagement explains the enthusiasm of the members toward one another and willingness to work toward the goal. Teamwork expresses how people worked together within the collaboration. These results demonstrate the interrelatedness of the aspects of success.

When asked how the collaborations could have been improved, respondents discussed the need for time, more resources, committed members, and a goal everyone shared. Funding is key, and in Colorado, access is local, and state funding is hampered due to competition and government funding limitations. As Harper et al. (2014) posited, funding is required for outcomes and sustainability of the work.

We built strong successful relationships that brought positive benefit to our community.

Successful relationships benefited the community and were constructed through communication, trust, and processes around a shared goal. These relationships are part of a social identity, impacting individual and group identity and perceptions, motivations, and behaviors (Stoner et al., 2011; Stümer et al., 2008).

Building relationships, benefiting communities, and learning how to collaborate are important outcomes for the current work and for setting up future opportunities. As was expressed by one member "As we do this more and see the positive results, it begets more trust for future collaboration."

In spite of our differences, we built something wonderful together.

Members strongly agreed their collaboration built something wonderful. With the level of agreement with this statement higher than the level for goal achievement, this finding resembles the collaborative advantage described by Vangen and Huxham (2003). This finding adds another measure to describe success to the literature: building something wonderful together. As documented by Ales et al. (2011) members may experience collective learning, while building an inclusive resolution to a messy problem, producing "wonder."

Wonder includes the idea that it is a great outcome and powerful energizer to build something between people of different organizations, perspectives, and experiences. The power came from success, equal voice, inclusion of diverse organizations and members, coming together to create a community benefit, and building relationships through the implementation of communication practices, trust, and a process.

The members recognized and felt the power of coming together. When asked about the impact of the collaboration, most of the members agreed on the greater collective impact.

Narratives described working across traditional organizational boundaries, with new partners and ideas. Words like remarkable, unique, and marriage were used to describe the feeling of building something wonderful, which resembles valued collaborative participation, identified by Endres and Weibler (2020). The idea of providing positive results for a community, both now and in the future, was regarded as wonderful. This power of together creating something wonderful is added to the literature as an important contribution of the collaboration process.

Summary of Success. Most of the members agreed their collaboration was successful, yet success was identified by a variety of measures. Success meant strong relationships, benefiting the community, community contributions, internal processes, resources, collective identity, and support for a shared goal. In addition, despite their differences, something wonderful was built. The results highlighted collective impact for the community, the individual nature of each collaboration, and how engaged members move the process forward, especially with a long-time horizon.

These results demonstrate the unique outcomes for success. Groups discussed how their collaborations obtained increased or joint funding, a change in legislation, and growth in programming. Others shared providing new or increased service to their communities, and the collective impact because of the members' efforts. Meeting small goals along the path to big ones was offered. Shared stories spoke of success and how "we" (members of the collaboration) succeeded in "our" efforts. When historic boundaries are removed, success occurs in the community, because people work together for a common good. Finally, built and sustained relationships between members were both a success and a significant outcome for the members and a positive benefit for their communities. The process of collaboration brings intrinsic and extrinsic value to members and their communities, and that is a measure of success.

CONCLUSION

As I have shown, interorganizational collaboration is a shared leadership process used by committed stakeholders within a problem domain to solve "messy" or complex issues. Resolution of complex problems is achieved through an iterative process, using first the initial elements for success, committed members, resources, and time, followed by the elements that emerge over time, including communication, trust, shared goal, defined process, and finally collective identity. When collective identity is achieved, the fluidity of the process and decision-making aids in outcomes, building capacity within the group, and leading to multiple definitions of success. Collective identity manifests itself externally because of the changes people have made internally (Stümer et al., 2008). These changes are brought about throughout the course of being members accepting each other as having an equal voice, developing the supporting processes, and committing to the shared goal (Carson et al., 2007). The outcomes of collective identity include members who spend the time in dialogue and discourse, and work through the difficult discussion and decision-making as equals.

The relationships built during collaboration may be as important, or more, than achieving the goal because of the longer lasting impact to the community. Collaboration builds capacity into a community, through the development of the relationships, sharing a common goal, having conversations and dialogue, ideation, and building trust within a problem domain.

Collaboration is a time consuming, difficult option to create shared leadership, build capacity into a group and a group defined community, and solve a messy problem. If it is the right approach, it can result in outcomes that go beyond just the resolution of the problem. Perhaps the reader can be lucky enough to have the following outcome: "In spite of our differences, we built something wonderful together."

REFERENCES

Ales, M. W., Rodrigues, S. B., Snyder, R., & Conklin, M. (2011). Developing and implementing an effective framework for collaboration: The experience of the CS2day collaboration. *Journal of Continuing Education in the Health Professions, 31*(S1), S13–S20. doi:10.1002/chp.20144

Austin, J. (2000). *The collaborative challenge.* Jossey-Bass.

Bunniss, S., Gray, F., & Kelly, D. (2011). Collective learning change and improvement in health care: Trialling a facilitated learning initiative with general practice teams. *Journal of Evaluation in Clinical Practice, 18*, 630–636. doi:10.1111/j.1365-2753.2011.01641.x

Carson, J., Tesluk, P., & Marrone, J. (2007). Shared leadership in teams: An investigation of antecedent conditions and performance. *Academy of Management Journal, 50*, 1217–1234. doi:10.2307/20159921

De Cremer, D., & van Knippenberg, D. (2005). Cooperation as a function of leader self-sacrifice, trust, and identification. *Leadership & Organizational Development Journal, 26*(5/6), 355–369. doi:10.1106/01437730510607833

Dibble, R., & Gibson, A. (2013). Collaboration for the common good: An examination of the challenges and adjustment processes in multicultural collaboration. *Journal of Organizational Behavior, 34*, 764–790. doi:10.1002/job.1872

Durugbo, C., Hutabaret, W., Tiwari, A., & Alcock, J. R. (2011). Modelling collaboration using complex networks. *Information Sciences, 181*(15), 3143–3161. doi:10.1016/j.ins.2011.03.020

Emerson, K., Nabatchi, T., & Balogh, S. (2011). An integrative framework for collaborative governance. *Journal of Public Administration Research, 22*, 1–29. doi:10.1093/jopart/mur011

Endres, S., & Weibler, J. (2020). Understanding (non)leadership phenomena in collaborative interorganizational networks and advancing shared leadership theory: an interpretive grounded theory study. *Business Research, 13*, 275–309. doi:10.1007/s40685-019-0086-6

Erakovich, R., & Anderson, T. (2013). Cross-sector collaboration: Management decision and change model. *International Journal of Public Sector Management, 26*(2), 163–173. doi:10.1108/09513551311318031

Fayard, A., & DeSanctis, G. (2010). Enacting language games: The development of a sense of 'we-ness' in online forums. *Information Systems Journal, 20*(4), 383–416. doi:10.111/j.1365-2575.2009.00335.x

Fenwick, T. (2012). Complexity science and professional learning for collaboration: A critical reconsideration of possibilities and limitations. *Journal of Education and Work, 25*(2), 141–162. https://doi.org/10.1080/13639080.2012.644911

Gray, B. (1989). *Collaborating.* Jossey-Bass.

Greer, P. (2017). *Elements of effective interorganizational collaboration: A mixed methods study.* Electronic Thesis or Dissertation. Retrieved from https://etd.ohiolink.edu/

Gupta, V., Huang, R., & Yayla, A. (2011). Social capital, collective transformational leadership, and performance: A resource-based view of self-managed teams. *Journal of Managerial Issues*, *XXIII*(1), 31–45. Retrieved from http://www.jstor.org/stable/25822536?seq=1#page_scan_tab_contents

Hamilton, F. (2010). Leading and organizing social change for companion animals. *Anthrozoos*, *23*(3), 277–292. doi:10.2752/175303710x12750451259057

Hardy, C., Lawrence, T. B., & Grant, D. (2005). Discourse and collaboration: The role of conversations and collective identity. *Academy of Management Review*, *30*(1), 58–77. doi:10.5465/amr.2005.15281426

Harper, C. R., Kupermine, G. P., Weaver, S. R., Emshoff, J., & Erickson, S. (2014). Leverages resources and systems changes in community collaborations. *American Journal of American Psychology*, *54*, 348–357. doi:10.1007/s10464-014-9678-7

Huxham, C., & Vangen, S. (2005). *Managing to collaborate*. Routledge.

Innes, J. E., & Booher, D. E. (1999). Consensus building and complex adaptive systems. *Journal of the American Planning Association*, *65*(4), 412–423. doi:10.1080/01944369908976071

Ivery, J. (2007). Organizational ecology: A theoretical framework for examining collaborative partnerships. *Administration in Social Work*, *31*(4), 7–19. doi:10.1300/JI47v3In04_03

Kramer, R. (2006). Social identity and social capital: The collective self at work. *International Public Management Journal*, *9*(1), 25–45. doi:10.1080/10967490600625316

Kramer, M., & Crespy, D. (2011). Communicating collaborative leadership. *The Leadership Quarterly*, *22*(5), 1024–1037. doi:10.1016/j.leaqua.2011.07.021

Mizrahi, T., Rosenthal, B., & Ivery, J. (2013). Coalitions, collaborations, and partnerships: Interorganizational approaches to social change. In M. Weil, M. Reisch, & M. Ohmer (Eds.), *The handbook of community practice* (pp. 383–402). Sage.

Mulder, I., Swaak, J., & Kessels, J. (2004). In search of reflective behavior and shared understanding by ad hoc expert teams. *Cyber Psychology & Behavior*, *7*(2), 141–154. doi:10.1089/109493104323024410

Oborn, E., & Dawson, S. (2010). Knowledge and practice in multidisciplinary teams: Struggle, accommodation, and privilege. *Human Relations*, *63*(12), 1835–1857. doi:10.1177/0018726710371237

Perrault, E., McClelland, R., Austin, C., & Sieppert, J. (2011). Working together in collaborations: Successful process factors for community collaboration. *Administration in Social Work*, *35*(3), 282–298. doi:10.1080/03643107.2011.575343

Petri, L. (2010). Concept analysis of interdisciplinary collaboration. *Nursing Forum*, *45*(2), 73–82. doi:10.1111/j.1744-6198.2010.00167.x

Purdy, J. M. (2012). A framework for assessing power in collaborative governance processes. *Public Administration Review*, *72*(3), 409–417. doi:10.111/j.1540-6201-2012-02525.x

Stoner, J., Perrewé, P. L., & Hofacker, C. (2011), The development and validation of the Multi-Dimensional Identification Scale (MDIS). *Journal of Applied Social Psychology, 41*(7), 1632–1658. https://doi.org/10.1111/j.1559–1816.2011.00770.x

Stümer, S., Simon, B., & Loewy, M. I. (2008). Intraorganizational respect and organizational perspective: The mediating role of collective identity. *Group Processes Intergroup Relations, 11*(5), 5–20. doi:10.1177/1368430207084842

Thomson, A. M., & Perry, J. L. (2006). Collaboration processes: Inside the black box. *Public Administration Review, Special Edition*, 20–32. Retrieved from http://www.indiana.edu/~jlpweb/papers/Collaboration%20Processes_Inside%20the%20 Black%20Box_Thomson%20%26%20Perry_PAR_2006%20Supplement.pdf

Vangen, S., Hayes, J. P., & Cornforth, C. (2014). Governing cross-sector, interorganizational collaborations. *Public Management Review, 17*(9), 1237–1260. doi:10.1080/14719037.2014.903658

Vangen, S., & Huxham, C. (2003). Enacting leadership for collaborative advantage: Dilemmas of ideology and pragmatism in the activities of partnership managers. *British Journal of Management, 14*, S61–S76.

Vila-Henninger, L. (2015). Understanding symbolic boundaries and improving quantitative analysis of social exclusion by improving the operationalization of boundary work. *Sociology Compass, 9*(12), 1025–1035. doi:10.1111/soc4.12334

Watson, E. R., & Foster-Fishman, P. G. (2012). The exchange boundary framework: Understanding the evolution of power within collaborative decision-making settings. *American Journal of Community Psychology, 51*(1–2), 151–163. doi:10.1007/s10464-012-9540-8

12

THE ROLE OF LEADERS IN CATALYZING COOPERATIVE BEHAVIOR IN THE GOVERNANCE OF NONPROFIT SECTOR SHARED RESOURCES: THE CASE OF EARLY CHILDHOOD EDUCATION

WENDOLLY A. ESCOBAR, ANGELA TITI AMAYAH AND MD HAQUE

INTRODUCTION AND PURPOSE

The nonprofit sector faces a significant challenge caused by diminishing public and private funding. Insufficient resources available to achieve their goals have forced nonprofit organizations to cooperate among themselves to pool their human and financial resources as well as to form public–private partnerships. Such cooperation depends upon leaders who are capable of catalyzing cooperation where competition or separation existed before. Drawing on lessons from the commons literature, this chapter focuses on the role of leaders as catalysts of such cooperative behavior in the early childhood education sector. Based on interviews conducted with 10 leaders responsible for public–private partnerships in this sector, the chapter proposes a framework of values and skills that successful catalytic leaders of cooperation require. These include passion, a keen ability to form significant and meaningful relationships, and the willingness to change in terms of mindset and outlook and to further develop capacity, knowledge, and skills. This framework will prove useful as the nonprofit sector increasingly is required to collaborate to survive.

BACKGROUND

The nonprofit sector is undergoing a major transformation. The operation of nonprofit organizations has become complicated, as nonprofit leaders encounter reduced funding, increased accountability measures and the increasing need to explore alternative funding opportunities that require nonprofits to become more collaborative. Nonprofits working in the early childhood education programs especially face serious funding constraints. In Southern California, for example, federal and state funding is sorely inadequate to provide quality early care and childhood education programs to the 2.5 million children who are eligible to attend such programs or to help families in need of support to send their children to these programs (Gould, Whitebook, Mokhiber, & Austin, 2019). Furthermore, it is unlikely that federal and state funds will ever be able to guarantee an allocation of money specifically dedicated to family engagement (Weiss, Lopez, & Rosenberg, 2010). Nonprofits have consequently been forced to find alternative ways to obtain the resources necessary to serve the families and children in need of such programs.

LESSONS FROM THE COMMONS

Successful self-governance of resources by the commons provides lessons to draw upon for successfully instituting cooperation and collaboration in the nonprofit sector to share and govern diminishing resources. Whereas Hardin's (1968) article, "The Tragedy of the Commons," argued that unmanaged shared natural resources would lead to their inevitable depletion due to overuse by individuals seeking their individual gain, economist and Nobel Prize winner Elinor Ostrom (1990) demonstrated that collective access to and ownership of resources does not necessarily lead to mismanagement. Ostrom argued that local self-governance institutions can successfully solve common pool resource problems. Individuals can cooperate to produce shared, long-term benefits deriving from such common pooled resources. While Hardin's original argument focused on common-property resources such as oceans, wildlife and other resources, a number of societal issues requiring shared financial and human resources such as those faced by nonprofits appear to fit the commons dilemma. Other scholars have suggested that a leader who articulates different ways of organizing to improve outcomes is necessary to achieve the success of the governance of shared resources (e.g., Gutiérrez, Hilborn, & Defeo, 2011). We submit that leadership, among others factors, plays a critical role in the sustainable management of commonly managed resources.

Leadership is a dynamic process of influence which involves an ongoing transaction between a leader and followers (Hollander, 1978). Leadership starts with a leader and the process of leadership cannot be separated from the person as leader. Therefore, in this chapter, we investigate the role of leaders as catalysts of cooperative behavior in the context of nonprofit organizations. Due to funding shortages, it is imperative that nonprofits in the field of early childhood education work toward identifying strategies that focus on leveraging existing resources to strengthen the family engagement support available for families of young children (Sharpe, Davis, & Howard, 2017). Stakeholders, funders, communities, and donors have begun to expect early childhood education programs to work more collaboratively to better utilize resources and deliver more results. Collaborative community efforts result in higher levels of performance and greater community impact due to cooperative behavior and pooling of resources.

THE ROLE OF LEADERS IN ADDRESSING COMMONS DILEMMAS

There is an abundance of evidence emerging from laboratory simulations that the tragedy of the commons can be averted through the cooperation of individuals. However, the question of the conditions that enhance cooperation in the field has not been fully answered (Vollan & Ostrom, 2010). In a study of forest user groups in Ethiopia, Rustagi, Engel, and Kosfeld (2010) found that groups with a higher rate of "conditional cooperators" were more likely to invest in forest patrols aimed at enforcing firewood collection rules. Rustagi et al. (2010) also showed that leadership, among other factors, influenced the success of cooperative management. Furthermore, Rustagi et al.'s study demonstrated that the proportion of conditional cooperators in a group is influenced by clan affiliation prestige and the leader whose prestige is a key to change the norms of the group.

Given that all members of the group may not have the same influence over processes and decisions on which the collective action is based, the role of leaders will vary based on power relationships and inequalities between individuals of the group. Leaders here are understood as individuals who have "a larger role than other group members in the establishment of goals, logistics of coordination, monitoring of effort, dispute resolution, or reward and punishment" (Glowacki & von Rueden, 2015).

Leaders as catalysts of cooperative behavior in nonprofit organizations in the field of early childhood programs need to establish multi-stakeholder partnerships to govern shared and limited resources. Research has concluded that leadership is often the most important factor stimulating synergy in multi-stakeholder partnerships, which suggests that weak or problematic leadership might lead to problems in such partnerships (Wilson et al., 2010). Furthermore, research found that leadership in multi-stakeholder partnerships is more complex than the non-multi-stakeholder partnerships (Bradshaw, 2009), imposing more demands upon the leader in such situations.

Nonprofit partnerships face many challenges due to a documented leadership deficit in the sector (Escobar, 2020). While there are key organizational and cultural considerations in partnership development, partnership leaders have a key role and must break away from traditional leadership models to more collaborative ones. The nonprofit sector has traditionally sought to change the world with limited financial resources and barely enough human capital. These organizations are skilled in leveraging existing community resources and creating collaborative spaces to do together what one agency cannot do individually. It is within this context that collaborative leadership is critical.

PERSPECTIVE OF PUBLIC SERVICE ORGANIZATIONAL LEADERS FROM EARLY CHILDHOOD EDUCATION

To understand the perspective of leaders from the nonprofit sector who are responsible for public–private partnerships, we[1] spoke with 10 public service organizational leaders in early childhood education that represented seven different nonprofit organizations serving communities in a large metropolitan city in Southern California. Each of these agencies receives state funding for different programming purposes and provides at least one type of educational support for families of children from birth to five years of age. One agency is considered a school site, wherein direct instruction to children across grades is provided, and the rest are nonschool sites that provide community-based support to families. The leaders that we spoke with range in title, role, and experience. Universally, they all work directly with families of young children as a part of their organizational role and are all bilingual.

We met with each leader individually and conducted a semi-structured interview with questions specific to their collaborative practices within the context of a public-private partnership. Some of the questions asked in the interview include:

1. Describe the reason(s) why this agency chose to participate in this partnership?

2. Describe the ways in which this partnership has been successful for all of the people involved.

3. How have you collaborated in this partnership?

4. How is the sustainability of this work addressed in this partnership?

5. How is leadership exercised and how is the collaboration initiated?

The interviews were scheduled directly with the interviewees and mostly held virtually to provide flexibility and comfort with the process. The interviews were audio recorded with permission and transcribed for accuracy. The final transcript was sent to each interviewee for review and clarification. Through these interviews, our aim was to help leaders in the nonprofit sectors better understand how they can accomplish their organizational goal through resource-based collaboration.

The following is a framework for collaborative leadership that serves to illustrate the role of the leader as a catalyst of cooperative behavior that emerged from our interviews. The framework illustrates three primary tenets that serve to successfully catalyze cooperative behaviors among groups of professionals in not-for-profit organizations. The tenets of this framework illustrate both the values that are at the core of collaborative leadership as well as characteristics that drive cooperative behavior.

Passion. Passion is an intrinsic characteristic of a collaborative leader that is extrinsically evident in the expressed desire to produce quality work and the personal commitment to supporting others (Escobar, 2020). Passion drives one's desire to be involved in and to see all aspects of an endeavor through. Passion is fuel for creativity, sparks innovation and is contagious when channeled in the right way. Passion drives excellence. Passionate leaders are willing and able to think outside of the box, with the ultimate goal of making an impact on those directly influenced by the work. As one participant explained:

> *I think honestly it was the gift of the agency to be able to choose something like this program and to really see it through. I think because it's a brand new position within [my] organization, we are learning more about what family engagement can look like. The freedom to explore this as a tool in the family engagement toolbox is a true gift. (Escobar, 2020)*

It is vital to the success of a collaborative partnership that leaders lead from a place of passion. Being equipped with knowledge and skills is not sufficient to complete tasks or reach outcomes without the passion necessary to apply them. Effective leaders possess an in-depth knowledge and understanding of what it takes to motivate and inspire their subordinates. Sharing their passion and vision for the work inspires others to connect, support, and share their own passions for the work. Passion creates an emotional investment, thereby developing the intrinsic motivation to seek positive results and effect change. When collaborative leaders share their passion, they inspire those around them to do the same. Bringing the passion to light serves to validate the collaborative work, the value that each individual brings to the project, and move the group toward a shared purpose and end goal. Sharing of passion leads to emotional investments in the work, thereby increasing the interest of the group toward attaining results.

Relationships. Nonprofit leaders need the appropriate knowledge necessary for establishing new working relationships, which includes negotiating mutually agreed upon clearly defined outcomes and goals for all collaborators. Taking measures to develop and negotiate an effective shared vision and goal with key stakeholders of the collaborative partnership while incorporating important data and outcome measures is a critical element of this process (Carnochan, Samples, Myers, & Austin, 2014). Collaborative partnership lends itself naturally to building relationships, particularly as projects are built out and developed over time. Relationships serve multiple roles in collaborative work.

Before beginning to identify and form new partnerships, leaders should try to learn about the best practices to identify and develop relationships with partner organizations. During the formation of new partnerships, leaders need to fully understand and align the strengths and weaknesses of the organization's resources, experience, and reputation. As one participant pointed out:

> So years ago, [our agency] had a vision of really enhancing family engagement strategies across our association and they were able to secure funding from [an outside private funder] to create my position that was to be really devoted to just that. By virtue of training, I was made aware of an opportunity through this [public-private partnership] and it seemed like an incredibly good fit. We thought, what an opportunity to start with these caregivers and really engage with them in more lasting and deeper ways. (Escobar, 2020)

Initially, the relationships between those involved in executing the work at an organizational level serve to move the work forward. They serve a catalytic function. Over time, as trust builds between professionals, a willingness to think about, act on, and evaluate the work grows. This strengthening of relationships over shared ideas and outcomes serves as a means of engaging in continuous quality improvement and allows the group to refine the work and increase its impact over time. These internal relationships also serve as a model for building relationships with external stakeholders, usually those who receive services as a result of collaborative work being done. It is these relationships that also serve as a measure of success within collaborative spaces, as a participant elaborated:

> I think that level of flexibility and freedom is really important when you're doing a program. I do appreciate that because with that freedom and flexibility there was also support. I felt like I could always go to [the grantee] for additional guidance and for help with connections. That relationship was central to the success of this program. (Escobar, 2020)

The relationships that develop out of the work being done between professionals and the community tell the story of the work and its impact. As relationships are built over time, trust is developed. Trusting relationships allow for deeper conversations about the impact of the work on those who receive services. Aside from promoting an increased willingness to share personal details and honest feedback in any formal evaluations that might need to be completed, relationships also provide the context within which people can share the true impact of the work that is being done. Relationships with parents are one such key component of positive impact.

> *It seems that the vision of [my organization] is a globalizing vision. We cannot do anything if we do not have parents who are like equitable partners and who help in the process. I think that one of the successes we have had here is that we have seen the interests, the needs, and the problems. It seems that the interest of our families is no longer just to come to the class and see what they can learn, but to give what is offered. (Escobar, 2020)*

The effects of having strong relationships as the foundation of collaborative leadership do not just happen by accident. Part of bringing out the highest levels of cooperation in others is building relationships with intentionality and purpose. The components of relationships that require attention include building trust, offering regular, face-to-face support throughout the various stages of the work, and consistently engaging in both formal and informal communications (Escobar, 2020). Interpersonal interactions that take place within the context of relationships should serve to validate the work being done as well as model the ways to build relationships with those outside of the collaborative space. Collaborative leaders understand that having an impact cannot be achieved without developing relationships with those around them.

> *They say it takes a whole village to raise a child. It also takes a whole village to improve a community. The more people we get involved, the more effective things will be. (Escobar, 2020)*

Change. Change is primarily the intended outcome of collaborative work. Collaborative leadership involves bringing individuals together for the purpose of effecting change. Change is not singularly experienced within the context of collaborative spaces. Change is prevalent across all levels, from those receiving services to those working collaboratively to plan and execute programming (Escobar, 2020). Typically, change is considered within the context of the end user. Those that benefit from collaborative programming typically experience change, which those doing the work try to track, quantify, and evaluate to inform future work. Change, however, is not just present among those who are receiving services. Change is also experienced among the professionals doing the work themselves.

I feel that even as a parent myself, I grew to understand the differ-ent perspectives of other families. Wow. We have the same chal-lenges. I'm making connections with those families and see them grow within themselves, which is also impactful. Families came together. They built those relationships and they were joking with one another. Just seeing that, [they're] making a change to help the children. (Escobar, 2020)

Within the context of collaborative work, change is defined as a shift in mindset, capacity, outlook, knowledge, and skills. According to Escobar (2020), change experienced by direct service professionals executing collaborative work is an indicator of a strong collaborative partnership. A tenet of collaborative leadership is the ability to inspire change, both internally and externally. Collab-orative leadership seeks out opportunities to share change experiences through relationship building and open, consistent communication (Escobar, 2020). Change is only evident when the story of change is told. Collaborative leaders recognize that telling such a story is important to motivating the larger group to continue moving forward with the work. Stories of change communicate impact, which motivate others to continue to do the work and achieve results.

We could see that they were making changes in their lives because they [would] come and tell us the following week, "Oh, I did this because of the class that you've covered." So, we knew that it was successful for them. It was also successful for me as a facilitator because I learned a lot too. Like the program says we were all learn-ers and we were all teachers. (Escobar, 2020)

It is important to note that these three facets of the framework for collab-orative leadership create optimal spaces for collaborative work when con-sidered together. There is not one specific characteristic that is worth paying more attention to than the others. All three facets are equally important to the efficacy of collaborative leaders.

CONCLUSION

The chapter presents the findings from 10 interviews of early childhood education nonprofit leaders. The interviews focused on their collaborative practices within the context of a public–private partnership. Based on these interviews, values and skills that successful catalytic leaders of cooperation require were identified: passion, a keen ability to form significant and meaningful relationships, and the willingness to change in terms of mindset and outlook and to further develop capacity, knowledge, and skills. Further research should investigate other variables that could influence the development of collaborative practices in a nonprofit context, as well as additional ways to improve cooperation in the field. Further research could also be initiated on the efforts of commons to form federations as an effort to expand the influence of commons on society.

NOTE

1. Wendolly A. Escobar was the principal investigator of this study which was conducted to complete her dissertation. Professor M. D. Haque was her dissertation chair while Angela Titi Amayah was her student reader. They closely collaborated to complete the research and for this reason they employ the pronoun "we" in this chapter.

REFERENCES

Carnochan, S., Samples, M., Myers, M., & Austin, M. J. (2014). Performance measurement challenges in nonprofit human service organizations. *Nonprofit and Voluntary Sector Quarterly, 43*(6), 1014–1032.

Escobar, W. A. (2020). Investing in family engagement: Understanding public-private *partnerships as a means of funding high-quality early childhood education* (Order No. 28001171). Available from Dissertations & Theses @ University of La Verne - SCELC. (2430673445). Retrieved from http://laverne.idm.oclc.org/login?url=https://search-proquest-com.laverne.idm.oclc.org/docview/2430673445?accountid=25355

Glowacki, L., & von Rueden, C. (2015). Leadership solves collective action problems in small-scale societies. *Philosophical Transactions Royal Society B, 370,* 20150010. doi:10.1098/rstb.2015.0010

Gutiérrez, N. L., Hilborn, R., & Defeo, O. (2011). Leadership, social capital and incentives promote successful fisheries. *Nature, 470*(7334), 386–389.

Hardin, G. (1968). The tragedy of the commons. *Science, 162*(3859), 1243–1248. doi: 10.1126/science.162.3859.1243

Hardin, G. (1998). Extensions of "The tragedy of the commons". *Science, 280*(5364), 682–683.

Hollander, E. P. (1978). *Leadership dynamics.* The Free Press.

Ostrom, E. (1990). *Governing the commons: The evolution of institutions for collective action.* Cambridge University Press. doi:10.1017/CBO9780511807763.

Rustagi, D., Engel, S., & Kosfeld, M. (2010). Conditional cooperation and costly monitoring explain success in forest commons management. *Science, 330*(6006), 961–965.

Vollan, B., & Ostrom, E. (2010). Cooperation and the commons. *Science, 330*(6006), 923–924.

PART III

LEADING SPECIFIC TYPES OF COMMONS

13

THE PEOPLES' VOICE CAFE: LEADING COLLECTIVELY AND HORIZONTALLY FOR MORE THAN 40 YEARS

SUSAN (SUSIE) J. ERENRICH

INTRODUCTION

Meta Mendel-Reyes, in her book, *Reclaiming Democracy: The Sixties in Politics & Memory* asks the following questions: How would a democracy in which we are all leaders actually work? Can we all be leaders? Do all of us even want to be leaders? (Mendel-Reyes, 1995, pp. 161–162). The answer to those questions at the Peoples' Voice Cafe (PVC), the subject of this chapter, is a resounding yes. The New York City arts-based institution has been leading from the commons for more than four decades. The commons, utilized in this context, is a form of community building and collaboration. The members of this special group are cultural activists, who have come together to agitate and instigate for systemic change, even though the victories are small. Their brand of community building refers to "the process of building relationships that helps community members cohere around common purpose, identity, and a sense of belonging, which may lead to social or community capital" (Korza & Bacon, 2010, p. 11).

In some respects, members of the PVC collective are the cornerstone of civic, social, and community change. By providing space and a platform to troubadours of conscience, the collaborative carries on the long traditional history of topical music in the area.

This piece is a personal examination of the legacy of the Peoples' Voice Cafe. Readers will be provided with an overview of the group. They will be exposed to an abbreviated nuts and bolts narrative of what a typical evening looks like. They will get a bird's-eye view of some of the inherent challenges of operationalizing an all-volunteer establishment that is horizontally led. And they will learn whether this form of the commons is sustainable during and after a pandemic subsides.

PORTRAITURE METHODOLOGY

Portraiture, a form of narrative inquiry, is the research method that is employed in this chapter. The qualitative approach pioneered by Harvard scholar Sara Lawrence-Lightfoot "combines systematic, empirical description with aesthetic expression, blending art and science, humanistic sensibilities and scientific rigor" (Lawrence-Lightfoot & Davis, 1997, p. 3). Social historian, Joseph Featherstone (1989), referred to portraiture as "people's scholarship" (Featherstone, 1989, p. 375). "[A scholarship in which] scientific facts gathered in the field give voice to a people's experience" (p. 375).

> We hear the sound of a human voice making sense of other voices, especially those not often heard, voices of women and of people of color. We trace the line of a story set in a historical context, placing the actors in a long-running moral and political drama. The text itself enacts the writer's deepest moral and political values, the eclecticism of method and material. (pp. 375–376)

Through the five components of the methodology: context, voice, relationship, emerging themes, and aesthetic whole, folks are able to bridge the social science of analysis, with the creative presence of voice, remembrance, and solidarity. Used here, it helps to highlight the powerful role that Peoples' Voice Cafe has played through a storytelling format that is accessible to the masses.

Sara Lawrence-Lightfoot believes that if members of academic communities want to broaden the audience for their work, then they must "begin to speak in a language that is understandable, not exclusive and esoteric … a language that encourages identification, provokes debate, and invites reflection and action" (Lawrence-Lightfoot, 2005, p. 9).

WELCOME TO THE PEOPLES' VOICE CAFE

On March 11, 2020, the lights went out and the doors were locked. It was the first time in more than 40 years that Peoples' Voice Cafe had to cancel the rest of its season. COVID-19 had turned New York City into a ghost town. People were dying, there was a calamitous economic downturn, and the suffering was mind-boggling. I received this cancelation notice from the booking committee – forwarded to all scheduled performers:

Peoples' Voice Cafe Cancellation Notice for all performances from

March 14 through May 16, 2020

Because of the very real threat that the COVID-19 corona virus poses to our audiences, our volunteers, and our performers, as well as to the larger community, the Peoples' Voice Cafe Board of Directors has reluctantly decided to cancel our shows scheduled for March 14 through May 16, 2020. We will then reassess the situation during our usual summer break. (Suffet, March 11, 2020 – email)

My show was the last of the season – May 16, 2020. It was a concert titled, *The Cost of Freedom,* to mark the 50th anniversary of the shootings on the Kent State and Jackson State college campuses. The event also served as the launch of a new anthology that I edited, *The Cost of Freedom: Voicing A Movement After Kent State 1970.* The evening was to be filled with topical songs performed by the award-winning husband and wife duo, Magpie (Terry Leonino and Greg Artzner), interspersed with dramatic readings from the collection. It wasn't to be. Health and safety come first.

OVERVIEW OF THE CAFE

The Peoples' Voice Cafe (PVC) is an all-volunteer collective that has provided quality entertainment to New York City for more than 40 years. Every Saturday night from September through May, the Cafe provides a space for the artistic expression of a wide variety of humanitarian issues and concerns. The collective was formed in 1979. It was a response to the changing political climate of the time. During that period, artists involved in social change efforts were experiencing a backlash, unable to secure paying gigs unless they altered or toned down their activist rhetoric. After numerous discussions with others, who had been shunned, or had to find alternative employment, artists from the New York City area decided to take matters into their own hands. Judy Gorman, a local singer-songwriter who was spearheading the charge, held the first meeting in her Manhattan apartment. A collective was formed and the artists searched for an appropriate space. Peoples' Voice Cafe was born.

The Cafe is currently located at 40 East 35th Street, in New York City (between Park & Madison). The venue rents space from The Community Church of New York Unitarian Universalists.

All shows start at 8:00 p.m. Doors open at 7:30. The Cafe does not accept reservations in advance. People need to come early to be assured of a seat. The Cafe can comfortably accommodate approximately 150 people. The gate is a $20 contribution – more if a person chooses, less if he/she can't – no one is turned away. If the person is a member of Peoples' Voice, then the suggested contribution is $12 (Fig. 1).

Peoples' Voice depends on its members for financial support. The basic membership contribution is $30 per year. The membership contribution for two people at one address is $40. Members are only asked to contribute $12 when they attend Peoples' Voice concerts. Folk Society of NY members,

Fig. 1. Peoples' Voice Cafe the Night of the Book Launch. Photo by Brad McKelvey.

students, and youth are also asked to contribute $12. Besides saving money when people become members, they are placed on the mailing list. Each month they receive a schedule of events for the entire year.

The Peoples' Voice Cafe also depends on its volunteers. Volunteers are needed to collect money at the door, work the refreshment table, set up chairs, assist with mailings, run the sound, publicize the shows, sell product for the performers, and bake.

In 2005, I joined the collective and began to do bookings for the horizontally led organization. From 2005 to 2012, I shared the booking responsibilities with another woman, and we worked as a team. I was responsible for bringing in artists with reputations that go beyond the borders of New York City and she continued to deal with local or lesser-known artists who have utilized the space in the past. The intent was to enable the Peoples' Voice Cafe to become more culturally viable and financially stable.

Popular artists were awarded an entire evening because they could fill the venue. Lesser-known artists shared the evening to guarantee a bigger house.

When I began my booking responsibilities, something appeared to be very wrong.

For an organization to be in existence, at the time, for a quarter of a century, I would have assumed that it would be a popular venue. Everything else was closed: Gerdes Folk City, the Gaslight, the Village Gate, and during my tenure in Manhattan, the Bottom Line, to name a few.

I discovered that there was a serious need for increasing visibility and resources. Even though the Cafe is into its 41st season, much of the public is still unfamiliar with the alternative coffee house, which has resulted in low attendance. Low attendance makes it difficult for Peoples' Voice Cafe to make its expenses. This also affects the quality of performers who agree to play. And it impacts the collective's reputation and integrity.

After the 2012 season, I moved back to the Washington, DC metropolitan area, but remained on the PVC Booking Committee. My responsibilities for the collective were minimized. Nevertheless, I still contributed and produced one or two events per year.

MAY 16, 2020

If there wasn't a pandemic, the concert to launch *The Cost of Freedom: Voicing A Movement After Kent State 1970* would have probably happened this way. After attending most of the shows I booked between 2005 and 2012, and hosting/producing at least a dozen more, I am familiar with the weekly drill.

When entering the space, I would have been hospitably received by my colleagues with cheery greetings and warm embraces. After a millisecond of small talk, the all-volunteer battalion would continue to equip the stage for the Saturday ritual. Members of the engineering team would conscientiously install cables, carefully assemble microphones and prep the board. Sound check would begin at approximately 6:30 p.m. – give or take a few minutes. Other enlistees would energetically spruce up the space, organize the product table, adroitly arrange chairs and tidy the foyer.

My singer–songwriter compatriots would arrive in the midst of the activity with a truck load of instruments. They would casually unpack their gear while I provided guidance for the team. There usually wasn't a minute to spare.

When sound check commenced, I would turn my attention to the entranceway. I would agonize about the weather impacting attendance for the show. It never mattered whether it was a bright sunny day or torrential rain. I wanted folks to come to the event. After all, this was New York City and there were literally thousands of opportunities to choose from (Fig. 2).

Fig. 2.   From Left to Right Is Magpie (Terry Leonino & Greg Artzner) and Si Kahn. Photo by Brad McKelvey.

I also fretted about marches, demonstrations, protests and social justice conferences conflicting with the PVC schedule. Given the composition of the PVC crowd, it could influence the size of the house.

A voice motioning me to the right side of the wooden rostrum for a microphone test would disturb my inner monologue and I would get on with the preparation for the evening. The vociferous sound would permeate the space and adjustments would be made and evaluated for quality control.

My musical associates and long-time confidants also monitored and appraised the ambience of the room testing their instrumental and vocal transmissions.

Shortly thereafter, theater goers would fill the seats, the lights would dim, announcements would be dispatched, and I would take my place at the microphone. *Good Evening Everyone.*

THE MAY 16, 2020 CONCERT GOES VIRTUAL

On Monday, May 4, 2020, *The Cost of Freedom* show went virtual. Since PVC was closed due to the pandemic, and the event scheduled for the Kent Stage on the actual anniversary of the shootings was also postponed, Magpie and I decided to present the historical musical tribute to all the slain and injured students at Kent State, Jackson State and beyond online. The emotionally powerful selection of songs about the Vietnam era, interspersed with dramatic readings from the newly released book, was meticulously and conscientiously recorded by the duo in their upstate New York home. Anyone in the world could tune in at their convenience to view the presentation. Of course, there is no replacement for a live happening.

I wasn't able to welcome fellow travelers to the last show of the season. I wasn't able to engage with the audience or hear the sound of thunderous applause following the execution of a beautiful song. There is no interlude with a virtual program. If the Cafe were opened, intermission is usually a time to mingle, devour some home-baked goodies, purchase merchandise, stretch my legs, and replenish my soul. And at the end of a person's virtual viewing experience, the audience doesn't jump to their feet for a prolonged, exuberant standing ovation. There is only deafening silence.

LOWS AND HIGHS FOR THE HORIZONTALLY
LED COLLECTIVE

Like any organization or horizontally led collective, Peoples' Voice Cafe has its challenges. Packed houses at the Cafe are infrequent affairs, but they do occur on rare occasions. Steve Suffet, the PVC Program Director and a member of the board, examined some of the group's difficulties in his September 2018 guest column for "The Grassroots Leadership & The Arts for Social Change Corner":

> *The first challenge is attracting and holding an audience. Filling seats in New York City on a Saturday night has never been easy. In addition to competing with other live music venues, the Peoples' Voice Cafe is up against Broadway and off-Broadway theater, comedy clubs, movies, and almost every other kind of entertainment you can imagine. In the past few years, however, the situation has grown even more daunting. For reasons that are murky, the average size of our weekly audience has been declining, and even many of our long-time subscribers are no longer attending as frequently as they once did. (Suffett, 2018)*

Not having a permanent residence has also impacted turnout. The makeshift theater housed at The Community Church of New York Unitarian Universalist is only visible to onlookers on Saturday evenings between September and May. The rest of the week pedestrians only see a building. And since the "multiracial, multicultural, and multigenerational" house of worship is closed due to COVID-19, there isn't a lot of action at the moment (ccny.org home page).

Not having a permanent home can also be problematic for folks who attend PVC shows. The gate supposedly opens at 7:30, but guests tend to trickle in before the recommended arrival time. There really isn't a space to hangout. And no one wants to wait outside on a frosty night or in a rainstorm while the Cafe readies the theater to welcome its patrons. So early admission is the only alternative even though it interferes with sound check.

The ingredients and composition of the space presents other hardships for PVC. The chairs are considerably hard and uncomfortable. The stage isn't elevated, so the artists and theatergoers are on the same level. This makes it difficult to watch the show. Only audience members in the front row have a bird's-eye view.

And at the half-way mark, when folks at the Cafe chat with friends, consume fresh baked snacks, leaf through the available music, and take a breather, it is also the point in the program where a number of spectators make their exit. For a predominantly older audience, two and a half hours sitting in an unpadded chair can take a toll on an aging body.

Additionally, there are no advanced ticket sales, so when artists commit to perform, they have no idea how much they will earn. Every so often, a luminary, like Roberta Flack, will accept a gig. In those rare cases, the Cafe can offer a small guarantee. The common practice, however, is 60% of the gate goes to the creators; 40% goes to the Cafe to cover the organization's expenses.

Other obstacles include having an inadequate publicity committee. Without sufficient advertising, it is difficult for PVC to compete with a considerable number of other venues in Manhattan offering marvelous productions at the exact same time.

Like most gathering spaces, nowadays, the Cafe entryway is wheelchair accessible. The bathrooms are also at everyone's disposal and conform to the Americans with Disabilities Act. In past locations, architectural complications hampering wide chairs from easily moving around in the space was a serious problem, especially with a maturing baby boomer crowd. These barriers, however, don't exist at the Community Church of New York.

In 2014, the Cafe finally incorporated and became a nonprofit organization opposed to being a membership group. Its 501(c)(3) status allows the all-volunteer collective to raise funds in addition to the unreliable financial support it enjoyed over the years. For instance, a basic membership subscription is $20 per year. The subscription rate for two people at one address is $30. Supporters receive a reduced rate to shows, and a monthly schedule of events. Although subscribers and nonsubscribers alike come into possession of the monthly schedule because it is a marketing tool. As a result, it isn't really a benefit.

With nonprofit legal status, the Cafe has economic stability, at least it did before COVID-19. It obtained some small grants to help bankroll its efforts and was able to secure tax deductible donations from individuals to help sustain the group.

Most essential to the Cafe is its front-line volunteers and organic style of horizontal leadership. Every representative in the collective has a job and everyone leads. It is a model for participatory democracy at its best and it has served the community well. Jobs include collecting entrance fees, selling refreshments, prepping the space before and after a show, assisting with mailings, running the sound, booking the artists, promoting the events, vending merchandise for the performers, balancing the books, and baking.

First and foremost, Peoples' Voice Cafe offers something different. It is the last nerve center for topical music in Manhattan. The Greenwich Village heyday has run its course and the commercial venues, so commonplace in the 1960s, have all vanished. Night spots like the Gaslight, Gerdes Folk City, Cafe Wha?, the Village Gate, and The Bottom Line, were snuffed out by neighborhood gentrification. PVC is in a unique position to make the coffee house the premier locale for artists committed to social change activism. This is especially true with the blossoming Black Lives Matter Movement.

Another differentiating characteristic of the Cafe is its recognizable egalitarian principles. There are no superstars on the bill. Every artist is considered equal regardless of fame outside of the PVC arena.

Cafe concerts are inexpensive. The suggested gate is $20 – more if you choose, less if you can't – no one is turned away. This firmly established practice of equitability makes PVC shows accessible to everyone regardless of financial status. On the other hand, what is great for patrons isn't necessarily great for artists. A smaller gate can affect the wallet of the performer making it impossible for some to accept a gig. On the bright side, however, a countless number of balladeers have welcomed the opportunity to play throughout PVC's more than forty-year history. Peoples' Voice Cafe is a cause and many of the troubadours that I have booked have wanted to support its mission.

AT PEOPLES' VOICE CAFE WE ARE ALL LEADERS

What follows is an abbreviated example of the "We Are All Leaders" PVC doctrine, which can even be illustrated in the case of *The Cost of Freedom*, the event that was never realized due to the pandemic. The scenario looks like this: During a previous engagement at the Cafe, Steve Suffet, a long-time associate of the collective and a PVC board member, asked me if I wanted to produce the last show of the season in 2020 to coincide with the fiftieth anniversary of the Kent and Jackson State shootings. Magpie and I were in the house that evening to launch another performance. I discussed the proposal with the husband-and-wife duo, prior to our soundcheck. We believed that it would be a fitting tribute to the slain students and a great way to launch the new book, *The Cost of Freedom: Voicing A Movement After Kent State 1970*. We agreed without hesitation.

In the coming months, leading up to the concert, Magpie and I met numerous times to discuss the selection of dramatic readings and songs. We were equal partners. Initially, I was responsible for organizing literary content for the event and Magpie was tasked with complimenting the powerful testimonials with representative tunes. Once COVID-19 took hold, our conversations shifted on-line. When all was said and done, together, we created a compelling tour de force. Publicity was sent to collective members and was promptly placed on the official PVC site.

That is as far as we got. If the show would have come to fruition, everyone on the evening's team would have gotten into their prospective roles to ensure its success. There would be volunteers at the gate to collect the entrance fee. Other volunteers would be in the back of the house with the baked goods. Someone would be at the merchandise table and the sound engineers would be setting up equipment for the event. Tasks and responsibilities in the collective are known at the onset. Everyone chooses to participate on a committee and the members within that group make decisions. Those decisions are coordinated and discussed by other parties. That way, everyone is in the loop and it leads to a rewarding night. No one, however, steps on anyone else's toes.

Virtual conversations always take place prior to a PVC program. It has nothing to do with the pandemic. It is the best way to get everyone on the same page. Our deliberations are civil. We share the same basic philosophy. We want to provide an accessible diverse community space for artists who are involved in humanitarian causes. We are an egalitarian operation. Our principles are evident in the way we operate. And as Meta Mendel-Reyes points out:

> *Through participation, we become more fully who we are, as individuals and as members of communities. Through participation, we become political adults, making decisions together about our collective lives. Through participation, we share in a movement culture of preparing meals together, of telling stories, of singing great songs, of being connected to a particular group of people, and to the activists who came before and who will come after us. (Mendel-Reyes, 1995, p. 163)*

This is what participatory democracy and horizontal leadership looks like.

The Peoples' Voice Cafe, however, is not the first organization to utilize a grassroots, bottom-up, horizontal leadership model grounded in participatory democracy. The "We Are All Leaders" paradigm was around long before the PVC existed and the field of leadership was an accepted area of inquiry. The terminology is different, but the fundamental principles are similar.

For instance, the Industrial Workers of the World (IWW), otherwise known as the Wobblies, were leadership practitioners and scholars in their own right. Near the beginning of C. Wright Mill's 1948 publication *The New Men of Power*, he related eyewitness testimony of an event that took place in Everett, Washington during the Free Speech battle waged by the IWW in 1917. When a ship full of Wobblies approached the shore, Sheriff McRae shouted out to them, "Who is your leader?" "We are all leaders!" was the response (Lynd & Grubacic, 2008).

Fred Thompson, an organizer for the IWW and onetime editor of its newspaper, *The Industrial Worker*, discussed horizontal, transformational leadership in a 1957 article, "The Art of Making A [sic] Decent Revolution."

> *Our hope is that workers will build large and effective unions that are run by the rank and file; that the structure of these unions will correspond to the actual economic ties between workers, so that workers on every job will be in a position to determine more and more what happens on that job; and through a collective class-wide structure, decide what happens in industry as a whole. It is in this way, as we see it, that the working class can reshape its world into something consistent with our better aspirations and with the technical capacities mankind has developed. (Kornbluh, 1998, p. 385)*

Group-centered leadership is also the backbone of the Highlander Folk School, now known as the Highlander Research and Education Center. Founded in 1932 in Monteagle, Tennessee, the organization is a place where "average citizens can pool their knowledge, learn from history … and seek solutions to their social problems" (Dunson, 1965, p. 28).

The unification of cultural expression with a horizontally led leadership-development training program, has been the main ingredient of the institution's educational agenda since its earliest days.

In the 1960s, the Highlander doctrine served as the prevailing instructional archetype for cultural activists who were deeply involved in civil rights work in the South. And 85 years later, Highlander still "serves as a catalyst for grassroots organizing and movement building in Appalachia and the U.S. South" (Highlander Center, n.d.).

Saul Alinsky, known as one of the great community organizers in the United States, framed the concept of horizontal leadership in terms of peoples' organizations. Like Highlander, education is a key component in peoples' organizations. It is the root of the transformational process:

> *In a People's Organization popular education is an exciting and dramatic process. Education instead of being distant and academic becomes a direct and intimate part of the personal lives, experiences, and activities of the people. Knowledge then becomes an arsenal of weapons in the battle against injustice and degradation. It is no longer learning for learning's sake, but learning for a real reason, a purpose. It ceases to be a luxury or something known under the vague, refined name of culture and becomes as essential as money in the bank, good health, good housing, or regular employment. (Alinsky, 1969, p. 173)*

There are literally hundreds of examples that illustrate the "We Are All Leaders" model. Only a few are mentioned here to provide readers with a conceptual frame. Peoples' Voice Cafe fits into this paradigm.

CLOSED UNTIL JANUARY 2021 – POSSIBLY SEPTEMBER 2021

On June 18, 2020, the following notice went out to the Peoples' Voice Cafe membership:

PEOPLES' VOICE CAFE CANCELATION NOTICE FOR ALL PERFORMANCES FROM SEPTEMBER THROUGH DECEMBER 2020

In mid-March, because of the COVID-19 pandemic, the Peoples' Voice Cafe canceled the remainder of our September 2019–May 2020 season. While we had hoped to resume our regular program this coming September, we now find that is impossible for three reasons:

- The COVID-19 pandemic continues to pose a danger to our volunteers, to our artists, and to our audiences.

- Community Church of New York, our venue, is currently closed, and we cannot count on it being open by September.

- We do not know when New York City and New York State will permit concert venues such as ours to reopen. Furthermore, even if the restrictions are lifted before September, both the Peoples' Voice Cafe and Community Church of New York have decided to be exceedingly cautious and reopen slowly.

> *Based upon these three factors, the Peoples' Voice Cafe Board of Directors has reluctantly decided to cancel all of our shows from September through December 2020. We regret that we have to take this action, but the Covid-19 pandemic is a force majeure, an extraordinary event that is beyond anyone's control. We will do our best to rebook the artists whose shows have been canceled, but it might take us more than a year to do so.*

> *As of now, we hope that the three shows we had booked for January 2021 will take place as scheduled. However, there is a very real possibility that we will have to cancel those shows as well. Even if we do not cancel those shows, we might have to impose some restrictions, such as limiting the size of the audience.*

At this point, we hope to resume our regular program no later than September 2021. In the meantime, we are exploring the possibility of presenting one or more shows online as live streaming video (PeoplesVoiceCafe@comcast.net, June 18, 2020).

Shortly thereafter, on June 22, 2020, the postponement of events was confirmed at the PVC board meeting I attended. The outbreak of COVID-19 impacted the horizontally led collective in a serious way. The cancelation of shows has taken the one-of-a-kind New York City coffee house out of circulation, but this is only temporary. The dedicated volunteers are in for the long haul. Possibly starting virtual programming to let folks know that they are alive and well. And they are determined to be on the front line of change when the Big Apple is opened for business again.

My time with the Peoples' Voice Cafe booking committee has been rewarding. It was not my first adventure with horizontal leadership and participatory democracy. It has been, however, long-lasting and transformational. I will continue to serve and look forward to a robust celebration once the organization gets back on its feet.

EPILOGUE

Since I originally wrote this chapter, on September 12, 2020, PVC hosted a Black Lives Matter Live Stream Concert. Performers for the evening included Dilson Hernandez, Suzanne Schmid with Your Reckless Mind, and Lindsey Wilson. There was a $12 contribution request to help support the performers, whose careers have been temporarily put on hold due to COVID-19. As stated earlier in this chapter, PVC has a "nobody turned away" policy, so the event was also held on the PVC Facebook page and Youtube channel. Additional livestream events are scheduled throughout the end of 2020. So, for now, PVC keeps on keeping on.

REFERENCES

Alinsky, S. (1969). *Reveille for radicals*. New York, NY: Vintage Books.

Dunson, J. (1965). *Freedom in the air: Song movements of the 60s*. New York, NY: International.

Featherstone, J. (1989). To make the wounded whole. *Harvard Educational Review*, *59*, 367–368.

Highlander Center. (n.d.). Our Story. Retrieved from www.highlandercenter.org

Kornbluh, J. (1998). *Rebel voices: An IWW anthology*. Chicago, IL: Charles H. Kerr.

Korza, P., & Bacon, B. S. (2010). *Trend or tipping point: Arts & social change grantmaking*. Washington, DC: Americans for the Arts.

Lawrence-Lightfoot, S. (2005). Reflections on portraiture: A dialog between art and science. *Qualitative Inquiry*, *11*(1), 3–15.

Lawrence-Lightfoot, S., & Davis, J. H. (1997). *The art and science of portraiture*. San Francisco, CA: Jossey-Bass.

Lynd, S., & Grubacic, A. (2008). *Wobblies and Zapatistas: Conversations on anarchism, Marxism, and radical history*. Oakland, CA: PM Press.

Mendel-Reyes, M. (1995). *Reclaiming democracy: The sixties in politics and memory*. New York, NY: Routledge.

Peoples' Voice Cafe. (n.d.). *Home*. Retrieved from www.peoplesvoicecafe.org

Suffet, S. (2018, September 13). The Peoples' Voice Cafe in New York City. *Interface Newsletter*. Retrieved from https://intersections.ilamembers.org/member-benefit-access/interface/grassroots-leadership/member-benefit-access-interface-grassroots-leadership-peoples-voice-cafe92

The Community Church of New York. (n.d.). About Us. Retrieved from http://www.ccny.org

14

OPEN DATA, DISTRIBUTED LEADERSHIP AND FOOD SECURITY: THE ROLE OF WOMEN SMALLHOLDER FARMERS

ÉLIANE UBALIJORO, VICTOR N. SUNDAY, FOTEINI ZAMPATI, UCHECHI SHIRLEY ANADUAKA AND SUCHITH ANAND

INTRODUCTION

According to Jeremy Rifkin in his 2009 book, *"The Empathic Civilization": Rethinking Human Nature in the Biosphere Era,* we have moved from the Age of Reason to the Age of Empathy. In a big data driven global context, how do we ensure no one is left behind? Digital literacy has become the critical skill to communicate and transact locally and globally. Fully harnessing digital technologies in service to humanity and the planet, however, requires unique collaborative leadership compared to a winner takes all profit-driven model.

This work builds on shared leadership theory by emphasizing

> *the need for members to co-lead each other. Also known by labels such as horizontal, distributed, or collective leadership, shared leadership theory views leadership as a set of actions, rather than a designated role. (Johnson, Safadi, & Faraj, 2015)*

Our intent is to illustrate distributed leadership in action toward zero hunger and poverty leveraging open data by highlighting an example of women smallholder farmers in Nigeria.

Agriculture in the twenty-first century combines technological, business, and social acumen, a combination that has been traditionally available. However, an additional layer that is disrupting how we engage in agriculture and nutrition has been the accelerated use of digital data and tools. These fourth industrial revolution tools are guiding when and how we grow food to how we make it accessible through markets and the value addition life cycle. This collaborative process is bringing together leadership across disciplines in ways that were unimaginable in the past. Power dynamics and ownership rights are shifting in ways that can ensure the marginalized and the poorest have equitable access to knowledge they contribute to as well as knowledge that helps improve their sustainable livelihoods.

Open data platforms involve shared co-creation, production, access, and use of digital commons. This chapter will examine examples of how open data policies and capacity development at local levels are helping to empower distributed leadership in women smallholder farmers and increase their livelihoods. We will also explore how land rights for women smallholder farmers powered by digitalization greatly influence the capacity to achieve the United Nations Sustainable Development Goal 1 (SDG 1) End Poverty and Sustainable Development Sustainable Development Goal 2 (SDG 2) Zero Hunger.

Dialogue related to open data ownership must actively include participation of vulnerable populations under climate threat, especially representation from the 800 million people who go hungry every night as well as the 2.7 billion who experience food insecurity. Their active participation in the articulations of rights and governance systems related to open data in agriculture and nutrition is critical to empathy and evidence-driven solutions to meet the biggest challenges we face in feeding a growing population. Africa's population, for example, is set to reach 2.6 billion by 2050 while the continent will also be responsible for half of the births on the planet between now and 2050. By 2035, half the world's workforce will be African (Swaniker, 2018).

In the context of a growing vulnerable African population, it is critical that digital technologies contribute in all ways possible to sustainable food production on the African continent and to ending rising levels of malnutrition. Empowering local smallholder farmers to improve their livelihoods and harness the new "gold" that data are being touted to be will require paradigm shifts that help end the digital divide and ensure benefits to the most marginalized for their contributions to data acquisitions, sharing, and use. How do we ensure that ownership rights do not accrue to the intermediaries that invest in databases, but to the persons who provide or use data, especially smallholder women farmers? What leadership models do we need to look at to promote equity-based governance models? Can inter-organizational open data charters, international treaties, national model laws and policies or a social certification scheme for open data be part of the solution? What are the critical roles and responsibilities that must be taken care of to raise awareness and build the needed capacity to resolve open data ownership challenges?

OPEN DATA FOR FOOD SECURITY AND THE COMMONS

Open Data comprises a critical concern of the commons and their leadership. An exploration of distributed leadership through the work of Global Open Data in Agriculture and Nutrition (GODAN) as well as other perspectives related to how leadership of the commons is changing our global relationship to agriculture, food and nutrition will highlight how this landscape is empowering female smallholder farmers around the world. Advocacy for open data use in advancing global food security and nutrition stems from the reality that farmers use of data-driven agriculture significantly increases their on-farm income. Leveraging collective wisdom to nurture sustainable food systems highlights the interdependence needed to address information asymmetry of vulnerable populations within a knowledge intensive agriculture framework.

Democratizing access to knowledge and insights from satellites to remote sensing instruments enhances sustainable agricultural practices by minimizing use of costly inputs, enhancing better use of natural resources, and better, less wasteful logistical connections to food value chains. When farmers have access to these sources of digital data, they are able to connect to local and global market spaces and knowledge acquisition toward thriving and sustainable livelihoods. Open Data for Agriculture and Nutrition communities are creating spaces to manage shared resources and services that enable harnessing digital technologies to achieve food security locally and globally. These open data communities are collaborative and transdisciplinary. This leadership is reshaping how we view sustainable food systems around the world and will continue to become more critical as global populations increase, especially in emerging countries, and demands on our planet's natural resources rise. Collaboration in Open Data for Agriculture and Nutrition is changing the governance of shared resources and services around the world for a more caring and food secure world.

STRENGTHENING LOCAL CAPACITY DEVELOPMENT FOR ZERO HUNGER THROUGH OPEN DATA

Globally, approximately 821 million people suffer from hidden hunger and micronutrient deficiencies due to the lack of nutritious meals (WFP, 2019). Moreover, more than 45% of deaths of children under the age of five are due to malnutrition owing to the lack of vitamin A, protein and zinc commonly found in animal source foods like fish and meat they have scarce access to in their diets (WHO, 2019). Hunger and diseases related to hunger are responsible for around nine million deaths a year. Over three million of these deaths represent loss of life of hungry and malnourished children (The World Counts, 2020). For those who survive nutrient deprivation, there is a significant impact on their physical health, psychosocial development, long-term opportunities and productivity (WFP, 2020). The threats to food security and nutrition have been linked to conflicts and instability, natural disasters due to climate change, economic slowdown, and policy failures (FAO, IFAD, UNICEF, WFP, & WHO, 2019).

Promoting food security and nutrition relies heavily on well-targeted and informative policies, which combine disaster risk management plans, robust social protection systems for the vulnerable, and inclusive socioeconomic and sustainable agricultural programs. GODAN helps to provide these policies through a global network that includes over 1,100 organizations (governments, international organizations, private sector and academia) from 118 countries across the world. Close to half of GODAN partner organizations are on the African continent. The GODAN alliance has deep expertise in agriculture and nutrition, ranging from genomes all the way to satellites, organizations big and small, with a unique range of expertise covering all aspects related to food, from farm to fork and beyond. GODAN has also demonstrated strong capacity building in Africa, tapping into a wide range of resources including the Regional Universities Forum for Capacity Building in Agriculture (RUFORUM) which is a consortium of 113 African universities operating within 38 countries spanning the African continent. This network has no hierarchy. Participation allows all to share and benefit from each other's knowledge and insights of collective good. As an example, when farmers have access to meteorological, soil and market data generated through these types of networks, their incomes often increase by at least 30%. Data they have access to are generated by experts and by farmer cooperatives and can come also from their own plots. All farmers are producers and users of data. Sharing and communication of data and insights generate value toward achieving SDGs 1 and 2 through distributed leadership.

SMALLHOLDER FARMERS

The world's estimated 570 million smallholder farmers provide over 80% of the food consumed in a large part of the developing world, contributing significantly to poverty reduction and food security (IFAD, 2013; OXFAM, 2017). Smallholder farmers do not compete on equitable terms in local, regional, or global markets. Smallholder farmers, although they are poor, play an essential role in the economic life of most developing countries. A study undertaken by GRAIN (2014), an international nonprofit organization that works to support smallholder farmers and social movements in their struggles for community-controlled and biodiversity-based food systems, identified six major themes that characterize this global population:

1. *"The vast majority of farms in the world today are small and getting smaller*

2. *Small farms are currently squeezed onto less than a quarter of the world's farmland*

3. *We are fast losing farms and farmers in many places, while big farms are getting bigger*

4. *Small farms continue to be the major food producers in the world*

5. *Small farms are overall more productive than big farms*

6. *Most small farmers are women."*

EMPOWERING WOMEN SMALLHOLDER FARMERS

Women are the face of smallholder farming and the workforce for food production. They constitute 60–80% of smallholder farmers in developing countries and produce 70–80% of food in African countries. Despite their contribution to agricultural production, they constitute less than 15% of the landowners (FAO, 2018), a reality which threatens their livelihoods, rights, and socioeconomic status (Chandra, McNamara, Dargusch, Caspe, & Dalabajan, 2016). Achieving a world without hunger will be far-fetched without equal land rights, access to critical inputs, and improved efficiency for smallholder farmers. According to the World Bank (2018), the world could get a bit closer to achieving the goal of zero hunger if smallholder farmer rights would be well-entrenched in the systems. This is especially important for rights related to gender. In many of these countries, women hold the majority share of smallholdings but have limited rights to land and other agricultural resources. Without closing the gender gap in land rights, access to agricultural resources (e.g., data, knowledge, tools and skills), capacity for self-determined decision-making and efficient supply chains (i.e., input and output markets), women remain disempowered and unable to contribute fully to agricultural production systems. In other words, land rights are critical to achieving measurable targets of SDG 2 Zero Hunger.

Women's land rights and tenure security are critical to gender equity, as a means to promote economic growth and development as well as to reduce poverty. These issues are gaining prominence in the international agenda since two of the SDG indicators (5.A.1 and 1.4.2) focus on women's land rights (Doss & Meinzen-Dick, 2018). The current inequality in land rights, in addition to lack of access to financial services, markets (i.e., input and output), agricultural training and education, suitable working conditions, and equal treatment, place women farmers in a disadvantaged position. The lack of security in land tenure prevents women from entering into contract agreements which are beneficial in terms of crop yields, earnings and long-term sources of income.

Moreover, having equal access to land rights can afford women the necessary collateral to access credit and for capital investments. Without these rights, female smallholder farmers are less likely to access social networks (membership in agricultural associations), economic inputs (buy and use fertilizer, quality seeds that are drought-resistant, etc.), and farming tools (e.g., water pumps). All these factors are necessary for increasing crop yields and building sustainable agricultural practices (Duckett, 2019). Closing the gender gap in rights and opportunities to land assets is ensuring that women are empowered to scale agricultural production and reap the gains from sustainable farming practices. Empowering women farmers, with the same rights and opportunities to productive resources as men, is increasing their agency and capacity to invest in their farms. Scaling this globally could increase their farm yields by 20–30% thereby lifting 100–150 million (12–17%) people out of hunger and raise the total agricultural output in developing countries by 2.5–4% (FAO, 2012).

Open data are helping level the playing field for female smallholder farmers by addressing the inequalities in the world related to land registration.

Open access knowledge platforms are giving women the opportunity to register digitally land in their name, securing their rights. Improvement in the rights to land assets is enabling women to *"reap a timely and fair return and be able to enforce their rights against non-holders"* (FAO, 1996). A lot of work still needs to be done to reach scale, but bright examples are encouraging. In Rwanda, a nationwide digital-based registry has secured rights to 11 million parcels of land for many smallholder farmers, many of them women. The open data available in the land registry highlight the fact that a higher number of women hold real rights on land compared to men now in Rwanda. This is transformational for Rwanda. Before 1994, women had no rights to inherit land in Rwanda. Now not only is open data allowing them to secure rights to land, but now women can leverage this asset "to get involved with new commercial ventures, investing and enhancing their properties or building rural enterprises" (GODAN, 2016, pp. 6–7). Open access to this data is reducing conflicts related to tenancies and proprietary land in the most densely populated country in Africa. This is helping secure and scale long-term social stability, equality and harmony powered by data. Open data are a critical element to the entire commons movement because it is supporting and scaling knowledge platforms that encourage people to have more power over their own lives. In the Rwanda case, 90% of those how have benefited from the land registry are low-income households and most are female smallholder farmers.

These great developments should not discount the urgent need for open data frameworks to have rules of usage and access to ensure ill-willed people cannot pollute the data, introduce garbage data, and mislead users, an issue that is growing at an alarming rate on social media today. Voluntary codes of conduct related to access and use of agriculture data are encouraging needed ethical frameworks for safe open data. GODAN in partnership with the Technical Centre for Agriculture and Rural Cooperation (CTA) and the Global Forum on Agricultural Research and Innovation (GFAR) have produced an agriculture code of conduct toolkit to facilitate stakeholder engagement for win/win shared co-created ethical frameworks. The toolkit helps stakeholders gain a better understanding of the differing needs and concerns of all actors, strengthening trust throughout the data value chain and enriching the commons. The practical benefits of the toolkit are having "scalable guidelines for everyone dealing with the production, ownership, sharing and use of data in agriculture" (GODAN, 2020).

OPEN DATA MAPPING EMPOWERMENT FOR WOMEN: THE UNIQUE MAPPERS APPROACH

Women's empowerment is central to open data mapping for sustainable agriculture at global and local levels. Data about where and who is empowered are also important. This allows knowing where and who owns a parcel of land for agriculture, a critical factor in securing loans based on land as a collateral. Empowering women to drive open data mapping in agriculture is a sure trigger of multiple and measurable targets of SDGs in developing African countries. Issues about women's land rights, agricultural sustainability and the SDGs can be tackled with open data mapping (Sunday, Ojo, Nathelia, & Anaduaka, 2020). Unique Mappers Network, Nigeria, leverages on open data mapping empowerment strategy to drive GODAN Action (an initiative to leverage standards, research and capacity), SDG targets and women inclusive community engagement. This approach impacts positively on knowledge about women land rights and agricultural sustainability and is being used to advocate for scaling of Open data infrastructure, in Nigeria and other low to middle income African countries in general.

Unique Mappers Network (UniqueMappersTeam) or UMT Network is a Nigerian registered nonprofit organization with a mandate and mission for Humanitarian Response and Community Development through:

1. *"Open Mapping using OpenStreetMap project in Nigeria*

2. *Mobile Data collection & Field Surveys for open data development*

3. *Open Source Geospatial Empowerment using GeoForAll Lab*

4. *Flying Lab/Community Drone Mapping for open data development*

5. *Participatory Citizens Science Projects for community engagement*

6. *Gender-Equality and Youth Empowerment using Open Data & Open Geospatial*

7. *Community Inclusive Empowerment for Sustainable Development Actions."*

UMT leverages community inclusive empowerment programs (using Open Data and Open Source Geospatial software) to drive GODAN Action for SDG2 (Zero hunger) in Nigeria. Unique Mappers' partnership with GODAN is anchored in the Open Data Capacity Development program for food security in Nigeria. UMT network provides map data that are open and accessible not just for disaster response, emergency crises, research, and economic development but also open data mapping that empowers women and smallholder farmers' land rights to achieve measurable targets related to the Sustainable Development Goals. UMT drives operational capacity for community engagement across the 36 states of Nigeria, with emerging Unique Mappers state chapters and Unique Mappers response teams in higher institutions in Nigeria and beyond.

Through GODAN Action, UMT drives open data capacity development that engages Unique Mappers-GODAN Ambassadors and Champions, inclusive women communities, youth in higher institutions as well as public and private sector stakeholders for a multidisciplinary nexus of National Open Data Initiatives (NDIs) that facilitate digitalization of agriculture, empowers female smallholder farmers as well as boost digital economy for sustainable agriculture. GODAN-Nigeria capacity development program for the NDI project in Nigeria is focused on providing critical geospatial data about the food supply chain that empowers smallholder women farmers, including women and girls who are involved in fishery and Agro-businesses.

Empowering women with open-source geospatial skills enables effective community engagement for open data capacity development for food security. Without geospatial skill empowerment, critical geospatial data about the location of a farmland, the size of such lands, crop types, supply chain values as well as who owns the land (land rights) would not be readily available. The empowerment of women in open data mapping also provides the opportunity for women to collect data as well as make it accessible through globally free-to-use platforms such as the OpenStreetMap. The Unique Mappers approach to women's empowerment in open data mapping is anchored on OpenStreet-Map techniques which enables open data acquisition as well as Geospatial Skill Empowerment for Women and everyone. Empowering women with geospatial skills also provides an opportunity to bridge the gender gap in the digital divide. It provides opportunity for women to freely share, use, and reuse data about land use, farmlands, land rights and whatever is mapped on the earth's surface. In addition, it provides the opportunity for women to be knowledgeable about their land rights and benefits, particularly for vulnerable rural African women, including widows (Sunday et al., 2020).

Ogrute Community is the epicenter of a hill called Ugwu Eru – more than 562 m above sea level (Photos 1 and 2). Ugwu Eru seasonally produces

Photo 1.   Location Details of Ugwu Eru Hill, Ogrute Community, Enugu-Ezike, Nigeria.

Photo 2.   Location Details of Ugwu Eru Hill, Ogrute Community, Enugu-Ezike, Nigeria.

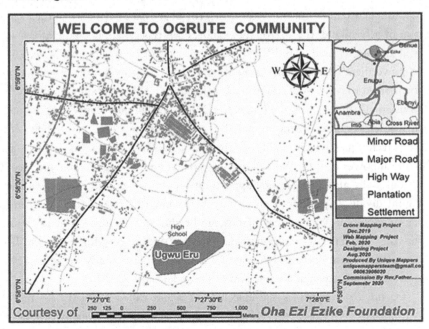

13 edible species of mushrooms. Mushrooms are globally known to be highly nutritious and very good for our health as they are packed with dozens of minerals and vitamins. Among the projects carried out by Unique Mappers with women inclusive participation around GODAN Action is the Ogrute Ugwu Eru Mapathon for SDG2 food security project in Ogrute Community Enugu-Ezike, Enugu State Nigeria (Photos 3–5). Open Data Mapping for Ogrute provided critical geospatial data for SDG-2 measurable targets. A survey for the assessment of the food value chain was administered to more than 100 sampled smallholder farmers in Ogrute. The supply chain value, benefits, productivity, frequency of consumption as well as the type of farming system and farmers land rights in the area were accessed during the community mapping of Ogrute. The assessment indicated that mushrooms grow mostly during the

Photo 3.   Ogrute Ugwu Eru Community Drone Mapping and Mapathon Organized by UniqueMappersTeam.

**Photo 4.   Ogrute Ugwu Eru Community Drone Mapping and Mapathon
Organized by UniqueMappersTeam.**

**Photo 5.   Ogrute Ugwu Eru Community Drone Mapping and Mapathon
Organized by UniqueMappersTeam.**

rainy season. More than 5,000 households, most of whom are smallholder
farmers that depend on mushrooms for subsistence and nutrition, were added
to OpenStreetMap as an open data map for Ogrute Community. This kind of
community mapping project provides opportunities for women's empowerment, especially, girls who can engage in drone mapping, mobile data collection

as well as digitization of data using geospatial skills (Sunday et al., 2020). As data science jobs gain importance in the digital economy, women's active participation ensures sustainable livelihoods for their families and communities.

Unique Mappers Network, also leverages the annual celebration of Open Data Day (ODD), International Women's Day (IWD) as well as the Let-GirlsMap campaign of YouthMappers Network, to provide opportunity for women empowerment with open data mapping to enable them to respond to vulnerable communities in Nigeria. During such events, Unique Mappers organize and host events to build capacity in geospatial skills by reaching out to women, girls, and youths in high school and tertiary institutions in various parts of Nigeria, working with female volunteers who lead the events (Photos 6–8). This is critical to minimize gender-based bias that prevents girls and women's safe exploration of scientific initiatives while creating a safe environment to learn. These events are also used to drive SDG 5 – Gender equality in the mapping community of Unique Mappers (Photos 9–12)

Photo 6.   Participants at the Unique Mappers International Women's Day (IWD) Open Data.

Photo 7. Participants at the Unique Mappers International Women's Day (IWD) Open Data.

EMPOWERMENT EVENTS

The COVID-19 pandemic has highlighted the need for safe ways of doing research, trading food while minimizing movement of people. This has created a unique opportunity for the Unique Mappers Network to advance GODAN Action of open data advocacy to achieving SDG 2 food security by accelerating the use of data science to grow, process, and deliver food in a timely way,

Photo 8. Participants at the Unique Mappers International Women's Day (IWD) Open Data.

Photo 9. Unique Mappers Women and Girls Empowerment Event Organized as part of International Women's Day and Open Data Day 2020.

Photo 10.   Unique Mappers Women and Girls Empowerment Event Organized as Part of International Women's Day and Open Data Day 2020.

Photo 11.   Unique Mappers Women and Girls Empowerment Event Organized as Part of International Women's Day and Open Data Day 2020.

Photo 12.   Unique Mappers Women and Girls Empowerment Event Organized as Part of International Women's Day and Open Data Day 2020.

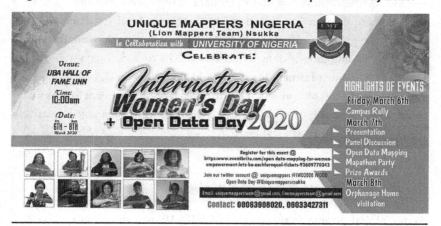

while increasing logistical efficiencies. Unique Mappers Nigeria collaborated with RichFood Foundation (a not-for-profit organization providing community response) to access data for COVID 19 household food interventions among the women farmers of Kpaduma village (Photo 13). Kpaduma village

Photo 13.   Heatmap of COVID-19 Pandemic Household Food Intervention in Kpaduma Village, Nigeria.

is a community consisting mainly of poor smallholder farmers in Abuja FCT, Nigeria. The impact of the COVID-19 pandemic necessitated food intervention for the community, and open data about where and how palliative measures are dispersed was critical to supporting local food security and proactive response to vulnerable women in the area. Female volunteers were empowered using mobile data collection toolkits to access data about these smallholder women farmers for household food intervention. Making such data open and accessible via ICT platforms enables government and humanitarian agencies to empower these rural farmers as well as manage proactively issues of food security at local levels.

CONCLUSION

As the global population navigates COVID-19, no corner on the earth is unaffected by the current pandemic. The potential effects on food systems could be devastating. What is clear is that until everyone is safe from the virus, we are all vulnerable. The urgent need to upend traditional corporate intellectual property is now. Humanity needs a bottom-up, open-source, open science, peer-to-peer knowledge sharing space to help uplift the most marginalized. The fourth industrial revolution has given us a powerful platform that can help connect over 570 million smallholder farmers to amazing tools that help increase sustainable food systems and local livelihoods. Distributed leadership can harness these technological breakthroughs in ways that cultivate our interdependence. What is needed is to start with the goal that open data can be the gold that helps us achieve the impossible, ending poverty and hunger globally. No one alone can do this; all of us can contribute in small and big ways together to solve these wicked problems.

> It is now possible for large groups of people to coordinate their actions, not just by bringing lots of information to a few centralized places but also by bringing lots of information to lots of places through ever-growing networks within and beyond. (Ancona, Malone, Orlikowski, & Senge, 2007, p. 93)

This distributed leadership builds on bringing sensemaking, relating, visioning, and inventing to serve a larger goal.

What is needed is for each of us to become our sister/brother's keeper across humanity. By understanding context, nurturing relationships widely across networks, a compelling vision of the future can be co-designed. We can than nurture this vision of the future from a common purpose. We can navigate the uncertainties that show up and cultivate an emerging plan we can each contribute our best to. What open data can promote at its best is the ethics of helping each other, by sharing our knowledge, so others can build on it for the greater good. Open data when used ethically celebrates community, collective leadership, diversity and encourages inclusion. When we know we need others, we approach our work with humility, ready to learn from others, to practice reciprocity. We open ourselves to our vulnerability. We open ourselves to the reality that we cannot solve complex problems like global food security and nutrition alone. We embrace the power of shared ideas. Cultivating leadership for the commons through digital data to grow global food security takes away our need to be heroic and nurtures our interdependence. This cultivation of leadership nurtures the open, transparent, and vulnerable parts of us that heroic leadership does not allow. Leadership for the commons values the needed one world consciousness that is required for science to serve compassionate care of all people, in ways that contributes to planetary health.

REFERENCES

Ancona, D., Malone, T. W., Orlikowski, W. J., & Senge, P. M. (2007). In praise of the incomplete leader. *Harvard Business Review*, 85(2), 92–100, 156. PMID: 17345683.

Chandra, A., McNamara, K. E., Dargusch, P., Caspe, A. M., & Dalabajan, D. (2016). Gendered vulnerabilities of smallholder farmers to climate change in conflict-prone areas: A case study from Mindanao, Philippines. *Journal of Rural Studies*, 50(2017), 45–59. doi:10.1016/j.jrurstud.2016.12.011

Doss, C., & Meinzen-Dick, R. (2018). *Women's land tenure security: A conceptual framework*. Research Consortium. Retrieved from https://consortium.resourceequity.org/conceptual-framework

Duckett, M. K. (2019). Empowering female farmers to feed the world. Retrieved from National Geographic: https://www.nationalgeographic.com/culture/2019/03/partner-content-empowering-female-farmers/

FAO, IFAD, UNICEF, WFP, & WHO. (2019). *The State of Food Security and Nutrition in the World 2019. Safeguarding against economic slowdowns and downturns*. FAO. Retrieved from http://www.fao.org/3/ca5162en/ca5162en.pdf

FAO. (1996). *Women, land tenure and food security. Sustainable Development Department*. Food and Agriculture Organization of the United Nations. Retrieved from http://www.fao.org/3/x0171e/x0171e07.htm#P556_66356

FAO. (2011). Women in Agriculture: Closing the gender gap for development. *The State of Food and Agriculture 2010-11* (p. 42). Retrieved from http://www.fao.org/3/i2050e/i2050e.pdf.

FAO. (2018). *The gender gap in land rights*. FAO. Retrieved from http://www.fao.org/3/I8796EN/i8796en.pdf

GODAN. (2016). Land rights in Rwanda: Transparency, land rights, land tenure regularisation. https://www.godan.info/sites/default/files/documents/GODAN_Success_Stories_Brochure_Issue_1.pdf

GODAN. (2020). Agriculture data Code of Conduct toolkit. Retrieved from https://www.godan.info/codes

GRAIN. (2014). Hungry for land: Small farmers feed the world with less than a quarter of all farmland. Retrieved from https://www.grain.org/article/entries/4929-hungry-for-land-small-farmers-feed-the-world-with-less-than-a-quarter-of-all-farmland

IFAD. (2013). Small holders, food security and the environment. Retrieved from https://web.archive.org/web/20130528223144/http://www.ifad.org/operations/food/farmer.htm

Johnson, S. L., Safadi, H., & Faraj, S. (2015). The emergence of online community leadership. *Information Systems Research*, 26(1), 165–187. doi:10.1287/isre.2014.0562

OXFAM. (2017). Financing Women Farmers: The need to increase and redirect agriculture and climate adaptation resources. OXFAm.org. Retrieved from https://reliefweb.int/sites/reliefweb.int/files/resources/bp-financing-women-farmers-131017-en.pdf

Rifkin J. (2009). *The empathic civilization: The race to global consciousness in a world in crisis*. ISBN: 9781585427659.

Sunday, V., Ojo, T., Nathelia, S., & Anaduaka, U. S. (2020). GODAN Webinar on "Empowering Women For Open Data Mapping in Agriculture: Implication for Land Rights and the SDGs in Africa". Retrieved from https://landportal.org/blog-post/2020/05/empowering-women-open-data-mapping-agriculture-implications-land-rights-and-sdgs

Swaniker, F. (2018). How to unlock the talents of young Africans: An entrepreneur from Ghana on the continent's growing population of young people. Retrieved from https://www.gatesnotes.com/development/fred-swaniker-on-africas-next-generation

The World Counts. (2020). How many people die of hunger each year. Retrieved from https://www.theworldcounts.com/challenges/people-and-poverty/hunger-and-obesity/how-many-people-die-from-hunger-each-year/story

UNDP. (2009). Capacity Development: a UNDP primer, p. 5. Retrieved from http://
www.undp.org/content/dam/aplaws/publication/en/publications/capacity-development/
capacity-development-a-undp-primer/CDG_PrimerReport_final_web.pdf

WFP. (2019). 2019 – Hunger Map. World Food Program.

WFP. (2020). *Empowering countries to achieve zero hunger*. Centre of Excellence:
World Food Programme.

WHO. (2019). Children: Reducing mortality. Fact sheets. Retrieved from
https://www.who.int/news-room/fact-sheets/detail/children-reducing-mortality

World Bank. (2018). Breaking the grass ceiling empowering women farmers feature
story. Retrieved from https://www.worldbank.org/en/news/feature/2018/03/06/
breaking-the-grass-ceiling-Empowering-women-farmers

15

LEARNING AND LEADING TOGETHER TO TRANSFORM THE WORLD: JESUIT HIGHER EDUCATION AND IGNATIAN LEADERSHIP FORMATION AT THE MARGINS

DUNG Q. TRAN AND MICHAEL R. CAREY

INTRODUCTION

According to the most recent Global Trends Report of the United Nations High Commissioner for Refugees (UNHCR) (2020), nearly "79.5 million individuals were forcibly displaced worldwide at the end of 2019 as a result of persecution, conflict, violence, human rights violations or events seriously disturbing public order" (p. 2). Of the displaced, only 3% of them could access higher education in 2018 (UNHCR, 2019). A college education furnishes an important foundation for promoting a culture of sustainable development, human rights, equality, peace, global citizenship, and appreciation of diversity and inclusion (United Nations, 2015). Given their enduring reputation for "promoting the common good" (Quan, 2017, p. 9) through their international network of colleges and universities, the Society of Jesus, more commonly known as the Jesuits, have stepped forward to co-create a global learning commons.

With their 500-year-old approach to transformative tertiary education that prepares discerning human persons for leadership and impact across myriad professions (Tran & Carey, 2018), Jesuit education is universally regarded as a global model of educational excellence (Casalini, 2019). In leveraging their international network of universities, ministries, and relationships, they are concretizing the social justice dimension of their educational mission by accompanying marginalized populations as they pursue higher education. Such populations include, but are not limited to, forced migrants and refugees as well as people experiencing extreme poverty.

Since 2010, an initiative initially known as, "Jesuit Commons: Higher Education at the Margins" (JC:HEM), and later rebranded as, "Jesuit Worldwide Learning: Higher Education at the Margins" (JWL), in 2016, is "one of several NGOs delivering higher education to refugees, internally displaced people, and others living at the margins" (Habash, 2020a, p. 8). Through a variety of formats blending on-site, online, and mobile delivery of instructional content harnessing the resources of nearly 200 Jesuit universities (and their alumni networks) across the globe, JWL

> [...] provides equitable high quality tertiary learning to people and communities at the margins of societies – be it through poverty, location, lack of opportunity, conflict or forced displacement – so all can contribute their knowledge and voices to the global community of learners and together foster hope to create a more peaceful and humane world. (Jesuit Worldwide Learning, 2021a, para. 2)

With internet access in short supply in most learners' locales, JWL depends on strategic partners to operate and maintain learning centers in host countries "while providing online education either through its own learning management system (LMS), JWL HeLP, or through the donation of an LMS from Georgetown University for its Diploma program" (Habash, 2020b, p. 151). Students download online course content and upload assignments at community learning centers via JWL-supplied tablets and Wi-Fi. The remotely delivered courses are created by subject matter experts and facilitated by faculty drawn from a "vast pool of global talent" from various disciplines and institutions that include "teacher training experts, newly minted associate professors, and recent refugee arrivals who bring with them academic credentials and additional layers of critical capacity and talent" (Griffin & McFarland, 2016, p. 14).

Consequently, the purpose of this chapter is to review the historical context and circumstances that contributed to the creation of such an innovative and Ignatian-inspired initiative and its sustainable development. Additionally, we discuss how JWL functions as a multidimensional global-leadership-on-the-commons and is animated by a distinctively Ignatian approach to educational formation. Finally, our chapter concludes with several brief stories of committed students and alumni who have emerged as on-site leaders serving as learning coordinators and tutors for JWL and their local communities.

HISTORICAL CONTEXT: THE JESUITS AND THEIR JUSTICE-MINDED APPROACH TO THE COMMON GOOD

According to Cesare Casarino (2008), the commons is "a collective and cooperative process of actualization of common...potentials [intellectual, spiritual, emotional, linguistic, and material, among others] that entails necessarily the mobilization of humankind in its totality" (p. 12) to concretize collective strategies of solidarity among diverse individuals and communities to enact structural social change. Although Casarino has expressed a preference for defining the commons "in terms of communication rather than community" (p. 12), common spaces such as cooperative community economic structures or a university knowledge commons can serve a profound and prophetic rhetorical role for communities clamoring for change. What is now known as Jesuit Worldwide Learning: Higher Education at the Margins and its nearly 500-year-old spiritual, pedagogical, and justice-minded heritage is one such educational knowledge commons worthy of sustained attention.

Within five decades of establishing the Society of Jesus in 1540, Ignatius of Loyola and the first Jesuits became a "worldwide missionary order, a major force in the sixteenth-century renewal of Catholicism, and created an educational system that transformed Europe and beyond" (Sparough, Manney, & Hipskind, 2010, p. 29). As noted in their updated organizational charter in 1550, after officially undertaking education as a signature ministry, the Jesuits pledged to "reconcile the estranged, compassionately assist and serve...and... to perform works of charity according to what will seem expedient for the glory of God and the common good" (de Aldama, 1990, p. 7). Though religious orders predating the Jesuits concretized a concern for the common good – "the sum total of social conditions which allow people, either as groups or as individuals, to reach their fulfillment more fully and more easily" (John Paul II, 1993, n. 1906) – the Jesuits' explicit and official commitment to the common good "was the first in the history of such institutions" (O'Malley, 2016, p. 154).

By 1773, when the Society of Jesus was globally suppressed by Pope Clement XIV, the Jesuits "operated some seven hundred schools of various kinds around the globe" (O'Malley, 2016, p. 155). Pope Pius VII reestablished the Jesuits in 1814, but the immense international network of schools never quite recovered "its earlier levels of prestige and influence" (Banchoff, 2016, p. 244). Since then, however, "the global and civic dimensions of Jesuit higher education have grown more tightly interconnected....[and] increasingly oriented to the global common good" (p. 239). With the Catholic Church's growing openness to dialogue with contemporary culture through the teachings of Vatican II (1962–1965), the Jesuits began to enlarge their perceived purpose of their schools: "to help prepare both young people and adults to live and labor for others and with others to build a more just world" (32nd General Congregation of the Society of Jesus, 1975, #60, para. 3).

In an effort to concretize their commitment to social justice, the Society of Jesus General Pedro Arrupe established the Jesuit Refugee Service in November 1980, specifically, as a response to the plight of Vietnamese refugees fleeing their war-torn country following the Fall of Saigon in 1975 (Bole, 2020). The focus on faith and justice in an increasingly global world continued under the leadership of Jesuit Peter-Hans Kolvenbach, who served as the 29th superior general of the Society of Jesus from 1983 to 2008. In a landmark address on the 25th anniversary of the 32nd General Congregation at Santa Clara University, Kolvenbach (2001) contended that "Jesuit universities have stronger and different reasons than many other academic and research institutions for addressing the actual world as it unjustly exists and for helping to reshape it" (p. 28). Building on these important insights, Fr. Kolvenbach's successor identified several distinctive strengths of Jesuit institutions. Within a crowded higher education market of competitors claiming to form justice-minded citizens for an increasingly globalized world, Jesuit higher education is distinguished by "a strong humanist ethos and a far-flung international network" (Banchoff, 2016, p. 253).

In remarks to representatives of nearly 200 Jesuit institutions of higher learning in 2010 at Universidad Iberoamericana in Mexico City, Jesuit Adolfo Nicolás (2010), the thirtieth superior general of the Society of Jesus, asserted that the primary challenges for the Jesuits are "the challenges of the world" (p. 8). Such challenges include a search for meaning – "Is life worth living?" – as well as "the challenges of poverty, death, suffering, violence and war" (p. 8):

> *When one can access so much information so quickly and so painlessly; when one can express and publish to the world one's reactions so immediately and so unthinkingly in one's blogs or*

micro-blogs; when the latest opinion column from the New York Times *or* El Pais, *or the newest viral video can be spread so quickly to people half a world away, shaping their perceptions and feelings, then the laborious, painstaking work of serious, critical thinking often gets short-circuited. One can "cut-and-paste" without the need to think critically or write accurately or come to one's own careful conclusions.*

When beautiful images from the merchants of consumer dreams flood one's computer screens, or when the ugly or unpleasant sounds of the world can be shut out by one's MP3 music player, then one's vision, one's perception of reality, one's desiring can also remain shallow....When one is overwhelmed with such a dizzying pluralism of choices and values and beliefs and visions of life, then one can so easily slip into the lazy superficiality of relativism or mere tolerance of others...rather than engaging in the hard work of forming communities of dialogue in the search of truth and understanding. It is easier to do as one is told than to study, to pray, to risk, or to discern a choice. (pp. 2–3)

Given the alluring convenience of immediate gratification through the confluence of consumer culture, social media, and moral relativism, Nicolás urged executive leaders of Jesuit higher education to "revitalize their commitment to *cura personalis* through attention to the deep spiritual, emotional, and social, as well as academic and professional, needs of students" (Banchoff, 2016, p. 253). For Nicolás (2010), high-impact Jesuit higher education "integrates intellectual rigor with reflection on the experience of reality together with the creative imagination to work toward constructing a more humane, just, sustainable, and faith-filled world" (pp. 5–6). He also noted that reflection on the experience of reality ought to include an abiding awareness of those on the margins, "especially the world of the poor" (p. 6).

THE ORIGIN AND PILOT PHASE OF JESUIT COMMONS

As evidenced in former Jesuit Superior General Nicolás' (2010) assertions, such a humanistic and socially-driven approach is what has kept issues of justice at the forefront of the Jesuits and their lay collaborators in a rapidly changing, technologically advanced, and globalized world for nearly 500 years. Continuing their enduring commitment and outreach to marginalized populations, "Jesuit universities in 2007 formed Jesuit Commons, a digital entity, as a global platform to share resources and connect institutions via the Internet" (Balleis, 2016, p. 233).

Nicolás (2010), in the aforementioned address to Jesuit higher education leaders in Mexico City, elucidated the need for such an ambitious initiative:

> *First, an important challenge to the learned ministry of our universities today comes from the fact that globalization has created "knowledge societies," in which development of persons, cultures and societies is tremendously dependent on access to knowledge in order to grow. Globalization has created new inequalities between those who enjoy the power given to them by knowledge, and those who are excluded from its benefits because they have no access to that knowledge. Thus, we need to ask: who benefits from the knowledge produced in our institutions and who does not? Who needs the knowledge we can share, and how can we share it more effectively with those for whom that knowledge can truly make a difference, especially the poor and excluded? We also need to ask some specific questions of faculty and students: How have they become voices for the voiceless, sources of human rights for those denied such rights, resources for protection of the environment, persons of solidarity for the poor? And the list could go on.*
>
> *In this connection, the work-in-progress of the "Jesuit Commons"…is extremely important, and it will require a more serious support and commitment from our universities if it is to succeed in its ambitious dream of promoting greater equality in access to knowledge for the sake of the development of persons and communities. (pp. 9–10)*

In response to Nicolás' call for collaboration, an ever-growing number of universities volunteered their assets to help broaden access to knowledge. Through discernment, discussion, and funding from an anonymous donor, Jesuit Commons became Jesuit Commons: Higher Education at the Margins (JC:HEM), an educational project officially sponsored by the Jesuits and "implemented in close collaboration with JRS [Jesuit Refugee Services] as a global partner" (Balleis, 2016, p. 234). According to Mary McFarland (2013), a co-founder and the first international director of JC:HEM, the notion of commons,

> – be it a virtual one – is much like a university commons area where people could walk through, travel through virtually, and when they had a high need, anyone who had a resource that would match that need would know about it and could come in (from the Jesuit network). (as cited in Topuzova, 2013, p. 144)

McFarland underscored that universities were "resource rich" (p. 144) in the sense of having access to education and educational resources.

With the support of resource rich "universities like Georgetown, Regis, and Gonzaga" (Griffin & McFarland, 2016, p. 12), the pilot phase (2010–2014) began with learning centers in Kenya, Malawi, Syria, and Jordan. During this early period, two academic programs, undergirded by the Ignatian pedagogical paradigm or simply Ignatian pedagogy, were created to serve students. A 45-credit liberal studies diploma from Regis University in Denver, Colorado and community service-learning tracks (CSLTs), a co-created response tailored to the emerging educational desires of and feedback from refugees and host community members – "the very essence of Ignatian pedagogy at work in teaching the Jesuit curriculum of liberal arts" (Balleis, 2016, p. 235). Through the time-tested and eminently adaptable Ignatian pedagogical paradigm, the interplay of student–teacher context, experience, reflection, action, and evaluation (Duminuco, 2000), learners are encouraged to leverage their experiences by engaging their "memory, imagination, and emotion to grasp the value of their learning, its relationship to other aspects of life, and any implications for future study" (Chubbuck, 2007, p. 243). In addition to the emergent community service-learning tracks, another manifestation of Ignatian pedagogy occurred in September 2013 shortly after the first 52 students received their diplomas in liberal arts. In a student-satisfaction survey, the inaugural graduates identified philosophy, logic, and Eastern religions as their favorite courses. Such unexpected favorites prompted what was then JC:HEM, "to solicit more feedback so, just as traditional universities, it could tailor the educational experience to student needs and interests" (Balleis, 2016, p. 235). As a result of this feedback, as well as communication among the larger community of educators, the organization of Jesuit Commons evolved.

FROM JESUIT COMMONS TO JESUIT WORLDWIDE LEARNING

In light of on-going input from alumni, current learners, local community members, faculty and administrators from partner Jesuit universities, corporate benefactors, and Jesuit officials, among others, Jesuit Commons: Higher Education at the Margins (JC:HEM) rebranded itself as Jesuit Worldwide Learning: Higher Education at the Margins (JWL) in 2016 (Balleis, 2020). A common work of the Central European Province of the Society of Jesus, which is comprised of the previous Jesuit provinces of Austria, Germany, Lithuania-Latvia, and Switzerland, the Jesuit leaders of the Central European Province and JWL chose Geneva, Switzerland as JWL's home base because of its close proximity to the international headquarters of the United Nations Human Rights Council (UNHRC), the International Committee of the Red Cross, the World Council of Churches, the World Health Organization, and the Jesuit Refugee Service.

In broadening its base of mission-aligned strategic partners, JWL

> *gained greater operational and organizational capacity to reach more marginalized communities and students, thereby becoming more cost-effective....[and making] the JWL model of online learning at the margins a truly scalable, transferable and sustainable worldwide service. (Balleis, 2018, as cited in Jesuit Worldwide Learning, 2018, p. 5)*

For instance, in December 2019, representatives from Fujitsu Ltd., Seitwerk GmbH, and AfB Social and Green IT met "at the Fujitsu tower in Munich to brainstorm ideas for JWL's five-year strategic framework, and to explore new opportunities for collaboration" (Jesuit Worldwide Learning, 2020a, p. 29).

Another example of cost containment is through the current organizational design of JWL. As an alliance of "three independent non-profit organizations based in Switzerland, the United States and Germany, operations and finances are jointly supported by a collaborative team across...entities" (p. 24). JWL's core staff of 23, many of whom are full-time, manage and organize "the academic delivery, IT, operations, human resources, administration and communication" so that JWL can serve "its 4,000 students worldwide" (p. 30). JWL's team includes a number of Jesuits, on-loan professionals from partner universities and organizations, high-achieving JWL alumni, and many volunteers.

As of February 2021, people at the margins of society are able to access higher education at JWL community learning centers in the following countries: Afghanistan, the Central African Republic, the Democratic Republic of Congo, Guyana, India, Iraq, Italy, Jordan, Kenya, Malawi, Myanmar, Nepal, the Philippines, Sri Lanka, Togo, and Zambia (Jesuit Worldwide Learning, 2021c). At the local level, JWL partner organizations allocate staff to JWL's community centers – another form of cost containment and sharing. For example,

> In 2019, [of the 414 individuals volunteering, supporting, teaching, tutoring and learning together with 4,000 students], there were 40 staff members provided by partner organizations dedicated to JWL. Among those are 10 Jesuits located in Sri Lanka, Myanmar, Afghanistan and Central African Republic. (Jesuit Worldwide Learning, 2020a, p. 30)

JWL's 16 university partners throughout the world "make their contributions in kind, for example, through the provision of volunteer faculty, academic and/or IT platforms and service" (p. 39). For instance, "In 2019, JWL had 207 international faculties online for the academic and professional courses" (p. 30). Many of the volunteer faculty were from Jesuit universities in the United States who taught "courses for the Diploma in Liberal Studies program accredited by Regis University in Denver, Colorado" (p. 30).

In terms of long-term sustainability, it is an open question as to how the knowledge commons that is Jesuit Worldwide Learning can endure when it relies on the generosity of committed university presidents. This will especially be important to monitor given the unexpected millions of dollars in novel coronavirus-related spending by universities. Continued creativity, strategic planning, entrepreneurial innovation, and on-going (corporate) benefaction will be critical for ensuring the long-term future of JWL.

STUDENT SUCCESS STORIES AND FUTURE FRONTIERS FOR JESUIT WORLDWIDE LEARNING

Along with the opportunities and challenges presented by the COVID-19 pandemic during 2020, JWL celebrated 10 years of making Jesuit higher education more accessible to learners on the margins, especially refugees, through blended online learning, and discerning strategic and sustainable ways forward.

In a recent report that quantitatively analyzed admission, completion, and retention data from the online Diploma in Liberal Studies, a program of 15 courses for a total of 45 credits conferred by Regis University, it was determined that, "Over the past 10 years, 433 of 1073 enrolled students have already graduated and a majority of the presently 305 active students are expected to graduate before end of 2021" (Jesuit Worldwide Learning, 2020b, p. 2). Although 335 students withdrew for a variety of reasons, including resettlement,

> *114 out of 335 who dropped-out never earned a credit and left right at the beginning of the program – they either left before actually starting, during the first course, or after failing the first course. (p. 5)*

Since one third of the students who withdrew did not earn a single credit, one possible conclusion is to co-create a "more rigorous admission process" that can more accurately access and predict a prospective student's "commitment and resilience" (p. 5).

Among the 60% of students who persisted to diploma completion, it was found that a vibrant and robust community learning center, especially ones managed by JWL graduates, were more successful in terms of student retention and graduation rates. According to the 2019 Jesuit Worldwide Learning Annual Report (2020a),

> *49 field staff work and support JWL as coordinators and learning facilitators in the community learning centers in Kenya, Malawi, Zambia, Iraq and Jordan. Many have dual roles and almost all are refugees and/or graduates or students of JWL programs. (p. 30)*

Part of this paying-it-forward phenomenon has been fueled by new educational opportunities to matriculate into undergraduate degree programs in management (Southern New Hampshire University, U.S.A.), sustainable development (Xavier University Bhubaneswar, India), and leadership (Creighton University, U.S.A).

Consider the story of Siamoy, who was among the first 12 Afghan students from the Daikundi Province to graduate in 2018 from the Diploma in Liberal Studies program, offered through the Bamyan community learning center in

Afghanistan. From that inaugural graduating class of a dozen, 10 of them, including Siamoy, received scholarships from Creighton University, a Jesuit institution in Omaha, Nebraska, U.S.A., to continue their tertiary education and earn a Bachelor of Science in Leadership. With the support of JWL, Siamoy and others are actively involved in leading the community learning centers as English tutors and peer academic advisers. In Siamoy's (2020) view, "studying Bachelors from Creighton University widened my understanding of society and helped me to challenge and cross many boundaries in recognizing plurality that exists in society" (as cited in Jesuit Worldwide Learning, 2020a, p. 21).

Among those in Creighton's undergraduate leadership program expanding Siamoy's understanding of society is Fowza. Originally from Somalia, she completed JWL's Diploma in Liberal Studies in 2018 while in Amman, Jordan. During her Diploma studies, Fowza (2019) deepened her desire to positively contribute to her local community, realizing that "our differences are what make us beautiful" (as cited in Jesuit Worldwide Learning, 2019b, p. 13). Following her Diploma graduation, Fowza also enrolled in the Bachelor of Science in Leadership program through Creighton University and joined JWL as the Amman community learning center coordinator and Liberal Arts Diploma facilitator. In this role, Fowza has been able to put her leadership studies into practice by honing her organizational skills and supporting peers along their educational journey. Fowza's ultimate dream is to start a JWL community learning center in Somalia (Jesuit Worldwide Learning, 2019a).

The third and final JWL student vignette in this chapter focuses on Regeza, an undergraduate student from the Dzaleka, Malawi refugee camp who is pursuing a Bachelor of Arts in Management through JWL's partnership with Southern New Hampshire University, U.S.A. A motivated person for the common good, Regeza (2020) was selected to participate in the inaugural African Drone and Data Academy in Malawi. He is interested

> *in aerial mapping of the Dzaleka refugee camp to create a flood model that supports improved construction planning and flood abatement in response to the chronic flooding that causes the destruction of many homes during the rainy season. (as cited in Jesuit Worldwide Learning, 2020a, p. 20)*

The inspiring (and still emerging) leadership development stories of Siamoy, Fowza, and Regeza qualitatively reinforce Rega's (2020) conclusions in a recent report accounting for the "challenges faced, the solutions adopted and the opportunities identified" (p. 1) during the early period of the COVID-19 pandemic. For Rega,

> *The human factor embodied by the centers in the field and by the support from local onsite facilitators and staff has proved to be a key element for the success of JWL mission: bringing Higher Education opportunities to the margins of this world. (p. 9)*

A coordinated effort by JWL leadership was made to

> *to check on students' basic needs, distribute bundles and devices, to activate new communication platforms and to ensure the LMS was working and students were able to access it, to arrange with the online faculty submissions' extensions, to extend the period of enrollment, and to circulate information at a global level. (Rega, 2020, pp. 7–8)*

For example, JWL global webinars are now held every two months so that leadership stakeholders such as Siamoy, Fowza, Regeza, and others throughout the world can listen, learn, and co-create community and social change.

CONCLUSION

For nearly 500 years, the Society of Jesus and their Jesuit institutions have harnessed their "global presence with a commitment to the care of the whole person and the cultivation of skills and knowledge to benefit the wider society" (Banchoff, 2016, p. 255). Guided by a world-affirming and transformative spiritual philosophy, Jesuit colleges and universities offer a strong humanistic ethos, an expansive international network of schools, and an integrative approach to educational formation. The Jesuit approach combines "intellectual rigor with reflection on the experience of reality together with the creative imagination to work toward constructing a more humane, just, sustainable, and faith-filled world" (Nicolás, 2010, pp. 5–6). Drawing a "direct link between pressing global issues and the aims of Jesuit higher education" (Balleis, 2016, p. 224), Adolfo Nicolás (2010), former superior general of the Society of Jesus, urged Jesuits and their lay collaborators to develop stronger and more strategic international partnerships to "address important issues touching faith, justice, and ecology that challenge us across countries and continents" (p. 11). Additionally, Nicolás encouraged Jesuit educational leaders to "search for creative ways of sharing the fruits of research with the excluded," so as to "counter the inequality of knowledge distribution" (p. 11).

What was initially called the Jesuit Commons: Higher Education at the Margins (JC:HEM) is one of the most notable success stories since Nicolás' (2010) seminal speech at the Universidad Iberoamericana in Mexico City. A collaborative alliance of "three independent non-profit organizations based in Switzerland, the United States and Germany" (Jesuit Worldwide Learning, 2020a, p. 24), what is now known as Jesuit Worldwide Learning (JWL) provides higher education to people on the margins of society through a variety of blended, global, and mobile learning formats. Since its founding by an international coalition of Jesuit colleges and universities in 2010, JWL has developed into "35 community learning centers across three continents and have reached more than 6,000 students from 40 nations" (Jesuit Worldwide Learning, 2019b, p. 2).

As evidenced by the preceding presentation, "cultivating a learning community of artful mentoring may indeed generate gardens of blossoming hope" (Mossman Riva, 2020, p. 120). Exemplary JWL alumni like Siamoy, Fowza, and Regeza, to name a few, are actualizing and practicing the humanistic ideals of their undergraduate leadership education at Jesuit universities and are actively engaged in a multidimensional process of leadership communing. They are collaboratively contributing to the broadening of access and availability of higher education at the margins to historically marginalized societies as community learning center coordinators and refugee camp construction contractors. As Siamoy, Fowza, Regeza and many others continue to flourish and inspire other JWL students, they are fulfilling the promise of an Ignatian-inspired leadership commons where all persons of good will can learn and lead to transform the world (Jesuit Worldwide Learning, 2021b) in a liminal space. Through the testimony of Siamoy, Fowza, and Regeza, such a threshold between past, present, and future has given birth to a commons-centric approach to Jesuit higher education that mirrors the life-affirming values most of humanity shares (Thompson, 2020).

REFERENCES

32nd General Congregation of the Society of Jesus. (1975). *Our mission today: The service of faith and the promotion of justice*. http://www.sjweb.info/documents/sjs/docs/D4%20Eng.pdf

Balleis, P. (2016). Global human mobility, refugees, and Jesuit education at the margins. In T. Banchoff & J. Casanova (Eds.), *The Jesuits and globalization: Historical legacies and contemporary challenges* (pp. 224–238). Georgetown University Press.

Balleis, P. (2020). *10 years of online higher education at the margins: A mission of the Jesuits.* https://www.jwl.org/en/news/detail/5d65cdaa-ffe6-11ea-b42f-002590812774

Banchoff, T. (2016). Jesuit higher education and the global common good. In T. Banchoff & J. Casanova (Eds.), *The Jesuits and globalization: Historical legacies and contemporary challenges* (pp. 239–260). Georgetown University Press.

Bole, W. (2020). *Still "walking with refugees," 40 years later.* https://www.jesuit-swest.org/stories/still-walking-with-refugees-40-years-later/

Casalini, C. (2019). Rise, character, and development of Jesuit education. In I. G. Zupanov (Ed.), *The Oxford handbook of the Jesuits* (pp. 153–176). Oxford University Press.

Casarino, C. (2008). Surplus common: A preface. In C. Casarino & A. Negri (Eds.), *In praise of the common: A conversation on philosophy and politics* (pp. 1–40). University of Minnesota Press.

Chubbuck, S. M. (2007). Socially just teaching and the complementarity of Ignatian pedagogy and critical pedagogy. *Christian Higher Education, 6,* 239–265.

de Aldama, A. M. (1990). *The formula of the institute: Notes for a commentary* (I. Echaniz, Trans.). Institute of Jesuit Sources.

Duminuco, V. J. (Ed.). (2000). *The Jesuit Ratio Studiorum: 400th Anniversary perspectives.* Fordham University Press.

Griffin, N., & McFarland, M. (2016). Higher ed at the margins: Cause for hope. *Conversations on Jesuit Higher Education, 49*(1), 12–14.

Habash, M. (2020a). Learning with students at the margins: Creighton University's pilot program with Jesuit Worldwide Learning 2017–2018. *Jesuit Higher Education: A Journal, 9*(1), 7–17.

Habash, M. (2020b). Five things you should know about Jesuit Worldwide Learning: Higher Education at the Margins. *Jesuit Higher Education: A Journal, 9*(1), 150–153.

Jesuit Worldwide Learning. (2018). *Annual report 2017.* https://www.jwl.org/media/download/cms/media/pdf/news/20181019-jwl-annual-report-2017-web.pdf

Jesuit Worldwide Learning. (2019a). *Annual report 2018.* https://www.jwl.org/media/download/cms/media/pdf/news/jwl-annual-report-online-2018.pdf

Jesuit Worldwide Learning. (2019b). *Media kit.* https://www.jwl.org/en/news/media-kit

Jesuit Worldwide Learning. (2020a). *Annual report 2019.* https://www.jwl.org/media/download/cms/media/pdf/news/jwl-annual-report-2019-website-final.pdf

Jesuit Worldwide Learning. (2020b). *Report on 10 years of the online Diploma in Liberal Studies for refugees and marginalized communities.* https://www.jwl.org/media/download/cms/media/pdf/news/jwl-report-on-10-years-online-diploma-opt-final.pdf

Jesuit Worldwide Learning. (2021a). *Mission.* https://www.jwl.org/en/home

Jesuit Worldwide Learning. (2021b). *Our vision.* https://www.jwl.org/en/what-we-do/our-vision

Jesuit Worldwide Learning. (2021c). *Where we are?* https://www.jwl.org/en/what-we-do/where-we-are

John Paul II. (1993). *Catechism of the Catholic Church.* http://www.vatican.va/archive/ENG0015/_INDEX.HTM

Kolvenbach, P. H. (2001). The service of faith and the promotion of justice in American Jesuit higher education. *Studies in the Spirituality of Jesuits, 33*(1), 23–27.

Loyola, I. (1991). The spiritual exercises. In G. E. Ganss (Ed. & Trans.), *Ignatius of Loyola: Spiritual exercises and selected works* (pp. 113–214). Paulist Press. (Original work published 1548).

Mossman Riva, S. (2020). Translating Ignatian principles into artful pedagogies of hope. *Jesuit Higher Education: A Journal, 9*(1), 106–121.

Nicolás, A. (2010). *Depth, universality, and learned ministry: Challenges to Jesuit higher education* today. http://www.sjweb.info/documents/ansj/100423_Mexico%20City_Higher%20Education%20Today_ENG.pdf

O'Malley, J. W. (2016). Historical perspectives on Jesuit education and globalization. In T. Banchoff & J. Casanova (Eds.), *The Jesuits and globalization: Historical legacies and contemporary challenges* (pp. 147–168). Georgetown University Press.

Quan, M. (2017). Introduction. In T. Jones & L. Nichols (Eds.), *Undocumented and in college: Students and institutions in a climate of national hostility* (pp. 1–11). Fordham University Press.

Rega, I. (2020). *Covid-19 and Jesuit Worldwide Learning: How we operated and what we learnt.* https://www.jwl.org/media/download/cms/media/research/20200731-covid-and-jwl-report-july-2020.pdf

Sparough, J. M., Manney, J., & Hipskind, T. (2010). *What's your decision? How to make choices with confidence and clarity.* Loyola Press.

Thompson, R. J. (2020). *Proleptic leadership on the commons: Ushering in a new global order.* Emerald.

Tran, D. Q., & Carey, M. R. (2018). Toward a discerning mind and heart: An Ignatian approach to workplace spirituality and spiritual leadership. In S. Dhiman, G. E. Roberts, & J. E. Crossman (Eds.), *The Palgrave handbook of workplace spirituality and fulfillment* (pp. 753–772). Palgrave Macmillan.

Topuzova, L. N. (2013). An interview with Mary McFarland, international director, Jesuit Commons: Higher education at the Margins. *AUDEM: The International Journal of Higher Education and Democracy, 4*(1), 142–148.

United Nations. (2015). Transforming our world: The 2030 agenda for sustainable development. https://sustainabledevelopment.un.org/content/documents/21252030%20Agenda%20for%20Sustainable%20Development%20web.pdf

United Nations High Commissioner for Refugees. (2019). *Global trends: Forced displacement in* 2018. https://www.unhcr.org/5d08d7ee7.pdf

United Nations High Commissioner for Refugees. (2020). *Global trends: Forced displacement in* 2019. https://www.unhcr.org/5ee200e37.pdf

16

TRADITIONAL LEADERSHIP ON THE COMMONS: MAIN CHALLENGES FOR LEADERS OF COMMUNITY ORGANIZATIONS TO GOVERN RURAL WATER IN RÁNQUIL, CHILE

CAMILA ALEJANDRA VARGAS ESTAY, NOELIA CARRASCO
HENRÍQUEZ, VÍCTOR MANUEL VARGAS ROJAS
AND LUIS GATICA MORA

INTRODUCTION

Water community organizations are essential for water management in rural areas in the majority of Latin American and Caribbean countries, including Chile. However, Chile is the only country in this region where water is traded as an asset and is subjected to property rights. Despite this legal context, the behavior of local leaders and the Water Committees management system consider water as a commons. Consequently, these committees face constant obstacles caused by the duality of water management systems present in the country.

For these reasons, this chapter aims to visualize the challenges faced by these committees in the context of increasing water scarcity to guarantee the local communities' and users' access to water. The study addresses the perspectives of leaders and members of Water Committees of the district of Ranquil, a highly vulnerable territory located in South-Central Chile. Some of the main challenges identified deal with issues such as water outages, poor water quality, and the presence of forest plantations. Equally important are some obstacles related to interaction with other stakeholders of the territory, the lack of support from the state, and issues within the committees' organization and members.

Notwithstanding such challenges, leaders, locals, and water users are aware of the importance of Rural Water Committees and how their management system has successfully managed water for many decades in rural areas. Therefore, maintaining and improving this traditional system is key to guaranteeing sustainable management of water as a commons in rural areas. Consequently, all new initiatives created to tackle water scarcity in rural areas must consider the perspective of a collective approach that originates from within local organizations to avoid issues such as discoordination, unenforceability, trust issues, among others.

BACKGROUND

Chile is one of the driest regions worldwide, with a continually growing demand for water due to human activities, such as extractive industries, silviculture, agriculture, and human consumption, among others. This has left many regions of the country with a high-water deficit and caused environmental degradation and socio-environmental conflicts (Aitken, Rivera, Godoy-Faundez, & Holzapfel, 2016). The multidimensional issues associated with water have intensified over the last few years, due to the progressive scarcity of this resource. The progressive increase of effects caused by the extractive industry in urban and rural territories has forced communities to review and redevelop the current unsustainable ways to manage the commons.

Even though we are facing water scarcity as a global issue, in the case of water in the rural areas, the problem of scarcity raises new problems and challenges for water community organizations who manage water in such areas. To better understand this issue in context, it is necessary to clarify two concepts that make this topic a unique and interesting one to visualize.

Chile has a duality of systems for managing water. There are many differences in the way water is administrated, perceived, and supplied in urban areas in contrast to rural areas. This is one of the main issues that makes water a controversial resource.

Chilean regulation and the implementation of the neoliberal economic model have enabled the privatization of water and left private sanitary companies to manage it (Hardin, 1968). However, in the case of rural areas, the management of water is the responsibility of water community organizations, which have implemented their traditional system that involves concepts such as collaboration, partnership, local governance, and a different type of leadership.

This type of management system has successfully and sustainably managed water for decades in rural areas. However, the extensive misappropriation of existing water sources by different stakeholders present in rural areas and the lack of water replenishment due to global warming have caused different problems and raised many challenges for these rural water organizations.

This chapter shares a study to understand the challenges faced by these organizations and also to illustrate traditional leadership that promotes the collaborative governance of water as a commons (Ostrom, 1990) from the perspective of the water organizations in the context of the current challenges associated with the water crisis and governance process in the territories (Delgado, Torres-Gomez, Tironi-Silva & Marin, 2015).

Therefore, to guarantee access to clean water for people living in rural areas and the sustainable management of the resource, it is imperative to establish institutional, organizational, and private collaboration. This collaboration must support the existing traditional systems used by the water organizations. Only in this way we can strengthen local governance and promote leadership on the commons.

COMMUNITY WATER ORGANIZATIONS

In rural areas of Chile, water is managed by community water organizations following a principle of water as a commons. These organizations are networks that share, manage, and ensure that water can be accessed by all the members. They do not replicate the relationship of provider and consumer that prevails in the urban areas. Instead, everyone involved in the management of water as a commons has a duty as a user or part of the network. In this case, the role of the government is only to support the water organizations and ensure that they are effectively following the Hydraulic Works Department requirements, albeit by a different means and with different leadership.

Rural water associations are community organizations of functional basis, ruled by neighbor's associations, under the Decree N°58, 1997 and the Law

N°19.418. Water Associations are legal and nonprofit organizations, and their members join and participate voluntarily. They can collect and administer the economic resources gathered from their respective members. These resources are used to restock materials, improve, or expand service facilities, and sign the necessary agreements and contracts to achieve the organization's goals. The associations are composed in their entirety of inhabitants and members of the community that use a common water source that is either superficial, such as springs or estuaries, or subterranean such as deep wells that supply water for hundreds of families.

According to the Hydraulic Works Department (HWD), an institution depending on the Ministry of Public Works and responsible for public policies in terms of rural potable water, there are nearly 1,900 organizations registered as water committees and cooperatives (Superintendencia de Servicios Sanitarios, 2019). However, according to the last report of the National Roundtable on Water, it is estimated that there are 950 Water Associations that are not working with the Hydraulic Works Department (HWD) (Mesa Nacional del Agua, 2020). Nonetheless, based on nonofficial records carried out in the Bio Bio and Ñuble Regions, it can be estimated that the quantity of Water Associations outside the HWD can be similar to the ones working with them. This means that these water associations operate under more vulnerable conditions, and most of them do not have sanitary clearance since they do not have treatment systems and only distribute untreated water.

Water in Chile is regulated by two laws: The Civil Code and The Water Code of 1981. The latter is the more controversial one, due to its market-based bias that allowed the privatization of water for the first time in Chile's history. Under the new Code, water itself is considered an asset independent from the land where it is located, allowing its commercialization (Larraín, 2012; Larraín & Poo, 2010). The conflict surrounding the access to water in the country is structurally linked to the application of the management model established in the Water Code of 1981 (Figueroa, 2013).

Nowadays, the pressures derived from climate change in territories with water shortage have highlighted both the state deficiencies in terms of the administration of the resource under market logic and the organizational weakness of Water Associations. There are different public instruments to finance and deal with rural communities' water needs, including contributions from private companies within the framework of their social responsibility processes. Nonetheless, the access to water for the rural population is still a problem that requires reviewing the principles of access to this resource – as an asset or/and as a right – and the institutional reformulations that guarantee sustainable management of common-pool resources (Ostrom & Hess, 2010).

In this context, the need to strengthen the HWD staff and professionalize the Water Associations led to the creation of the Rural Sanitation Services Law in 2017 (Law 20.998). However, the regulation for the application of this law is very recent (October 2020), so the process to strengthen water associations has not started yet.

In Chile, as in many other places in the world, rural water is a resource in dispute, from the perspective of values, and this value conflict is caused by incompatible belief systems. On one side, there is the action of the state and its administration of water as an asset; on the other side is the relationship and use of water by the communities and families as a commons. This translates into disorganized and unfocused systems of institutional governance (Mesa Nacional del Agua, 2020), which were designed from the perspective that sees communities only as consumers of a service. Despite these opposing proposals, both strategies have proven insufficient to guarantee fair management of water. This is one of the main issues for the constitutional debate in Chile in 2021 and 2022 (Moraga, 2019).

All these actions take place in Chile at the same time as an ongoing constitutional deliberative process, where the citizens' concerns are particularly focused on environmental matters. All these concerns were expressed starting with the "social outburst" of October 2019 (Reyes-Mendy, Valenzuela Calderón, & Chaura Vega, 2020). In this manner, the water crisis is a key topic in public debates, in institutional administration, and especially in community administration. In this context, local leaders must deal, not only with the management of their community water services but also incorporate new perspectives to maintain informed and efficient leaders within their communities. For this reason, they require new ways to understand social and legal processes, dedicate more time and effort to study, and have updated information.

Consequently, our study aims to provide a better understanding of how the current national context in terms of water availability, political policies, regulations, the involvement of the state or other private or institutional stakeholders, among others, are affecting the role of Water Associations and we carried out a specific study to achieve this goal.

DESCRIPTION OF OUR STUDY

Location Background and Current Situation

Before we begin describing this study, it is necessary to situate and incorporate some geographical information about the location where our study takes place. Our study is based on the district of Ranquil located in the west of part of the Ñuble Region in South-Central Chile. The main water supply of the Ñuble Region is the Itata River; this area is also called the Itata Valley (Fig. 1).

In the Ñuble Region, there are around 689 Water Committees, which supply water to 146,929 people (INE, 2017). Rural water is essential in this area and for the communities in the study not only for supplying water to people but also for their livelihood since small-scale farming is the productive base of rural family agriculture.

However, in this region, the issue of water scarcity is worsening, especially in the most rural areas. Year after year, the lack of rain and scarce

Fig. 1.   The Following Map Illustrates the Areas Mentioned Above in the Itata Valley, Ñuble Region.

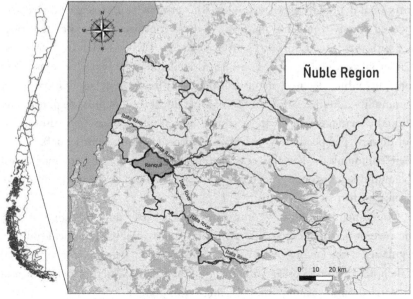

replenishment of water tanks make water availability and accessibility difficult. Recently, the region's water deficit has increased to 50% (Baeza, 2017). Considering that this region has the largest percentage of the rural population in Chile, 30.6% (INE, 2017), the situation is critical. Thus, the committees and their leadership are even more important in this context of crisis.

The Itata Valley as many other valleys in Chile is known for its viticulture, which was one of the main economic activities in the area for many decades. Many economic activities are surrounding the Itata River, such as agriculture, livestock, hunting, viticulture, and forestry. Nonetheless, since 2006, the forest activity acquired more prominence due to the installation of the Industrial Plant of Cellulose Nueva Aldea in the area and brought new effects in the territory.

One of them is the rapid expansion of forest plantations in the last decades. For instance, in 1994, 19% of the territory was covered by farms and 30.46% by forest plantations. However, by the year 2015, 52.52% of the territory was covered by forest plantations and only 9% by farming activities (Agencia de Sustentabilidad y Cambio Climatico, 2018). This has not only caused important changes in the land use of the district of Ránquil but also has affected the development of other productive activities in the area and explains the power dynamics from different stakeholders in the territory. Other effects brought by the Cellulose Plant are conflicts with the community due to air pollution caused by the plant's fumes, bad smell, and bad water quality.

All of these aspects condition and affect local governance, especially considering the number of stakeholders present in the territory and the different water uses. For this reason, the social processes related to water involve necessarily the interaction among diverse stakeholders in the territory and can lead to conflicts for their use (Larraín & Poo, 2010; Ostrom & Hess, 2010). Moreover, to guarantee the sustainability of water resources, particularly to guarantee its access for human consumption, there is a need for collaboration, articulation, and leadership.

Without disregarding the interactions between the stakeholders and the predominant forces in the decision-making processes and access to water, it can be observed that community work is becoming more important than ever. In other words, water scarcity has not only caused a lack of water, but also brought new challenges and demands for the inhabitants, community organizations, and above all, for their leaders.

Methodology and Data Collection

A previous study carried out in a forest micro basin in the district of Rán-quil, with the participation of its Water Committee, evidenced aspects related to local knowledge about water from the perspective of local communities (Vargas, Carrasco, & Vargas, 2019). The challenges for the governance and leadership resulting from this study set a start point for the research included in this chapter.

To understand the challenges identified in previous studies and to visual-ize the perspective of local leaders and inhabitants, we used different sources, such as interviews, participant observation, and participatory online research to collect the information.

Firstly, the sample selection was built considering, as the main criterion, that they were leaders of a committee and members of the Communal Union of Ránquil. This is a community organization that groups all the Water Com-mittees of the district. The interviews with secretaries, presidents, treasurers, and users of the committee were carried out in February 2019.

Secondly, participant observation was conducted during the six sessions of the Voluntary Agreement for Watershed Management (hereinafter referred to as AVGC) carried out in 2018, in which the Water Committee's leaders and Communal Union participated along with representatives of the regional government, forest companies, and the cellulose plant. This agreement was signed in Ránquil in January 2018 and coordinated by the Sustainability Agency for Climate Change that depends on the Economic Development Agency (CORFO in Spanish). Its content was created through a participatory process carried out in 2017. This process included the participation of repre-sentatives from public organizations, local universities, and the municipality, including the participation of Water Committees' leaders of the district. The main goal of this agreement is to "build and implement a local governance process to advance collectively toward the sustainable development that emphasizes the integrated management of the water resources in Ránquil" (Agencia de Sustentabilidad y Cambio Climatico, 2018). From these events, it was possible to identify the characteristics and the challenges of the leaders facing the requirements caused by the water crisis and the difficulties for fair governance of water in the territory.

Thirdly, the process of participatory research online carried out through the project SIMOL (Local Monitoring System) enabled us to work collectively with a group of twenty people, including leaders, students, teachers, members of Water Committees. This online research covered some questions about the characteristics of water leadership, their attributes, and challenges.

The data collected helped to organize the analysis of the challenges faced by the water leaders. Through the systematization and analysis of the three sources mentioned above, it was possible to gather their needs, learnings, proposals, and questions to advance toward a local water governance model that emphasizes the community attributes and allow them to act collaboratively. Management can help to face challenges such as water scarcity and promote new forms of governance of the commons.

FINDINGS IN RÁNQUIL

Critical Issues Calling for Leadership

1. Outages
After the systematization of the data collected from interviews, we identified that the most common everyday issue in rural areas of Ránquil is the repetitive outages of the water supply. During the summer, the situation is critical since the number of outages increases and the restoration time can vary from a couple of hours to a week in the most affected areas. In some cases, the outages are planned and programmed, and they only last a few days or a couple of hours in the best-case scenario. However, in general, most water outages are unexpected and are a permanent concern for the users, especially during summertime. These outages affect the users' daily life and the irrigation of vegetable gardens and plants. Nonetheless, for the leaders of Water Associations, the outages cause them a lot of pressure since they receive calls from neighbors when this happens, especially in the summertime.

2. Water Quality
In addition to the outages, some leaders of Water Committees that are not part of the Hydraulic Works Department state that in many cases the water quality is not good, but they do not always have the resources to drink water from other sources, such as bottled water. A fraction of the participants described that sometimes the water is brown due to the presence of sediment

in the water. In these cases, leaders must be especially diligent in organizing
the community for cleaning or repairing activities.

3. The Effects of Forest Plantations

On the other hand, from the perspective of leaders, most of them agree with
considering forest plantations as primarily responsible for the water scarcity
in the territory. Some users state that the high amount of water consumption of forest plantations and the cellulose plant is evident in the river's
water level. In addition to water scarcity, leaders mention that there are
some other effects caused by the plantations, such as drought and damage
to the fauna due to the use of pesticides. Only one interviewee ($n = 17$) has a
positive impression of forest plantations. Besides the effects on the amount
of water consumption, the interviewees mention that there is no protection
of watercourses since the plantations are everywhere. They also mention
the change of land use from farms to forest plantations. This aspect was
repeatedly mentioned in the AVGC sessions where participatory observation was carried out. In said sessions, an agreement from forest companies
and public organizations was achieved to restore special conservation sites
for water sources. Nonetheless, this is a medium and long-term agreement
that requires great coordination efforts that have not been fully developed
in the territory.

4. Articulation with Other Stakeholders

Forest Company

One of the findings from the interviews and observant participation was the
relationship of local communities with the forest company. Locals mentioned
that the company did not fulfill prior agreements with the communities and
local organizations, which implicates permanent tensions and negotiations.
This assessment from the leaders regarding unfulfilled agreements by the
main industry in the district, also reveals the presence of a sense of community or commons that appeal to obtaining answers to dignify the inhabitants
as a union rather than compensation for particular individuals.

Municipality

Regarding the relationship with the municipality, many users state that they
are unhappy with the institution. They mentioned that the institution only

acts when there is a critical situation causing a feeling of abandonment and inattentiveness regarding the water issue. Nonetheless, in most cases, leaders are aware of projects or plants to face water issues, including governance processes such as AVGC and SIMOL. Thus, leaders recognize institutions and processes, but they also understand the importance of strengthening the community as a fundamental aspect of water sustainability.

Hydraulic Works Department – State

In terms of the relationship with the state representatives and institutions on which the leaders rely for funding and support, they mention that their main obstacle to fulfill their role comes from the slow process of the state. Some urgent projects will enable the catchment, distribution, and treatment of water, but the approval and execution take years. Furthermore, they mention a lack of funding and tools to support committees that are not self-sustainable by the contributions of their members and who cannot pay higher fees due to their socioeconomic status. Lastly, another concern that affects the leaders socially and psychologically is the lack of answers from the state in critical situations of scarcity, in which new studies and investment are urgent to update their infrastructure.

OTHER FINDINGS

Everyday Practices to Deal with Scarcity

In terms of the everyday use of water among the members of the committee, there are some practices carried out by them to save and reuse wastewater from laundry and shower for irrigation purposes, such as plants and small vegetable gardens. Also, leaders identify some changes in the people's everyday practices that show more awareness of the scarcity. For example, their showers are brief, and they avoid leaving the water running when washing their hands, teeth, or the dishes. Although these practices are small changes, at the same time they are a sign of a decline in life quality making rural life more difficult.

Last but not least, there were some other aspects identified by the participants including the need to increase the supply capacity, technical support for the Water Committee operator and the community, raising funds, and building trust among users and leaders, and involving people who are committed to water management.

The Role of Water Committees

The operation of different Water Committees in the district is varied. On the one hand, some Water Associations work very efficiently in every aspect (coordination, communication, execution of works, maintenance, meeting attendance, etc.). On the other hand, there are some committees that do not work as efficiently and some conflicts can be found between the leaders and members that affect greatly communication and community coordination.

Most of the users and leaders recognize the importance of Water Committees for the users since they know that without participation, they would not have access to drinking water. Nevertheless, they mention some reasons why some Water Committees work differently than others. The main reasons are the lack of commitment from Water Committees' members and users to attend meetings and pay the monthly fees, lack of awareness from users who waste the water, and the need for a committed board of directors. This aspect was repeatedly mentioned in the AVGC sessions. Leaders insisted on the importance of design and implement dissemination and training activities that could help them to motivate the informed participation of the population.

Experiences of Water as a Commons from the Leaders and the Governance Process

One of the main findings of this study shows that despite the regulation of the state and institutions, the community vision and sense of water as a common and a basic universal right prevails in them. In this interstice, leaders must face the challenges inside and outside their communities through constant interaction with public and private agents for the proper operation of local water systems. From the interviews, we could collect and understand the issues caused by the water deficit in the district of Ránquil and the disposition of their leaders for the defense of water as a commons.

The leaders of Water Committees that carry out their duties from the perspective of collaborative leadership agree on three main aspects to understand their roles:

a) To maintain this form of leadership, leaders must have a sense of responsibility toward their neighbors and build trust with the users.

b) They must maintain a form of communication that allows them to act on behalf of the benefits for the community.

c) The leaders must understand that their leadership is not more important than the participation of the users or members of the committees.

From the perspective of a collaborative leadership approach of water as a common, leaders have an important role in the management of water. However, it is equally important that the users and members of the committees are aware of the use of water, besides attending meetings and paying the fees. Therefore, Water Committees are an example of collaborative leadership that is not comprehended from the individuality but the collective and their common interests and problems.

The concerns mentioned by the leaders, users, and members of Water Committees in Ránquil constitute an important source for the challenges in the redesign of water governance in Chile. Initiatives such as AVGC and SIMOL hope to become a space to support this new governance model, establish serious institutional commitments, and involve more participation from the user's organizations and committees. The water crisis in the last few decades has evidenced that one of the main weaknesses in the water access systems in rural areas is the coordination between institutional representatives and the organizations' leaders, especially the rural users that are economic and socially vulnerable.

CONCLUSIONS AND IMPLICATIONS

Lessons and Challenges for the Leaderships of Water as a Commons

The information obtained through this study illustrates the premise that rural water in Chile is a common-pool resource in dispute but conditioned by different systems of institutional governance, and by the effects of the change of land use that replaced traditional productive activities, such as the production of monoculture plantations at a large scale in their territories. From a social standpoint, community water management seems to be the main alternative to face the challenges of the climate crisis and guarantee the availability of this resource for the people who depend on it for personal, domestic, or farming use. Certainly, this entails changes and adjustments in the manner of organization in the management of Water Committees, and therefore new competencies and abilities for their leaders.

Consequently, all new initiatives created to tackle water scarcity in rural areas must consider the perspective of a collective approach that originates from within local organizations to avoid issues such as discoordination, unenforceability, trust issues, among others. Even though there are some Water Committees that are not working as efficiently as others, their management system has worked for many decades and all efforts should aim to improve their traditional ways and support their important roles in the conservation and sustainable management of water.

One of the main implications from the findings was the need to visualize the challenges faced by Water Committees' leaders to fulfill their roles. Only then we can find ways to facilitate their duties and at the same time promote the creation of new leadership based on the commons in rural territories. For this reason, we included the following infographic summarizing the main proposals from leaders of the territory during the development of the project SIMOL (Fig. 2).

These principles enable the analysis of institutions from within and provide ideas and proposals to improve them and emphasize the need to be respected by all stakeholders in the territory. For this reason, strengthening the Water Committees is essential, especially counting with leaders that aid the empowerment, counsel, and training of committed users who can improve the management tools and water governance in the territory. This is the only way to move forward toward the construction of robust models capable to face the governance challenges.

Based on the information obtained from the interviews, it can be confirmed that Water Committees are capable to successfully manage their water resources. However, there are some issues related to the effectiveness of the management that can affect the work inside the committees as well as the participation in processes of articulation and governance with other stakeholders of the watershed. The public administration has scarce resources and in most cases is managed in a disorganized manner and without the proper technical consultation or local pertinence. This situation worsens the condition of the vulnerability of the rural population subjected to this type of politics.

The study analyzed shows that even though in Chile water is considered as an asset and is commercialized, rural community organizations have preserved a collaborative way to manage water as a common. The legacy of

Fig. 2. What Are the Challenges for Water Leaders in Ránquil? (SIMOL, 2020). Author's translation.

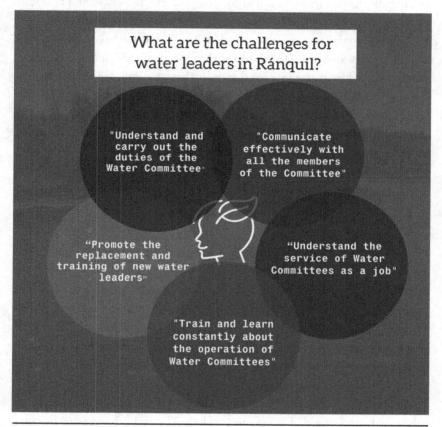

values and ecopolitics that the Water Committees pass on became more relevant when we analyze it in the context of a dispute between interests, productive scales, and sociocultural models of water usage, as exemplified in the study with the forest industry. The results of the analysis conducted to illustrate the complex and varied nature of the challenges to face governance in this type of setting. Also, they encourage paying more attention to the local and social adaptation processes the global water crisis faces.

Our proposal to understand the leaderships of water as collaborative leadership focused on the collective and common interests can be adjusted to adaptation processes for the climate crisis. Nonetheless, these processes do not only include the communities, local users, or water committees, but also institutions and policies that must be updated and coordinated to benefit efficient, pertinent, and timely management. These processes also involve the sciences and academia in general to guarantee a new political science interface in which the territories and local knowledge and practices have an important place. In this way, it is possible to imagine new ways of governance.

From our point of view, these leaders can be considered as evidence of our collective sense and relationship with water that never faded despite the efforts to consider water as a market asset that was imposed by the neoliberal model installed in Chile from the democratic backsliding of 1973. The collaborative leaderships of water as a common are the start point and patrimony to reevaluate the sustainability of water from its multiple implications for the society, ecology, and above all, the territories.

FINAL THOUGHTS

The pandemic of 2020 has evidenced many aspects regarded in this chapter. The multidimensional vulnerability of the rural population has exacerbated, and the water crisis has become a priority in public and territorial agendas. Based on the importance of handwashing as the main preventive action against the COVID-19 virus, it is essential to provide access to water for all people, particularly people who live in rural areas, where access to health care facilities is already limited. From this point of view, the pandemic has pressured a variety of institutions to prioritize, even more, the importance of access to water for everybody.

Additionally, to existent inequalities, the communication gap between the urban and rural worlds has become evident. The lack of access to Internet providers or bad mobile network coverage has affected the participation of people living in rural areas. The pandemic has visualized even more the uncertainty of a potable water supply in rural areas and the great inequalities between the population living in rural areas with the ones in the cities.

Water as a commons and public resource is a transversal civic claim in Chile nowadays. From the social outburst of October 2019, a social and political process has started in Chile to reevaluate the ways the natural resources are managed in the country. In this complex and challenging scenario, collaborative leadership of water as a common are especially valued. This implies that changes in the public institutions and administration in the territories must be reformulated. This is what we hope to happen in Chile through the constitutional process that begins in 2021.

ACKNOWLEDGMENTS

Monitoring of watersheds and other forest ecosystems linked to human consumption of water in South-Central Chile", Code: 3041331211 Agreement between the Ministry of Agriculture and Forest Institute of Chile.

Project: ANID/FONDEF ID19I10121 "Sistema de monitoreo para la participación local en la gestión integrada de cuencas" SIMOL.

Thank you to cartographer Walter Valdivia for the creation of the map used in this chapter.

Members of the Communal Union of Water Committees of Ránquil, for your fundamental collaboration on this research project.

REFERENCES

Agencia de Sustentabilidad y Cambio Climatico. (2018). *Acuerdo Voluntario de Gestión de Cuencas Ranquil*. Recuperado de https://www.ascc.cl/resources/uploads/documentos/archivos/668/convenio.pdf

Aitken, D., Rivera, D., Godoy-Faundez, A., & Holzapfel, E. (2016). Water scarcity and the impact of the mining and agricultural sectors in Chile. *Sustainability, 8*(2). doi:10.3390/su8020128

Baeza, E. (2017). *Situación hídrica de la provincia de Ñuble, Región del Biobío.* Retrieved from https://obtienearchivo.bcn.cl/obtienearchivo?id=reposito rio/10221/24258/2/Informe_Agua_Regi%C3%B3n_Atacama_Final.pdf

Delgado, L. E., Torres-Gomez, M., Tironi-Silva, A., & Marin, V. H. (2015). Local adaptation strategy to climate change for equitable water access in Chilean rural zones. America *Latina Hoy-Revista De Ciencias Sociales, 69*, 113–137. doi:10.14201/alh201569113137

Figueroa, D. (2013). *Legislation on use of water in agriculture. Chile.* Retrieved from Washington DC: https://hdl.loc.gov/loc.law/llglrd.2013417719

Hardin, G. (1968). The tragedy of the commons. *Science, 162*, 1243–1248.

INE. (2017). *Censo de Población y Vivienda.* INE.

Larraín, S. (2012). Human rights and market rules in Chile's Water Conflicts: A call for structural changes in water Policy. *Environmental Justice, 5*(2), 82–88. doi:10.1089/env.2011.0020

Larraín, S., & Poo, P. (2010). *Conflictos por el Agua en Chile. Entre los Derechos Humanos y las Reglas del Mercado.* Chile Sustentable.

Mesa Nacional del Agua. (2020). *Primer Informe de la Mesa Nacional del Agua.* Retrieved from https://www.mop.cl/Prensa/Documents/Mesa_Nacional_del_Agua_2020_Primer_Informe_Enero.pdf

Moraga, P. (2019). *La protección del medio ambiente: reflexiones para una reforma constitucional*. Editorial Jurídica de Chile.

Ostrom, E. (1990). *Governing the commons: The evolution of institutions for collective action*. Cambridge University Press.

Ostrom, E., & Hess, C. (2010). *Private and common property rights*. Edward Elgar Publishing Ltd.

Reyes-Mendy, F., Valenzuela Calderón, M., & Chaura Vega, C. (2020). *¿Cómo pensar los desafíos ambientales de cara a una nueva Constitución?: preocupaciones ambientales en tiempos de cambio constitucional*. Retrieved from https://doi.org/10.7764/datasetUC/CCG-UC.11534/29406

SIMOL. (2020, November 1). Desafíos para la gestión local del agua. Retrieved from http://sistemademonitoreolocal.cl. Accessed on December 10, 2020.

Superintendencia de Servicios Sanitarios. (2019). *Informe de Coberturas del Sector Sanitario 2018*.

Vargas, V., Carrasco, N., & Vargas, C. (2019). Local participation in forest watershed management: Design and analysis of experiences in water supply micro-basins with forest plantations in South Central Chile. *Forests, 10*(7). doi:10.3390/f10070580

17

LEADERSHIP OF THE COMMONS IN BOSNIA AND HERZEGOVINA: PROTECTING NATURAL RESOURCES AND RECLAIMING PUBLIC SPACE

EDIN IBRAHIMEFENDIC

INTRODUCTION

In this chapter, I will explore the types of leadership that have emerged in Bosnia and Herzegovina during the social and civic movements for the protection of rivers and public spaces. I have focused my research on two examples. The first example is Kruščica, a village in central Bosnia in the municipality of Vitez that continues to fight against the building of a dam in the river that serves as the source of the inhabitants' lives. The second is the action by an "elite group" in Sarajevo to reopen the National Museum or *Zemaljski muzej* (originally named "Landsmuseum" during the Austro-Hungarian period, the name of the museum was a translation from German, but from its founding the museum was conceptualized as a national museum). Through these two examples, the ideas of collective leadership and elite leadership will be explored and redefined according to the circumstances in which they emerged as the most expeditious approach to achieving goals.[1]

These two cases serve also as examples where leadership can take a group from a protest to a movement. Protests are generally organized by those who are in a less favorable position politically (women in Kruščica, employees of the museum) and are attempting to influence decision makers through media and public support. They are not, that is, using their power directly but rather indirectly vis-à-vis a broad public. If individuals in such a protest want to achieve better results, they need to endure and transform their protests into a social movement. As Tarrow (2011) pointed out "social movements are those protests that survive and function for a longer period" (pp. 9–12). In both the cases of Kruščica and the National Museum, protesters formed a social movement that eventually reaped tangible and impactful results. Furthermore, in both cases, the processes of resistance and self-governance remain ongoing. The women in Kruščica continue their fight to maintain the right to use the water from their river and prevent the construction of the dam. The National Museum has reopened but still faces many financial and managerial issues including the final arrangement through which the state will provide financing and possibly oversight.

COMMONS AS POLITICAL STRUGGLE

For these case studies, I will employ the definition of commons proposed by Tomašević, Horvat, Midžić, Dragšić, and Dakić (2018) for social and civic action undertaken by citizens in order to have a voice in their lives and well-being. As these authors contended, commons can in these cases be defined as:

> the political act of claiming commons through conflict against com-
> modification, commercialization, privatization and state enclosure
> of goods for the benefit of a few. This kind of commons definition
> is more political and conflicting compared to the classical definition
> of commons used for governance cases...In this definition, struggle
> against privatization and statization is the constitutive element of com-
> mons, and the definition allows authors to explore conflict over access
> and control of some specific resource, as well as to analyze various
> actors that engage in conflict and the discourse that they use. (p. 116)

BACKGROUND

The dissolution of Yugoslavia resulted in several wars for independence in the countries that comprised the broader nation. The 1992 to 1995 war in Bosnia and Herzegovina (BiH) is considered to have been the most violent. Among the many war crimes and atrocities committed in BiH, the siege of Sarajevo, the genocide in Srebrenica, the destruction of Old Bridge in Mostar and the rape and concentration camps in Prijedor are considered by the international community to have been the most horrible.

While the Dayton Peace Agreement that ended the war in BiH brought apparent peace, it left a deeply divided country. The Agreement and Constitution that followed established a consocialist country divided by Bosniak Muslim, Serb Orthodox, and Croat Catholic ethnic groups, called constituent peoples. The Federation of BiH is comprised of Bosniaks and Croats. The Serbs claim parts of the country which they call "the Serb Republic" and share the rotating presidency and other key political offices with Bosniaks and Croats. The Constitution of Bosnia and Herzegovina identifies Bosniaks, Croats, and Serbs as constituent people and limits certain aspects of political rights only to them. All other citizens of Bosnia and Herzegovina are identified as others. The ethnopolitical divisions have for years limited civic oriented activism and although there is cooperation within nongovernmental organizations (NGOs) and the larger civil society, such civic activism, an essential feature of democracy, still has not reached desired levels. There is even a phenomenon of a so called Civil Society Organizations (CSO) linked with political parties and described as civil society organizations whose range of activities is conditioned by attitudes and policies of certain groups within the society, and changes according to them. They adapt to the desires of specific political parties and represent them through their activities under the mask of representing the "interests of citizens." Unfortunately, their presence in everyday life in BiH is great, and they stage so many promotion activities that many citizens place the entire civil society in their politicized context. Their task and goal is to draw in supporters and voters, and they rarely organize any activities in periods between election campaigns (Dimitrovic, 2011, p. 7). The ethnic homogenization causes people to vote for nationalistic parties and nationalistic policies although there is enormous dissatisfaction with the local and national political situation. As a result, some scholars claim that the conflict that caused the civil war in fact never ended but that it remains a "frozen conflict" (Perry, 2019). As in many post-conflict countries, another reality that has limited civic activism in BiH is the lack of legitimacy of the civic sector (Puljec-Shank, 2015) .

Given the complexity of the socio-political situation in BiH, leadership, in order to be truly effective, has to be exercised on important and commonly held causes above ethnic divisions and outside the politics of the government in order to maintain its legitimacy in the eyes of the public. Most CSOs are not focused on decision-making processes but are rather driven by the decisions of a few people inside them, who are most commonly founding members. A CSO mapping study carried out by the Mission of the European Union described the general environment in CSOs as "post authoritarian." The study also pointed out that the small membership in CSOs is a major weakness that further damages their legitimacy (Mapping study of CSO's in BiH, 2016). The collective and elite leadership collective exercised in the two case studies of Kruščica and the National Museum proved to be legitimate because of the fact that the leaders did not represent any particular political interest but rather represented the will of the people.

THE CASE OF KRUŠČICA

Background

The government of BiH has attempted to attract foreign investment and entrepreneurship as necessary strategies of economic development. However, like many other countries in the Balkans, BiH remains poor and undeveloped. While economic growth exists, it is still very slow and huge proportions of the population have not yet seen any effect from it. The low economic growth is a byproduct of the inability (or unwillingness) of political elites to use resources in effective and transparent ways. This inability is compounded by corruption and the fact that political parties are entrenched in business interests. Although the political leaders distinguish themselves from the communist regime in former Yugoslavia by asserting that the economy is free from the influence of special interests in contrast to the previous regime controlled economy, this is not in reality the case. Numerous cases of corruption and nepotism have plagued the economy which has not been able to absorb the huge numbers of unemployed. Furthermore, corruption has been facilitated by the rapid transition from a socialist, publicly owned system to a nonliberal economy with very weak enforcement mechanisms.

Investment in the Energy Sector

BiH is one of the few countries in the world that still has wild rivers, which are appealing sources for hydroenergy. The government planned huge investments in this sector that initially were accepted by the public because such investments could attract increased foreign investments, generate increased local capital, and boost the economy. However, the changed scope (the number of small dams that was planned in BiH was 186 two years ago (Sofić Salihbegović, 2019)) and the consequences of these investments were not discussed publicly. It was eventually revealed that the government had approved plans for 333 hydropower plants on BiH's 244 rivers (De Launey, 2018). For many small impoverished communities, the idea of certain investments looked promising, but as numbers increased (an estimated 2,800 dams are in the process of being constructed in the wider Balkan region (Nelson, 2017)) and their environmentally destructive effects of pollution and irreparable damage were known, community resistance grew (Gallop, 2020). While there were numerous protests alongside NGOs and communities fighting in courts, these instances were isolated with none receiving the public attention that Kruščica did. In many cases, the involvement and consultation of the local communities were delayed, the plans lacked clarity and there existed potential breaches of procedure.

Through my work as an attorney for the Human Rights Ombudsperson for BiH, I have noticed similar approaches used by investors, not only in BiH, but in different countries. Such investment projects are at first mentioned only in numbers – such as millions invested, hundreds employed – but their real scope and effects are rarely mentioned – dams built, streams destroyed and channeled, and, due to automatization, the fact that completed dams consist of small hydroelectric plants that employ sometimes only two or three employees. Sometimes activists are portrayed as jealous of others' wealth and indifferent to community welfare in their efforts to "hinder progress." Kruščica was in many ways a breaking point in the public perception of this issue.

Plans to Build Dams in Kruščica River

The Government of BiH approved plans to build two small dams and hydropower plants on the river Kruščica, which villagers claimed would cause irreplaceable damage and negatively affect their daily life and livelihood. The river provides drinking water for 100,000 people in Zenica, 50,000 people in Vitez, and more people in the surrounding areas (Patagonia, 2018). Moreover, the villagers pointed out that the process of consultation to build the dam as required by law was not followed despite claims to the contrary. The law required that a series of meetings be held with local inhabitants but they never took place. Only a small number of locals had been informed of the plan.

As a consequence of their dismay over these plans, and inspired by the successful resistance movement that the neighboring community of Fojnica had launched in 2012 (Patagonia, 2018), the community joined together to protest these plans. Women in the community called each other when the first construction machine showed up and formed a human barricade so the machine could not access the river. Women constructed a wooden shelter in front of a bridge that led to the entrance to the river, built a fire for warmth, and stayed there in shifts for 24 hours a day. On the night of August 23, 2017, the police attempted to forcibly move the women from their shelter and small bridge so the investors could move machines into the construction site. When the women refused to move, the police beat the women and violently moved them (Arnika, 2017). The women reported in the 2018 movie *Blue Heart: The Fight for Europe's Last Wild Rivers* (Patagonia, 2018) that they stood vigil instead of their men because they knew the police would beat up and do terrible things to their men, but they did not expect the police to do the same to them. The media reported the event as police brutality and excessive use of force (the local police later conducted an investigation and found that the police acted in accordance with their mandate and regulation) with photographs depicting bruised bodies and injuries. The public became sympathetic to the protestors and opposed to the government and began to support the protests.

Despite the violent police attack, the inhabitants of Kruščica showed no willingness to back down. They continued with the blockade of the construction site and guarded the small bridge that leads to it for over one year. Their next step was to hold elections for their community and to extend communication and contacts with other groups facing a similar situation, as well as NGOs fighting court cases. For the first time, women ran for positions on the community council. After more than a year and a half, they were able to annul the construction permit, forcing local authorities to start new proceedings to obtain approvals for the dams and hydropower plants.

Interestingly, the fight to protect their river superseded local ethnically divided prejudices and politics. Vitez is the municipality in which the community of Kruščica is located. Vitez was one of places that was the most negatively affected during the war and the location of many war crimes. In this municipality, divisions between Bosniaks and Croats are still rigid. Almost all aspects of social life are divided. Local schools, for example, are still segregated and function under the system "two schools under one roof."

The same building is used by two separate schools, one that enlists almost entirely Bosniak children and the other exclusively Croat children, and the children are taught separate histories and learn ethnic prejudice. Nonetheless, the local women who led and were mostly represented during protests were able to avoid getting involved in this everyday divisive and partisan politics. The village's population is drawn from Bosniak and Croat communities and both communities are supportive with women in the movement coming from both. Another indication that the women have avoided divisive issues is how, according to Alma Midžić, members refrained from support of those charged or sentenced for war crimes. Certain members within the movement obtained prominent political roles like Tahita Tibold who was elected as the first woman ever as the head of the community council. She continued to stay involved in the movement and exchanged information and met with the group as well as informing others through her smart phone.

I have categorized the leadership practiced in Kruščica as collective leadership due to the practices among the participants who have created a complex, dynamic multilevel process involving an exchange of information, not only through meetings but by creating a group on the instant messaging application "Viber" where they posted ideas and news. In this way, they were able to use their skills and resources collectively in the most expedient way in order to accomplish their goal. As such, their leadership practices represented

> a complex, multi-level, dynamic process that emerges at the cross-roads of a distribution of the leadership role, diverse skills and expertise within the network, and the effective exchange of information among team members in order to capitalize on and coordinate their role behaviors and expertise. (Friedrich et al., 2009, p. 935)

The people cooperated to achieve a shared goal while maintaining high levels of legitimacy and the ability to resist all kinds of manipulation that many much stronger, better-funded movements were not.

Even the local governments in BiH could not ignore the issue any more (Vejnovic, 2018). Many local communities in the meantime have openly stated that they are against such dams and hydroenergy plants and legislative bodies in BiH have adopted are or in a process of adopting resolutions and laws aimed to stop further construction. On June 23, 2020, the Parliament of BiH decided on a moratorium on hydropower projects in the country. No new approvals will be given and projects that were approved will be audited to see whether their approval was legally admissible (Eichelmann & Arning, 2020).

With their persistence and strategy, the women of Kruščica were not the first in BiH to begin this struggle but they were the ones that turned mere reaction to the news of the construction to preventative action to stop it. Azra Hromadžić (2015) has noted that in such a context, local people often highlight the difference between "people" and "politicians," illustrating that people want change while politicians do not. Activism in such communities is often perceived as unwanted and unneeded because, according to their beliefs, everything is predestined. Thus, the power and influence of the hydropower resistance movements must be acknowledged as a breakthrough in manifesting the "power of the people." As the women of Kruščica are a group of individuals who worked tirelessly to achieve their goal, they have become a source of inspiration to other groups to work together. Today, the coalitions for protection of rivers are much stronger and better merged than ever before.

THE NATIONAL MUSEUM OF BOSNIA AND HERZEGOVINA

The campaign to stop construction of the dams illustrated collective leadership and a "bottom up" approach in which communities and NGOs fighting to protect the environment forced the government and political parties to step in and remedy the situation. On the other hand, the campaign to reopen the National Museum faced completely different challenges in overcoming several issues that had led to its closure.

The 1995 postwar consociational state structure in BiH concentrated powers in the two sub-state entities of the Federation of BiH and the Serb Republic and left the state itself with very limited jurisdictions. Jurisdiction over cultural life was divided between the state and the sub-states which functioned according to ethnic rivalry. Consequently, the National Museum, which from its beginning was conceived to encompass the whole history of BiH, fell between the cracks in the ethnonationalist paradigms. The museum found itself in a legal vacuum, without proper funding, since the Federation and the Serb Republic could not agree on a co-funding agreement and the state's hands were tied. Furthermore, since the museum was located in Sarajevo in the Federation largely inhabited by Bosniaks, the Serbs and Croats began to see the museum as a tool that Bosniaks were using to impose their culture on the other two (Gavrankapetanović-Redžić, 2018). As museum director Adnan Busuladzic explained, "There are two opposing ideas on how this country should be organized. This society is at war over those ideas and nobody cares about a museum" (Cerkez, 2012). Gorcin Dizdar, a scientist who studied monumental medieval tombstones in the Balkans argued that

> *if there was any "fault" that led to its closure, it is that the museum is one of the main symbols of the state...Our political system is simply created to bolster the differences among the main ethnic groups – the Muslims, Serbs and Croats. Under such a system, nobody feels responsible for the state and its symbols. (French Press Agency, 2015, para. 10)*

Furthermore, the museum and its employees got caught in the cultural wars that took place as BiH transitioned from a socialist regime to a neoliberal economy. Capitalism bred a new class of rich elites who exercised an inordinate influence on government policy. Culture was of less importance than profit to them. Culture became the domain of the middle class and museum employees became the symbol of a dying socialist culture dominated by government control. These employees were denigrated in public as being "old school," not able to adapt to the modern imperative to globalize, largely because they did not speak and write English, and incapable of finding ways of making the museum profitable within the capitalist paradigm (Gavrankapetanović-Redžić, 2018). Lack of state financing due to budget cuts, combined with criticism of museum employees who did not receive their salaries for the three years, led to the closure of the museum in 2012 for the first time in the 124 years since its establishment. Despite not receiving their salaries, museum employees continued to go to work in the museum after its closure to take care of the collection which they were emotionally and intellectually attached to.

After the Dayton Peace Agreement, the international community dominated the reconstruction of BiH as a consocionalist capitalist state. Their emphasis was on establishing the economic and political foundations of such a state that fit within the model of the European Union. Culture remained of little importance. As Hajdarpašić (2008) noted in his chapter, "Museums, Multiculturalism, and the Remaking of Postwar Sarajevo," when Jacques Paul Klein headed the United Nations mission in 2001, his involvement regarding the National Museum was very limited. Klein used his own very strong personal influence and religion to support the exhibition of the jewel of the

National Museum, namely the *Sarajevo Haggadah*, which had been brought to BiH in the fourteenth-century from northern Spain by the Jewish exodus from Spain during the Inquisition. Klein was not interested in the larger issues the museum faced nor of resurrecting the rich culture of the country. Unfortunately, he set an example of the priorities that BiH was to emphasize in their state building process. In light of this, we might say that the international community – if we speak about leadership through example – showed an approach similar to that of a strongman in Eastern Europe: autocratic and functioning outside of a system.

In 2015, the Sarajevo-based NGO *Akcija* implemented the "I am the Museum" (*Ja sam muzej*) campaign to reopen the museum, which one of its employees claimed began "out of a willingness to address the impasse the Museum had reached in 2012 followed by a three-year closure of its premises, and a deeply negative image of the Museum among the public" (Gavrankapetanović-Redžić, 2018, p. 86). The campaign, partly funded by international donors, attracted influential Bosnian artists and musicians, civil society leaders, foreign ambassadors, and cultural buffs around the world. There were more than 500 media articles published about the campaign.

The campaign included portraits and stories of the museum's workers, literary works about the museum from notable authors and regional writers and essayists working on shifts for the museum, something that supporters of the campaign did regardless of whether they were public persons, famous artists, ambassadors, or regular citizens to illustrate their commitment to solving the urgent problem of funding. In the environment where everything is political and culture is viewed through a nationalistic lens, the project did absolutely the opposite and many institutions and individuals committed themselves to this issue.

Jasna Kovo was one of three persons who developed the initial idea of the campaign, which grew into a large social movement, along with Aida Kalender and Ines Tanović. While reflecting on the campaign, Kovo said that if at that time all three of them were not engaged in the CSO "Akcija," which had a rather large grant from international donors for projects in culture, they would not have been able to push approval for the campaign through. In an interview she said that there are some things you can get by spontaneous action but something of this size would be impossible. The funding helped them to organize focus groups with culture workers in all of BiH regarding their priorities. The lowly and abandoned status of the National Museum was repeatedly raised. "That gave us legitimacy," emphasized Kovo. Even greater legitimacy for the campaign came from the workers in the Museum who embraced the campaign wholeheartedly. Kovo reported that they chose the name for the campaign, "I am Museum," to create an obvious identity between themselves and the museum. They started organizing first the exhibition about museum workers who were working and protecting the country's common heritage despite the fact that they had not received their salaries for three years. This exhibition attracted the attention of culturally aware individuals in BIH and around the world who felt great empathy for these workers who were sacrificing themselves for the good of the museum.

In 2015, the museum reopened its doors. While it is still struggling, it has taken huge steps forward. One of the core breakthroughs caused by the campaign has been the (public) perception of museums not only as buildings but as something one is attached to as part of their common heritage. If people have a common past, a heritage that links them in the present, their future is connected as well. Bosnians can challenge the ethnocentric narrative and find common ground, despite the obstacles. While nationalism might control our present, we cannot let them divide our past and create further divisions in our future. Museums have many purposes – educational, cultural, historical – but they are foremost our bonds with the past. They show that our present is changeable and we are in control of it.

Leaders were distributed throughout the campaign and exercised distributed leadership as defined by Gronn (2002). The aggregated leadership of the campaign were "dispersed among some, many, or maybe all of the members... (and) allow[ed] for the possibility that all organization members may be leaders at some stage" (Gronn, 2002, p. 429). However, I chose to define the leadership of the campaign an "elite leadership" for two reasons. First, the campaign was better organized and planned than actions initiated by other CSOs. Hence, it stood apart, appearing elite. The people behind the campaign understood that the campaign had to be different and better organized than any protest before in order to have an impact. Second, a small group of cultural professionals created the campaign outside of the dominant narrative in BiH, emphasizing the relevant national issues at stake. The slogan, "I am Museum," is in a way a subversive act in a country where the first and foremost identity of everyone is with an ethnic group, a country where the most well-known collective body is its presidency in which political elites are in a perennial political stalemate.

If the political elite in a country like BiH act mostly to maintain the status quo and function only with international oversight because of the perception that the country is politically immature and unfamiliar with democratic processes, then the country needs another elite outside of the political realm. Such an elite, in this case a cultural elite, practices elite leadership which turns the spotlight on a major success story in which people have taken charge of a situation the government has failed to solve and hence gives hope to the people that things in the country can change for the better.

Today, we understand elite leadership to be a class of rich and influential individuals, but we should also take into account the narrower sense of that term – that is, the people who have earned respect or good results in their professions. By using the slogan, "I am Museum," these so called "cultural elites" have achieved an identification with the National Museum and created a sense of commonality. Furthermore, by emphasizing the position of museum employees, they highlighted not only the museum's problems but those facing workers in the wider culture industry. As Gavrankapetanović-Redžić (2018) concluded:

> The engagement with culture, as a collective good ignored by the political administration, was presented by those who were engaged in the project "I am the Museum" as citizen activism. That one portion of citizens see themselves as those who need to actively engage in political actions for the benefit of the collective points to the status of culture as a marker of distinction in a society that is still being dynamically transformed…Dealing with culture and cultural heritage, in terms of production or preservation, gradually becomes a statement about one's willingness to engage with something that the "small, wealthy elite" ignores, but the middle-class (or at least some of its members) considers important. Culture is symbolically appropriated through activist engagement, such as the "I am the Museum" campaign, and serves as a medium for regaining social and political legitimacy in opposition to those in the dominant class who possess more important economic capital but lack cultural and social capital. (pp. 86–87)

CONCLUSION

When we compare the two examples I have discussed in this chapter, it is possible to see how the leadership that emerges in a protest or campaign or social movement shapes the behavior of the participants, their relationship with each other, and the scope of their influence, direct and indirect. Kruščica started as a protest and then became a local movement and after that a part of a larger national movement to protect natural resources. From its beginnings, the campaign,

"I am Museum," took into account the situation and obstacles to change and built up the campaign by attracting people from around the world. The group of professionals led the campaign in a way that did not attract followers but rather participants. The campaign did not grow vertically but rather horizontally.

In the past 25 years, BiH has seen many initiatives in the civil sector (Tijana Dimitrovic, 2011). While few have had resounding success, we can say that they at least anticipated some tangible change. Of course some initiatives – like those dealing with the past, the acknowledgment of war crimes, or constitutional changes – have been very complex, sensitive, or political. In many ways, people who were linked with them would find themselves in situations where their affiliations with a certain group or political party would undermine their work. For this reason, the leadership in the commons qua social movements in two above-mentioned cases is significant. In tackling important causes, leadership can be collective or collective and elite at the same time. This allows for a more inclusive approach that cannot be put within the context of everyday politics. Even in a divided country like BiH, the commons can serve as an opportunity to build something larger and overcome the divisive legacy of war.

In his essay, "*U miru*," ("In peace") the famous Bosnian writer Dževad Karahasan (n.d.) explained how humanity needs to stop seeing nature as something to conquer but rather something we must live with in partnership. He reflected on his childhood during socialism and remembered a teacher speaking about new dams and hydroelectric plants and "scientific optimism" that dictated that everything is achievable through technical exploration and that water is something to use for progress. He contrasted this utilitarian approach to nature he was taught with the emerging recognition that nature is to be protected rather than exhausted. Perhaps the protection of common resources and leadership that is arising from the protests and movements will ignite new optimism in a divided country such as BiH and as well in a world where we need once again to connect with each other.

NOTE

1. My research is based on three interviews conducted in 2020, including of Alma Midzic, Tahira Tibold, and Jasna Kovo. Alma Midzic is academic and activist and has been involved in many projects related to the commons in Bosnia and Herzegovina. Tahira Tibold is an activist in Kruščica. Jasna Kovo has been involved in many campaigns and has published several articles and participated in different research projects.

REFERENCES

Arnika. (2017). Riot police forcibly remove residents defending river against hydropower. Retrieved from https://english.arnika.org/news/riot-police-forcibly-remove-residents-defending-river-against-hydropower

Cerkez, A. (2012). Bosnia's national museum closes after 124 years. *CNBC.* Retrieved from https://www.cnbc.com/2012/10/04/bosnias-national-museum-closes-after-124-years.html

De Launey, G. (2018). "They dammed everything" – Bosnia's hydropower gone sour. *BBC News.* Retrieved from https://www.bbc.com/news/world-europe-45470309

Dimitrović, T. (2011). Challenges of civil Society in Bosnia and Herzegovina, Social Inclusion Foundation in Bosnia and Herzegovina, April, 2011. Retrieved from http://www.sif.ba/dok/1392298597.pdf

Dževad Karahasan. (n.d.). Essay "U miru". Retrieved from http://penbih.ba/2020/10/dzevad-karahasan-u-miru/

Eichelmann, U., & Arning, A. (2020). Historic decision for rivers in Bosnia & Herzegovina. Save the Blue Heart of Europe. Retrieved from https://www.patagonia.com/stories/save-blue-heart-europe-balkan-rivers-story/story-28991.html

French Press Agency. (2015). Bosnians turn out to save country's oldest museum. *Daily Sabah.* Retrieved from https://www.dailysabah.com/feature/2015/09/14/bosnians-turn-out-to-save-countrys-oldest-museum

Friedrich, T. L., Vessey, W. B., Schuelke, M. J., Ruark, G. A., & Mumford, M. D. (2009). A framework for understanding collective leadership: The selective utilization of a leader and team expertise within networks. *The Leadership Quarterly, 20*(6), 933–958.

Gallop, P. (n.d.). A tale of two communities successfully resisting the Balkan hydropower tsunami. Bankwatch. Retrieved from https://bankwatch.org/story/a-tale-of-two-communities-successfully-resisting-the-balkan-hydropower-tsunami

Gavrankapetanović-Redžić, J. (2018). Culture, memory, and collective identities in the (re)making: The National Museum of Bosnia and Herzegovina. *Acta Slavica Iaponica, 39*, 71–90.

Gronn, P. (2002). Distributed leadership as a unit of analysis. *Leadership Quarterly, 13*(4), 423–451.

Hajdarpašić, E. (2008). Museums, multiculturalism, and the remaking of postwar Sarajevo. In R. Ostow (Ed.), *(Re)Visualizing national history: Museums and national identities in Europe in the New Millennium* (pp. 109–138). University of Toronto Press.

Hromadžić, A. (2015). *Citizens of an empty nation: Youth and state making in postwar Bosnia and Herzegovina* (pp. 136–137). University of Pennsylvania Press.

Mapping Study of CSOs in Bosnia and Herzegovina. (n.d.). Retrieved from http://europa.ba/wp-content/uploads/2016/11/Mapping-study-of-CSOs-in-BiH.pdf

Nelson, A. (2017, November 27). Balkan hydropower projects soar by 300% putting wildlife at risk, research shows. *The Guardian.* Retrieved from https://www.theguardian.com/environment/2017/nov/27/balkan-hydropower-projects-soar-by-300-putting-wildlife-at-risk-research-shows

Patagonia. (2018). *Blue Heart: The fight for Europe's last wild rivers.* [video]. Retrieved from https://www.youtube.com/watch?v=OhmHByZ0Xd8

Perry, V. (2019). Frozen, stalled, stuck, or just muddling through: The post-Dayton frozen conflict in Bosnia and Herzegovina. *Asia Europe Journal, 17*(1), 107–127.

Puljec-Shank, R. (2015). Civil society in a divided country: Linking legitimacy and ethnicity of civil society organizations in Bosnia and Herzegovina. Research Gate. Retrieved from https://www.researchgate.net/publication/277268841_Civil_society_in_a_divided_society_Linking_legitimacy_and_ethnicness_of_civil_society_organizations_in_Bosnia-Herzegovina

Sofić Salihbegović, A. (2019, January 3). Zašto tolike nove hidroelektrane u BiH? *Deutsche Welle – DW.* Retrieved from https://www.dw.com/hr/za%C5%A1to-tolike-nove-hidroelektrane-u-bih/a-47739194

Tarrow, S. (2011). *Power in movement: Social movements and contentious politics* (3rd ed.). Cambridge University Press.

Tijana Dimitrović, Challenges of civil Society in Bosnia and Herzegovina. Retrieved from http://www.sif.ba/dok/1392298597.pdf

Tomašević, T., Horvat, V., Midžić, A., Dragšić, I., & Dakić, M. (2018). *Commons in South East Europe: Case of Croatia, Bosnia & Herzegovina and Macedonia.* Institute for Political Ecology

Vejnovic, V. (2018). European Parliament warns Balkan countries to stop destructive hydropower. *Bankwatch Network.* Retrieved from https://bankwatch.org/blog/european-parliament-warns-balkan-countries-to-stop-destructive-hydropower

18

HOPPING THE HOOPS OR BUILDING A COMMUNAL CULTURE AS THE MOST SIGNIFICANT PILLAR OF LEADERSHIP OF THE COMMONS

KATJA HLEB, MIHA ŠKERLAVAJ AND DOMEN ROZMAN

INTRODUCTION

Dunking Devils is a world-famous Guinness World Record holding Slovenian acrobatic basketball team which has been performing since 2004. Given the extreme and highly dangerous acrobatic stunts the Dunking Devils perform, the group provides an excellent example of how responsible leadership and communal culture are critical to ensure group cohesion and the safety of its acrobats (see, e.g., https://www.youtube.com/watch?v=CBgPOSsEUis&t=42s).

To observe how responsible leadership and communal culture are developed, we conducted an in-depth case study to trace and describe the growth process of the Dunking Devils community along with leadership emerging through a few pivotal moments in the 15 years of their existence. We included the moments of crisis – last among them the coronavirus crisis of 2020 – that Dunking Devils turned into a springboard for the whole community to a new organizational model.

Employing a grounded theory research method, we illustrate how Dunking Devils believe that the core that sustained the group and has brought it huge worldwide success, is their deliberate emphasis on communal culture. Additionally, we propose that by observing the case of Dunking Devils we can see how one of the critical companions to this kind of culture is responsible leadership of self and others. After doing a thorough qualitative analysis of the material provided by Dunking Devils, we believe that in their case there is a synergistic relationship between communal culture and responsible leadership. Important for the emergence of responsible leadership was the strong presence of authenticity and the international context of their performances, which put pressure on the group to be excellent. These elements were intertwined with multiple instances of community underlined in verbal, written, behavioral or group values.

The core contribution of our study is shedding light on the possibly more responsible leadership practices of the future as the values of social responsibility and sustainability become more widely shared. These practices may be useful for all organizations and even more so for those involving high risk where, firstly, much is at stake (i.e., the level of danger manifested in the Dunking Devils' performance); and secondly, the crowd or client metaphorically votes for the success of the organization, or lack thereof. With so many high-risk elements involved, such organizations such as Dunking Devils need to commit to excellence or stop performing. Excellence derives in large part from responsibility.

In addition, we demonstrate how the process of communal culture development can be (or has to be) a forerunner of the success of the organization and its sustainability. To ensure its long-term sustainability, Dunking Devils has been organically growing and adapting its purpose to its environment, transitioning from a high-end entertainer to an educational agent in society, beginning again with culture as a central pillar of its community. The findings of our case study are also significant for the study of leadership and communal culture in the commons where responsibility is one of its foundational principles.

THE STORY OF DUNKING DEVILS

Japanese hall full of fans waiting in the dark. Neon lights on moving human bodies start to switch on. The crowd's ecstasy goes viral. Domen, a head of Dunking Devils, is silently observing. He knows how many times things did not go well in the past and is well aware of the single most important factor gluing his men together in a singular, synergic and possibly devastatingly dangerous activity, namely, responsible communal culture.

Dunking Devils is one of the world's leading acrobatic groups that started out as a small commons of teenage amateur basketball acrobatic performers, having little acrobatic, basketball or management skills. With utter dedication and special kind of community building system, they have sustained and grown over the past 15 years from a few amateurs to a group of 100 members, age 15 to 35. They have performed more than 2,000 shows in 50 different countries while their videos have been viewed more than 500 million times.

Dunking Devils has reinvented their business model three times and made their last big shift during the coronavirus crisis. Today they have their own academy and a strategic plan to enter the infotainment industry. Six of their members are involved on a full professional basis and their CEO Domen Rozman is a TEDx and executive conferences speaker. The Dunking Devils motto is: "There is one true direction. Up!" and they set a clear example of a commons of performers very successfully adhering to the cause they all find valuable and worthy.

COMMUNAL CULTURE

We coin the term "communal culture" as the culture built and intertwined in the community around a shared interest, serving as its glue and pivotal axis. In the in-depth case of Dunking Devils, the terms "community," "communal," and "team" manifested in every set of data and on multiple occasions. Theoretically, a comparable term was coined by Mintzberg (2009), featuring the case of Pixar. Mintzberg (2009) defined "community-ship" as a term standing between individual leadership on one side and collective citizenship on the other. Community-ship makes the use of leadership that is of an engaged and distributed nature.

Kegan and Lahey (2016) described a strategic approach to communal culture which manifests in a win-win situation for both individuals and the organization. They coined the term "deliberately developmental organizations" (DDOs) that are shaped by (a) "edge" or developmental aspirations, (b) "home" or developmental communities and (c) "groove" or developmental practices. When addressing the betterment of organizations, Kegan and Lahey applied the simple equation of better me + better you = better us for aggregating and applying the individual level data to the organizational level data (Humprey & LeBreton, 2019).

RESPONSIBLE LEADERSHIP

Responsible leadership is a newer leadership theory (Hannah et al., 2014) and represents a key leadership component of corporate social responsibility (Matten & Moon, 2008, 2020). Waldman, Siegel, and Stahl (2020) defined responsible leadership as

> *an orientation or mindset taken by people in executive level positions toward meeting the needs of a firm's stakeholder(s). As such, it deals with defining those stakeholder(s), assessing the legitimacy of their claims, and determining how those needs, expectations or interests can and should be best served. (p. 6)*

Taking a more socio-relational approach, Maak and Pless (2006) defined responsible leadership as

> *a relational and ethical phenomenon, which occurs in social processes of interaction with those who affect or are affected by leadership and have a stake in the purpose and vision of the leadership relationship. (p. 103)*

It is the art of building and sustaining good relationships with all relevant stakeholders" (p 104). As such, a responsible leader's "core task is to weave a web of inclusion" (Maak & Pless, 2006, p. 104) where leaders engage themselves among equals.

Stakeholders include far more than the firm's stockholders and include personnel, clients, and customers, as well as society writ large and the environment. Waldman et al. (2020) argued that the conceptualization of responsible leadership is based on two primary manifestations, namely the strategist and the integrator. The strategist orientation concerns itself with the direct interest of the organization and shareholders whereas the integrator orientation concerns itself with all relevant stakeholders (Freeman, 1984; Freeman et al., 2010), whose interests are affected by policies and actions of the firm. Strategists, the authors argue, have less developed ethical outlooks and a linear focus, while integrators are highly ethical, think in paradoxes, are responsible, authentic, and have a global outlook. Integrators consider all stakeholder interests as highly authentic, beneficial to the firm in the long term and not subject to strict cost-benefit analysis. A leader's personal involvement with stakeholders is the norm. Integrators have all the characteristics of the strategists plus the additional ones associated with responsible leadership.

Responsible leadership's proposed dimensions include: (a) development of mind (b) paradox vs. linear either/or mindset, (c) responsibility vs. accountability, (d) authenticity and personal involvement and (e) international and cross-cultural perspectives. The two versions of responsible leadership, strategist and integrator, in theory differ on these four dichotomies (Waldman et al., 2020). The integrator manifestation of responsible leadership is discussed in this chapter in relation to the Dunking Devils.

In the in-depth case study of Dunking Devils, we have found solid evidence of the three proposed antecedents of responsible leadership as defined

Table 1. The characteristics of Integrator and Strategist mindsets in responsible leadership construct (Waldman et al., 2020).

1. Development of the mind: neuroscience and developmental psychology offer an explanation of the default states of the brain and the meaning making as the developmental property

2. Paradoxical mindset: bringing together and harmonizing the contradictory needs of diverse stakeholders

3. Responsibility/vs accountability: R= feels responsibility toward stakeholders whose interests are affected by the policies and actions of the organisation. A= feels accountability towards stakeholders only.

4. Authenticity: high concern for authenticity through leadership.

5. International and cross cultural perspectives: different approach to leadership according to geographical position; for example, Scandinavian approach differs significantly from more traditional culture by being more cosmopolitan in its outlook.

by Waldman et al. (2020); (a) the responsibility component, (b) the authenticity component, and the (c) international and cross-cultural perspectives component. We conjecture regarding the existence of the development of the mind and a paradox mindset (Fig. 1).

Fig. 1. Theoretical Frame of Responsible Leadership Construct.

METHODS AND DATA

We studied communal culture and responsible leadership using an in-depth case study method and grounded theory approach (Charmaz, 2014; Glaser & Strauss, 1967; Strauss & Corbin, 1990). The emergence of Dunking Devils' communal culture is abundantly documented in their *"Culture diary,"* a collection of written documents about the development of the culture. Additional data consisted of personal diaries, emails exchanged, personal notes of its founders and charter members, semistructured interviews with Dunking Devils founders and charter members, podcasts with the Dunking Devils CEO, observation with involvement, and video analysis of Dunking Devils publicly available content consisting of reality shows, vlogs, productions, public engagements like Britain's Got Talent, TED talks and open executive conference speeches.

BUILDING COMMUNAL CULTURE

The communal culture of Dunking Devils was demonstrated in the data collected by: (1) the high importance or high value ascribed to community in words and deeds; (2) the level of sophistication describing community and communal culture in the documents reviewed; (3) the relations among the three most important groups of agents that include: (a) the community core comprised six fully professionally committed members, (b) hired managers and investors, and (c) the community as a whole; (4) *"the team;"* (5) care for the next generation of acrobats; (6) clearly defined communal core values; and the (7) context, consisting of psychological safety and resilience.

Throughout the data set, there is a strong presence of a strong communal culture that is consistently highly valued. In the three pivotal documents written by Dunking Devils, community and communal culture is widely discussed. It is a *conditio sine qua non* for Dunking Devils and there is a general agreement upon the fact that *"community"* is the central pillar of a long-lasting success. The word *"community"* is used often and deliberately in Dunking Devils documents and letters, assuming its importance for the writer and for the reader of the document.

Relations among the three groups of key agents – the community core comprised six fully professionally committed members, hired managers and investors, and the community as a whole – are clearly described and reoccurring. The relationship between the community core and the hired managers is based on the perception by the core that they need outside expertise because of their own lack of competency in certain areas. As their competency develops, they begin to perceive that they no longer need the outside expertise. In a sense, the illusion about the power of the external agent loses its grip and the relationship terminates in a more or less abrupt way. Hence, over time the relations between the core group and outside experts last for a shorter duration, become less emotionally charged and spiral into not being needed. The core group expressed a deep level of introspection about these relationships. For example, the Dunking Devils CEO said:

> *"It is like a self-reflection. It is interesting to me. I think, I am aware of, if I know the pattern; if I am being responsible it would be good to avoid God like relationships in the future. As we are just ending a 15-year cycle."*

and

> *"how we have again and again chosen ourselves before someone external, that has been warm at first; how shall I put it, useful at first, and then it became a threat."*

The relationship between the core group and the community as a whole is the single biggest potential threat to the community. This relationship is *"open," "taken all the best care of," "attended to immediately and with all needed care in case of conflict."* Although hierarchical due to the large number of community members, accessibility to top managers is communicated clearly and regularly. The feedback loop confirms that the core group is accessible, illustrated by the way that younger members of the community openly come with suggestions, complaints, and troubles to all levels of community members.

> *"The team" is a crucial element of Dunking Devils. Both respondents in semistructured interviews mentioned communal culture 14 times and 13 times respectively either directly or indirectly. The narrative that stressed the existence and/or importance of communal culture was:* "we are THE TEAM," "even in most dynamic times the core remained solid," *and* "after not addressing the 2017 crisis immediately, we have corrected that approach in the coronavirus crisis time and called the big community meeting instantly."

The Dunking Devils Academy, a structured place for the young to belong as long as they follow a few clear norms, demonstrates the importance of the communal culture being transferred from generation to generation. One such core norm is *"tease with love."* Whenever someone makes a mistake, they are *"teased with love."* This norm is highly regarded and often practiced in all directions. The aim of the *"tease with love"* concept is to teach the community members that they are acceptable as they are, that they belong, and that the community has their back, especially on their weak spot. Besides, the members of the community are aware of the healing, relaxing, and bonding features of good humor shared in a trustworthy circle. Summer camps are a clear community building activity, as are tours, which are very demanding.

Characteristics that underlie the group's strong communal culture include the resilience of the core Dunking Devils community, even in times of lack of expertise, competence, resources, or direction and the collective ownership of success. Self-praise regarding success catalyzes teasing with love during which the individual claiming success is asked to deeply reflect upon the fact that only together could success be claimed.

Psychological safety is a strong and deliberately bred construct in the community, played out as kicking the young emerging leaders out of their comfort zones. Mistakes are expected in such a scenario and are observed from afar. In such a way, every member can and does learn through their own visceral experience.

Three core values are considered serious and important building blocks of communal culture. The CEO perceives them as the connection mechanism at the very deepest level of the community psyche. The three values include: *"team work, the only one right way is up, and the value of experience."* In-boarding and not on-boarding takes place, the concept described in the case of Marvel (Harrison et al., 2019). People can fully opt in with Dunking Devils' community and still keep other identities played out elsewhere, intact.

Fig. 2 represents timeline of pivotal points in Dunking Devils community building.

EMERGENCE OF RESPONSIBLE LEADERSHIP

Throughout the data set, there is a strong presence of signs and building blocks of responsible leadership. Especially high importance or high value is consistently placed upon responsibility. Data show that signs of responsibility being

Fig. 2. Timeline Presenting Pivotal Moments in the Dunking Devils Community Building.

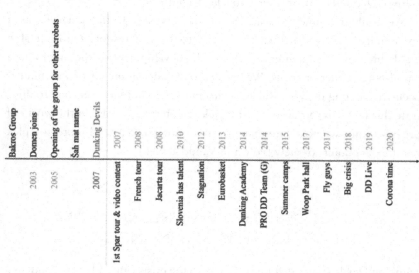

either reinforced as a norm or lived are commonplace. Numerous examples demonstrate verbal or written affirmation of responsibility – teaching by example, lecturing about responsibility to paying sources (like executive conferences) or big audiences (like TED talk). A few examples are: *"shows are a pressure so big that it is difficult to imagine," "the moment of big decision* (such as whether to commit to Dunking Devils professionally) – *six members decided to fully commit,"* and, *"we decided we would self-manage ourselves and stop hiring people we attributed power to they did not possess."*

Authenticity and personal involvement are also norms aspired to consciously and deliberately. As explained by one of the respondents:

> *"When not many spectators show up for the performance, ... many hours of video analysis taught me I shall never let my face fall down, I shall do it for me, for the boys, for the gang, for fun, I shall be me all the time, many people watching or few."*

The international and cross-cultural characteristic of responsible relationship posited by Waldman et al. (2020) functions in regions of the world more open to the practice of responsible leadership compared with other accepted leadership approaches. We argue that in the case of Dunking Devils, who are all young digital natives, trotting the globe for a good decade most days of the year, illustrates that the group manifests the international and cross-cultural characteristic of responsible leadership.

We could not find evidence in documents that Dunking Devils as a community exercises the last two characteristics of responsible leadership highlighted by Waldman et al. (2020), the development of the mind and a paradoxical either/or focus. We speculate that development of the mind is occurring among the youthful acrobats, but we do not have the data to illustrate this fact. Given that the youth lack long-term expertise in the world of organizations, we postulate that they have not yet mastered more complex paradoxical points of view (Pole and Vande de Ven).

IMPACT OF THE CORONAVIRUS CRISIS ON THE DEVELOPMENT OF DUNKING DEVILS

Dunking Devils responded immediately to the crisis caused by the pandemic during which they could not travel for performances. Instead, they made several major changes in their operations including: (1) holding live screened trainings, led by one member of the community per day; (2) organizing a big community meeting as soon as it was possible (5th of May 2020) to reinforce the communal culture; (3) drafting a detailed document encompassing vision/mission statements for 2020–2025 and in-depth self-reflections, (4) organizing swift adaptive change of their business proposition that prevented a cashflow loss, (5) filming, producing and on 9/11 posting one of the best Dunking Devils productions ever made, and (6) bringing to fruition the NBA show with the Slovene NBA champion Luka Dončić.

The reaction to the 2020 coronavirus crisis and the video productions that followed are very symbolic of Dunking Devils communal culture. An immediate call of the meeting of the whole community and a profound, real time anonymous survey distributed to its members cemented the community during a period when they were self-isolating and hence disconnected. Virtual trainings re-bonded the group and maintained their necessary fitness. A swift transformation of their business model to selling production and social media skills to big domestic corporations prevented a major loss of income. Their new vision statement describing the 2020–2025 timeframe capitalized on *"an empty space where contemplation is possible."*

During this period, Dunking Devils was able to produce videos they had planned for before but never realized. One video turned the tallest chimney in Europe – the symbol of past pollution and a call for carbon free production in the 2050 future – into a source of huge athletic achievement covered with Hollywood level production (see: https://www.youtube.com/watch?v=l IPgGk4lu7E&feature=youtu.be). The second video, a Dunking Devils show with the NBA together with the Slovenian NBA champion Luka Dončič, was a long-time dream come true (see: https://www.youtube.com/watch?v=r2d Qxn3iprk&feature=youtu.be). Hence, in the year where most have struggled in so many ways, Dunking Devils with their attitude of *"The Team"* (*"Ekipa"*), their three solid, clear, and reinforced values, and their deeply rooted responsibility and the *"one way-up"* approach have been able to "up their game" to an even higher level.

THE RELATIONSHIP BETWEEN COMMUNAL CULTURE AND RESPONSIBLE LEADERSHIP IN DUNKING DEVILS

The communal culture and responsible leadership of Dunking Devils are intertwined in a synergistic relationship. We demonstrate and provide the evidence for this synergistic relationship by referring to several demonstrative statements from the documents studied and representing this relationship in Fig. 3. The connections between communal culture and responsible leadership are explained in Fig. 3.

Connection a/A: Dunking Devils places a strong, direct (in narrative) and indirect (in coherent behavior) emphasis on community and the communal

Fig. 3. The Connections Between the Concepts of Communal Culture and Responsible Leadership.

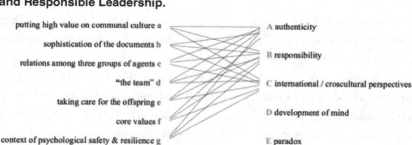

culture. In their words, authenticity, to be who you are at all times, is a necessary building block for such a community to endure and grow.

> "When we fell in crisis after the Fly guys, we called in the whole community for the meeting and talked completely naked, completely vulnerably and with the anonymous questionnaire, for as long as anyone had anything to say."

Connection a/B: Communal culture and responsibility seem to be intertwined in order for the common young people to stay together successfully for a period of 15 years.

We fundamentally bring all of them up to be leaders. To be the leaders of their own life and then to help lead others. How long it takes a person to take on that role, is entirely up to their personal development span."

> "When we filmed Fly Guys, we neglected our own community, the one that means so much."

Connection a/C: Communal culture glues the members together also when spreading their influence through their performance worldwide.

> "We have grown constantly ever since. More and more members to the community. More tours, longer tours. We have developed in those as managers, as leaders."

Connection b/A: Dunking devils demonstrate the authenticity of their innermost thoughts and feelings in their spoken and written words. The statement below comes from an interview and is documented in written form.

> "In our vision we jotted down that we wanted our own park, our own domicile hall, where we can train well."

Connection b/B: We would consider the termination of the relationship with the first professional manager as an example of addressing a sensitive situation very authentically and responsibly.

Connection c/A: The relations among people that found their way to Dunking Devils are of utmost importance to the group. They are in no way left to coincidence. To the contrary, they are established and maintained with vigor and attention. Authenticity of both sides of the relationships is in their words a prerequisite for this to happen.

"We break barriers deliberately. I need every youth to know, they can come any time to any of us and tell wholeheartedly what is wrong, what bothers them. We want them to know they can be who they are in our community."

Connection c/B: All of the documents we reviewed that were written by Dunking Devils during their formation indicate a commitment to responsibility for a clear open, honest and timely communication with managers.

Connection d/A: The value of the team and the need for their members to be authentic is emphasized in the material we reviewed. One of the most picturesque pieces of evidence is found in the narrative after the performance on the tall chimney in which they said they could never do such a thing were they not true to themselves and their teammates. Interviews offered additional insight, like this one:

"When one grows from the position of one among equals to the leader, one gets to lead 5-6 people. You delegate and they respect you. They don't quarrel with you. But you need to communicate as a friend, not as some top-down authority."

Connection d/B: The connection between the concept of the team and responsibility is probably one of the most obvious synergistic relationships between the two concepts. The activity Dunking Devils undergo in their performances is very dangerous to say the least. The absence of team spirit, and the responsibility for self and others is essential in order to keep safe and often even alive.

Connection d/C: We can even assume that 30 performances in 35 days in a distant country for young people in their late teens and early twenties cannot happen without real team spirit and friendship. There is data available supporting this assumption in all of their documents. Max, many times the "leader of the way" expressed it simply:

"Tours have connected us. They are the catalyst of friendship."

Connection e/A: We as researchers wondered whether this sub-relationship is the core of the leadership among young people working together for a long time toward a very demanding goal. The authentic care of the young, when one is still very young themselves (maybe not always young chronologically but immature in some other aspect), might be the key to how commons can lead and be led, both simultaneously, successfully.

"I was the youngest for a long time. I played a role of a damsel for a long time. It suited me. It was easy. Then I was appointed the role of a "tour leader" and all hell broke loose. We had 30 performances in 35 days. It was very very tiresome. I had little sleep. All the time I was thinking about what to do next. However, I grew as a leader enormously. I was very thankful for this to have happened later. I was 'The Leader of The Tour (voda puta)'"

Connection e/B: Further, responsibility in leading youth is demonstrated by the following:

"We started to take care of our offspring. Without them we would no longer exist."

"Young people are deliberately thought of as a responsibility at our summer camps. It is a planned part of the curriculum."

One of the clearest examples of this point would in our opinion be the amount of time and effort spent on repairing the damage done after Fly Guys was filmed and the young Dunking Devils were sidelined and neglected. In 2017, Dunking Devils was invited to film the *Fly Guys* series. As it was a big international project that could have offered a much bigger window into the world, they grabbed the opportunity. It was a very demanding task, athletically and organizationally and only the older members took part. During the filming, the older members abandoned their regular meetings with the rest of the community. Consequently, the Dunking Devils community started to show the signs of crisis and deterioration. In late 2017, the CEO and the core team realized what had happened and made a concerted effort into rebuilding trust and community. Beginning in January 2018, Dunking Devils have held a number of all-community meetings where the core team provided the space for all the community members to vent their frustrations, in written and spoken form and to re-energize the communal culture. The older members did whatever it took to correct their mistake with the young and restored their trust fully in three months.

Connection e/C: Young members are soon to be taken on international tours. What is more, they are given responsibilities – even more than they can handle – and are protected in silence by the older and more experienced members. The international arena is bred into every member's veins the moment they can handle it.

Connection f/A,B: The awareness of the importance of clear, common, and openly discussed values, the time dedicated to these and the seriousness of an open discussion about them is an illustration of the communal values being practiced authentically and responsibly.

> *"I am usually the one that keeps track of our agreements being lived out. Are we acting with integrity? Are we sticking to our core three values?"*

Connection f/C: We feel safe to say that Dunking Devils' values are travel proof and that they are practiced the same when they perform in Japan, in the U.S., in Slovenia, or in Greece.

Connection g/A, B, C: Psychological safety, resilience in the context of authenticity, responsibility, and international context are consistently practiced and Max and Domen provide an example for each in their narratives below:

> *"People stay as every single member is heard at Dunking Devils. Emotionally and physically. Besides, we do cool stuff."*

"Teasing with love" as one of the commonly communicated building blocks of the Dunking Devils is a demonstration of psychological safety being established in a very responsible, proactive, measurable, and corrective manner.

> *"We bring opportunities internationally that young can not easily get elsewhere."*

CONCLUSION AND RECOMMENDATIONS FOR GOING FORWARD

Across seven complex sources of data, we identified a few critical building blocks and sustaining mechanisms of communal culture and responsible leadership in the Dunking Devils community. We found that the communal culture is one of the keys to the sustainable and resilient nature of the organization researched. The communal culture is deliberately built, nurtured, and preserved and is perceived as the main pillar and core asset of the community. Another key feature is responsibility and leadership, both groomed in its members and the community as a whole all the time, from the very beginning of the group's existence or individual inclusion, and literally in every moment.

> *"To hit the basket is a personal responsibility and in that moment one is a leader of his/her own act upon which the success of the whole depends."*

Authenticity and personal involvement are present to a large degree and so is international context, key components of responsible leadership as defined by Waldman et al. (2020). Development of the mind and paradox thinking are still to be developed in the entire group, although the CEO manifests these characteristics.

Dunking Devils are planning on leveraging the platforms, networks, and high pace digital outlets to bring awareness and knowhow of personal excellency and the power of collective collaboration to many. Appealing to the generations of the digital era, having limited attention spans and requirements for a fast pace, Dunking Devils seems to have a significant comparative advantage to more traditional systems.

From our point of view, these and more are the arguments worth discussing under the umbrella of the leadership of the commons, specifically addressing the collaborative part of the leadership practiced in the domain of knowledge and educational entertainment or as some call it, edutainment. As we perceive the viable future directions for organizations, community may be in part a model for future organizational cultures. Additionally, the study of self-made youth can offer new insights into leadership models appropriate for the generation born in 2000 and beyond.

ACKNOWLEDGMENT

We would like to thank the Dunking Devils community for selflessly and abundantly sharing their information with historic and reflective value. It has astonished us again and again how deeply rooted a culture of contributing to the community at large is among these relatively young people.

REFERENCES

Charmaz, K. (2014). *Constructing grounded theory. A practical guide through qualitative analysis.* Sage; 2006/2008.

Freeman, E. R. (1994). The politics of stakeholder theory: Some future directions. *Business Ethics Quarterly*, 4(4), (Oct., 1994), 409–421.

Freeman, E. R., Parmar, B. L., & Harrison, J. S. (2010). Stakeholder theory: The state of the art. *The Academy of management annals*, 3(1), 403–445.

Glaser, B. G., & Strauss, A. L. (1967). *The discovery of grounded theory; strategies for qualitative research.* Aldine.

Hannah, S.T., Sumanth, J. J., Lester, P., & Cavarretta, F. (2014). Debunking the false dichotomy of leadership idealism and pragmatism: Critical evaluation and support of newer genre leadership theories. *Journal of organizational behavior*, 35, 598–621.

Harrison, S. H., Carlsen, A., & Škerlavaj, M. (2019). *Marvel's blockbuster machine.* Harvard Business Review.

Humprey, S. E., & LeBreton, J. M. (2019). *The handbook of multilevel theory, measurement, and analysis.* American Psychological Association.

Kegan, R., Lahey, L., Miller, M. L., Fleming, A., & Helsing, D. (2016). *An everyone culture: Becoming a deliberately developmental organization.* Harvard Business Review Press.

Kish-Gephart, J., Treviño, L., Chen, A., & Tilton, J. (2019). *"Behavioral business ethics: The journey from foundations to future"*, Business Ethics (Business and Society 360, Vol. 3, pp. 3–34). Emerald Publishing Limited.

Matten, D., & Moon, J. (2008). "Implicit" and "explicit" CSR: A conceptual framework for a comparative understanding of corporate social responsibility. *Academy of Management Review*, 33, 404–424.

Matten, D., & Moon, J. (2020). 2018 decade award invited article. Reflections on the 2018 decade award: The meaning and dynamics of corporate social responsibility. *Academy of Management Review 2020*, 45(1), 7–28.

Mintzberg, H. (2009). *Rebuilding companies as communities.* Harvard Business Review.

Maak, T., & Pless, N. M. (2006). Responsible leadership in a stakeholder society – A relational perspective. *Journal of Business Ethics*, 66, 99–115.

Mintzberg, H. (2009). *Rebuilding companies as communities.* Harvard Business Review.

Strauss, A. L., & Corbin, J. (1990). *Basic of qualitative research: Grounded theory procedures and techniques.* Sage.

Waldman, D. A., Siegel, D. S., & Stahl, G. K. (2020). Defining the socially responsible leader: Revisiting issues in responsible leadership. *Journal of Leadership and Organizational Studies*, 1–16.

19

JOB COMMONS: THE OVERLOOKED DIMENSION OF COMMONS LEADERSHIP AND GLOBAL AND LOCAL GOVERNANCE

JAN HURST

Commons scholars and activists promote the local and global governance of common resources, whether environmental, cultural, knowledge, or public goods (Cogolati & Wouters, 2018; Ostrom, 1990). Yet they fail to consider jobs as a commons resource for sustaining everyday lives. The job indifference allows millions of people to languish in rich and poor countries without the hope of finding work alongside precarious underemployed workers and unpaid feminized domestic care workers. The global unemployment count already reached 190 million by early 2020, and the International Labor Organization (ILO) warns this may double following the global capitalist crisis and economic slowdown post Covid-19 pandemic (UN, 2020). The ill-preparedness for the pandemic exposed the fragility of work without local job governance to plan and protect job futures. Workers who sustain society, moreover, are at the bottom of a job status ladder and are undervalued and unrewarded despite fulfilling essential roles during crises such as the global pandemic.

Capitalism maintains job rationing for profit and savings, yet our most common need is for worthwhile jobs in abundance. Shifting priorities requires an ethical awakening and transnational solidarity, similar to how recent civil rights protests are forcing leaders to disrupt the status quo and address structural racism. Commons conceptualization is a useful entry point to problematize jobs at a higher level of abstraction so that political and civic leaders, communities, policymakers, and institutions can link job struggle to the commons for personal and social survival.

This chapter argues the case for redefining leadership on the commons for jobs. A "job commons" is broadly defined here as the commonization of jobs, whereby people seeking waged-labor can access local commons-protected jobs. These jobs exist in addition to competitive job markets and would be locally self-organized and self-governed to ensure that everyone seeking employment could find a job. A key question is whether a job-centric commons can secure human dignity and incomes wherever worthwhile jobs are needed most and support multi-racial working classes to sustain livelihoods through work, not just wealth.

Hence, the chapter has two aims: (1) to justify the case for a job commons; and (2) to identify the empirical building blocks to deliver a job commons so that leadership in community, political, social, and technological fields can shape the paradigm into reality for socio-economic justice while protecting the planet. Three sections follow: "Commons: Working for Whom?" section examines commons oversight of jobs in an historical context; "Redefining Leadership on the Commons for Jobs," section argues why job supplies need commons leadership; and "Job Commons: Reform for the Commonization of Jobs," section explores how job commons applied might bridge job gaps and everything else that concerns jobs, so everyone who wants to work can participate.

COMMONS: WORKING FOR WHOM?

Generally, "commons" definitions represent cooperative actions to protect global and local variants of the "common good." Yet the common need for jobs is often overlooked by scholars despite jobs being essential for sustaining livelihoods, self-determination, and collective wellbeing (see, e.g., Fig. 1 "A Map of the New Commons," in Hess, 2008, p. 13; Rose, 2019). The commons movement has focused more on "cultural commons," defending open access to public goods, knowledge sharing, creativity, digital space, and "environmental commons," protecting natural resources and stewarding consumption quotas in nature.

Commons struggles also overlap with political struggles in mass organizing, from localism (socialist), decentralization (liberal), to smaller government (conservative) which tends toward centrism in practice. Anti-capitalist (anarchist) lifestyles, on the other hand, promote self-help, self-rule, and social economy, from eco-villages to urban cooperatives. However, anti-state post-capitalist imaginings overlook the common need for waged jobs, not just reciprocal or communal labor. These imaginings leave uncertainty regarding how job supplies can engage all skill levels, as well as challenge discrimination, environmentally harmful growth, and labor devaluation. And, therefore, they remain defeatist about state and civil society's role protecting jobs as a commons, while ensuring jobs protect all commons.

"Labor as a commons" literature, for example, does not concern job creation for the masses. Rather, it emphasizes self-managed "new cooperativism" in worker ownership firms (Vieta, 2016). Cooperatives, thereby, are "… an *organizational commons*, the labor performed is a *commoning practice*, and the surplus generated a *commonwealth*" (italics in the original, see de Peuter & Dyer-Witheford, 2010, p. 45). Azzellini (2018) cites international examples of workers using commons-pool resource approaches to recuperate small to medium size firms facing closure. This allows for greater solidarity, self-management, equal remuneration, flatter hierarchies, less monitoring, and additional support from child-care to shared cooking. But even social enterprises cap labor in competitive capitalist states, and their lack of access to credit stifles their ability to scale up.

Some view commons for sharing wealth (Hardt & Negri, 2009) or as a management principal "…by which a resource is made openly accessible to all those in a community regardless of their identity or intended use" (Frischmann, 2005, p. 1022). Peter Linebaugh, a historian, considers the commons "the theory that vests all property in the community and organizes labor for the common benefit of all" (2008, p. 8). Commons is thus a relatable framework for securing job provision for downstream benefit. This is especially true given that disposable human potential is staggeringly expensive and a wasteful by-product of capitalist society with a fallout that is perversely lucrative for pharmaceutical and welfare industries (see Hawken, Lovins, & Lovins, 1999, pp. 48–61; Yates, 2011). Establishing common norms for zero waste of human potential, however, needs a peremptory process – a moral social contract founded by orderly governance and principles of *jus cogens* through international law (Weatherall, 2015). Designing "cosmopolitan localism" is also questionable without jobs (Manzini & M'Rithaa, 2017, pp. 33–35). Barchiesi (2012), however, warns against addressing a global working class, as global north and south have different labor histories, post-colonial oppression, allegiances, and forms of capitalist resistance.

Commons Leadership in Labor History

Historically, labor was integral to commons for social, environmental, and economic survival. Only modern definitions overlook labor and turned commons heritage into a narrative about the preservation of natural habitats. In England, for example, the "Charter of the Forest," a separate amendment to the second reissued Magna Carta in 1217, restored access to the forest, which made subsistence a community obligation, not as a given, but to allow free commoners to draw from the land and secure housing, food, work, raw material, customs, and medicine (Standing, 2019). For four centuries, the forest charter had greater relevance to "working class" politics. Nonetheless, the Magna Carta is only commemorated for protecting individual freedom and property rights (Linebaugh, 2008). Likewise, Europe's professional guilds, commons, as well as religious and charity systems regulated social order (De Moor, 2015, pp. 24–25).

However, feudal hierarchies began privatizing common land for production and hunting and began taxing politically excluded peasants (van der Linden, 2017). Protests led to peasant wars in Germany (1525) and Austria (1626). Although overthrown by militia, the peasant demands in twelve articles for reform, from civil liberties, paid labor, to restoring commons access, has helped seed human rights ideology, along with other social movements worldwide. Environmental groups continue to wrestle private interests from common liberties, such as, access to land, water, leisure (parks, festivals, allotments) and the right to roam, or they restrict public access in order to protect certain species (Harvey, 2011, p. 102). However, the fight for livelihoods has been lost as a commons endeavor. Then again, commoning practices support anti-capitalist alternative economies to reproduce autonomy, democratic confederalism, eco-feminism, cooperative working, community sharing, and problem-solving (De Angelis, 2014, pp. i74–i79). Examples include regional social movements with unique conditions and history, from the Zapatista movement in Mexico (Stalher-Sholk, 2014), to the Rojava revolution in North and Eastern Syria (Colasanti, Frondizi, Liddle, & Meneguzzo, 2018). A job commons, however, cannot bypass markets or development regimes, and whether it progresses as a reformist or autonomous movement will depend on local history and context (see Kousis & Paschou, 2017).

Job Supply Fault Lines: A Recent History

In the past century, leadership responses to capitalism's "growing pains" allowed global economic injustices to persist. Universal job insecurity, however, needs structural change (Azmanova, 2020; Cato, 2009). For example, U.S. New Deal job programs, following the 1929 financial crash, helped modernize infrastructure and services, but high unemployment and racial discrimination continued (Gilmore, 2002, p. 18). Only World War II (WWII) mobilized resources including land, labor, and capital to close employment gaps. Post WWII inspired greater equity for trade unions, welfare, and progressive taxation, but collective consciousness did not extend to a right to work.

Late adoption of Keynesian mixed economy policies in the 1960s provided economic stimulus after capitalism became stressed, but this stimulus was short-lived as public works and full employment were never grounded (Tcherneva, 2012). The late 1970s oil slump squeezed profits, increased inflation, recession, labor unrest, and trade union and industrial power declined. In the 1980s, neo-liberal economics set political agendas to enterprise public services, but financial unrest continued (Glyn, 2007). The late 1990s "battle" to escape markets and state oppression through technological commons was a non-starter, as monopoly firms captured open cost-free layers of the internet, colonized commerce, mined its users, extended market power through automation and outsourced production without employee negotiations. In western spheres, standard fulltime work is transitioning into flexible but precarious nonstandard contractual employment without unionization or collective bargaining, supposedly to reduce costs of dismissal and increase productivity and profitability.

Commons Leadership: Lost Vision for Job Futures

Leadership on the commons, therefore, could commonize socially productive jobs to serve nations and citizens well and protect job futures. The labor theory of value based on wages, rent, consumption, and profit hides capitalist structures that cannot sustain the common good (Collins, 2016; Lutz, 2002). Jobless "solutions," moreover, like the universal basic income (UBI)

(Van Parijs & Vanderborght, 2017), a wage compensation, is arguably defeatist, since it "…benefits the West and does not challenge the world system, which provides the wealth for their social safety net" (Andrews, 2018, p.193). Even the labor economist Guy Standing (2019, pp. 339–341) proposes a Commons Charter and redistributive "commons dividend" for sharing wealth and appreciating leisure without a jobs vision. Then again, Susser and Tonnelat (2013) define urban commons as a shared collective endeavor involving: (i) labor, consumption and public services, (ii) public space, and (iii) art. They link labor to collective identity in production and consumption, social movements, union protest, and public service provision. They see women fronting commons progress and "decent life" guarantees comprising collective production, from housing to caring professions; devolution of power from national to city management and locally designed public services (pp. 109–111).

However, leadership on the commons does not connect commons values, such as, participatory democracy, cooperative processes bridging social welfare, or private and public markets with job acquisition. Online communities want highly structured protocols with loose coordination and different commitment levels to equalize the means of production (Fuster Morell, 2014). But commons seen as a techno-sharing economy has gender implications given that male open-software developers dominate digital solidarity (Schweik & English, 2012, p. 45). Online labor markets also saturate demand as global competition undercuts high and low-skill wages and algorithms reproduce discrimination. Furthermore, even commons such as Local Exchange Trading Schemes, Time Banks, and other barter currencies have job distribution limits, including for degrowth (see Dittmer, 2013).

No Green Job Fix Yet

The struggle for jobs is also spatial and context specific and solutions need global cooperation. Proposals for "Green New Deal" jobs in the Western hemisphere (Pettifor, 2019), for example, raise consciousness for environmental commons. But green products, from solar panels to electric cars are metal and mineral mining intensive, and often damaging at source, from habitat destruction, water pollution, and deforestation to health impairment. Norway, for example, bans misleading "green" car advertisements (Zink & Geyer, 2016). And, while demand for Chinese processed lithium and copper;

the most efficient electrical conductor for batteries is soaring, its excavation undermines Chilean plains eco-structure, and cobalt from Central Africa and the Democratic Republic of Congo implicates child labor. Poor countries' low paid workers, thereby, subsidize richer countries low-carbon products. Hence, Antal (2014) questions whether full employment is compatible with green goals if jobs growth increases consumption. Arguably, raising living standards for all needs a job commons paradigm for collective responsibility and confronting jobs issues head on.

REDEFINING LEADERSHIP ON THE COMMONS FOR JOBS

This section makes the case for redefining leadership on the commons for jobs, arguing why job policy and collaborative governance have grown outmoded. The section, thereafter, considers how a job commons paradigm might be delivered.

Why Leadership on the Commons Needs a Jobs Outlook

A bold humane vision for leadership on the commons is essential, given that capitalism's hallmarks include unemployment, growing income inequality, employment discrimination, domestic debt fueled growth, environmental damage, and exploited laborers and children in raw material production. Even when skill-level is equal, job acquisition depends on where you live, and what you look like, and job progression depends on where you work. Making jobs a priority is not to denounce postwork theorists who criticize over-working, pointless jobs, moral posturing for a work ethic, or working-class nostalgia (Frayne, 2015; Graeber, 2018; Weeks, 2011). But paid work in a money-exchange economy has psychosocial benefits beyond unpaid work, wage compensation, or welfare (Jahoda, 1982). Waged-labor is how societies organized for centuries. Collective responsibility to distribute jobs more fairly is required and is why a commons outlook applies. Job provision, therefore, might be seen as "contributive justice" (Timmermann, 2018, pp. 94–95).

Hence, several scholars defend a job guarantee (Darity, 1999, p. 496; Mitchell & Wray, 2005) not to preserve capitalism, but because unemployment impairs health and wellbeing (see Davies, Homolova, Grey, & Bellis, 2019; Farré, Fasani, & Mueller, 2018; Voßemer et al., 2018). Some call for a shorter working week as the amount of paid hours needed to recoup wellbeing may not be great (Kamerāde, Wang, Burchell, Balderson, & Coutts, 2019). Others propose combining a basic income and public works offer (Fitzroy & Jin, 2018) or job governance to support universal work (Hurst, 2020). Many fear too much state intervention will usurp private sector innovation and create inflation and public spending deficits. Yet public funded research brought many innovations to market, from the touchscreen to GPS (Mazzucato, 2013).

Modern Monetary Theorists (MMTs) say governments can spend and control inflation and enact the right policies for individual and collective benefit (Armstrong, 2019; Nersisyan & Wray, 2019). But right- and left-wing politicians are unwilling to plan permanent job provision. The former deny labor power in class struggle and espouse free enterprise, despite corporate welfare exceeding social welfare (Jensen & Malesky, 2018). The latter, especially in the global north, want workplace democratization, employee ownership, worker's concessions, and a low-carbon "Green New Deal" job creation program. But even Roosevelt's 1930s "New Deal" environmental project, responding to the Great Depression and mass unemployment, excluded local people (see Maher, 2015). Arguably, job futures need commons status and protection, not ad hoc politically dependent programs absorbing only a fraction of the labor surplus, or promoting communitarianism, such as the UK's "Big Society" (see Caffentzis & Federici, 2014, pp. i97–i98), a failed idea to transform communities through volunteering, without considering jobs.

Job Policy outside the Commons

Economies periodically slide, but "business as usual" policies are insufficient even during periods of growth, as neither the private sector nor self-managed provision can absorb labor surplus. First, the micro and macroeconomic theories influencing political leaders' fiscal and monetary policies, from corporate welfare, job programs, education, re-skilling to entrepreneurship cannot create enough jobs for all who seek work. Even the unifying arms of the United Nations (UN) Sustainable Development Goals (SDGs) lack aspiration for local job supplies, despite headline "solutions" from economic growth to boosting tourism (Hurst, 2020), which will remain subdued despite the Covid-19 vaccine. Job security had already deteriorated under the International Labour Organisation's "decent work" agenda, as globalization and off-shoring lowered wages and exacerbated inequality.

Second, expecting people to retrain for jobs is unrealistic, as capitalist circuitry is anti-productive and anti-participatory, given competition creates job market enclosure and labor surplus. Human capital theory, for example, seeks to activate individuals to improve employability through work preparation, skills attainment, continuous learning, and entrepreneurship (Kuddo, 2012). But supply-side policy masks the abandonment of full employment goals (Raffass, 2017). Dobbins' (2018) letter to *The Guardian* explains

> [*that*] *labor market supply of trained workers automatically creates its own demand from employers is a hoax, evidenced by rising underemployment. This neoliberal orthodoxy has enabled governments to avoid crafting an industrial strategy to repair the social damage left by deindustrialization. (May 7th, 2018)*

Neoliberalism also allows the mass incarceration of black people to conceal the job dearth and level of unemployment, especially, in the USA where the "prison-industrial complex has become a venue for profit" (Calathes, 2017, pp. 448–449). Institutions, moreover, downplay the lack of a demand-side response for people needing employment support, whether through disability or transitioning from prison (Frøyland, Andreassen, & Innvær, 2019; Richardson & Thieme, 2020).

Third, job generation policies targeting "less-skilled" workers are not effective (Freeman & Gottschalk, 1998). For example, (i) employers are reluctant to hire disadvantaged workers despite wage subsidies, (ii) jobs created in enterprise zones in disadvantaged areas are usually taken by commuters, (iii) expanding public sector jobs through conditionality tied to welfare can be stigmatizing or result in jobs lacking progression, (iv) improving pay through profit-sharing or minimum wage can reduce benefits elsewhere, or employers make people redundant, and (iv) distributing jobs through work-sharing or affirmative action hiring does not address the shortage of opportunity and underlying disadvantage.

Fourth, robotic technologies advance job creation for the "productivity effect" to substitute repetitive tasks, increase quality and output, and reduce labor for continuous profits. But people still desire meaningful work, not only for money, but health benefits, social bonding, and influencing decisions for a greater good (Smids, Nyholm, & Berkers, 2020; Steger & Dik, 2010). But many jobs are also mired helping others to flourish (Veltman, 2016, pp. 142–171). Welfare provisions make capitalist accumulation less offensive and subdue dissent, as they are rooted in precapitalist religious traditions, but uneven welfare distribution and associated stigma denies giving job seekers uniform voice, representation, and power. How we resolve this dilemma is hardly confronted, as even the "right to work" under the *United Nations 1948 Declaration of Human Rights* lacks progress (Branco, 2019), commons representations, or job governance.

Collaborative Governance Is Not a Jobs Remedy

In recent decades, public leaders have expected collaborative governance to democratize decision-making in overlapping hierarchies, markets and governing networks adapting to political ideas and events (Cerny, 2017; Deacon, Macovei, Van Langenhove, & Yeates, 2009). Yet governance is also the means to sustain the status quo and careers coping with complex policy issues, governing mandates, and market-conforming funding regimes that fragment provision and enterprise public sectors. It coerces governance actors to interpret job supply problems as agents of neo-liberal globalization. Consequently, networks governing labor geographies have limited structural power, labor agency, and resistance (Coe & Jordhus-Lier, 2011; Hurst, 2016).

To achieve the UN's "decent work" agenda, for example, requires policy dissent, power diffusion, and structural unity across diplomatic, technical, legal, national, regional and community, an unlikely outcome without a universal job governance framework. Appeals to strengthen employment protection, therefore, will remain fragmented (Wright et al., 2019). As governing institutions contracting-out culture forces service providers and interest groups with less power to compete for service level agreements that restrict leadership agency, autonomy, and voice, and tackling problems together. "Networks of labor activism" may still compete (Zajak, Egels-Zandén, & Piper, 2017). Even global commons scholars detach environmental governance from regional youth unemployment, international division of labor, widening income disparities and discriminations (Brousseau, Dedeurwaerdere, Jouvet, & Willinger, 2012). In short, there is no job-centric governance disrupting capitalism for the greater good.

JOB COMMONS: REFORM FOR THE COMMONIZATION OF JOBS

Arguably, reform means raising consciousness for "job commons" – a new arm of commons scholarship with countermovement potential for tackling the global job dearth and employment marginalization. A partnership for jobs and the commons is essential for nature and human coexistence. Job supplies deserve new thinking, as programs overlook the gravity of the job dearth situation that impacts the same cohorts. The UK Conservative government, for example, claims 13,500 new "Job Entry: Targeted Support (JETS)" coaches will help 250,000 people impacted by Covid-19 to quickly find work (DWP, 2020). Yet with only 433,000 job vacancies in August 2020, and 1.398 million people unemployed (the actual count will be much higher), many job seekers will not find work, or will be coerced into self-employment, or "zero hour" contracts to meet JETS goals. Whether a "job commons" environment can commonize jobs to counter capitalism's antiwork practices and worker alienation should be considered. This does not mean working against the state and markets, rather it means making them work to support the commons, as their collective responsibilities are due. Hence, this section will clarify what can be done to counter inhumane job organizing, what commons-centric job creation would look like, how it can be delivered so people can earn without further exploitation, and who might pay and commit to sharing job solutions.

Establishing Job Commons

Civic and elected leaders with funding power would need to establish a job commons environment with public, social, legal and governance obligations to ensure all who want to work can contribute to society. They might, for example, instigate job governance, job generating policy, and job protections using a universal work charter and five components as a guide (Fig. 1).

A good economy would also reflect job values that address universal concerns (Knoedler & Schneider, 2010). Table 1, for example, compares job values in a spectrum of anti- and pro-job common values. Public leaders, thereby, can influence a shift to the latter if the former prevails. Job competition would still endure in chosen career paths or sectors dependent on skill specialism or temporary help jobs. But jobs "working for the commons,"

Fig. 1.   Leadership Components in the Job Commons Environment.

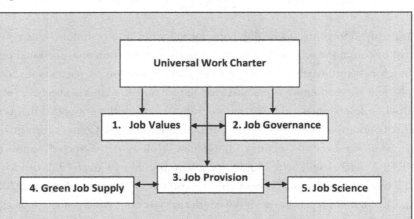

Universal work charter: Universal standards incorporate five components; each
to assist provision of local jobs on demand for the common good:

1. ***Job values***
   - Institutions and civil society develop a social job licence to protect
     common values and labor rights with moral and legal representation.
2. ***Job governance***
   - Governance infrastructure regulates universal basic service (UBS) jobs so
     people can counter employment discrimination and thrive.
3. ***Job provision***
   - On-demand UBS jobs applicable to local needs secure agriculture, food
     production, affordable house building, sanitation, internet, postal,
     transport, and care, from early years to end-of-life. So called "low-skilled"
     jobs transform into high-value jobs with world class standards and role
     prestige like civil service or military jobs.
4. ***Green job supply***
   - Jobs supporting national-local self sufficiency and circular economy
     lessen environmental damage from growth, consumption and transport
     emissions.
5. ***Job science***
   - Universities support analysis of demographic job need, and harness
     design technologies for sectorial wellbeing and ecological productive jobs
     in disadvantaged places.

Table 1. **Spectrum of Job Values.**

Anti-job Commons	Pro-job Commons
• Supports job scarcity for profit motive.	• Supports jobs in abundance for wellbeing.
• Sustains ceaseless extraction.	• Sustains human and natural habitats.
• Devalues jobs maintaining society.	• Values jobs maintaining society.
• Reduces employment protection.	• Increases employment protection.
• Emphasizes self-responsibility and activation finding work and improving employability.	• Emphasizes individual and collective responsibilities addressing structural unemployment and discrimination.
• Competition sanctions job distribution.	• Job governance sanctions job distribution.

while not compulsory, would grant sufficient job security for everyone else needing permanent waged-labor delivering universal basic services (UBS), from care, shelter, infrastructure, health, food to environmental protection. These occupations could be "commonized" not nationalized, as local production for the commons would support real need rather than financialization and support a spectrum of ability. Job planners could develop social licenses for commons jobs, ensuring international standards raise the worth and remuneration of so-called "low-skilled" jobs.

Jobs in common would be honored, protected, and stabilized in thematic occupational job streams supported by local job governance and collective decision-making managed through rotation and gender quotas. Freedom to engage in creative commons innovation would also be supported. But whether a commons collaborative economy is (i) governed through self-organization and (ii) jobs are commissioned through public and private sectors are a matter for job governance and civil society negotiation (see examples in Guttmann, 2019).

Job Commons Postdisasters

Job commons would be well prepared to respond to unemployment post natural or man-made disasters, by scaling up UBS, redeployment, and social interactions. The social distancing requirement of the Covid-19 pandemic, for example, has stymied supply and demand and has proven to be disastrous for countries dependent on consumption-led growth. In some countries, recourse has been to furlough workers with time-limited government-backed wage compensation and business loans. Moreover, women in service sectors have been disproportionately unemployed during the pandemic (ILO, 2020, pp. 8–11). Yet, demand remains for essential public and private works with safe distancing, from medical and care support, disease prevention, infrastructure repairs, shelter security, onshore food production, low-carbon heating, flood-protection, education to wellbeing and artistic endeavors. Longer-term planning would develop circular economies, de-carbonized infrastructure, and factories of the future with shorter supply chains, zero waste in fresh produce and provision of eco-efficient goods, services, and training (Cullen, Allwood, & Borgstein, 2011; Thiede & Herrmann, 2019), especially, as green economics failed to develop socially productive job ecology, what social economists call "social provisioning" (Figart & Mutari, 2008). Arguably, the same moral outrage felt when natural habitats cannot sustain, must also apply to human habitats needing jobs.

Challenges

Applying job commons raises many technical issues for localities, occupations, social protection, and labor organizing. First, thousands of people will need low-carbon UBS job creation near residential settings. Community job planning would need to negotiate with common markets and resourcing, and youth input for job designing. Job rotas could be mainstreamed if roles oversubscribe in places with high unemployment. Uneven job opportunities and climate change already force migration; hence job commons implementation needs global governance perspectives for sharing responsibilities and knowledge to reduce the brain drain. Universities could also evolve job sciences to help locales identify, manage, and regulate job solutions. Second, social welfare will still need protecting. Although job commons would counter welfare stigma, bureaucracy, and sanctions, it is not welfare replacement and the right *not* to work must remain. Frictional unemployment, moreover, is a normal occurrence when transitioning between jobs. Welfare provision, however, could expand under commons job creation, setting international standards for a "care" revolution. Third, job commoners would decide how labor organizations can best serve workers for economic democracy in commons-UBS industries. This may combine institutionalization, self-governance, and the social solidarity economy

(Guttmann, 2019). In Argentina, for example, unemployed labor unions evolved into self-managed government funded cooperatives employing 250,000 workers to improve local infrastructure, subsequently demanding higher wages and resources for extra-community activities (Kaese & Wolff, 2016, pp. 53–56). Instead of expecting poor people to resolve their own employment problems through entrepreneurship, looking harder for work, or attaining education and skills, a job commons approach, as mentioned above, would provide locally relevant UBS to protect citizens against a lack of demand. It also requires permanent investment in eco-social infrastructure.

Who Pays?

The first option of funding would be traditional public budgeting to spread costs by co-opting communities to manage UBS at lower costs than highly paid managers. Reducing joblessness would also reduce associated welfare and health costs, from addictions, crime, debt, family breakdown, forced migration, homelessness, illness, to premature death. Budgets would divert to supplement UBS occupations for greatest community impact, such as, securitizing shelter. With more people working who want to work, the earned income on demand would circulate expenditure through the economy, increase tax revenues, and expand supply chain demand in competitive and noncompetitive markets.

A second option under progressive MMT auspices (Wray, 2015) would be government spending proportional to job common needs. Examples include the way public borrowing compensates financiers hedge fund losses when investment bubbles and financial derivatives crash or disasters like Covid-19 need extra funding. A financial commons would assure the masses that government rhetoric for "balancing the budget" and austerity is a myth. The challenge would be to convince the public that borrowing for the job commons economy is equally as important as sustaining corporate welfare. As long as inflation is kept under control, governments with sovereign currency can borrow to pay for whatever they want without going bankrupt. Taxing assets, land, property, excessive tech wealth, and financial transactions like share-trading could also contribute to a job commons fund. In other words, a job commons could be made affordable.

But MMT economists and financial sectors must find answers to help north and south share risks.

CONCLUSIONS

This chapter advances an account of a job commons paradigm given leadership on the commons is failing to address the global jobs dearth. It asks leaders to confront the logic of capitalism, meaning a system that cannot marshal enough jobs for all job seekers. People with surplus capital or careers with long-hours culture want less-work intensive societies, but the majority of people on low income or no income seek more work. Consequently, job supplies need protecting as a universal commons given jobs remain central to how we sustain our lives and express ourselves. Job security, however, is eroding and neither right nor left leaning politics can boost enough jobs through business as usual "policy solutions," from corporate welfare, active labor market policies, microfinance, entrepreneurship, to job programs. Despite the striving for global and local governance, moreover, job supply problems fester on the ground.

Rather, leaders are managing unemployment as a human capital problem informed by skills-mismatch theory, which assumes jobs are plentiful and that people need only acquire the right skills or keep up with new technologies. Technological advancements, however, are hardly tackling job scarcity. As capitalist efficiencies for profit thrives on competition, labor rationing, and uneven opportunities. Access to jobs for those who want to work, should be a reality for all people, yet the universal need for job distribution to sustain livelihoods goes unheeded.

Conversely, job commons would encourage collective responsibility for shaping job ecology, removing uncertainty for job seekers and countering negative aspects of globalization, and welfare blaming. Securing permanent local jobs to fight poverty and discrimination is not impossible through a job commons environment, as outlined. It requires leaders with integrity to recognize the failings of transnational neoliberal politics and operationalize job commons as a means to connect citizens to local job governance, universally valued job infrastructure, and meaningful UBS jobs with international standards and job solidarity. In this way, leaders can apply job commons as a universal principle for achieving humane and progressive responses to local job needs, and a sustainable economy for citizens.

REFERENCES

Andrews, K. (2018). *Back to black: Retelling the politics of Black radicalism for the 21ˢᵗ century*. Zed Books Ltd.

Antal, M. (2014). Green goals and full employment: Are they compatible? *Ecological Economics, 107*, 276–286.

Armstrong, P. (2019). Keynes's view of deficits and functional finance: A modern monetary theory perspective. *International Review of Applied Economics, 33*(2), 241–253.

Azmanova, A. (2020). *Capitalism on edge: how fighting precarity can achieve radical change without crisis or utopia*. Columbia University Press.

Azzellini, D. (2018). Labour as a commons: The example of worker-recuperated companies. *Critical Sociology, 44*(4–5), 763–776.

Barchiesi, F. (2012). Liberation of, through, or from work? Postcolonial Africa and the problem with "job creation" in the global crisis. *Interface: A Journal for and About Social Movements, 4*, 230–253.

Branco, M. C. (2019). Economics for the right to work. *International Labour Review, 158*(1), 63–81.

Brousseau, E., Dedeurwaerdere, T., Jouvet, P. A., & Willinger, M. (Eds.). (2012). *Global environmental commons: Analytical and political challenges in building governance mechanisms*. Oxford University Press.

Caffentzis, G., & Federici, S. (2014). Commons against and beyond capitalism. *Community Development Journal, 49*(1), i92–i105.

Calathes, W. (2017). Racial capitalism and punishment philosophy and practices: What really stands in the way of prison abolition. *Contemporary Justice Review, 20*(4), 442–455.

Cato, M. S. (2009). *Green economics: An introduction to theory, policy and practice*. Earthscan.

Cerny, P. G. (2017). The limits of global governance: Transnational neopluralism in a complex world. In R. Marchetti (Ed.), *Partnerships in international policy-making* (pp. 31–47). Palgrave Macmillan.

Coe, N. M., & Jordhus-Lier, D. C. (2011). Constrained agency? Re-evaluating the geographies of labour. *Progress in Human Geography, 35*(2), 211–233.

Cogolati, S., & Wouters, J. (Eds.). (2018). *The commons and a new global governance*. Edward Elgar Publishing.

Colasanti, N., Frondizi, R., Liddle, J., & Meneguzzo, M. (2018). Grassroots democracy and local government in Northern Syria: The case of democratic confederalism. *Local Government Studies, 44*(6), 807–825.

Collins, J. L. (2016). Expanding the labor theory of value. *Dialectical Anthropology, 40*(2), 103–123.

Cullen, J. M., Allwood, J. M., & Borgstein, E. H. (2011). Reducing energy demand: What are the practical limits? *Environmental Science & Technology, 45*(4), 1711–1718.

Darity, W. Jr (1999). Who loses from unemployment. *Journal of Economic Issues, 33*(2), 491–496.

Davies, A. R., Homolova, L., Grey, C. N. B., & Bellis, M. A. (2019). Health and mass unemployment events – Developing a framework for preparedness and response. *Journal of Public Health, 41*(4), 665–673.

De Angelis, M. (2014). The commons: A brief life journey. *Community Development Journal, 49*(suppl_1), i68–i80.

De Moor, T. (2015). *The dilemma of the commoners: Understanding the use of common-pool resources in long-term perspective.* Cambridge University Press.

de Peuter, G., & Dyer-Witheford, N. (2010). Commons and cooperatives. *Affinities: A Journal of Radical Theory, Culture, and Action, 4*(1), 30–56.

Deacon, B., Macovei, M. C., Van Langenhove, L., & Yeates, N. (Eds.). (2009). *World-regional social policy and global governance: New research and policy agendas in Africa, Asia, Europe and Latin America.* Routledge.

Department for Work and Pensions. (DWP). (2020). *Nations job hunt JETS off.* Press release, 5th October 2020. London: DWP. Retrieved from https://www.gov.uk/government/news/nation-s-job-hunt-jets-off

Dittmer, K. (2013). Local currencies for purposive degrowth? A quality check of some proposals for changing money-as-usual. *Journal of Cleaner Production, 54*, 3–13.

Dobbins, T. (2018, May 7). Why a job guarantee would benefit us all. Letters to *The Guardian.* Retrieved from https://www.theguardian.com/society/2018/may/07/why-a-jobs-guarantee-would-benefit-us-all

Farré, L., Fasani, F., & Mueller, H. (2018). Feeling useless: The effect of unemployment on mental health in the Great Recession. *IZA Journal of Labor Economics, 7*(1), 8. doi:10.1186/s40172-018-0068-5

Figart, D. M., & Mutari, E. (2008). Work: Its social meanings and role in provisioning. In J. B. Davis & W. Dolfsma (Eds.), *The Elgar companion to social economics* (pp. 287–301). Edward Elgar Publishing Ltd.

Fitzroy, F., & Jin, J. (2018). Basic income and a public job offer: Complementary policies to reduce poverty and unemployment. *Journal of Poverty and Social Justice, 26*(2), 191–206.

Frayne, D. (2015). *The refusal of work: The theory and practice of resistance to work.* Zed Books Ltd.

Freeman, R. B., & Gottschalk, P. (Eds.). (1998). *Generating jobs: How to increase demand for less-skilled workers.* Russell Sage Foundation.

Frischmann, B. M. (2005). An economic theory of infrastructure and commons management. *Minnesota Law Review, 673*, 917–1030.

Frøyland, K., Andreassen, T. A., & Innvær, S. (2019). Contrasting supply-side, demand-side and combined approaches to labour market integration. *Journal of Social Policy*, 48(2), 311–328.

Fuster Morell, M. (2014). Governance of online creation communities for the building of digital commons: Viewed through the framework of the institutional analysis and development. In B. Frischmann, M. J. Madison, & K. Strandburg, (Eds.), *Governing knowledge commons* (pp. 281–312). Oxford University Press.

Gilmore, R. W. (2002). Fatal couplings of power and difference: Notes on racism and geography. *The Professional Geographer*, 54(1), 15–24.

Glyn, A. (2007). *Capitalism unleashed: Finance, globalization, and welfare*. Oxford University Press.

Graeber, D. (2018). *Bullshit jobs: The rise of pointless work, and what we can do about it*. Penguin books.

Guttmann, A. (2019). The social solidarity economy: Discerning its theory to accommodate the commons. *Review of Applied Socio-Economic Research*, 18(2), 43–57.

Hardt, M., & Negri, A. (2009). *Commonwealth*. Harvard University Press.

Harvey, D. (2011). The future of the commons. *Radical History Review*, 2011(109), 101–107.

Hawken, P., Lovins, A. H., & Lovins, L. H. (1999). *Natural capitalism*. Little Brown & Company.

Hurst, J. M. (2016). *The impact of networks on unemployment*. Palgrave Macmillan.

Hurst, J. (2020). Job supplies in disadvantaged neighbourhoods: Role of universal work. In W. Leal Filho, A. Azul, L. Brandli, P. Özuyar, & T. Wall (Eds.), *Decent work and economic growth. Encyclopedia of the UN Sustainable Development Goals*. Springer. doi:10.1007/978-3-319-71058-7_65-1

International Labor Organization (ILO). (2013). *Resolution concerning sustainable development, decent work and green jobs*. The general conference of the ILO, 102nd session, June 19th 2013. ILO. Retrieved from https://www.ilo.org/ilc/ILCSessions/previous-sessions/102/texts-adopted/WCMS_223785/lang–en/index.htm

International Labor Organization (ILO). (2020). *ILO Monitor: Covid-19 and the world of work, fifth edition*. Updated estimates and analysis, 30th June 2020. ILO. Retrieved from https://www.ilo.org/global/topics/coronavirus/impacts-and-responses/WCMS_749399/lang–en/index.htm

Jahoda, M. (1982). *Employment and unemployment: A social-psychological analysis*. Cambridge University Press.

Jensen, N. M., & Malesky, E. J. (2018). *Incentives to pander: How politicians use corporate welfare for political gain*. Cambridge University Press.

Kaese, F., & Wolff, J. (2016). Piqueteros after the hype: Unemployed movements in Argentina, 2008–2015. *European Review of Latin American and Caribbean Studies*, (102), 47–68.

Kamerāde, D., Wang, S., Burchell, B., Balderson, S. U., & Coutts, A. (2019). A shorter working week for everyone: How much paid work is needed for mental health and well-being? *Social Science & Medicine, 241,* 112353. doi:10.1016/j.socscimed.2019.06.006

Knoedler, J., & Schneider, G. (2010). An institutionalist vision of a good economy. *Forum for Social Economics, 39*(3), 259–267.

Kousis, M., & Paschou, M. (2017). Alternative forms of resilience. A typology of approaches for the study of citizen collective responses in hard economic times. *Partecipazione e Conflitto, 10*(1), 136–168.

Kuddo, A. (2012). *Public employment services and activation policies.* Social protection and labor discussion papers 1215. World Bank.

Linebaugh, P. (2008). *The Magna Carta manifesto: Liberties and commons for all.* University of California Press.

Lutz, M. A. (2002). *Economics for the common good: Two centuries of economic thought in the humanist tradition.* Routledge.

Maher, N. M. (2015). 'Work for others but none for us': The economic and environmental inequalities of New Deal relief. *Social History, 40*(3), 312–334.

Manzini, E., & M'Rithaa, M. K. (2017). Distributed systems and cosmopolitan localism: An emerging design scenario for resilient societies. In A. Skjerven & J. B. Reitan (Eds.), *Design for a sustainable culture: Perspectives, practices and education* (pp. 29–37). Routledge.

Mazzucato, M. (2013). *The entrepreneurial state: Debunking public vs. private sector myths.* Anthem Press.

Mitchell, W. F., & Wray, L. R. (2005). *Full employment through a job guarantee: A response to the critics.* Centre for Full Employment and Equity, Working paper 39. University of Newcastle, Australia. Available at SSRN 1010149.

Nersisyan, Y., & Wray, L. R. (2019). *How to pay for the Green New Deal.* Levy Institute Working Paper No. 931. Levy Economics Institute of Bard College.

Ostrom, E. (1990). *Governing the commons: The evolution of institutions for collective action.* Cambridge University Press.

Pettifor, A. (2019). *The case for the green new deal.* Verso.

Raffass, T. (2017). Demanding activation. *Journal of Social Policy, 46*(2), 349–365.

Richardson, L., & Thieme, T. A. (2020). Planning working futures: Precarious work through carceral space. *Social & Cultural Geography, 21*(1), 25–44.

Rose, C. M. (2019). Thinking about the commons. *International Journal of the Commons,* Arizona Legal Studies Discussion Paper, No 19-24. doi:10.2139/ssrn.3487612

Schweik, C. M., & English, R. C. (2012). *Internet success: A study of open-source software commons.* MIT Press.

Smids, J., Nyholm, S., & Berkers, H. (2020). Robots in the workplace: A threat to – or opportunity for – meaningful work? *Philosophy & Technology, 33*(3), 503–522. doi:10.1007/s13347-019-00377-4

Stahler-Sholk, R. (2014). Mexico: Autonomy, collective identity, and the Zapatista social movement. In R. Stahler-Sholk, H. E. Vanden & M. Becker (Eds.), *Rethinking Latin American social movements: Radical action from below* (pp. 187–207). Lanham, MD: Rowman & Littlefield.

Standing, G. (2019). *Plunder of the commons.* Penguin Books Limited.

Steger, M. F., & Dik, B. J. (2010). Work as meaning. In P. A. Linley, S. Harrington, & N. Page (Eds.), *Oxford handbook of positive psychology and work* (pp.131–142). Oxford University Press.

Susser, I., & Tonnelat, S. (2013). Transformative cities: The three urban commons. *Focaal, Journal of Global and Historical Anthropology,* (66), 105–121.

Tcherneva, P. R. (2012). Permanent on-the-spot job creation – The missing Keynes Plan for full employment and economic transformation. *Review of Social Economy, 70*(1), 57–80.

Thiede, S., & Herrmann, C. (Eds.). (2019). *Eco-factories of the future.* Springer.

Timmermann, C. (2018). Contributive justice: An exploration of a wider provision of meaningful work. *Social Justice Research, 31*(1), 85–111.

United Nations (UN). (2020). *Covid-19 impact could cause equivalent of 195 million job losses, warns ILO chief.* UN News [On-line] April 8, 2020. Retrieved from https://news.un.org/en/story/2020/04/1061322

van der Linden, M. (2017). European social protest, 1000–2000. In S. Berger & H. Nehring (Eds.), *The history of social movements in global perspective: A survey* (pp. 175–209). Palgrave Macmillan.

Van Parijs, P., & Vanderborght, Y. (2017). *Basic income: A radical proposal for a free society and a sane economy.* Harvard University Press.

Veltman, A. (2016). *Meaningful work.* Oxford University Press.

Vieta, M. (2016). Autogestión: Prefiguring a 'new cooperativism' and the 'labour commons'. In *Moving beyond capitalism* (pp. 77–85). Routledge.

Voßemer, J., Gebel, M., Täht, K., Unt, M., Högberg, B., & Strandh, M. (2018). The effects of unemployment and insecure jobs on well-being and health: The moderating role of labor market policies. *Social Indicators Research, 138*(3), 1229–1257.

Weatherall, T. (2015). *Jus cogens: International law and social contract.* Cambridge University Press.

Weeks, K. (2011). *The problem with work: Feminism, Marxism, antiwork politics, and postwork imaginaries.* Duke University Press.

Wray, L. R. (2015). *Modern money theory: A primer on macroeconomics for sovereign monetary systems* (2nd ed.). Palgrave Macmillan.

Wright, C., Wood, A., Trevor, J., McLaughlin, C., Huang, W., Harney, B., & Brown, W. (2019). Towards a new web of rules: An international review of institutional experimentation to strengthen employment protections. *Employee Relations, 41*(2), 313–330.

Yates, M. (2011). The human-as-waste, the labor theory of value and disposability in contemporary capitalism. *Antipode, 43*(5), 1679–1695.

Zajak, S., Egels-Zandén, N., & Piper, N. (2017). Networks of labour activism: Collective action across Asia and beyond. An introduction to the debate. *Development and Change, 48*(5), 899–921.

Zink, T., & Geyer, R. (2016). There is no such thing as a green product. *Stanford Social Innovation Review*, Spring 2016. [On-line]. Retrieved from https://ssir.org/articles/entry/there_is_no_such_thing_as_a_green_product

INDEX

Ability, 168
Accelerating rates of change, 200
Action, 160
Adaptability in networks, 7
Adaptive management, 192, 198–199
Affective perception, 124
Agriculture, 274
Allostasis, 69
Ambivalent intimacies, 37–44
Animal rescue, 177–178
    cat commoning in the shadows,
        186–187
    collaborations, 181–183
    connecting with collaborators,
        180–181
    dogs own our commons, 184–185
    encouraging others, 187–188
    reaction, 183–184
    working, 178–180
Animal Rescue Foundation
    (ARF), 182, 184
Anti-capitalist lifestyles, 365
Architecture, 74
Articulating principles, 76
Articulation with other stakeholders,
    320–321
Autoethnography, 177
Awareness, 163

Benevolent leadership, 15, 143
Bioinspired thinking, 70
Bisse de Saviesse, 1–2
Black Lives Matter protests, 61
Blurred lines, 33–37
Bonds, 31
Bosnia and Herzegovina (BiH), 329–330
    Federation, 331
    government, 332
    National Museum of, 336–340
    socio-political situation in, 331–332

Boston Common, 2
Brian Henning's Ethics of Creativity, 15
Building relationships, 236
Business Roundtable, 99–100

Capitalism, 26, 98–101, 115, 337, 363
Capitalist corporate bodies, 97–98
Care, 32–33, 163
    ethic, 48–52
    as foundational ethic of leadership
        on the commons, 29
Cash nexus, 41
Cat commoning in the shadows,
    186–187
Causality principle, 97
Change, 250–251
Charismatic perspectives of
    leadership, 82
Chile, 312–313, 315
Civil Code, The, 314
Civil society organizations (CSO), 331
    mapping study, 332
Co-created communication, 227
Co-creating conscious action, 148
Collaboration, 181–183, 223, 233
    elements of, 224–232
    outcomes of successful, 233–237
Collaborative community, 245
Collaborative governance, 372
Collaborative leadership network, 192
Collaborative partnership, 248
Collective action, 84–85, 90
Collective identity, 19–20, 223, 229–232
Collective intelligence, 169
Collective leadership, 120, 329
Collective-choice rule, 200–201
Colorado Collaboration Award
    competition, 19, 223
Commensalism, 72
Commitment, 236

Committed members, 225
Common pool resources (CPRs),
       4–5, 196
Commoners, 3, 157, 162, 168, 170
Commoning, 19, 51, 104, 114, 207
   purpose, 104–105
   rights of resource ownership,
       105–106
   scarcity or abundance–orientation to
       time, 106
Commons, 1–3, 6, 13–14, 18, 33, 82,
       88, 207–208, 297, 364–369
   conceptualization, 363–364
   leading specific types of, 20–26
   at odds, 98–101
   as political struggle, 330
Commons leadership, 12, 69–70, 76–77,
       367–368
   dimensions, 70–73
   in labor history, 366–367
   in practice, 73–75
   principles, 76
Communal culture, 25
   building, 350–352
   development, 346–347
   methods and data, 350
   and responsible leadership in
       Dunking Devils, 355–359
Communal intelligence, 169
Communal Union of Ránquil, 318
Communication, 227
Communion, 33
Communitas, 18–19, 206–211
   and culture, 213–215
Community, 3, 33–34, 350–351
   community-ship, 347
   responsiveness, 143
Community service-learning tracks
       (CSLTs), 301
Compassion, 145–146
Complex adaptive systems (CAS), 8
Complexity leadership, 8
Conditional cooperators, 245
Conscious contention, 147–148
Conscious conversations, 15, 143
   co-creating conscious action, 148
   conscious contention, 147–148
   conscious listening, 145–146
   conscious questions, 147
   conscious space, 146
   cultivating conscious wisdom,
       148–149

Conscious listening, 145–146
Conscious questions, 147
Conscious space, 146
Conscious wisdom, 148–149
Consciousness, 164–165
Consequentialism, 151
Contextual intelligence, 166
Contextual thinking, 165
Convening leadership, 17
   adaptive management, 198–199
   challenges, 199–201
   convenor, 192–193
   convenors from all sectors, 196
   convenors way of thinking, being,
       and acting, 194–196
   on the commons, 191–194, 196–198
Convenors, 17–18, 192–193
   from all sectors, 196
   way of thinking, being, and acting,
       194–196
Conventional leadership, 69, 102
Cooperatives, 365
Corporate-commons leadership, 97
   capitalism, corporations, and
       commons at odds, 98–101
   ecocentric model, 107–110
   hybrid model, 111, 114
   implications, 115–116
   leadership, 101–106
   Patagonia, 110–114
Corporations, 13–14, 98–101
Cost of Freedom:Voicing A Movement
       After Kent State 1970, The,
       261–262
Courageous covenant, 146
COVID-19
   crisis, 217
   pandemic, 286
Credit slips, 42
Crossing borders to the commons,
       215–216
Cultural commons, 364
Cultural diversity challenge, 199–200
Cultural elites, 340
Culture, 213–215, 337
Culture diary, 350
Curiosity, 147

Darwin's theory of evolution, 138
Dayton Peace Agreement, 331, 337
Debt, 32, 36, 44–45
   relations, 31

Decision-making processes, 165
Decommodifyng housing, 145
Defined process, 229
Degenerative systems
    in place, 61–65
    regenerative systems vs., 60–61
    worldview, 62
Deliberately developmental
        organizations (DDOs), 347
Discernment, 148–149
Discursive engagement, 140
Distributed leadership, 9, 19,
    214–215, 273
Dogs own our commons, 184–185
Dunking Devils, 345–346
    Academy, 352
    impact of coronavirus pandemic on
        development of, 354–355
    story of, 346–347
Duty, 32

Early childhood education, 243–244
    leaders in addressing commons
        dilemmas, 245–246
    lessons from commons, 244–245
    public service organizational leaders,
        246–251
Ecocentric identity, 112
Ecocentric model, 107–110
Ecology, 71–72
Economic systems, 32
Educational systems, 65
Einstein's theory of relativity, 138
Elite leadership, 329
Embeddedness, 71
Empathy, 145–146
Empowerment events, 286–290
Engagement, 236
Environment shaping, 75
Environmental commons, 364
Environmental movement, 5
Equipotency principle, 10
Ethic of certainty to ethic of creativity,
    138–141
Ethical sensitivity, 143
Ethics of the commons, 150–153
Exchangers, 40–41
Exchanges, 38
Experiences of water, 322–323

FabLab movement, 2
Facilitative leadership, 7

Favelas, 119
    considerations, 130–132
    leaders, 119
    leadership moment in, 125–130
    method, 120–125
    residents, 126
Feminine caring, 49
Followers, 83
Forest plantations, effects of, 320
Framing
    through language and artifacts,
        88–89
    for meaning-making and collective
        action, 84–85
Free-rider problem, 86
Frontline/border posts, 208

Generalized reciprocity, 40
Gifts, 32, 34–36
    reciprocities, 40
    relations, 37
Global Forum on Agricultural Research
        and Innovation (GFAR), 279
Global Open Data for Agriculture and
        Nutrition (GODAN), 21–22,
        275–276, 280–281
Global resonance, 168
Globalization, 191
Governance, 7
Governing the commons, 86
Great Lakes Commons, 2
Green New Deal jobs, 368–369
Group rituals, 230
Group-centered leadership, 21, 268
Guadalupe County Humane Society, 179
Guifi. net, 82–83, 85, 87–91
Guilt, 32

Hackerspace movement, 2
Hardin's model, 86
Harmonizing values in tension, 147–148
Heroic-centered perspectives of
        leadership, 82
Highlander doctrine, 269
Homeostasis, 69
Homo economicus, 5
Huerta system of irrigation, 1
Human action framework for leading
        proleptically, 160–162
Hybrid proposal, 114
Hydraulic Works Department
        (HWD), 314

Hypernorms, 139–140
Hypothetical reasoning, 140

"I am Museum" campaign, 339–340
Immunity, 33
Industrial Worker of the World (IWW),
    21, 268
Informal organizers, 119
Integral theorists, 164
Integrated reporting (IR), 73, 76–77
Integrating rituals, 212
Integrative Social Contract Theory
    (ISCT), 139
Intentionality, 108–110
Interlinked CPRs, 200
International Labor Organization
    (ILO), 363
International Monetary Fund, 4
International Women's Day (IWD), 285
Internet, 89
Interorganizational collaboration,
    20, 223
    elements of collaboration, 224–232
    findings and implications, 233
    outcomes of successful
        collaborations, 233–237
Itata Valley, 317

Jesuit Commons
    to Jesuit Worldwide Learning,
        302–303
    origin and pilot phase of, 299–301
Jesuit Commons: Higher Education at
    the Margins (JC:HEM), 296,
    300, 302, 307
Jesuit education, 295
Jesuit Refugee Services (JRS), 300
Jesuit Worldwide Learning: Higher
    Education at the Margins
    (JWL), 22–23, 296, 307
    Jesuit commons to, 302–303
    JWL HeLP, 296
    student success stories and future
        frontiers for, 303–306
Jesuits, 295
    historical context, 297–299
Job commons, 26, 363–364 (see also
    Commons)
    challenges, 376–377
    establishing, 373–375
    postdisasters, 375–376

redefining leadership on commons
    for jobs, 369–372
Job Entry: Targeted Support (JETS), 373
Job policy outside the commons,
    370–372
Job supply fault lines, 367
Justice to care, 44–48
Justice-minded approach to common
    good, 297–299
Justifiable hypernorms, 140

Keynesian mixed economy
    policies, 367
Knowledge
    societies, 300
    technologists, 216
Kruščica, 329–330, 332
    investment in energy sector, 332–333
    plans to build dams in Kruščica river,
        333–336

Labor as a commons, 365
Language, 35
    of informal reciprocities, 43
Laws of retribution and punishment, 45
Leaders, 83
    in addressing commons dilemmas,
        245–246
    in process, 7–8
Leadership, 69, 81, 157, 160,
    245, 329
    creating spaces to unfold collective
        practices and build collective
        agency, 90–91
    critical issues calling for, 319–321
    in favelas as collective process,
        122–123
    framing for meaning-making and
        collective action, 84–85
    framing through language and
        artifacts, 88–89
    Guifi. net, 87–88
    implications for, 91–93
    needed for commons, 59–60
    patterns, 52
    process philosophy and, 83–84
    Som Energia, 87–88
    struggle of conceptualizations and
        definitions, 85–87
    studies, 70
    theories, 81

Leadership moment, 14, 120
  concept, 123–125
  in favela, 125–130
Leadership on the commons, 6–7
  care as foundational ethic of, 29
  complexity leadership, 8
  leadership on peer-to-peer network
    commons, 9–10
  leading from nature, 9
  lifecycle, 16–20
  network leadership, 7–8
  reflections on, 26–28
  reimagining, 10–11
Leading oneself
  critical abilities of, 166–167
  leading with others leading
    community proleptically, 165
  through values of commoning, 165
Leading proleptically, 157–158
  consciousness, 164–165
  critical abilities of leading oneself,
    166–167
  human action framework for,
    160–162
  leading community and society,
    169–171
  leading oneself, leading with
    others leading community
    proleptically, 165
  leading oneself through values of
    commoning, 165
  leading with others proleptically,
    167–169
  opening oneself to future, 163–164
  preparing oneself to, 162–163
  prolepticism and, 158–159
Learning, 7
Learning management system (LMS),
  296
Les Rites de Passage (1960), 208
Liminality, 208–209
Linux open-source operating system, 2
Local communities, 23
Lost vision for job futures, 367–368
Low-skilled jobs, 375

Maker movement, 2
Management theory, 64–65
Masculinist abstraction, 49
Meaning-making, 13
  framing for, 84–85

Mediated ritual interaction, 212
Micro-social norms, 139
Midwives, 195
Mindfulness, 163
Modern monetary theorists (MMTs),
  370, 377
Multi-stakeholder partnerships, 246
Museum, 329
Mutualism, 72
Mutualistic commons leadership, 77

Narratives, 237
National Museum, 329–330
  of Bosnia and Herzegovina, 336–340
National Open Data Initiatives
  (NDIs), 281
Nature, 60, 67
Negative reciprocity, 38
Neighborhood associations, 121
Neoliberalism, 371
Network convenors, 194
Network leadership, 7–8
Non-market communities, 51
Nongovernmental organizations
  (NGOs), 331
Nonprofit organizations, 121
Nonprofit partnerships, 246
Nonprofit sector, 243
Ñuble Region, 316

Obligated leadership, 48–52
Obligations, 31, 143
Ogrute Community, 281
Ogrute Ugwu Eru Mapathon, 283–284
Open data
  for food security and commons, 275
  mapping empowerment for women,
    280–285
  platforms, 274
Open Data Day (ODD), 285
Open-source data, 21–22
OpenStreetMap, 281, 284
Organizations, 83
Outages, 319
Ownership, 105

Paradigm shift, 11–16
Parasitism, 71–72
Passion, 247–248
Patagonia, 110–114
Pattern-recognizing algorithms, 71

Peer governance, 214
Peer-to-peer (P2P), 2
  leadership on peer-to-peer network
    commons, 9–10
Peoples' Voice Cafe (PVC), 257–261
  cancelation notice, 269–271
  lows and highs for horizontally led
    collective, 264–266
  may 16, 2020, 261–263
  Portraiture methodology, 258
  "We Are All Leaders" PVC doctrine,
    266–269
Perennial tension, 141
Pierre Bourdieu's approach, 41–42
Place relations, 127–128
Polycentric governance structures, 23
Portraiture methodology, 258
Positive engagement, 143
Power, 72
Power over, 72
Practice of Courageous Covenant, 150
Practice of Discernment, 153
*Practice of Harmonizing Values in
  Tension*, 152–153
Primitive communities, 51
Primitive societies, 35
Prisoner's dilemma, 87
Process philosophy, 13, 83–84
Productivity effect, 371
Prolepsis, 158
Proleptic leaders, 16
Proleptic leadership, 161
Prolepticism, 158–159
Prosperity, 110
Prosumers, 10
Protests, 329
Psychological ethical identity, 139
Psychological safety, 352
Public service organizational leaders,
  246–251
Punitive justice, 46
Purpose, 130

Reactive listening, 146
Reflective listening, 146
Regenerative leaders(hip), 9 (*see also*
  Convening leadership)
  challenge for, 66–67
  essential for common good and our
    future, 67
Regenerative systems, 12
  degenerative systems *vs.*, 60–61

framework, 65
  leadership needed for commons,
    59–60
  worldview, 62
Regional Universities Forum for
    Capacity Building in Agriculture
    (RUFORUM), 276
Relationality, 108
Relationships, 70–72, 248–250
Religious traditions, 164
Residents, 127–128
Resources, 226
Resources, 73
Responsible leadership, 102–104,
    106–108, 348–349
  communal culture and, 355–359
  emergence, 352–354
Responsive listening, 146
Restorative justice, 46
Restoring trust, 51
Retributive justice, 46
RichFood Foundation, 289
Rights of resource ownership, 105–106
Rituals, 211–212
Road Warriors, 18, 206–207, 209
Rural water associations, 313–314

Sarajevo Haggadah, 338
Scaling up, 199
Scarcity
  everyday practices to deal with, 321
  or abundance–orientation to
    time, 106
Schwartz's analysis, 48
Science, 86
Sense of agency, 97
Shared goal, 228–229
Shared identity, 212–213
Shared leadership, 19, 223, 273 (*see also*
    Responsible leadership)
Shared purpose, 124, 128–130
Shared rituals, 212
SIMOL project, 318–319
Smallholder farmers, 277
Social accounting, 13, 76
Social bonds, 31
Social capital, 20, 37, 39, 41, 105
Social credit, 37
Social intelligence, 166
Social movements, 24, 330
Social outburst, 315
Social provisioning, 376

Social relationships, 212
Society, 3
Society of Jesus, 297–298
Solutions Group, 195
Som Energia, 82–83, 85, 87–88, 90
Spirals of positive change, 149–150
Spiritual depth, 143
Spiritual discernment, 167
Spiritual intelligence, 166
Spirituality, 167
Stakeholders, 100, 348
    network, 192–193
State, 3
State corporate bodies, 97–98
Stubborn optimism, 16–17, 184
Subsidiarity in governance, 7
Successful relationships, 236
Sustainability, 150, 162
Sustainable development goals (SDGs),
    21, 77, 371
    SDG 1, 274
    SDG 2, 274
Symbols, 211–212
System of Systems (SoS), 74–75
Systems Engineering, 73–75

Talionic law, 45
Team, 351
Teamwork, 236
Technical Centre for Agriculture and
    Rural Cooperation (CTA), 279
Theory U, 163
Time, 225–226
Traditional leadership, 313
Tragedy of the Commons, The, 4,
    85–87, 115, 197, 244
Transferability, 42
Trust, 37, 168, 228

Ubuntu, 5
Ugwu Eru, 281–282
Unique Mappers Network (UMT
    Network), 280–285
    in Nigeria, 22
United Nations (UN), 371
United Nations High Commissioner for
    Refugees (UNHCR), 295
United Nations Human Rights Council
    (UNHRC), 302
Universal basic income (UBI), 368
Universal basic services (UBS), 375, 377
Urban commons, 368

Value, 35
Value-infused leadership of
    commons, 137
    conscious conversations, 143–149
    ethic of certainty to ethic of
        creativity, 138–141
    ethics of the commons, 150–153
    identifying values in tension, 141–143
    spirals of positive change, 149–150
Viber, 335
Vitez, 334
Voluntary Agreement for Watershed
    Management (AVGC), 318

Warriors, 195
Water Associations, 315
Water Code of 1981, The, 314
Water Committees, 316, 318, 322
Water community organizations,
    311–315
    findings in Ránquil, 319–321
    lessons and challenges for leaderships
        of water as commons, 323–326
    location background and current
        situation, 316–317
    methodology and data collection,
        318–319
    other findings, 321–323
Water crisis, 315
Water outages, 23
Water quality, 23, 319–320
We Are All Leaders PVC doctrine,
    266–269
Wergild, 46
Wikimedia, 2
Wikipedia, 2
Wikispeed, 2
Wobblies (*see* Industrial Worker of the
    World (IWW))
Women smallholder farmers, 273
    empowering, 277–279
    empowerment events, 286–290
    open data for food security and
        commons, 275
    open data mapping empowerment
        for women, 280–285
    strengthening local capacity
        development for zero hunger
        through open data, 276
Work, 206
Workers in distributed spaces, 206–207
World War II (WWII), 367